LIBRARY PUBLIC RELATIONS

LIBRARY PUBLIC RELATIONS

Edited by

Sreenidhi Iyengar

ANMOL PUBLICATIONS PVT LTD

NEW DELHI-110 002 (INDIA)

ANMOL PUBLICATIONS PVT LTD
4374/4B, Ansari Road, Daryaganj
New Delhi-110 002

Library Public Relations

First Edition 1996

ISBN 81-7488-326-6

PRINTED IN INDIA

Published by J. L. Kumar for Anmol Publications Pvt Ltd, New Delhi and Printed at Mehra Offset Press, Delhi..

Contents

Preface

Of late Library and Information Science has gained crucial and significant place in the area of knowledge and learning.

Library holds an important centre stage in all institutions of learning as well as in public life.

The present book is a significant addition to the literature on library science. Here some useful, informative and valuable articles have been compiled and collated which are substantially based on the writings of some experts in the field of library science. Main topics dealt herein are: Library Public Relations; Public Relations in Librarianship; Public Relations of the Public Library; Public Relations and Publicity; Public Services Abroad; etc.

No doubt, this volume will prove informative and useful handbook to all professional librarians besides the scholars and academics in the field.

— **Editor**

1

Introduction

THE PUBLIC Library is created and organized to give the fullest and most consequential service possible to the greatest number of citizens, in the belief that the worth of a book is in its use and that books and people should be brought together in meaningful relationship. In introducing this book containing different chapters on the management of the library's public services activities, four general viewpoints are pertinent for the entire staff to share: a sense of purpose, a substantial knowledge of books, the desire to serve and a willingness to please.

A Sense of Purpose

We will discuss library objectives and functions and outline a programme for serving the whole community. To some persons such topics appear theoretical, difficult or unimportant. But no public library achieves greatness unless both the board and the staff have a clear sense of purpose, keyed to the spirit and needs of the times. This sense of purpose is at its strongest when knit into the fabric of the organization through staff experience and discussion based on observation of other libraries, on reading and on close attention to each reader's success in finding maximum service.

This applies particularly to public service personnel. After a few months' employment, each employee should be able to tell his friends and family reasonably well what the library is trying to do. But the library's overall purpose will come alive only if he can see how his own department's work and indeed his own job relates to that purpose. The difference between the man who was cutting stone and the one who was helping to build a great cathedral is paralleled in libraries. Is the desk assistant simply handing out books, or does he feel that he is helping people to lead fuller and richer lives? As new problems and conditions arise in each person's work, the best solutions are those which reflect the overall purpose of the library to serve its clientele.

A Knowledge of Books

Next to knowing what he is doing and why, a staff members needs knowledge of the library's varied forms of print and non-print. Unless he knows books and how to find them and how to find out about them, he is poorly prepared to serve the public. Knowledge of books means an ever-growing acquaintance with titles and their authors, bibliographical history, library call numbers and physical locations, but especially their contents and their values, uses and present and past popularity with readers. This requires reading many books—in part or in whole—and reading about books. Those who lack a real interest in books, the habit of reading and the vision and conviction that books can be powerful helpers to citizens may well ask themselves whether they are in the right occupation.

Some perception of the intellectual content of books marks the professional from the technician, the more effective from the less effective, and the subject literature specialist from the generalist, because it enables the librarian to compare materials on the same subject but of different form, and intelligently to use each alone or in combination with others. Every librarian needs to have this spark of knowledge, or he might as well be handling shoes or canned foods. Such knowledge has its roots in librarian's formal education, but it must be updated by continual reading, by in-service training, by book discussion, and by authorization to read important books and journals on library time. A good librarian reads eight to ten hours a week on his own time. Without such knowledge of books the library staff does a poor job in selecting new titles for purchase, in cataloguing and classification, in compiling booklists, in handling group activity programmes and in serving individual readers.

A Desire to Serve

Seven decades ago, individual librarians laboured in a wilderness of new problems and public indifference, but they were dedicated missionaries. Public libraries are accepted today, but many library employees do their work routinely. If public libraries were supported by readers' fees and there were direct competition for those fees, each public service staff member would no doubt act as though his salary depended on the quality of service he rendered, and on the number of repeat customers he developed. The reader should feel that the assistant he meets is interested in him, diligent to understand his problems, and anxious to see that he gets what he wishes. These impressions and attitudes, and the quality of service received, make up the reader's mental image of the library. In short, good service means that the customer gets what he wants or the next available thing to it, but is not sent away empty-handed.

The librarian can promote the desire to serve by development of a formal policy statement, by appropriate in-service training by appointing and promoting persons imbued with the spirit of service, by systematic observation, by assuring himself that supervision is good in each department and branch, by soliciting staff members' and patrons' comments and reactions, and most of all by his own attitude and example. What the chief makes clear that he expects done first and best will probably be so treated by his colleagues.

A Willingness to Please

"Willingness to please" encompasses a whole list of specifics, from courtesy to patrons to modern and attractive furniture and surroundings. Many public libraries are less than distinguished in this regard, probably not as good as the average retail store. Simple courtesy includes good telephone manners, the pleasant smile of greeting, remembering a patron's name and reading tastes and willingness to stop a routine job, or talking to a colleague, to serve a patron. An assistant should check to be sure that a patron is served when he is referred from one desk or department to another, and he should never seem bored when he has to explain to one more reader how to use the card catalogue or other tool. All these are factors of great moment to readers. Courtesy is invaluable, and it costs nothing.

Perhaps public libraries need not pick beauty queens for circulation desk assistants but there is no denying that personable men and women will be more pleasing to readers, other things being equal. Good grooming and a smart appearance are highly compatible with good education, cultural enthusiasm and knowledge of books, and would seem as desirable at the library's most conspicuous service point as in any successful appliance dealer's salesroom—and for the same reason. Best of all is the friendly, outgoing personality which warms all it touches, a prime consideration in recruitment and appointment of public service staff. What happens when a staff member meets and serves a patron is the acid test of a library's service programme and of its whole administration. The patron should feel that he is being treated with courtesy by one who is alert, pleasant, competent, and interested in his problem.

Concept of Public Relations

For many who, Thirty years ago, considered "propaganda" to be a naughty word, "public relations" today has a similar sinister connotation.

They, and their younger contemporaries, say that he propagandist, as well as the press agent and publicity director, has merely changed his title to that of public relations counsel. These "wonder children of the age" are called hidden persuaders, pressure boys, masters of the Invisible Sell, space grabbers, ballyhoo boys, hucksters, cunning manipulators of the mind, malicious engineers of public consent, master of the art or science of getting one's own way—in short, generally, socially undesirable characters.

By contrast, the hundreds of thousands, if not millions, of persons who perform public relations functions today contend that their activities are of great social benefit. They take credit for having converted business and industry completely away from the "public be damned" attitude and say that they have humanized business, helped give it good manners and, most important, a conscience; and that they have taught it that he profits most who serves best. They define public relations as simply doing the right thing and letting people know about it, applying the golden rule in everyday activities while not letting one's light shine un-noticed under a basket. To them, sound public relations means the daily application of common sense, common courtesy, and common decency in accordance with a continuous programme of enlightened self-interest through good works which not only earn one a good reputation but cause him to deserve it as a good neighbour.

Curse or blessing, organized public relations is a product of the times. It is an inevitable consequence of large population growth, urbanization, impersonalization, and complexity in all social, economic, political, and other aspects of modern life. No scientific means have yet been devised to determine accurately the extent to which public relations may have contributed to the confusion of our times, or how much, on the other hand, it constructively assists the frustrated victim of complexity to grope his way toward an understanding of contemporary social forces. Whether, as its adverse critics assert, public relations has provided a dangerous weapon for "sharpies" and others out for "a fast buck," or, as its defenders assert, it has applied appreciable restraints to the "dog eat dog" economic system, it, nevertheless, is true that much of the discussion regarding public relations really pertains to the system of which it is a part rather than to the tool itself. Perhaps public relations should be considered as a symptom or symbol of a highly complex and impersonal social order.

Certain it is that to be heard today one must shout. Newspapers no longer have sufficient space in which to tell all the news that's fit to print and wouldn't have it even if they discontinued all their comic strips and other features. Community newspapers, news magazines, news letters, and other media of communication have filled the gap only partially. The voice which wants to be heard must speak up for itself; it no longer is possible to relay on others to find you out and present your point of view for you.

Modern public relations, however, involves much more than devising ways and means of obtaining widespread and continuous publicity. In fact, the best advice a public relations counsel might give a client could be assiduously to avoid the limelight. *Webster's New International Dictionary* succinctly defines the scope of modern public relations thus: "The activities of an industry, union corporation profession, government or other organization in building and maintaining sound and productive relations with special publics such as customers, employees or stockholders and with the public at large, so as to adapt itself to its environment and interpret itself to society."

By contrast, press agentry is merely attracting attention to yourself, usually with only immediate or short rate results in mind. The term was first applied, a couple of generations ago, to agents employed by circuses, theaters, dramatic companies, and the like to attract audiences. They did so by such advertising methods as billboards, handbills, news releases, parades, barkers, free sideshows, and passes to influential customers who would help start the trek toward the big tent, museum, or arena. These show business press agents engaged in extravagant claims and considerable amount of fakery which was expected, received with good humour, and enjoyed as part of the fun.

Some press agentry, of course, exists today, but it usually is not upon the advice of a scientific-minded public relations counsel. Instead, as in the past, it is by someone seeking a quick specific return as the lovesick swain who chained himself to a radiator in the attempt to help his girl friend get a singing engagement. Public relations counsel-inspired publicity stunts are more far reaching in purpose and are a part of a long range programme. Anniversary banquets, public exhibits, lecture series, and educational programmes are within this category. Most organizations with well developed department of public relations engage in a considerable amount of public service. They provide material—much of it excellent audio-visual educational aids—to schools, study clubs, civic organizations, and the public at large. This material contains a minimum of "puffery" or none at all. Some of it contains information which, it is hoped, will help build attitudes which ultimately, usually indirectly, will redound to the advantage of those who finance it. Much of it merely is intended to help create goodwill toward the disseminating agency.

There is no attempt to disguise or deny the fact that the Department of Public Relations of a business corporation is expected to contribute to the ultimate prosperity of the organization, or that a public relations agency employed by a motion picture star or politician tries to win fame and/or fortune for its client. Labour unions have gone in for public relations to try to win public support for themselves as well as to influence legislators and other public officials. Government sells itself on a big scale to the voting public by providing and publicizing services. Crude methods of press agentry or publicity-seeking however, have generally been abandoned by the experts in the field as the broader concept of public relations has evolved. Publicity today is just one department within any public relations outfit, whether it be an agency serving many clients or a part of a large industrial organization. Individuals who depend upon keeping their names known still expect their publicity man to obtain frequent mention for them in the gossip columns and public prints generally, and particular industries, businesses, and trade associations still "plant" or try to inspire articles in magazines and other publications. Much of the cynicism which exists in some places regarding public relations is due to the increasing difficulty of determining what is and is not primarily publicity inspired. When a candidate for public office shows up at a clam bake, it is taken for granted that he is seeking votes as well as nourishment. It is not so easy to detect motives when public figures show up at public functions, visit hospitals, autograph baseballs and programmes, make charitable and philanthropic contributions, lend support to this or that cause, make public statements, etc.

As students of public opinion formation and other aspects of human behaviour, however, public relations counsel do not rely solely on incessant publicity, through advertising or the media of communication. They are much more scientific than that in their appraisal of what makes for enduring success. Thus, they consider not just the mass public but also the special publics with which their clients deal, on which they rely. Such publics include a company's employees, its stockholders, suppliers, neighbours, and customers. Public relations counsel, it is obvious, did not create these or other public relationships. No individual or institution can avoid having public relationships, and it is trite to point out that everyone with whom one has contact forms an opinion of him, which can be either beneficial or harmful. In the long run, it is a satisfied employee or customer who does the most for a business. If your employees say, "It's a good place to work," or your customers declare, "They give you a square deal," you are immune to the effect of any press agentry or publicity stunts in which your competitor can engage.

It is good public relations activity when:

A department store provides adequate rest rooms;

A filling station attendant cleans your windshield and puts air in your tires;

A congressman answers his crank mail courteously;

A mayor presides at a cornerstone laying;

A music store loans instruments for a public school concert;

A college publicly recognizes the work of a scholar;

A newspaper provides a speaker for a men's club;

The management of a factory sends a letter congratulating an employee on a wedding anniversary;

A large corporation sends easy-to-read annual reports and personal letters to minority stockholders;

A chain store manager participates in community affairs; or

A fire department welcomes school children on a field trip.

Hart, Michigan, businessmen and farmers annually sponsor a Mexican Homecoming Fiesta for the entertainment of migratory cherry pickers.

Such activities are open and above board. Their purpose, to build good will, is obvious but not resented. What is resented is any attempt to disguise the nature of an activity as through a "front" organization, ostensibly operating objectively in the public interest but actually supported, often secretly, by those who expect to benefit by its operations. In 1929, one of the most extravagant public relations stunts of all times occurred when the President of the United States and many other notables went to Dearborn, Michigan to help celebrate Light's Golden Jubilee. Ostensibly, it was to honour the aging Thomas A. Edison, which it did. It was however, the brainchild of the electric light industry's public relations director. He was Edward L. Bernays, nephew of Sigmund Freud and, next to Ivy Ledbetter lee, the leading pioneer in this field. His *Crystallizing Public Opinion,*[1] published by Boni, Liveright in 1923, was the first full-length book defining this new way of "engineering consent" by means of "public relations counsel," a term Bernays invented.

Today, these public relations counsel work closely with personnel managers who may be under them. Public relations can take a great deal of the credit for making workers happier on their jobs. Enlightened P.R. men are not strikebreakers or union busters and they do not resort to "gimmicks" to keep labour pacified so as to prevent unrest, for such methods do not have lasting effect. It is certainly true that a large segment of the business and industrial world has learned this lesson the hard way after many decades of bitter conflict, and that some elements have not learned it yet. Public relations men with broad perspectives, however, have supplanted strong labour unions and protective governmental agencies as the principal influence upon management, into whose planning sessions they now are being admitted in increasing numbers, to go to the roots of discontent on the part of either employees or customers rather than to devise ways of circumventing situations needing reformation.

Similarly, in its policies toward the general public, the public relations-minded organization is today generally open-handed. For example, in their early days, both the railroads and the airlines did their best to make difficult the work of newspaper reporters attempting to obtain information regarding accidents. Today, they realize that the goodwill they thereby would lose makes the effort dangerous. Full cooperation in the handling of such news has replaced concerted efforts to suppress or cover-up the facts. Greatest credit for effecting this change generally is accorded the late Ivy Ledbetter Lee, who was employed by the Rockefeller interests early in the century after a series of public investigations and exposes by the so-called muckrakers in several widely circulated magazines had caused widespread distrust of big business. Lee recognized that the "public be dammed" attitude no longer was workable, if it ever had been, and he persuaded his clients to end the policy of secrecy which previously had been orthodox. Some who call themselves public relations counsel today still may act occasionally, or even frequently, as censors or "cover-up" artists, attempting to prevent or counteract an unfavourable response to some incident without going to the roots of its cause. Such practitioners, however, are decidedly not up to date or in tune with the times. The most effective public relations, may it be repeated, is now pretty generally recognized as that which takes "the long view" and which recognizes that the effects on sales or reputation are indirect and difficult to measure. There is rapidly increasing recognition that you can "phony it up" just so long but that the day of reckoning comes inevitably. The only sound first step in any effective public relations programme is to "put the house in order."

The informational and propaganda efforts of the federal government during both world wars provided great impetus to commercial public relations. Not only were thousands of persons given training in public relations techniques, but also great strides were made in the development of scientific methods of studying public attitudes and opinions. This work has been continued by private agencies and by an increasing number of colleges and universities. Communications is now recognized as a so-called discipline within the social sciences. Market analysis, public opinion polling, and content analysis are among the subjects studied quantitatively by these new scholarly experts on communications. Motivational research is the name given to efforts to determine the potential receptivity by particular audiences of advertising and other appeals. Bernays defines the function of the public relations counsel as to "interpret the client to the public and the public to the client."

Since most communications research to date has been primarily to benefit the person who has something—a commodity or an idea—to sell, the need for greater public understanding of what is happening is beginning to be felt. Since the short-lived (1937-41) Institute for Propaganda Analysis, there has been no large-scale organized effort to educate the general public to the purposes and/or methods of the special pleader.

Today, the only effective antidote to any public relations efforts which are "bad" is counter-efforts which are "good," just as it long has been known that the best defense against propaganda is counter-propaganda. Minority groups, especially those with small bankrolls—a characteristic of minority groups—are learning to use this new weapon in self-defense in order not to lose whatever is at stake by default. Granted that the large and powerful have the advantage; they would have it, public relations or no public relations. More and more, social agencies and professional groups have been getting off their supercilious high horses as regards public relations and are festooning their public facades. Voices that make no attempt to be heard are ineffective. Even a death rattle may have some influence on posterity.

If public relations is motivated behaviour, good manners, smart actions to make people like you, then certainly it can be practised by ethical individuals and institutions for good and social useful ends as well as for strictly monetary purposes. If this sounds like, "If you can't lick 'em, join 'em," that's exactly as it is supposed to sound. A few more cheery "good mornings" and smiling "good byes" in freshly painted and well lighted highbrow dens would make life decidedly more pleasant. It is not possible to consider public relations as a fad or a bogie which will pass or go away if you wait long enough. As has been said, it is impossible to exist in any society without public relationships, anyway. A policy to have no conscious public relations is a public relations policy itself. Few persons or institutions can achieve much without being liked, at least by the right people. Liking often grows out of understanding and understanding is based on information. The "inner glow" which comes from anonymous do-gooding may be great compensation, but to be content with it is vouchsafed only to those who already have established themselves.

The best public relations is that which has an altruistic motive, which takes a broad view of the place of the practitioner in the social order and has a sense of social responsibility or at least enlightened self-interest. The greatest potential danger of a thoroughly public relations-conscious public is the artificiality in the behaviour of persons toward each other which it might entail. Today, it already is difficult to know what is publicity stunt and what isn't, and that goes for a great deal of charity and philanthropy as well as for banquets, mass meetings, and other newsworthy affairs. Even when the motivations of the sponsors of such events do not seem to be ulterior, publicity seekers may take advantage of such occasions to grab the limelight they provide. It is to conjecture whether anyone who relies upon public favour for a livelihood today can fail to be conscious of his public relations in everything that he does. If this means that his behaviour will always be circumspect, good. It is to shudder, however, to contemplate a world in which nobody ever joined anything, never went anywhere, never said anything or did anything without a careful weighing of the possible effect upon his economic well being. Quite a few persons active in public affairs, who have virtually reached this stage of behaviour already, have complained bitterly over the fact that they must struggle to retain the small amount of privacy which they want for themselves. If nothing is ever "on the level"—meaning done without conscious purpose to improve the status of the perpetrator—the spontaneity and nonconformity which have been responsible in the past for so much of what is today considered good shall have disappeared.

Encouraging evidence that man is not so easily converted into a mental automaton has been provided by numerous political elections in which the public relations effort was overwhelmingly in behalf of one candidate or party but the people voted the other way. This indicates that basic attitudes and opinions are not so easily manipulated as the would-be manipulator would like to have it. Kermit Eby recalls that in 1944, when he was educational director for the Congress of Industrial Organizations, he was instrumental in the distribution of forty million pieces of literature on behalf of the candidacy of Franklin Delano Roosevelt. Surveys showed that F.D.R. got 71 per cent of the CIO vote. He also got 68 per cent of the AFL vote although that organization distributed virtually no literature in his behalf. In *Harper's* for June 1957, R.L. Heilbronner[2] revealed that an expensive campaign to make Cincinnati "United Nations conscious" was "a gigantic frost" because "most people don't give a damn about most things, unless those things are part and parcel of their concrete lives."

Maybe skillful public relations conducted by groups without axes to grind could make people "give a damn" about the United Nations and many other things. The public relations profession (if that is what it is) cannot be blamed for all of the ignorance and indifference—the anti-intellectualism—of our times. Even if it were not scapegoating to declare the opposite, the alternative is not to allow victory by default. Just as the automobile, nuclear power, etc., can be used for good or bad purposes, so can public relations. It may be true that your good public relations is my bad public relations. That, however, is merely tantamount to acceptance of the fact that modern life in this democracy is characterized by competing, conflicting interests all wanting to be heard.

What is the alternative to becoming public relations-conscious today? Ideally, it would be to work for a smaller, simpler society. Historians and anthropologists tell us, however, that such societies are not without their hates and fears and tensions, albeit on a smaller scale and at a slower pace.

Like it or not, public relations is a development of our contemporary culture. It's the way those who depend on widespread favourable acceptance by others operate in an age when face-to-face relationships are minimized. The public relations-conscious organization has to study itself constantly to ask, "Am I doing the right thing?" Good ethics may be a natural consequence of such inquiry. A professional attitude may become predominant to the delight of the socially-minded pragmatist.

REFERENCES

1. E. L. Bernays, *Crystallizing Public Opinion.* New York, Boni, Liveright, 1923.
2. R. L Heilbronner, Public Relations—The Invisible Sell. *Harper's,* 214 : 23-31, June 1957.

2

Public Relations in Librarianship

PUBLIC relations is with the public. It is the relationship of your library with its borrowers, with the non-borrowers of your community, with your trustees or library committee, with dealers, collectors, salesmen of equipment; with scholars and contest solvers, with your staff and the administration for which you work. Public relations is with the public, and as true as in its Biblical context is the admonition, "Whatsoever you do unto the least of these. . ."

"Course or blessing," C.D. MacDougall calls public relations. Either is possible. For your public relations is what you make it. It cannot be shuddered at and wished away, but it can be welcomed and made to serve you well. It is with you every minute of every day. It is waiting at your library doors. It is observing the cleanliness of your hallways and public rooms. It is reacting to the service of all your staff, listening in on telephone conversations, reading your mail. It follows you home, into your personal life. It accompanies you on all your ventures into the life of your community.

Public relations has been endowed with a kind of twentieth century magic by the corporations and their P.R. officers. Neither the corporations nor the P.R. men invented public relations. It has been with us since the beginning of trade. But the American business man has learned the foolishness of *caveat emptor* as a motto, has learned the dead end of selling wooden nutmegs. He has made the good will of his public part and parcel of the assets of his business. Public relations is as much a part of the daily life of a library as it is of any business. Perhaps more so, for a library is not self-supporting and depends, even more than the usual business, primarily on the good opinion of its patrons. It is day-to-day building of the atmosphere of goodwill in which a library (or a business) can operate most widely and most effectively to give the best possible service to its public. As R. L. Heilbronner[1] wrote in *Harper's Magazine* for June 1957: "In a word, public relations covers a lot of acreage-blurring out into advertising, slopping over into selling, dipping down into publicity, and touching—or at least aspiring to—the 'making' of public opinion itself."

Edward W. Barrett, dean of Columbia University's School of Journalism, praises J.W. Hill, himself the ungowned dean of American P.R. men, for seeing "public relations as broad management function-more precisely . . . as the management function of giving the same organized and careful attention to the asset of good will as is given to any other major asset of the business."[2] Public relations may well be the most important asset—"the priceless ingredient," to quote the phrase that one firm's advertising programme has made famous—for bad public relations can cancel the good of every other asset.

With a knowledge of experiences of other libraries and other types of organizations, public relations becomes perforce a do-it-yourself programme. Public relations is the asset; is the programme, most expressive of the individuality, the personality, of each separate library. It may be patterned emulatively, but never imitatively. It must be done according to the needs of your library. It must express as attractively (and as accurately) as possible your library to the public.

First, public relations must be properly fitted into the administrative pattern of your library. Few libraries can afford the services of a special public relations officer. For those that can, fine. University and college libraries often can work through a campus public relations office. In some cases, a city P.R. man is available to public libraries. Where a trained professional is available, it is an error both factual and tactical to direct public relations except through that individual. In other cases, public relations must be conducted as an auxiliary responsibility of the librarian or delegated to some other member of his staff. In both of these alternatives, however, it remains a function of management and the responsibility of the librarian.

A library's policies in many fields must be worked out thoroughly and wisely by the librarian and his governing board. Once worked out, policy must be implemented by actions which elucidate it in every function for the library and by every member of a library's staff. The right hand must know what to expect of the left hand. It is of basic importance for good public relations that all staff be kept as fully informed as possible, both of long-term library policy and immediate newsworthy developments which relate to that policy. If not with a single voice, the library must at least speak in a consistent accent.

The extent of a library's services and resources must be well enough known for any and every employee to respond with accurate answers or definite and proper referrals to patrons' questions. There is hardly a greater disservice that library can do its public relations programme than to permit an employee to answer an inquiry with a "that's-not-my-business" type of reply. It matters not how extensive a library's services are if the attainment of those services becomes a dismaying pursuit of referrals from one functionary to another. Good service is the handmaiden of good public relations. This does not mean that every library must provide every service. It does mean that whatever service a library provides must be done well. A well considered "no" can be much more effective public relations than an ill considered yes."

Public relations is as important within your organization as it is without. Staff relations are a part of public relations. Ability to work with a governing board is a part of public relations. And, once these relationships are satisfactorily established, each member of your staff, each member of your board becomes a part-time P.R. man for your library. But the more apparent aspects of public relations are those outside your management family. Public relations is with the public, but each library has several publics. There is its public which borrows books. There is a public made up others in the same profession. There is a public, in some libraries at least, of scholars or professional users of materials.

Relations with the general borrowing public are broadest, most demanding, and, yet, easiest. Here the field is reasonably well defined. Here publicity (and publicity must be positively delimited as only a small aspect of public relations) can be effective. Here patrons' response is quickest and most vocal; if you are taking the wrong tack, someone will tell you so. Librarians generally have done good work with publicity, but it is too easy to forget that not all publicity is good publicity.

Publicity begins at home—or, at least, in the library profession itself. Staff news sheets, exhibits, guides to exhibits are all part of a library publicity programme. The incidence of library publicity material of this type pitched at a kindergarten level is more appalling than appealing. Is it necessary that adult human beings approach the problem of announcing a staff party as if they were writing for the amusement of low grade morons? The same approach pervades much of the material issued in the name of recruiting for librarianship. Unless librarians write as intelligent people, how can intelligent people be recruited to the ranks of librarianship? The cute crack, the quick quip are devices best left to the experienced writer or to the professional adman. In the hands of the tyro, they too soon become an over-sweetened syllabub, more fluff than substance and inclined to cloy. But staff news sheets can be informative, can be cleanly written and neatly printed. Recruiting pamphlets can be intelligently and attractively devised. Exhibits, can be artfully and artistically arranged. If these things are done well, they make for good public relations. But there is no middle ground. It is better that they not be done at all than that they be done badly.

Newspaper publicity must be controlled within the management function of public relations, but it is practicably possible to delegate responsibility in this area. It is helpful both to the library and to a paper that one person be responsible for newspaper publicity. A minimum of experience can establish a satisfactory working relationship between a library and a reporter. He will know what he wants. It is your business to give him the facts. Handout journalism has been a corollary development of public relations as a profession. It is certainly not its healthiest aspect. Make information available to newspapers, but don't try to style it for them. Reporters are better reporters than are librarians.

Notices and articles in the library press are another aspect of continuing public relations. The unfortunate proliferation of library periodicals makes complete coverage impossible, cuts down the readership for any single journal, and lowers the average quality of writing on librarianship; but this is, nevertheless, a legitimate area for use in furthering public relations. Wide knowledge of one's own profession and of his colleagues in it is a prerequisite for general recognition of librarianship as a profession. Librarians are inclined to write too much solely for other librarians, talk too much to other librarians. Participation in national, regional, and local organizations of professional librarians is good public relations, particularly if such organizations reach other professions and the public in general. Individual participation by staff members is also good for a library. Individuals should be encouraged in membership in civic groups, professional organizations in specific subject fields, and in activity in community projects. As useful as professional exchange is, articles in the non-library press, speeches before Rotary, Kiwanis, and other civic or special interest groups are especially rewarding.

Publicity and participation are merely vehicles of public relations. The public as a mass can be effectively reached through newspaper, radio, and television. The public as a special force in promoting the welfare of a library can be better and more directly reached through individual participation in the widest possible variety of activities. Public relations as a continuing function is a more important and a slower process. It is axiomatic that repeated incidental mention of a celebrity is more important to his reputation than one large splurge of publicity about him. Every time the library is mentioned favourably, every time an individual connected with the library appears in the community in a favourable light good public relations are being built. Every time a library is listed among the acknowledgments in a published book, every time an individual sees a creditable publication from the library, every time an organization or an individual is helped by the library's services, the library increases in stature. The cumulative effects are unlimited: better budgets, adequate staffing, more books, finer buildings, easier recruiting—in a word: better libraries.

"Good will" is often listed in corporate assets as valued at $1.00—not because it is worth little but because it is an intangible beyond practical evaluation. Good will is priceless. It is public relations that build good will. Libraries are a public or institutional service, tangible examples of good public relations on the part of a municipality, a corporation, or an educational institution providing information and recreational resources to its constituency. Librarianship is a service profession. If librarians are to emphasize their work as a profession, interpreting as well as making available knowledge, this emphasis must be based on good service. It must be quality service at all levels of operations. Good service, conceived to support community and institutional goals, will automatically result in good public relations. Good public relations will create lasting good will.

Developing a Library Public Relations Programme

The art of public relations is not new for it has been practised ever since the beginning of time. At an earlier date, it was probably known as "understanding" or "getting along" or "good will" or even "putting your best foot forward" and "doing good and getting credit for it." It was only when it became a science, some twenty odd years ago, that it came to be considered, by some, as a mysterious, wonder-working short cut that could solve any problem and produce any desired effect. The term, unfortunately, has also often been used, without real meaning or understanding, to describe flash-in-the-pan publicity stunts and programmes that smack only of press-agentry and nothing more. This may account for the suspicious or cynical eye with which some people view what they, incorrectly, term "public relations."

There are many definitions of public relations but one of the most succinct was formulated by two experts in the field, J. H. Wright and B. H. Christian, who said: "Modern public relations is a planned programme of policies and conduct that will build public confidence and increase public understanding."[3]

In analyzing this definition it becomes readily apparent that there are three important words to be considered. The first is "planned". An effective programme has to be planned. It cannot be sporadic. It must be continuing function that is in operation not only day by day but year after year. The second word is "policies" and this implies the direction in which an agency is moving and will move, the aims and extent of services, the manner in which it cooperates with opinion forming groups and the position it occupies or hopes to occupy in a given area or community. "Conduct" is the third word and this refers to the behaviour of an entity in the social pattern as well as to the behaviour of everyone associated with it from top management down through the ranks.

Public relations is often referred to as a management function. This is true, to a certain degree, for policies are set by management or the administrative officers but it is the staff or the employees who carry out these policies. One cannot function without the other. A good programme of internal relations is the base on which good public relations are built. An employee or staff group that works harmoniously, with an understanding of the objectives and the methods by which these objectives are to be accomplished, is of the greatest importance.

A good programme of internal relations begins with the employees—all of the employees. Their attitudes affect cost, efficiency, and service but their effect does not stop there. They also influence consumer and community attitudes and help to shape public opinion.

After examining the real fundamentals upon which good public relations are built one comes to the realization that no organization or institution can function, fully and successfully, without putting these fundamentals into practice. Libraries must apply these principles to merit public understanding and support. Only then will people make the maximum use of resources and services and provide adequate support, for libraries of all kinds and sizes.

Libraries have been practising public relations for years but in the post-war period the library's responsibility to the community or group it serves has grown enormously. In a rapidly changing world, libraries are faced with many new and different kinds of competition, not only in the areas of service and communication, but also in the areas of finance and personnel. Social, scientific, and economic changes have brought a host of new challenges as well as problems. Often, the very existence of a library depends upon how well it meets these changes. Because of these conditions, it is advisable to take long look at the existing public relations programme in every library to determine whether it is adequate, and if it is not, how it can be improved.

Such soul-searching is common in industry and merchandising and is often accomplished by means of surveys, polls, interviews, and research studies. Most libraries can neither afford the time nor the money for such large-scale projects. A simple method has been devised, however, for agencies who wish to conduct their own surveys. It requires a certain amount of time and an even greater amount of honesty on the part of the administrative officers, which include the board of trustees or directors and the librarian. Department heads and staff members are invited to participate, at some point in the programme, and make valuable contributions to the whole.

These are six questions to be asked and answered when evaluating an existing library public relations programme:

1. Is there anything wrong with the activities of this institution?
2. Is there anything wrong with the objectives of this institution?
3. What is our policy toward the public?
4. What policies have caused misunderstanding, if any?
5. Have you done everything we can to promote good will?
6. How much does the public really know about this institution?

Some of these questions apply specifically to public relations and others apply to internal relations and these, of necessity, must be answered and discussed first, for good public relations thrive only on good internal relations.

After the institutional aims and objectives have been subjected to the searchlight of truth it may seem feasible to adopt an entirely new plan, or new ideas and planning may be added to those parts of the existing public relations programme that have proved to be sound and productive. Any plan should be elastic enough to meet changing attitudes and conditions. Some aspects of every programme will be concerned with long-term usage and others will be adopted for short-term usage. An ideal library public relations programme does these things:

1. Evaluates public attitudes and public needs.
2. Forms policies and procedures identified with these attitudes and needs.
3. Explains policies and problems to its publics.
4. Develops programmes and services that will earn public understanding and support.

Evaluating public attitudes and public needs is the library's first responsibility. It must know that people in a given community or area need to help them lead fuller lives and to help them meet everyday problems in the home, the school, at work, and in their social environment. Generalizations about people's needs are known to most librarians. They know that the first desire is for security. People want to know how to raise their families, how to acquire and keep a home, how to better themselves financially and socially, and how to understand and get along with other people. Their secondary interests include hobbies, group activities, and leisure-time pursuits. But one cannot generalize about attitudes. These cannot be taken for granted. A librarian must know what the people in his community are thinking and how they feel about almost everything. This knowledge can be acquired only by personal contact with people and groups at all levels. In the past, some librarians have been accused of living in an ivory tower but every progressive librarian knows that such a state of isolation is not possible in modern society.

Policies and procedures are developed after the evaluation of public attitudes and needs has been completed. A willingness to help and work with both the individual and the group and to encourage interest and participation in library activities is the first step toward gaining public understanding and support. The fact that library has anticipated and met the needs of an individual or a group soon becomes common knowledge. Word-of-mouth publicity is a powerful force that costs nothing and is often more effective than many high-priced publicity campaigns.

Publicity is the tool that is used to tell the story of the library and to explain its policies and problems to its publics. It is not the purpose but an important tool of public relations that is used to create an intelligent, informed, and favourable public opinion. Much of the success of any institution depends on the process by which people are kept informed. The publicity family is a large one and includes newspapers, magazines, films, radio, television, photographs, special programmes, public speeches, exhibits, books, book lists, reports, posters, publications, special events, meetings, and that all important word-of-mouth publicity. Libraries use publicity to gain or retain public sentiment behind a budget plea, promote good will, obtain gifts of books and money, spread information about library facilities, increase circulation, build up reference use, interest definite groups of people, promote attendance, direct people to the library and dozens and dozens of other large and small projects.

Publicity techniques are not difficult to master and many libraries have learned to use the methods and media once regarded as the sole property of business. Librarians have learned, too that there is no hocus-pocus about writing releases for newspapers or spot announcements for radio and television. There are certain basic techniques to be followed and these can be learned with the help of books plus careful study of the publicity outlets in each community. In recent years, some librarians have made use of planned programmes and publicity materials with considerable success. Many feel the subscription cost of these materials is far less costly and more effective than what they are able to produce themselves, at a like cost.

Many libraries enlist the cooperation of individuals and groups to help publicize services and policies. These may be within the library framework, such as a group of libraries pooling materials and talent for newspaper and radio news or for displays or booklists. Individuals and groups out of the library framework might include the Friends of the Library or the local gas and light company or newspaper editor, or the display manager of a department store or anyone else who helps to publicize the library, either directly or indirectly. Many libraries reach a wider audience more effectively and economically because of interest and cooperation on the part of individuals and groups who have already been "sold" on the library.

While a library has an active educational mission it cannot stop at providing suitable books and maintaining a competent staff just for the casual visitor. A library must be more than a mere purveyor of books. Special programmes and services that will earn public under standing and support are the concern of many libraries. A large library may possibly sponsor a dozen such programmes while a smaller library may concentrate on a single programme. Some of the special services and programmes that have been successfully developed by libraries in recent years include work with teen-agers, older adults, shut-ins, new citizens, parents, businessmen, and newcomers to the community.

No programme, however, is undertaken without careful consideration of the needs and interests of the community or area the library serves. There would be no point in sponsoring a Great Books programme in a community where the people need desperately to learn and understand the English language, just because a library somewhere else has undertaken such a programme. It would seem equally foolish to undertake an elementary course in the English language in a community where people had long since mastered the tongue. This not only applies to programmes but to services, also.

Some special programmes and services are worked out with the assistance of interested individuals and community groups and are cooperative in nature. This, often, takes much of the pressure of time and work from the library staff and at the same time, creates the best possible kind of public relations.

Who can say how much good public relations will cost a library? No one can budget public relations. It is an intangible that is part and parcel, bone and sinew of every organization and institution. One library may have thousands and thousands of dollars to spend on personnel and resources while a smaller library may have one-tenth as much at its command. But the smaller library may have the better public relations because the librarian and the staff have learned that having a lot of money does not guarantee good public relations. Public relations is an individual thing. It expresses the personality of a library. Public relations is a slow-building process which calls for attention tact, and a consideration of every day matters. In other words, it is a programme of service.

REFERENCE

1. R. L. Heilbronner, Public Relations—The Invisible Sell. *Harper's Magazine,* 214:24, June 1957.
2. E. W. Barrett, Business of Building Good Will. [Review] *Saturday Review,* 41:21, Jan. 18, 1958.
3. J.H., Wright, and B. H. Christian, *Public Relations in Management.* New York, McGraw-Hill, 1949, p. 3.

3

Objectives and Functions of the Public Library

A VISITOR from abroad standing in the midst of busy American public library is impressed by the sight of so many men, women and children hurrying about to get books and information, or quietly reading and studying in the various departments, or asking for reference help at the service desks, or walking out with the books they have borrowed. He observes that most of these individuals get personal help, but that no one inquires the name, the status, the politics or religion or the purposes of any one of the library users. Each user comes and goes as an individual. Each is equally entitled to the most effective help the library can give. Objectives and interests are as numerous as the crowd. Our visitor is looking at a unique manifestation of the democratic process, the freedom of each citizen to read and to think as he may decide for himself, about any subject he chooses.

These millions of Americans are borrowing more than 550 million books a year from 8,000 public libraries. As users and taxpayers, the purposes, the operating methods, and the management of public libraries should be of interest to a wide range of these citizens.

The public library's functions and programmes derive from the conviction that books and other printed matter as well as certain audio-visual materials are powerful, indispensable agents for bringing enlightenment, new knowledge, encouragement and inspiration to every member of the community.[1,2,3] One function remains constant: to provide and service materials for enlarging the mind and dispelling prejudice and ignorance. "This implies the necessity of making access to the truth easy and rapid for anyone who seeks it. For the overwhelming majority, the quickest and easiest access to the world's best thought it through the public library."[4] This means very recent facts and ideas as well as the wisdom of the ages; the library must be current as well as retrospective.

As one newscaster sees them: "Today's libraries are much more than books alone. They are also art reproductions, music recordings, language aids, motion pictures, microfilms, meeting rooms for discussion groups. . . . They are beehives of activity . . . busy humming market places of ideas where the fields of interest are not narrowed to the educational or the cultural, but limitless as the span of man's own consciousness: a veritable treasure chest of facts and follies . . . a kind of intellectual service station . . . ."[5] This puts some secondary activities on a par with primary functions, but it gives the feeling of the modern busy library.

Every earnest person desires to live and work in the firm belief that this occupation is important and useful to society; librarians are no exception. Most of them choose their profession because they are convinced of the salutary influence of books and reading, and most of them realize that through the library's materials and services they can greatly serve their community.

Value and Formation of Goals

In serving its community a library should freshly study and formulate what it should or should not attempt. With specific objectives it can plan its immediate and long-range programme. Goals determine daily decisions and make book selection more effective. They influence the internal organization, the selection and assignment of staff members, the quality and kind of service. In turn they also determine the extent of its public support, and establish criteria to measure result.

Goals, or objectives, should derive from many sources: from the librarian's knowledge of present trends and problems in society; from his awareness of what goes on, nationally, in education and in cultural and intellectual fields; from national and local library leaders who have the background of discussion, debate, observation and experience. The staff members who are in constant contact with library users should have the right to participate in drawing up a statement of purposes and programmes.

Such a statement of goals needs to be written out, needs to be realistic, and must depend always upon the library's resources and funds; it must be possible to achieve the goals. The statement needs periodic review in the light of results achieved and of changes in the local situation. It should be compared with current developments elsewhere, but not distorted by temporary fads and enthusiasms. It should be comprehensive but aimed at a unitary concept of the library's purpose, and not diffused in scattered questions, problems or ideals.

Unified goals lead to Policies. *Policies* govern programmes and procedures. Goals deal with the larger aim: what the library hopes to accomplish. Policies are general directions as to what activities shall be undertaken, on what scale, with what emphasis. *Programmes* are the framework for activities, showing how in general the latter are to be planned, organized and managed. An activity is a specific operation or event undertaken or sponsored by the library. *Procedures* relate to operational details of activities. *Standards* are officially adopted or widely accepted measures by which to evaluate results; they may be derived from reliable data, or they may be rule-of-thumb dicta based on trial and experience.

The Background of Present Objectives

One can hardly understand and appreciate the philosophy and prevailing objectives of a profession without knowing what led up to them. Libraries stemmed from the ideal of improving society, a purpose or goal widely accepted. The ideal goes back to national belief, prevalent since colonial days, in "the improvability of human nature." Many books deal with this stimulating viewpoint, sometimes called "social Darwinism in American thought." Franklin and Washington and their colleagues in organizing our government held this ". . . concept, characteristic of their time, of the indefinite perfectability of man and his institutions, the belief that man could determine the main line of his progress, and the opinion that institutions existed to further progress, and that education was one of the principal means."[6]

This continuing, altruistic American conviction underlies social legislation and other public effort to ameliorate living conditions in the face of indifferent, the compromisers and the reactionaries. Under the influence of this conviction, librarians assume that the library is a potent factor in forwarding education and economic and social progress. They see evidence each hour of each day that library's materials are a positive influence in the thinking and in the lives of their fellow citizens.

A Philosophy of Librarianship

Much has been written on the lack of "a philosophy of librarianship"[7]. Most librarians are not deeply concerned about this; they are preoccupied with daily service and performance. Any statement of the basic philosophy of the American public library has to be supplemented by occasional fresh interpretations of its applications as adjusted to the times. Each year this democratic institution undergoes unforeseeable changes, as to appeal, modernity and efficiency, which aim to keep it in line with the constant procession of new problems, purposes and methods of American and world society. Consequently a librarian does well to study such considered statements, for example, as the two on national goals and purposes, which appeared in 1960.[8,9] Similarly, the returns from the 1960 census provide a new set of facts which indicate changes in the character and situations and therefore in the attitudes and needs of the population. Some inevitable results in library planning have already been forecast.[10]

Among recent developments following the Public Library Inquiry of 1947-50 have been the passage of and results from the Federal Library Services Act of June, 1956 and its five-year renewal from July, 1961. Following carefully worked-out plans based on the American Library Association's 1956 standards for public library service, appropriations were increased so that in 1961 Federal funds $7 million were matched by more than $9 million in state funds and about $4 million in local funds, a total of about $20 million annually. The number of counties without library service was cut from 319 to 200, basic reference collections have been strengthened and general services improved in many individual system.[11] Great progress is being made in drawing small-town and village libraries into a rapidly increasing number of regional systems. There are the widening and gratifying results from National Library Week, inaugurated in 1958. There has been radical improvement in general appearance and interior planning in scores of recent library buildings. Never has so much careful research been going on in so many aspects of librarianship as today, partly stimulated by grants for individual projects from the Council on Library Resources. These indicate that library leadership, nationally and in many states, is disposed and able to develop dynamic library programmes which can propel books and libraries into the heart of what goes on in this nation.[12] Only continued planning and effort can keep libraries moving ahead to close the gap between needs and actualities. One major objective is to bring weak little libraries into large systems. The need to accelerate this is suggested by the following Table 3.1, for fiscal 1960. It shows that 5,768 of the 8,190 identified libraries in the

U.S., or 70 per cent, are in communities of less than 10,000 population. This had grown from 4,486 in 1955.

Objectives in More Detail

Among topics and problems which engage the attention of library leaders in the 1960's, are these:

1. The need for a general shift of attention from elaborate organization toward reaching and serving the great population which still does not read or use books in any substantial way, through creative and imaginative programmes for extending the adult reading habit and informational service.

2. A more active role for the library in the community as an intellectual powerhouse and rallying point, partly achieved through more

TABLE 3.1.
Number and Per Cent of Public Library Systems, by Size of Population Served, Aggregate U.S. : Fiscal Year 1960*

Population served	*Number of libraries*	*Percentage of total*
Total	8,190	100.0
Less than 1,000	1,574	19.2
1,000-2,499	1,874	22.9
2,500-4,999	1,209	14.8
5,000-9,999	1,111	13.6
10,000-14,999	591	7.2
15,000-24,999	610	7.5
25,000-34,999	311	3.8
35,000-49,999	287	3.5
50,000-99,999	369	4.5
100,000-499,999	217	2.6
500,000-999,999	28	.3
1 million and over	9	.1

*From Table 2 in Frank L. Schick and Doris C. Holladay. *Statistics of Public Libraries Serving Populations of 100,000 or More: Fiscal Year 1960.* 24 pp. Nov. 1961. U.S. Office of Education. OE-15033.[13]

effective public relations and publicity. The essentially passive library cannot be allowed to continue undisturbed in its inertia.

3. Greater understanding of the individual reader and of the potential reader — his motivations, his reaction to books, reading and libraries, as preface to improved service. Studies directed by Lowell Martin, 1962-1965, at Baltimore, may produce important new facts to help on this.

4. Extended recruiting and better training for more librarians and clerical workers, in library schools and elsewhere, including on-the-job training, and the training of part-time and volunteer workers in smaller libraries.

5. More specific standards and measurements by which to evaluate how good a job is being done in each aspect of the work.

6. More attention to research on what libraries are doing, why, at what cost, and how staff members can be deployed more effectively to accomplish major objectives.

7. The need for speeding up the creation of regional and large cooperative library organizations, with able central staffs and strong collections to serve widely-spread smaller service points which should be federated for greater economy and usefulness.

8. Continued effort by library organizations to increase state and federal financing of public libraries beyond whatever increases can be secured from local government.

9. The need for serving more effectively the increasing throngs of grade and high school pupils seeking reference help, because even good school libraries are not likely to have the variety of materials which a public library has or to be open for pupil use as many hours—all this while greatly developing adult informational reading and reference services to more than equal to library's service to children and young people.

10. Increased emphasis on efficient methods of finding information, cooperative bibliographic enterprises, and use of machines if not too costly, or simpler devices, to accelerate the recording and rendering of more detailed information needed by a constantly more specialized clientele.

In a sense the library has a monopoly on certain distinct and unique objectives and services: reading, study, information and reference help. It can profitably concentrate on these. Whatever overlaps and duplicates what other institutions and agencies can or should do better or more logically diverts attention, funds and endeavor from these basic activities.

The *Post-War Standards for Public Libraries,* issued in 1943 by A. L. A., stimulated library services everywhere by defining objectives and describing desirable accomplishments. The most recent considered formulation of objectives in somewhat specific form appears in the opening pages of *Public Library Service . . . 1956,* resulting from two years' study by an able committee of A. L. A.[14] This statement, with a few omissions, follows here:

Functions of the Public Library

The modern public library collects the printed and audio-visual materials needed to conduct the individual and group life of its constituency. It organizes and makes them convenient and easy to use. It interprets and guides the use of materials to enable as many persons as possible to apply in their daily lives the record of what is known. Lack of any one these—collection, organization and distribution, interpretation and guidance—results in sub-standard library service. . . .

"Provision of materials means more than occasional availability. It means a supply sufficient to make the library a dependable source for more people most of the time. In addition to books, the public library selects and provides pamphlets, documents and other nonbook sources in printed form, and films, tapes, discs, and other non-print recording of knowledge and opinion.

"The materials are provided:

— To facilitate formal self-education of all people in the community.
— To enrich and further develop the subjects on which individuals are undertaking formal education.
— To meet the informational needs of all.
— To support the educational, civic, and cultural activities of groups and organizations.
— To encourage wholesome recreation and constructive use of leisure time.

Services

"All activities of the library are designed to facilitate use of resources-to remove barriers, to invite use, to guide reading toward the goals of each individual.

"Services provided by the public library must be planned in relation to other facilities in the community served. Standard for service must recognize the necessary variations in library programmes required by differing communities.

"The services performed by the modern library are as follows:

- Logical organization of materials for convenient use through shelf arrangement, classification, and catalouging.
- Lending of materials so that they may be used in the location and at the time suited to each individual.
- Provision of information service designed to locate facts as needed.
- Guidance to individuals in the use of educational and recreational material.

Assistance to civic, cultural, and educational organizations, in locating and using materials for programme planning, projects, and the education of members.

Stimulation of use and interpretation of materials through publicity, display, reading lists, story hours, book talks, book and film discussion, and other appropriate means either in the library or in community organizations.

"The materials, services, personnel, and physical facilities of the public library cover the interests of all ages and groups in the population. Starting with the very youngest, the pre-school child needs special resources and help. The fast-growing group of children of school age constitutes another important part of library responsibility. Teenagers and young adults, the challenging group approximately thirteen through nineteen years of age that is making the transition from home and school to adult life, constitute still another distinct responsibility. The various groups and interests in the adult population—the parent, the farmer, the businessman, for example—should be reflected in materials and services. The library responsibility extends to those aspects of the well-being of older and retired people that can be served by library facilities. It is to be expressly understood that each standard in this document applies to all ages and groups, and that a standard is not achieved if its provisions are met for one part of the population but not for another.

"Below these minimum functions of modern library service the child and citizen are denied reasonable opportunity to develop . . ."

The Primacy of Print

By 1955, citizens of the United States were borrowing more than 500 million books a year from their public libraries, not to mention what they borrowed from school, college and other libraries. On the basis of population in the areas served, this amounted to 4.2 books per capita compared with 3.4 volumes per capita in 1950. By 1960 the total figure had doubtless exceeded 550 million.[15]

Even more impressive, national book sales amounted to $1,100 million in 1960, compared with $500 million in 1952.[16] The popular demand for paperback books grows fastest of all; sales are now at the rate of a million a day, and include an increasing proportion of non-fiction and good fiction. There is also the enormous vogue of book club patronage, and the more than half billion circulation for each issue of the 8,000 various U.S. periodicals now published. Yet the total impact of all forms of reading, including newspapers and magazines, is far behind the pervasiveness of such popular mass media as radio, TV and movies. Of six nations included in a 1957 Gallup poll, only 17 per cent of U.S. citizens had been "reading a book at the time of interview," while in Canada 31 per cent, Australia 33 per cent, West Germany 34 per cent and England 55 per cent were "reading a book at present." Still more disconcerting, the per cent in the U.S. had dropped from 21 per cent in 1949. Only 39 per cent in the U.S. had read a book during the last year, whereas in Finland 64 per cent had.[17]

The public considers book service to be the public library's province, and books its reason for existence. Books, reading and study afford opportunities for improvement and relaxation and sources of information not obtainable through ubiquitous radio and television sets and other popular time consumers. Some books have profoundly influenced the destiny of all nations.[18] They have deeply affected the lives of countless individuals. Hitler feared books enough to burn them, and U.S. Information Service libraries in a few foreign lands are still being attacked by those determined to stiff the diffusion of knowledge and the spread of new ideas. Instead of taking a defeatist attitude, librarians should endeavour to help change the popular attitude, to too light response to books and too little inclination to read and study. In the present concern for national progress and production, public libraries are a prolific source for objectives, ideas and facts to help the intelligent public in its enterprises. They deserve for more recognition and financial support than they have anywhere received.

Libraries are directly affected and encouraged by the tremendous increases in school and college enrollment: grade school, from 22 million in 1950 to 31 million in 1960, and probably 38 million by 1970; high school, from 7 million in 1950 to 9 million 1960 and probably 15 million by 1970; and college, from 2 million 1950 to 3.5 million in 1960 and perhaps 6 million by 1970. M.A. degrees have climbed from 58,000 in 1950 to 87,000 in 1960 and probably will be 163,000 by 1970; doctor's degree from 6,600 1950 to 10,500 in 1960 and perhaps 20,000 by 1970. These figures indicate a widespread desire for preparation for more intensive and specialized occupations. They result, in part, from the modern emphasis on national scientific research and development, on which $1.8 billion was spent in 1945 but $12 billion in 1959 and probably $22 billion by 1970.[19] In 1960 also 35 million persons were enrolled in adult education classes, [20] and over 35 million women were women's club members.

A Relentless Drive to Dispel Ignorance

Unless librarians have a conviction that "the things of the mind". are highly important to each citizen's development and satisfactions in life, they can hardly have a profound belief that their books and libraries are very important; their own philosophy and objectives are thereby greatly diminished.

Growth of the reading habit and of all library service has been retarded by widespread disrespect for schools, teachers, books and libraries; for the trained and open individual mind; for the scientific approach to any subject; for the talented, imaginative, highly motivated person who can discover, invent, organize and lead society forward; and for the individual who can concentrate on thinking out a problem or an idea by himself, instead of rolling smoothly along with the herd. No school or college can offset the deficiencies of culturally underprivileged homes. The homes of many wealthy and intelligent parents lack motivation toward intellectual interests. "Ours is a society which does not honour reading . . . If Johnny's parents don't read, why should he submit to the rigors of acquiring that discipline? When his parents learn to read, Johnny will learn."[21] These attitudes, shared by large segments of the populations, have a profound influence on the importance that a library places on its own services. A recent encouraging sign is the occasional town or city which now awards the high school's initial, heretofore a sign of athletic prowess, to the few who get highest scholastic marks.

What Good is a Book in the 1960's?

One major contribution of reading is that it concentrates one's mind directly on the carefully recorded thoughts of others. These thoughts do not flit across the screen, or sound for a second in one's ears and then dissipate without being comprehended. Ideas, information, even stories reflecting human nature and character, wait on the printed page, to be read, reread, pondered, reconsidered in all their depth and richness, until their full meaning and significance leave an indelible impression.

The psychological value of concentrating and of quiet reflections is very great, as shown in numerous studies on the correlation of high reading ability with high scholastic marks. Reading and close attention are not easy. But the accomplishments of great men and famous women as well as the hard-won advances in arts and sciences always have depended and always will depend on concentration and close application. Despite the values of radio, TV, movies, discussion groups and other means of communication, it is only at their infrequent best that they are conducive to reflection and substantial thinking. Though a book is the best visual aid ever devised, constructive mass media have their place, and audio-visual materials must be recognized as an aid to understanding; at present they are rapidly developing as a supplementary device for class instruction.

Though facts and ideas are more easily available to the population than ever before, books are likely to play a correspondingly greater part in American life, because:

1. Only books provide the substantial portion of definite information which people need frequently to pursue their various objectives.

2. Only books provide the substantial aesthetic and emotional experience of appreciating well-written interpretations of life, and looking into the minds and souls of the character described. Compare for example the satisfaction of reading *Treasure Island,* or *Gone With the Wind,* or *Anna Karenina,* which enlarge and enrich, with their brief portrayal on TV or in the movies, usually curtailed or altered. To be sure, a good movie plus the notable book it derives from, or a play, or a musical production plus a textual explanation and evaluation of it make a combination more rewarding than either alone.

3. No other medium can let the demands of the content, rather than some outside consideration, dictate the length of the presentation. Thus, to deal with an idea of any scope and with the intensity it deserve only the book will serve. Most subjects, descriptions and characterizations can be handled adequately only by having time enough and material enough to do them justice. The reader is the one, and he deserves to be, to decide how slowly or how fast he will go, how much skimming and how much intensive repetition he will indulge in, and when and for how long he will put his mind to the matter.

4. Only the book, i.e., print, can eliminate the distraction of the personality of the actor or the broadcaster and the awareness of commercialized or group pressure, as in most programmes on TV, movies and radio. Though occasional exceptions are highly encouraging, to anyone who reads with enjoyment and attention these extraneous influences on and from mass media are distracting, exasperating and often belittling and intolerable.

5. Only book, i.e., print, makes it practicable for the ordinary citizen to turn back to what he saw, read; heard even a few days ago, and lay his hands upon it so that he can follow up some idea, question, objective that has been sticking in his mind as worth pursuing. "Last week's movie, yesterday's newspaper, this morning's TV show, are for all practical purposes gone forever," so far as helping him with what he wishes to look into further.[22]

6. Only books and print meet the need of the individual who wishes to inquire, think and act on his own chosen subject, for his own reasons and in his own way, instead of being influenced or controlled by group or herd thinking and objectives. Often it is only in books that he can examine all sides of a subject.

7. Only the book, among major communication media, encourages the highly desirable habit of quiet, relaxed thinking and reflection. "The rising demand for mental skills and the burgeoning of knowledge, put heavy pressure on school children . . . If children are to be eager learners and thinkers, adults must set an example ."[23] Reading parents make reading children. And libraries should be not only places of learning but places of delight.

What Books have done for Individuals

It avails little, in today's society, to recall the powerful part which books have played in the lives of many great men and women, including Lincoln, Ford, Edison, Westinghouse, Pasteur, Livingstone, Franklin, and as portrayed in hundreds of biographies. It could be argued that all this is from bygone days and totally different conditions, if it were not that this procession keeps on today, as in the recent case of Benjamin Fairless,[24] and many others who could be identified by librarians if they were asked. If, for example, any good library in a city of over 100,000 population currently publicized its wish to prepare a public exhibition of materials, products, inventions, art work, handicrafts, or writings, the ideas for which came from the local library's books and other materials, a surprising number of worthy, interesting examples would be brought forward. All these persons, in days gone by and today, had one priceless ingredient in their satisfactions in life, namely a powerful objectives backed by a deep conviction and determination. A gathering of such cases by libraries is badly needed as ammunition for library programmes aimed at individuals, and as a reminder that books count more than ever for local and national progress.

Objective: To Serve Individuals

A good library works closely with all community organizations. It will take a position of leadership, not necessarily through its librarian heading up some group or activity which puts him in news headlines or on a public platform to argue a cause, but through its initiative in encouraging various community organizations in constructive program mes, as a phase of adult education. But the library administrator cannot overlook or neglect his continuing obligation to the individuals who already come and those who can be encouraged to come to the library seeking services which are as yet not good enough in any respect.[25] For the library should attract and serve a far greater proportion of the population than has been reached so far in any community, enabling them to use library materials for reading and study to an extent not yet attempted anywhere. Many of these prospective patrons belong to organizations only vaguely aware of what the library can give them. As citizens who should participate actively in discussion meetings on vital current topics, they need to develop their individual mental powers by reading and studying material chosen on their own initiative on which to base their own thinking, as a preface and supplement to competent discussion.[26]

As Wakeman says, "Librarianship involves great challenges. We claim that our purpose is to supply 'the right book to the right reader at the right time.' Yet the extraordinarily intimate and delicate transactions involved in reader's advisory work are now conducted with only the shallowest understanding of why and how individuals are affected by what they read."[27] This idea of paying attention to the individual is in sharp contrast to the mass transfer of information and impressions, for example over TV and radio. Thomas Finletter has stated: "When I think of ten million passive spectators, all watching one man on a television screen, all listening at the same time to one persuasive voice, I am a little frightened . . . The thinker-for-himself comes, stubborn and alone, to wring his own meanings and fill his own needs . . . The public library seeks not to enforce the one idea upon the many, but to open to each individual user the unnumbered wealth of intellectual resources from which he can serve not another's ends, but his own."[28]

It should be a major objective for public libraries to recognize and aid the individual as such, even though he is most easily reached through a groups. As Ulveling points out, "More than a century ago, libraries were organized to serve individuals. . . . That libraries can and do still hold uppermost their service to individuals is their greatest strength."[29] The greatest possible number of schoolchildren deserve to be taught to read easily and with enjoyment. Thereafter they need continual aid, in school and especially in adulthood with individual reading programmes. Libraries should give constant stimulation to adults to read for information, for cultural self-development, for citizenship, for recreation. The public library shares this objective with the school and college library. It therefore needs to have a keen interest in and understanding of methods and problems in teaching reading, and in the humanities, as part of its own background for service.

There is wide current discussion of the old question: how far is it the public library's function to serve children and high school pupils who have or should have excellent school libraries? Any study of what pupils ask for, how they fare, why they seek more public library help rather than less when they have good school libraries, will indicate that the public library has a continuing social obligation to serve these young people as fully as it can, while it also helps to create and strengthen their school libraries.[30] But the majority of the population is over twenty-one, and these adults deserve the major share of the library's attention.

Obligation to the Gifted

It seems also incumbent on librarians to discover and encourage those many gifted persons in and out of school, of every age and in every social and economic level, now largely ignored or considered "squares," who have the brains, background, ability, ambition, character and vision requisite for becoming tomorrow's leaders. This objective is compatible with increasing and improving library services to the sizable segment of the population already using them, and at the same time reaching out to attract more recruits into the circle of library users. Excellence can be sought and attained in a context of concern for all. Specific programmes for the gifted, in schools and colleges, are constantly being inaugurated and are producing results.[31] The public library can do as much, by giving all the help possible to those readers who seem to have special promise, and assigning someone in each library of any size to be specially responsible. "Reading is the *sine qua non* of the gifted child's intellectual development. . ."[32] and no doubt this is equally true of adults.

The Library's Prime Educational Function

Books and reading have a powerful influence on society. Convinced of this, the library under real leadership can become an active, effective educational centre primarily for individual learning, and in a secondary way for group discussion and lectures. Not content with serving those who take the initiative in asking its aid, it needs to embark on a continuing programme to encourage citizens in every walk of life to use books and print in ever more effective ways. There is now a clearer view than hitherto of the library's obligation to promote the use of books of an informational, inspirational and self-educational nature. At the same time it can foster the reading of excellent fiction and other recreational books. There is no incompatibility in such a dual conception of service.[33] With all the high school patronage, involving mainly books designated "adult," the present overwhelming and increasing proportion of juvenile circulation, especially from bookmobiles and branches, is poor evidence of any deep conviction that adult education through books is a major objective, as most librarians claim that it should be. Many intelligent adults have had negative experiences at their libraries, and library promotion has not yet become effective enough in the face of other adult distractions.

Adult Education through Groups

Though public schools and other agencies are active in adult education, certain forms of adult education can perhaps be fostered and carried on in the public library more effectively than anywhere else. The climate of informality, the library's tradition of neutrality, the availability of rooms and the fact that libraries and librarians are looked to for community intellectual initiative and enterprise—these place on the library some responsibility to be a leader in promoting lectures, discussion meetings and other group programmes, if it can afford them. At least it can encourage and house them. Some of them may well be carried out elsewhere; in which case the library can cooperate or serve as co-sponsor.

Public libraries need to encourage group discussion, which can do so much to contribute varying viewpoints. While many librarians feel that such discussion often tends to be superficial, open discussion should challenge one to think more carefully, and it should be preceded and followed by some reading and study. Unfortunately it does not seem to engender much study. The extent to which staff time and therefore salary funds should be devoted to initiating, guiding, presiding at, teaching staff members and other citizens how to lead and participate in group discussion is widely questioned. Are public libraries under obligation to plan and manage public discussion? A great deal has been done by many librarians, through letters, phone calls, personal suggestion and encouragement, at slight expenditure of time and with no special organizational setup or salaried position, but by a little fore thought, to make scores of organizations aware that their discussion meetings will be welcomed under the library roof (if it has any meeting room), that the librarians will gladly help prepare programmes as well as references on discussion topics and that the library greatly desires that these programmes shall lead to reading and study.

The point of these paragraphs is that a prime library objective is at stake. If group programmes divert the time of a staff that cannot do justice to book and informational service, it would seem only fair to postpone them, except by way of encouragement to meet in the library.

Many libraries which complain of inadequate personnel are neglecting purposeful readers because part of the staff and the budget is absorbed in group and audio-visual programmes, which they apparently consider the most important aspect of "adult education." As a medium for continuing adult education nothing yet developed is so effective as books and reading. In a large western city library with administrative leadership so weak that it received less than fifty cents per capita, one of the ablest of the few trained competent and vital staff members was transferred from essential adult informational service to give full time to audio-visual and group programmes, even though patrons coming for book service were grossly neglected. In 1961, of the forty largest libraries, twelve were spending from 17 per cent to 25 per cent, one of them 32 per cent, of their inadequate "books and materials" budgets for audio-visual material; no doubt the related salary costs were in proportion.34 The resulting neglect of main-line services in such situations is criticized by many librarians, who do not for a moment claim that printed materials are the only media for transmitting knowledge.[35,36]

Librarians need not become obsessed by social, economic and citizenship problems, which comprise only a segment of the legitimate interests of a community. "A world in revolution does not permit us to delay," said a librarian in 1946; but fifteen or twenty years later the world appears even more in revolution. Obviously libraries should emphasize contemporary problems, and have increasingly done so, such as through the "Great Issues" and "Goals for Americans" programmes, and in a multitude of ways. But alertness of libraries to public problems is only one among many perennial obligations, even admitting that not all subjects are of equal importance. The time-consuming lengths to which some librarians would go to accomplish social changes through library programmes for the aged, for example, are discussed by Barnett under the heading "Beyond Librarianship."[37]

Confusion as to Adult Education

In cooperation with other agencies, the librarian should encourage the citizens in his community to study and discuss current problems. Reading and study are essential to any profitable discussion. They are adult educators, too. Our point is that a library's own boundaries of activity and responsibility have limits; its leaders should place first emphasis on their major service. Obviously the library staff must try to know what is happening today, and why, and foresee trends and be leaders of their community into a better next year. In its positive educational influence the library and the librarians cannot be aloof from community affairs and thinking; they should participate in the major community council.

The public schools and colleges in many cities and towns have been America's free and democratic meeting place for public discussion, and many of them are sponsoring discussion meetings.[38,39] Librarians can encourage this. "Hundreds of thousands of adults are joining reading classes each year . . . due . . . to the greater demands for competent reading that present-day life makes on an increasingly large proportion of our population." The U.S. Office of Education estimated 35 to 40 million adults enrolled in classes for 1961-62.[40] Most of these classes are held in public school, college or university extension buildings. A vital part of library philosophy is a warm regard, active support and systematic cooperation with American public school system, which does not spring from or foster religious, social or economic distinctions, is controlled by locally chosen citizens, and is giving renewed attentions, to the mentally gifted and to basic intellectual studies. The library will not neglect other schools and educational enterprises.

Renewed Conviction: The Books as Educators

The temptation to spread out too widely and superficially has diverted many librarians' attention from the needs of the great population which looks to its libraries for individual service and printed informational, cultural and inspirational help, which only the public library can give. As Schick and others have pointed out,[10] the demands for this from the adult public give every indication of accelerating. Many librarians need to regain their basic conviction that their books, reading and study services are of surpassing social and educational importance. The present programmes and performance of many libraries do not reflect a steady determination to promote these ends. Libraries may profitably emulate the paper-manufacturing company which initiated the prize-winning series of full-page colour advertisements "Send Me a Man Who Reads," which ran in national magazines of 1960-61. These reported that high-salaried leaders in various fields, and college scholarship winners, are reading for more than the less successful persons in their fields - "Men who read more achieve more," and "Reading is often a mainspring to leadership."[41]

Librarians have the responsibility of such leadership, to persuade their communities as to these basic values and to encourage high purposes and ideals and not be swayed by powerful clamour to do the superficially popular thing, or to buy and circulate destructive but popular books.

The tremendous growth of good reading by children, even during the last fifty years, has been greatly influenced by the library profession, but also by the book trade and by Frederic G. Melcher, its long-time leader and a library enthusiast. He was the moving spirit in the Boy Scout reading programme and its outgrowths Children's Book Week and National Library Week. He gave and publicized the annual Newbery and Caldecott Awards to stimulate better-written and better-il lustrated books for the young. When librarians feel discouraged and wonder what can be done to improve situations, they may profitably consider what the conviction, determination enthusiasm, resourcefulness of one person can accomplish in what, in Melcher's case, seemed at first a very indifferent world. Librarianship today needs a Frederic Melcher for adult reading.

NOTES & REFERENCES

1. Robert D. Leigh, (ed.) *The Public Library in the United State.s* 1950. Columbia Univ. Press. This is the summary report of "The Public Library Inquiry," a three-year objective study of all aspects of the subject, made by a group of social scientists.
2. William S. Learned, *The American Public Library and the Diffusion of Knowledge*. 1924. Harcourt. Still valid as an educator's stimulating interpretation of his careful inquiry into the operating and services of many libraries.
3. Nelson B. Henry, (ed.) *Adult Reading*. 1956. (*55th yearbook, Nat' l* Society for the Study of Education. Part 2.) Univ. of Chicago Press.
4. Gerald Johnson, "Role of the Public Library", *Introduction to Public Library Service*. A.L.A. 1956.
5. NBC's newsman Alex Dreier, July 13, 1958, marking the opening of the Annual Conference of the A.L.A.
6. Leonard D. White, *The Federalists: A Study in Administrative History*. 1948. Macmillan, p. 6.
7. J. Periam Danton, "Plea for a Philosophy of Librarianship." *Library Quarterly*. 4: 527-551. Oct. 1943.
8. Life (Chicago). *The National Purpose., 146 p. 1960. Holt. paper.*
9. President's Commission on National Goals. *Goals for Americans: Comprising the Report. . . and Chapters Submitted for Consideration. .* .372 p. 1960. Prentice-Hall. paper.
10. Frank L. Schick, ed. *The Future of Library Service: Demographic Aspects and Implications. Library Trends.* v. 10, no. 1, p. 3-67, July 1961; no. 2, p. 71-286, Oct. 1961. No. 1 on Population Trends. No 2 . a symposium of 17 papers on major aspects of public, school, college and special libraries and what seems to be ahead for each. A study of unusual consequence for policy and planning. See also Robert O'Brien. "The U.S. in 1970; Forecast of Things to Come." *Reader's Digest*. 78: 25-29. Jan. 1961.
11. *Wilson Library Bulletin*. 36: 87-88. Oct. 1961.

12. Lowell A. Martin. "Library Service to Adults." *Library Quarterly.* 25: 1-14. Jan. 1955. Reviews recent trends as well as accomplishments. It notes that recreational reading service is an essential part of a well-balanced library programme.
13. This bulletin contains much information beyond that implied by its title. The 1955 figure for comparison comes from note 15, below.
14. *Public Library Service: A Guide to Evaluation, with Minimum Standards. . .* 74. p. 1956. A.L.A. Supplemented by *Costs of Public Library Service in 1959.* 15 p. 1959. (Prepared by A.L.A. Public Libraries Division. Co-ordinating Committee on Revision of Public Library Standards. In references below, this publication and its supplement will be referred to by short title only.)
15. Rose Vainstein. *Statistics of Public Libraries: 1955- 56.* (Chapter 5. *Biennial Survey of Public Libraries: 1954-56.*) 102 p. 1959. U.S. Office of Education. p. 25. Reports a circulation of 489,519,000 from only 6,153 of the 7,871 libraries questioned: the Library Services Branch estimates that full returns would have brought the total above one half billion. Subsequent annual statistical tables, including one for 1960, justify the estimate for 1960. *Publishers' Weekly* had a mailing list of 9,000 public libraries in 1961.
16. *Publishers' Weekly.* 180: 26-27. July 17-, 1961. See also Robert B. Downs. "Books Are Here to Stay". *A.L.A. Bulletin.* 51: 665-672. Oct 1957.
17. "Latest Gallup Figures," and "Why Do We Lag ?" *Publishers' Weekly.* 171: 61. May 27, 1957.
18. Robert B. Downs, *Molders of the Modern Mind; 111 Books That Shaped Western Civilization.* 396 p. 1961. Barnes & Noble.
19. *Publishers' Weekly, 179: 22. Jan. 2, 1961. For later estimates see P.W.* 179: 20-24. March 6, 1961.
20. *Ibid., 177: 11. May 23, 1960.*
21. Gordon G. Dupee, "Can Johnny's Parents Read?" *Saturday Review.* 39: 5.7, 34. June 2, 1956. See also George Gallup. "You Can't Get Ahead Today Unless You Read." *Ladies' Home Journal. 77*: 44+ Aug. 1960. Also Mary C. Austin, et al. *The Torch Lighters: Tomorrow's Teachers of Reading.* 191 p. 1961. Harvard Univ. Press. "The Harvard-Carnegie Reading Study" aims to make reading play a much greater part in the teacher-training. Also *The National Interest and the Teaching English.* 140 p. 1961. National Council of Teachers of English. (Champaign, Ill.) A nationwide study of the status of reading

in the curriculum, the causes of shortcomings and their improvement, including reading promotion. Also Nelson B. Henry, ed. *Development in and Through Reading: 60th Yearbook of the National Society for the Study of Education.* Part 1. 406 p. 1961. Univ. of Chicago Press.

22. The foregoing points are in part drawn and modified from Lester Asheim, "Mass Communication and the Book."*Pioneer.* (Library Bureau.) Sept.-Oct. 1959. p. 2. Also Peter S. Jennison. "Today's Challenge to the Book World." *Library Journal.* 82: 2319-2325. Oct. 1, 1957. For an objective study of contrasting values of various media, see Lester Asheim. "Reading and the Newer Media." *A.L.A. Bulletin.* 55: 148-152. Feb. 1961.

23. Mrs. James C. Parker (National President of P.T.A.). *N.Y. Times.* May 24, 1960.

24. *Reader's Digest.* v. 76. March 1960. Inside front cover. For a quick summary of the influence of books on many famous persons including some still living, see the 26-p. Chapter 5 of Donald A. Laird. *The Technique of Getting Things Done.* 310 p. 1947. McGraw-Hill. See also footnote 41 below.

25. Samuel Simon. "Looking Back Is Forward Looking." In Wayne S. Yenawine, ed. *Library Evaluation.* 46 p. 1959. Syracuse Univ. Press. paper. p. 30-46. Cites pros and cons on an expensive group and A.V programme in a library which cannot afford enough books or trained informational staff to meet reader demands.

26. See Errett W. McDiarmid, "Crusade for an Educated America." (President's address) *A.L.A. Bulletin.* 42: 289-293. July 1948.

27. John Wakeman, "Greatest Challenge." Editorial. *Wilson Library Bulletin.* 35: 252. Nov. 1960.

28. Thomas Finletter. Quoted in Benjamin Elkin. "Are We Trying to Do Too Much ?" *Illinois Libraries.* 42: 192-193. March 1960. See also William H. Whyte, Jr. *The Organization Man.* 429 p. 1956. Simon. Also Henry M. Wriston. *Academic Procession.* 1959. Columbia Univ. Press. p. 192-194, on a college president's struggles, "against all the pressures. . . in the other direction," to provide students the opportunity for a "private life of the mind."

29. Ralph S. Ulveling. "Lose Not Our Greatest Strength." *Iowa Library Quarterly, 18: 242-246. Jan. 1961.*

30. Leonard H. Freiser. "Dr. Shaw and Toronto's Children." *Library Journal.* 86: 1947-1949. May 15, 1961. Listed here rather than in Chapter 22 because it explains understandingly a major public library function

which needs fresh evaluation. Also, Harold L. Hamill's remarks as president, Public Library Association, in *Operation LAPL.* July 1961. p. 1, 2. Los Angeles Public Library.

31. Besides numerous books for educators, such as Ruth Strang's *Helping Your Gifted Child.* 1960. Dutton, see *The Pursuit of Excellence: Education and the Future of America.* (The "Rockfeller Report" on Education). 49 p. 1958. Doubleday. Also "Emphasis on Excellence," in Carnegie Corporation of New York *Quarterly. 7:* 1-7. July 1959. Reviews activities in numerous schools and colleges. Also John W. Gardner (President of Carnegie Corporation). *Excellence.* 171 p., 1960. Harper. More specific suggestions in Howard W. Winger. "The Library Looks at the Gifted." *Illinois Libraries.* 42: 287-296. May 1960. Also Lillian L. Batchelor, ed. "The School Library and the Gifted Child." *A.L.A. Bulletin. 52:* 93-108. Feb. 1958; articles by eight school libraries and teachers exploring specific aspects some recognizing the obligation to call also on the public library for supplementary materials. These articles were also issued as an A.L.A. reprint.

32. Lillian L. Batchelor, "Setting a Reading Climate for the Gifted." *Library Journal,* 86: 319-325. Jan. 15, 1961.

33. See note 12, above.

34. *Salary Statistics for Large Public Libraries for 1961.* 2 p. processed sheet. Enoch Pratt Free Library.

35. Sarah L. Wallace, "An Air-Conditional Nightmare." *Wilson Library Bulleirn* 35: 703-705. May 1961.

36. Samuel Rothstein, "Reference Service: The New Dimension in Librarianship." *College and Research Libraries.* 22: 11-18. Jan. 1961. Substantial discussion of the major issues in public library informational services supporting the Public Library Inquiry of Dr. Robert Leigh that the public library should emphasize services that the mass media are not equipped to give.

37. Abraham N. Barnett, "Beyond Librarianship: A Critique of Rationales of Special Library Service to the Aged." *Library Quarterly.* 31: 178-186. April 1961.

38. Marilyn Russum, "Adult Education: Cinderella of the Sixties." *Saturday Review.* 44: 58-59. May 20, 1961.

39. *Adult Education in American Education Week. . . 1960.* 21 p. Summary. U.S. Office of Education. Also *Public School Adult Education, A Guide for Administrators and Teachers.* 155 p. 1956. National Asso'n of Public School Adult Educators. Washington.

40. *N.Y. Times* Aug. 27, 1961. See also William S. Gray and Bernice Rogers. Maturity in Readings? Its Nature and Appraisal. 273 p. 1956. Univ. of Chicago Press. p. 13. Uses carefully prepared objective criteria to analyze numerous adults' reading experience, their motivation and outcomes.
41. This series is available free in large reprints for pasting in schools and libraries from Education Dept. Box 1. International Paper Co., 220 East 42nd St., N.Y. 17.

4

A Career Service in Librarianship

By a career service in librarianship is meant that the library secures and retains the service of the best-qualified persons among those available, and that they are assisted and motivated to grow in personal and professional stature and to make their maximum possible contribution to the work of the library, and to the profession. The career objective applies to all employees, including those not in the professional service, and in any kind of library. It depends not on the availability of large funds but rather on the desire and determination of the trustees and librarian. It is not accomplished by the stroke of a pen or indeed ever wholly achieved; it is a frame of mind, a conviction that each employee has a career ahead, a goal by which to determine policies and procedures. It is better applied altogether than only in part, but better in part than not at all. It represents a break with the traditional attitude in many public libraries but it is in agreement with the research, modern thinking, and to a large extent the actual practice in American business and industry.[1]

For lack of space we cannot review the relevant developments in industry, as recounted in the enormous literature of industrial relations. Three main points summarize the present-day thinking on the role of the individual employee in a work setting.[2] First, each employee is an individual with his own strengths and limitations and his own unique personality; he wants to be recognized as such and be remembered by his own name. People are all alike in that they are all different. No employer can escape the problem of having to cope with at least the normal range of individual differences, and employee centered supervision result in greater production than does work-centered supervision.

Second, no one likes to live or work by himself. People belong to groups; they want to be accepted by their fellows, and to have their approbation and support. Recognition of the social fabric so created is one of the great discoveries of this recent period of industrial research. This informal social system exists and is very powerful, as in holding down productivity sometimes and in frustrating official rules and orders; relatively little is known as to how to utilize it purposively, save that management must somehow work within the limits imposed by its existence.

Third, everyone shares in the desire to be an effective member of the official team, to be vital part of something larger than himself and of which he can be proud. When stimulated and recognized this is what develops in men a fierce loyalty—whether to the combat unit of an army or to the production group of a factory. People tend to be happiest and most productive in a work situation where they can contribute creatively within the limits of their ability in ways which are socially approved and appreciated.

WORKING CONDITIONS

Salaries

A public library seeking to recruit and retain outstanding employees has to pay salaries commensurate with those of other libraries, of other occupations requiring approximately the same training, and of other local employers. Otherwise, few applicants will show up and seldom a well-qualified one. Low salaries in libraries are responsible for the drab and inadequate personnel who in turn create in people's minds the characteristic image of librarian. The problem should be attacked from both ends; salaries should be raised and every library should raise it level of acceptable work performance. Only the former is considered at this point.

Library salaries have always been low, largely because trustees and administrators failed to win public recognition of the value of library service, and partly because of the predominance of women as library employees. "Exploitation" is the word to describe the salaries long paid to custodians, library assistants and professional librarians. The continued shortage of librarians, more than anything else, has helped to improve starting salaries for library school graduates. In most cities they are not yet up to the salaries paid to school teachers, school librarians, and to members of many other professions with comparable education and experience. And teachers by and large earn less today than do other professional groups, and have gained less in purchasing power in the last fifty years than have most other occupations.[3] In 1955 the median monthly salary of 8,808 professional librarians in public libraries was only about $5 a week more than the average earnings of all production workers in manufacturing industries that year[4]. Since most libraries fail to advance salaries for the middle and top ranks in even the same relative amounts as for starting salaries, experienced employees find themselves earning little more than newcomers and with hardly any range of possible increase.

The librarian should work out a sound salary plan and insist on its adoption by the trustees and city officials, with periodic revision of the schedule in keeping with current conditions. A salary plan includes (a) salary range, viz., a minimum salary, a maximum salary and designated intermediate steps for each grade of position as defined in the library's position classification plan; and (b) a set of rules for the application and operation of this salary schedule.[5] Such a salary plan is to be preferred to secret payroll and the resulting favouritism in paying different salaries for essentially the same work. The many thorny technical problems should be resolved in consultation with the whole staff or with staff representatives, preferably helped by an experienced personnel officer.

Should the maximum salary of one grade be less or more than the minimum of the next higher grade, and by how much? Usually the former is preferred, so that the promotion from one grade to another will mean an increase in salary. But in the higher grades of service where promotions will be few, and wherever the total salary range of a given grade is limited, an overlap in the salaries paid for positions in two adjoining grades is inevitable. Typically the annual increments are too small; they should be at least $150 (equal to 7 cents an hour), and larger for the higher grades, so that they constitute a proportionate percentage increase of the minimum salary for the grade. How much difference should there be in the pay scale for different grades of positions? This depends on human judgment, the pressure of shortages and competition for certain types of skills. One good method is to establish a fair salary range for one or two key classes, e.g., junior professional librarian, and then work up and down the scale. It also turns on the number and amount of increments, and on whether salaries for different grades overlap.

Rules for the Salary Plan

To apply such a salary schedule, a set of rules should be drawn up in consultation with other staff members, be submitted to the board and city officials, and upon their approval be published for all to see. Besides definitions of terms, it should provide for periodic review of the salary schedule, for new appointments at minimum salary of the grade in question (with exceptions permitted in unusual cases), and for the treatment of individuals whose present salary does not fall exactly into the salary steps of the new schedule. An important policy to incorporate concerns the basis on which salary increments will be granted, either automatically (as is generally true of teachers) or on the recommendation of the librarian as the result of service ratings or other judgments of individual efficiency. Any plan should recognize that some employees are better than others. Automatic increments (or even semi-automatic, i.e., to be granted unless vetoed) are far easier to administer than discretionary, but they discourage excellence and lower the library's efficiency and morale. In addition, individual merit increases, longevity pay, and the requirement of continued academic study every five years or so to qualify for further increases should be included in the rules.

A salary schedule should be reviewed annually, desirably as part of a long-term (five-year) plan, and necessarily just before the next year's budget is decided. First, every present position and its performance needs scrutiny, to assure that every dollar is well spent at present; it will often be possible by work simplification to divert the time of present higher-paid persons to more profitable effort. Funds may be saved by using better supervision and work assignments to reduce the total number of positions, especially by closing small inefficient branches. Inevitably additional funds will be needed because public demands increase. There is only one way to get them—ask for them, justify the request and fight for them. Head librarians too often fail in this elementary duty—to design the best possible presentation of the need, defend it vigorously before the trustees and persuade them to use their every ounce of political strength with government officials tax bodies to get the money needed for salary increase. Obviously when a city raises the salaries of all governmental employees the trustees should see to it that the library employees are included as they surely will be in any across-the-board cuts.

One main argument can be used—even though city officials try to brush it off: the comparison of the library's present salaries with those of local firms and other libraries. In most cities the actual average salary of library employees is low enough to shock many people; library typists and other clerical workers seldom have as good a pay scale as in other local offices. Sources of data on salaries paid by other public libraries include the latest benchmark study of the national scene,[6] the annual statistics issues of many state library bulletins,[7] the annual compilation by the Enoch Pratt Free Library of *Salary Statistics for Large Public Libraries,*[8] the annual survey of salaries received by library school graduates,[9] the pool of salary data of forty-three public libraries, maintained by the Detroit Public Library,[10] *The Municipal Year Book,*[11] and *Public Library Abstracts.*[12] The National Education Association conducts comprehensive surveys of teachers' salaries every two years.[13] For local salaries of clerical and nonprofessional employees, see the studies of the U.S. Bureau of Labor Statistics as published in its bulletins or in the *Monthly Labor Review,* and the salary surveys by the National Office Management Association.[14] A survey of salaries paid throughout the community to persons in various standard positions may have been made by the local chamber of commerce or manufacturers association or by the state government. Best of all would be a salary survey done by and for the local units of government; it is almost sure to lead to salary increases for public library employees.

A salary schedule may be improved by raising the minimum on one or more grades or raising the maximum, increasing the number or size of increments, adding a cost-of-living bonus or longevity step increases, etc. There are ways to increase average salaries without directly changing the salary schedule; e.g., reclassifying positions from one grade to another, providing for automatic movement from one grade to another (as of junior librarians), reducing the work week (though this can only match what is generally accepted locally) or adding fringe benefits (as increased travel funds). But real take-home pay needs to be increased absolutely and relatively, now and in the future, to keep up with inflation, and to compete with salaries of other occupations. A staff of any quality or spirit will not lie down and accept local difficulties in achieving salary goals as absolving the librarian and trustees of their responsibility, especially if other city employees with the same or lesser qualifications are better paid.

Tenure

Formal guarantee of tenure or of employment beyond the probationary period is common for teachers but unusual in public library. Under civil service, removal can only be done as provided by the rules. Not enough library employees, however, are dismissed for inefficiency, and few without justification. The attitude is sometimes found that, because salaries are low, ineffective employees will not be dismissed; this means that the low salaries paid are no saving but are largely wasted.

A basic desire of people at work is to be assured of continued employment and to be protected from personal favouritism or caprice, politics or other factors unrelated to merit. Several librarians have been victims of controversy over ideas and censorship. The A.L.A. has a number of good statements aimed at preventing dismissal or other punishment for personal opinions or professional treatment of unpopular or controversial subjects.[15] On the other hand little is done to disturb the tenure of employees who are not competent. Permanent tenure for such persons is costly. It is contrary to the spirit of the career service idea, even though the public schools and the civil service are still more subject to this difficulty than are public libraries, because their tenure system is established by law and procedures for removing an employee are complex and almost unworkable. The informal system of tenure in public libraries should be retained and cherished, precisely because of the flexibility it permits. But to it should be added provision for systematically recording observations of each employees's efficiency (see "Service Ratings" below), and a stated policy of separating from the employ of the library any person incapable of maintaining reasonable efficiency. Only the trustees may dismiss a library employees, but this they should be prepared to do on recommendation of the librarian, supported by recorded facts.

Fringe Benefits

Factors other than salary may have direct monetary value. Fringe benefits of a generation ago favoured white collar workers over industrial workers. Unionization and other influences have put blue collar workers far ahead of office and professional personnel in regard to fringe benefits.[16] Some fringe benefits have double effect on compensation because of their relationship to the Federal income tax. A hospital insurance premium paid by the employer is worth not only its face value to the employee but also the additional income tax the latter would have to pay if his salary had been increased and he had paid the premium himself. As a rule of thumb, fringe benefits represent from 15 to 20 per cent of the annual total outlay for salaries.[17] Over the long run all American workers can expect increased fringe benefits; public library employees have to catch up with other workers.

The forty-four work week is now standard in public libraries, and some are beginning to require less. The coffee break, approximating ten minutes for each half day of work, is well entrenched and perhaps justified if used to relieve fatigue. The five-day week is also standard now, but most public libraries expect employees to work at least one or two nights a week without extra pay. Overtime work in libraries is rarely paid for directly (let alone by time and a half); usually the employee is granted compensatory time off. The number of paid holidays ranges more widely; six is the usual minimum.

Paid vacation, once the distinguishing prerogative of white collar workers, is now part of the compensation of almost all American employees. In public libraries, four weeks' paid vacation is standard for professional librarians, and two weeks for other library employees. Some libraries require each employee to take his whole vacation in the summer months when reader demands are at an ebb; others permit taking vacation at any time of the year, with the advance approval of the supervisor. Leaves of absence without pay are usually available to library staff members, but not leave with pay except for a few days to attend professional meetings. Increasingly staff members are helped by the library's travel funds, especially if they are serving on committees of state and national associations. Transportation paid for by the library is exempt from the Federal tax of 10 per cent.

In health and welfare, library fringe benefits are weakest of all. Paid sick leave is common, usually at most for one day a month and cumulative for a few years at least, and not to be used except for serious illness. About two-thirds of all American workers now have hospital and life insurance by virtue of their employment,[18] but such protection is missing almost completely in libraries; in most cases, it will require authorization by state law. Credit unions are usually available in the larger cities, often through organizations of municipal employees; as yet they touch only a minority of all public libraries. Severance pay, bonus and profit-sharing plans, and other such benefits are not found in libraries.

Retirement

Today most employees in all occupations are assured some continued income after retirement. And most public libraries, except the very small ones, have some provision for staff retirement; in any library without reasonably adequate retirement benefits, the trustees and librarian should press for a change.[19]

Librarians tried to establish their own private retirement plan in the 1930's.[20] But for all state and local government workers, including librarians, the great breakthrough came with the development, within the last twenty-five years of statewide retirement system for public employees, found now in many states.[21] A majority of all public library employees are covered by them. The library or the local unit of government applies to join the plan. It then pays in (a) the deductions from employees' current pay; (b) its matching contributions and pro-rata share of administrative expenses; and (c) the annual amount necessary to cover the prior service of those on the payroll when the plan was adopted, so that they can secure of full pension when they retire based on their total length of employment. Retirement benefits will vary with rates of contributions, age of retirement, the scope and variety of benefits offered, etc.

Such an actuarily sound retirement system is more expensive than generally realized. To keep solvent, most state plans offer relatively modest benefits (say around 25 per cent of final average salary), and their purchasing power has been steadily reduced by inflation. As a result, the second breakthrough in retirement benefits for public employees came in 1954 when Congress amended the Federal Social Security Act, opening to them the Old-Age and Survivors Insurance programme. This is conditional on each state adopting appropriate legislation [22] and on a vote of the employees concerned. The combination of social security and of a state or local retirement plan will in general result in pension of from a third to half of the final average salary; for this, the library's payments are or soon will be about 10 per cent of total salary expenditures. Still to be desired are interstate agreement to make it possible to transfer pension and retirement credits from state to state.

The individual library has one key decision to make—the age of compulsory retirement. Age sixty-five is the usually accepted point for compulsory retirement.[23] Reduced Federal social security benefits are available even at age sixty-two, and they are payable in full at sixty-five. Evidence indicates that loss or retention of ability is not measured always by chronological age, and that forced retirement has adverse effects on many people whose lives are focused on their jobs, unless they are oriented in advance to change their interests and habits. Life expectancy is increasing (at sixty-five one can expect to live another twelve or fifteen years), and the number who are sixty-five or over is becoming such a large percentage of the total that their support will be burdensome unless at least the most competent can continue working.

But on the average people do begin to lose their vigor by sixty-five, and become more conservative and less willing to experiment. Since older people tend to hold higher-level positions, their failure to retire blocks promotion of younger staff members and reduces the effectiveness of the library to solve new problems. Furthermore the usual public library retirement system makes it impossible for an employee within ten or fifteen years of retirement to consider taking another job, though that might be better for both him and the library, since he would lose the benefit of his employer's contributions to the retirement fund. General failure of libraries to dismiss ineffective staff members calls for a compulsory cut-off date to limit the time these hidden pensioners may linger. Provision is often made to continue the services of extra-valuable nonexecutive persons, recommended by the librarian to the board, on a year-to-year basis, perhaps for less than full time or in a less exacting position. But any librarian reluctant to retire at sixty-five, as a precedent for other, does his library a disservice and deprives it of the vigor and freshness of viewpoint likely to be contributed by a younger successor.

EMPLOYEE DEVELOPMENT

Job Enlargement

A main ingredient for an effective career service is systematic development of each employee's potential abilities, by such means as job enlargement, service ratings, in-service training and personal adjustment. The first step is to discover the individual's combination of qualities and abilities, and then to see that his work assignments give him a chance to perform ever more difficult and more responsible duties. This helps satisfy a basic psychological need for growth. Each employee should in time learn something about the jobs done by others in his work unit, as by a transfer, and this good insurance against the sudden loss of a staff member.

A transfer of an individual from one position to another in a given grade usually means some alternation in duties but no necessary change in pay. It may be initiated by the librarian, perhaps to give an employee a chance to make a better adjustment on the new job; by the supervisor of a vacant position, as to secure someone with special skills; by the employee's present supervisor, to be relieved of someone who is not effective; or by the employee himself, to secure new experience or to be located more conveniently. Transfers are often neglected as a method of employee development and tend to be used only for those of mediocre performance and to encourage them to leave. When a vacancy occurs, consideration should be given first to any present employee holding a position in the same grade of service who desires the transfer, provided he meets the qualification desired for the vacancy.

Promotions

A promotion means reassigning an individual from a position in a given grade to another position in a higher grade, usually involving a change in duties[24] and better pay. It is the best form of job enlargement for an employee of competence; it benefits the individual and the library. To what extent should vacancies be filled by appointment from outside the staff or by promotion from within? Promotion from within is the epitome of a career service; it can result in chain reaction of promotions down the line and it has a powerful effect on staff morale. Women librarians continue to work after marriage in ever larger numbers and even after they have children, and the long-range prospects for promotion are ever more important to them. Furthermore, it reduces training time and eliminates the hiatus while a new person learns his way around.[25]

On the other hand, appointment from the outside tends to introduce new ideas, and is necessary if there is no qualified person on the staff. In the history of almost every library there are times when key positions are better filled by appointments of new people with outstanding leadership qualities than by promotion of people who are passable but not able to push the library ahead. Appointment to an upper-level position should be made in anticipation of what will be forthcoming in the future and not as a reward for what was done in the past. Clearly, to promote from within requires the presence of competent persons with growth potential, in lower positions on the staff. As long as a high standard of selection is maintained, so that each present staff member is competing for the position not only with his colleagues but with people outside the staff, the policy of promotion from within is desirable and is recommended.

Should the basis of promotion be merit alone or length of service? Seniority does not necessarily bring to the top those persons best qualified for promotion, and should not be a major factor in determining promotions. All vacancies above the entering level should be announced to the staff, inviting applications but stating also that the position will not necessarily be filled by promotion. Personnel records are rarely complete, up-to-date, or well-organized for this purpose even in large libraries,[26] and careful study of the whole staff should be made in the case of each vacancy to find the person who will most strengthen the library at the given point. When an obvious candidates is passed over for another, he should be given an explanation of the reasons.

Shall only present members of a given department be considered for a vacancy in the department, or shall all persons be eligible who hold positions in the grade below that of the vacancy? While the obvious line of promotion is certainly from assistant head to headship of a department, the basic principle remains: every person promoted should be so selected because he appears to be better qualified for the position than any of his colleagues or anyone outside the staff. Too many professional librarians can secure promotion only by taking an administrative position, when they really do not like nor are they fitted for administrative duties as well as they are for some other aspect of the work. If in general they could be promoted only to the one position immediately superior to their own, that would be a negation of the spirit of a career service.

In choosing the person to be promoted, of those who meet the minimum qualifications, the informed judgment of the supervisor of the vacant position should weigh heavily, supplemented by the opinions of selected other supervisors and of the librarian, and by the record of the various candidates, including service ratings received and in-service training taken. The probationary period is important and should be used, when the promotion involves duties substantially different from those previously performed.

A library's professional prestige, and specifically its drawing power in recruitment of staff, is greatly influenced by whether appointees to upper-level positions are outstanding people or only mediocre. Promotion from within is a desirable part of a career service, if it results in the promotion of those best qualified of all who are available. Every experienced library administrator knows that the search for people to promote has to be continual and far and wide, and that the higher the level of a given position, the more difficult and important this search becomes. A good librarian tries to have an understudy for every key staff member including himself.

Service Ratings

By service ratings is meant the periodic assessment by a supervisor, in a prescribed fashion, of an employee's job performance and efficiency, with comments on his potential ability. Sometimes called merit rating, its application in libraries has been less controversial than in teaching but is no less difficult. Unless an effective system is worked out, or if ratings are not made at all, superficial, subjective and possibly biased opinions will be used by supervisors and the librarian, as in judging a new employees' work, deciding whether a staff member is to be promoted or recommending an employee for a merit increase. The problem is not whether but how to rate work performance fairly. Most people want to know where they stand with their supervisors. Many methods and forms have been developed,[27] including the 1948 A.L.A. "Personnel Service Rating Report," still available for purchase.[28] It is possible and even desirable to devise a local system and form, after studying some of the literature on service ratings.[29]

Service ratings are not such valid measures of performance that important decisions should be made solely from them; the rating should be only a part of the total data considered. Their chief value in act lies in their use for counseling the individual employee, in letting him know where he stands and in helping him to improve. A rating every six months is sufficient even for new employees, and annually or less often for employees of long standing. Mutual discussion by all who will make the ratings will help to reduce the wide differences of individual supervisor. Any service rating plan should require that the rating report be shown to and discussed with the employee. Supervisors are reluctant to make objective ratings, and then have to show them to the employee. But the worker can benefit only by discussing details of the report on his work with his supervisor. The interview should not stress his weaknesses and limitations—that is discouraging; it should be a constructive, good-spirited stocktaking of his work, with suggested ways to improve it. Both parties will fell encouraged when a series of interviews shows progress and successful adjustment. From these counseling interviews the wise supervisor can learn much about each assistant and much about his own effectiveness as a supervisor.[30] He may be courageous enough to let his assistants rate him, anonymously, as supervisor.

In-service Training

In-service training, offered to employees on matters of direct practical concern with their work on paid time and without cost to the employee, has become a standard practice in many public libraries. In-service training can take many different forms other than the traditional class or group with the supervisor as instructor. The library's staff manual and staff news bulletin and current library magazines are in-service training devices, as are committees, special projects, experiments, tours of branches or departments, staff meetings, discussion groups and planned job rotation for new professional employees.[31] A public library of twenty-five employees or more should expect to conduct one or more training programmes for its staff all the time. Training classes for apprentices or for persons trying to qualify for employment have largely been abandoned,[32] because of the expense involved, the difficulty of finding candidates and the turnover. Today many libraries in larger cities arrange for library schools to give library science courses by extension, and have persuaded local educational institutions to develop courses for non-professional library assistants.

Personal Grievance Adjustment

As long as people work together, some will have real or fancied grievances and unusual problems, in contrast to others who carry on happily and effectively. One's colleagues are human and are therefore different one from another. The librarian needs to get to know each one to try to understand him, and to treat him with respect for the integrity of his personality. As part of career service, a person of stature and judgment should be designated in each library to whom employees in trouble or with grievance can talk and get help, someone willing and able to make himself readily available, to keep confidential what he is told in confidence, and to offer a sympathetic ear without trying to run other persons' lives. It is a basic assumption that the librarian will deal with his colleagues honestly and fairly and in the best interest of the library and of all concerned. He will be interested in any situation which leads a member of the staff to feel that he has been abused or unfairly treated, and he will try to correct it. The tensions of today often grow from a misunderstanding, or a personality conflict, but sometimes there is real injustice. The first step is to uncover the difficulty and to have every employee know that he can go to a qualified person for a hearing, even if the source of his difficulty lies outside his job; people's work life and private life are very much interdependent, both for the normal person and the neurotic.

The library may have a complaint against a staff member, for malicious gossiping, for continual inability to get along well with his colleagues, for repeated tardiness or other poor work habits, or for other more or less serious reasons. An interview should be held by the appropriate supervisor after reviewing the facts available, and considering the possible alternatives. One objective is to seek with the individual the cause of his poor behaviour and to find possible corrective actions or factors, with the intent to salvage the individual and to retain his services, if they can be made minimally acceptable. It may prove important to give an official reprimand or warning that failure to improve his conduct or work performance will lead to some designated action, such as a transfer, demotion or dismissal.[33]

Then there is the person who makes less than an acceptable contribution to the work of the library; even doing his best is not good enough. Perhaps he should never have been hired or promoted, but there he is. Often the employee's work has declined gradually over the years; it would be impossible to dismiss him after years of service to the library and with no other source of income. Such a person (and what if it is the librarian?) should be transferred to work where he can least slow down the library's operation. The key factor in the adjustment of a person to his job would appear to be the degree of challenge or motivation which his work offers to his unique combination of talents and limitations. One possibility then is to seek from the individual his own self-knowledge as to what he likes and wants to do; possibly a transfer to that can be arranged. Or the situation may result from the discouragement and frustration of long years of failure to advance; job enlargement is a possible help. Business and industry, and other professions too, have this problem. All of them have created jobs for people who need to be moved out of the main stream of activity but cannot be dismissed. One test of a chief librarian is his ability to solve such a personal problem with creative imagination and courage. And the many different kinds of cases call for almost as many different types of approaches, e.g., the beginner, the devoted but average worker, the older employee who is beginning to slow down,[34] the person who is not promotable,[35] the problem employee.

On the other hand there is the equally important but more pleasant obligation on each librarian to assist in the personal adjustment of his colleagues by an appreciative word for unusual ability and good work. It is sad but true that so often the cases of poor adjustment of staff members necessarily get the head's attention, but he has to remind himself to identify and seek out those who are doing a good job. Everyone needs and responds to recognition. Staff morale is in effect a group judgment of the personal adjustment of its members. It reflects the extent to which they are happy in their work, and feel at one with one another and with the library. Morale is essential for successful performance, but it is not easy to secure, and certainly not by any few or simple methods or devices. Morale is the result of many actions and of intangible relationships, such as devotion and zeal in the work shown by a library's leaders and communicated to all the others. Like happiness, staff morale is not something which can be sought for and created directly. It is not related to wealth or ease of living. Often it arises and grows precisely because of success in overcoming hurdles, and is evident only after the circumstances which occasion it are past.[36]

Some aspects of personal adjustment apply especially to the professional librarians on the staff. Their potential contribution is great, but they also need some special consideration with regard to time and encouragement for professional reading, activity in professional associations, study and writing, and professional growth in general. They have an obligation to observe in letter and spirit the librarians' code of ethics,[37] and to give unstintingly of their physical and mental abilities in the maintenance and improvement of the library's service programme. But they need the unceasing support of the trustees and of the librarian in securing an adequate salary schedule, all the usual fringe benefits and desirable working conditions, and an opportunity to participate actively, even more than other staff members, in the long-term development of the library.

DEMOCRATIC ADMINISTRATION

Much of the talk about democratic administration usually means little more than that the administrator asks the opinions of some subordinates before he makes a major decision. This is only consultative administration. The acid test of democratic administration is whether the chief shares with his colleagues the power to make decisions. A few points will be brought out here, as relating to a career service.[38]

Democratic administration assumes and requires a free flow of relevant information through normal channels. People who are to share in making decisions must have access to the same and to all the needed facts, as by printed personnel rules, a staff bulletin and reports on board meetings. Just as important but more difficult is to get a free flow of information upward, since people tend not to tell the chief what he won't like to hear. As a result he should be sensitive to the signals of stress and trouble, such as the grapevine.

Most people will like democratic administration, and profit from it, and improve the library's service, if the pace is not too swift. One good way to begin is to delegate authority for routine decisions to the lowest effective level. This not only relieves the work load of the librarian and the department heads but builds up staff confidence and judgment derived from experience. Personnel policies and working conditions constitute another area in which decisions are of importance to all and the viewpoints of all need to be considered. Polices for the operation and long-range planning of the library should also be based on the thinking of at least the professional staff. This helps prepare them for supervisory and administrative positions, and enables the chief to make a stronger recommendation to the board when a given proposal has the endorsement of the staff and incorporates their views and experience.

Not that democratic administration is easy or infallible. It requires patience and skill from the librarian, as well as a conviction that it's worth it; and it takes time. It cannot be used to dodge all decision making or the other responsibilities of leadership. Staff members have to become accustomed to new ways of thinking too, and to learn that they may disagree with the chief without penalty. The department head or librarian may even have to learn a new technique: how to listen, and like it, to frank statements and questions in an open meeting, without wincing or embarrassment when they conflict with his own ideas or previous decisions or seem to reflect on his wisdom and ability. An effective staff organization helps in this regard, and is a basic necessity for democratic administration. The end result of the process can be said to be administration by objectives and not by orders.

EVALUATING THE LIBRARY'S PERSONNEL SITUATION

Written Statements of Personnel Policy

The objective of personnel administration is to secure for the library a staff notably qualified as to education background, personality, ability and efficiency, and devoted to improving the library's service to its community. How can a library's performance in this regard be measured? To evaluate anything there has to be a yardstick or a measuring device to ascertain whether the X factor in question exceeds or falls short of the standard.[39] In this case the yardstick with which to compare actual practice is a statement of local personnel policies officially adopted. If it has been stated policy to fill upper-level positions by promotion from within, whenever there is no better candidate available outside the staff, the percentage of such vacancies filled by promotion is easily calculated; what is more important, and can be done at least subjectively, is to compute the percentage of such appointees year by year who were outstanding and the percentage who were not. Similarly a judgment can be made as to the quality and ability of new professional, clerical and custodial staff members each year, to compare with what should be the policy—to discover and recruit highly—qualified and able employees at entering levels. A written statement of library personnel policies is essential for orientation of new employees and as a base for developing democratic administration. The preparation of such a statement brings up many questions in any library on which staff discussion will be profitable.[40] Without such a statement of policies one can hardly judge to what extent they are being observed.

Data on Turnover and Sick Leave

It helps to keep data on some measurable factors, such as turnover. Separation and accession rates per year are calculated by averaging the number of non-temporary positions on the library's payroll four or more times in the year and dividing that figure into the number of employees with permanent appointment who left or joined the staff. Separation rates can be analyzed to identify trouble spots, e.g., as to cause of separation (preventable or non-preventable), by library agency or department, and by the main groups of positions, such as professional librarians or junior library assistants.

What is a desirable rate of turnover? American industry has had an average separation rate of over 40 per cent a year in recent years;[41] as far as the few available data indicate, public library personnel turnover rates have in recent years been around 20-25 per cent, very similar to the Federal Government's turnover rate.[42] Even this is above the suggested optimum of 15 per cent.[43] Turnover is expensive, $200 to $500 per separation and mostly in hidden costs,[44] and high turnover is disastrous to good library service. The complete absence of turnover is also an unfavourable sign since it means that there are no vacancies to be filled by promotion and no influx of new people with new ideas. But for a long time the problem has been that of too high a turnover.

In general the record of paid sick leave taken by staff members provides an indication of morale and of job satisfaction; often there are comparable figures on sick leave available for local government offices or business firms, but not usually for other libraries. However any library can compare its own turnover and sick leave rates in one year with the same data for other years, and get an indication as to whether its performance in this respect is improving or declining.

Exit Interviews

A third practical approach to evaluating personnel administration, and the administration of the library, is through an exit interview by the librarian or personnel officer with every person leaving the employ of the library.[45] If the employee is encouraged to speak freely of his work experiences, much of value can be learned about trouble spots in the library's personnel programme. Exit interviews serve other purpose too, such as routine review of necessary steps in effecting the separation, giving the employee a last chance to ask questions and make suggestions, providing some official and personal recognition of his leaving the library's employ, and perhaps even persuading him not to leave.

The Ultimate Criterion

It is an assumption that good personnel administration will result in maintaining and improving the library's programme of community service. That is the ultimate criterion and it is not easy to judge objectively. Though causality is difficult to establish and impossible to prove, the librarian and ultimately the trustees need to review from time to time whether the leadership, the devotion, the morale, the effectiveness of the staff as a whole and of each department are improving or not. Is there a goodly proportion of the staff who are recognized locally and by their colleagues in other libraries as outstanding in ability and character? In the usual library there are some down-to-earth criteria for the everyday rating of the staff by the public which it serves: Do readers, especially adult readers, enjoy coming to the library partly because they respect and admire the staff members and like to do business with them? Is there even one, or are there maybe a dozen staff members who are looked up to by the community as knowing a great deal about the contents and qualities of books, and as personifying the public's recognition of the high cultural value of the library and its materials? Is the community really proud of the library staff, not merely in a vague way, but because when each reader has come for materials, for information, for help he has found able, devoted staff members in whatever department he has looked for them?

It may be that a new and different approach in personnel administration should be taken, since it is easy to become absorbed in routines and techniques, and to neglect the continuing search for outstanding employees, even before positions become vacant. The responsibility for not losing sight of the end goal is primarily that of the librarian.

NOTES & REFERENCES

1 Leonard D. White. *Government Career Service*. 99 p. 1935. Univ. of Chicago Press. An excellent statement.

2. See Edward C. Bursk (ed.), *Human Relations for Management: The New Perspective.* 372 p. 1956. Harper. 17 articles from the *Harvard Business Review.* Also Henry C. Lindgren. *Effective Leadership in Human Relations.* 287 p. 1954. Hermitage House. Also Chapter 11, "The Theory of Industrial Democracy." In William H. Knowles, *Personnel Management: A Human Relations Approach.* 488 p. 1955. American Book Co. p. 225-45. Also Thomas G. Spates. *Human Values Where People Work.* 246 p. 1960. Harper. Traces progress for 45 years as to feelings and experiences of all levels of workers.
3. Beardsley Ruml and Sidney G. Tickton, *Teaching Salaries Then and Now; A 50-Year Comparison with Other Occupations and Industries.* 93 p. 1955. Fund for the Advancement of Education. *Bulletin No.1.* N.Y.C. p. 40-44. Also "The Financial Rewards of Teaching." *NEA Research Bulletin.* 38: 49-55. May 1960.
4. Hazel B. Timmerman (ed.) *Salaries of Library Personnel, 1955,* 46 p. 1956. p. 3 Also Table C-1 of "Current Labor Statistics." U.S. Bureau of Labor Statistics, *Monthly Labor Review.* 79: 486. Apr. 1956.
5. David W. Belcher, *Wage and Salary Administration.* 503 p. 1955. Prentice Hall. Also "The Library's Pay Plan: A Statement of Principles." Adopted by the A.L.A. Council in July 1955. *A.L.A. Bulletin.* 49: 530-531. October 1955. Also A.L.A. Board on Personnel Administration. *Position Classification and Salary Administration in Libraries.* 1951. A.L.A. p. 48-58. Also North Carolina Library Association. *North Carolina Public Library Personnel Manual. University of North Carolina Institute of Government.* 1959. p. 11-19.
6. Hazel B. Timmerman, *op. cit.*
7. For example, see each April's issue of *News Notes of California Libraries.*
8. Also reprinted in the *American Library Annual.* Bowker.
9. Donald E. and Ruth B. Strout, "Higher Salaries, More Vacancies." *Library Journal.* 86: 2266-2272. June 15, 1961.
10. Kathleen B. Stebbins, *Personnel Administration in Libraries.* 1958. Scarecrow Press. p. 17.
11. "Table VII. Salaries of Selected Municipal Officials in Cities Over 10,000 Population: 1961." In *The Municipal Year Book: 1961.* International City Managers' Association. 1961. p. 156-158.
12. Published quarterly since Jan. 1960 by the Indiana Univ. Division of Library Science, and available free.
13. N.E.A. *Salaries and Salary Schedules of Urban School Employees,*

1960-61. Research Report 1961-R17. In process. Summarized in *NEA Research Bulletin* 39: 67-74. Oct. 1961.

14. *Office Salaries: A Guide to 1960 Salary Rates.* 40 p. 1960. (Survey Summary No. 24) National Office Management Association. Willow Grove, Pa. Data on the salaries of 600,000 employees in 23 jobs in over 9,000 companies in 136 cities.

15. *Tenure in Libraries: A Statement of Principles,* Adopted by the Council of the American Library Association, June 21, 1946. *A.L.A. Bulletin.* 40: 451-453. Nov. 1946. *Also Tenure in Libraries: A Statement of Principles of Intellectual Freedom and Tenure for Non-professional Library Employees.* 3 p. mimeo. 1947. A.L.A. Both statements are in Appendix II of A.L.A. Board on Personnel Administration. *Personnel Organization and Procedure: A Manual Suggested for Use in Public Libraries., 1952. A.L.A. p. 42-51.*

16. Edith B. Kidney, *Fringe Benefits for Salaries Employees in Government and Industry.* (Personnel Report No. 542) 33 p. 1945. Civil Service Assembly of the U.S. and Canada. Also William R. MeIntyre. "Fringe Benefits." *Editorial Research Reports.* Aug. 19, 1959. p. 613-29. For information on current practice in American cities in regard to hours worked, overtime, group insurance, sick leave and paid vacations, see "Municipal Personnel Data." In *The Municipal Year Book:* 1961. p. 161-189.

17. The money value of fringe benefits rose steadily from 15% of payroll in 1947 to 25% in 1959, in the case of 108 companies surveyed 7 times in the 13 years. See *Fringe Benefits:* 1959. 1960. Chamber of Commerce of the United States, p. 28-29.

18. See Alfred M. Skolnik and Joseph Zisman, "Growth in Employee Benefit Plans, 1954-57." In *Social Security Bulletin.* 22: 7. March 1959.

19. In 1949 almost three-fourths of all public library employees were in a retirement plan, and this was before the general extension of Federal Social Security to government employees. See Lily M. David, *Economic Status of Library Personnel:* 1949. 117 p. 1950. A.L.A. p. 52. Also Municipal Finance Officers Association, *Public Employee Retirement Terminology.* 21 p. 1956. And *Retirement Plans for Public Employees.* 46 p. 1958. Also Herbert Goldhor (ed.), *Retirement for Librarians.* 136 p. 1951. A.L.A. Still useful though increasingly out of date.

20. Renato Paul Bartolini, "The American Library Association Retirement

Plan." p. 80-94. in Herbert Goldhor (ed.), *Retirement for Librarians.*

21. In 1957 of over 5.5 million state and local government employees, 84% were under retirement plans; almost a third of these were in 27 state administered general coverage retirement systems. See p. 1 and 4 of U.S. Bureau of the Census, *Employee Retirement Systems of State and Local Government.* (Vol. IV, No. 1, of 1957 Census of Governments) 49 p. 1959. GPO. Also Julius J. Marke. "State Retirement, Certification and Pay Plans for Public Librarians, 1960," in Wyllis E. Wright, (ed.) *American Library and Book Trade Annual:* 1961. 1960. Bowker, p. 24-26.
22. By 1958, 33 states had passed such laws which directly included public libraries. See Julius J. Marke. *op. cit.*
23. Of 1,137 cities of over 10,000 population each, 586 (52%) have a compulsory retirement age–70 in 364 cities and 65 in 203. See *The Municipal Year Book: 1959.* International City Managers' Association. 1959, p. 164.
24. An exception occurs when a given position is reclassified to a higher grade, in recognition of substantial changes already made in the duties of that position; the individual holding that position is then officially promoted to the reclassified position.
25. *Building Better Promotion Programmes.* Personnel Management Series. No. 2; rev. ed., 34 p. 1958. U.S. Civil Service Commission. One of the few good statements on the subject. Four informed and experienced administrators answer the question "To What Extent Should Executive Position Be Filled from Outside?" In *Personnel Administration.* 20: 46-49. Jan.-Feb. 1957.
26. See statement by L. Quincy Mumford on the decision to continue posting notices of vacant positions, in Library of Congress *Information Bulletin.* Aug. 20, 1956. p. 443-44.
27. Such as recording critical and characteristic incidents in the daily work of an employee; see John C. Flanagan and Robert K. Burns, "The Employee Performance Record: A New Appraisal and Development Tool." *Harvard Business Review.* 33: 95. 102. Sept.-Oct. 1955.
28. Reprinted in Appendix IV, A.L.A. Board on Personnel Administration. *Personnel Organization and Procedure.* 1952. p. 54-59.
29. M. Joseph Dooher and Vivienne Marquis, *Rating Employee and Supervisory Performance: A Manual of Merit-Rating Techniques.* American Management Association, 192 p. 1950. Also Virgil M. Rogers (ed.) *"Merit Rating" for Teachers ?* Syracuse University Press.

79 p. 1959. Includes a "Selected Bibliography" with 100 references. The important reference in library literature is Edwin B. Colburn, ed. *Personnel Rating Procedures of American Libraries,* the report of the A.L.A. Division of Cataloging and Classification's Committee on Administration, available for loan on microfilm from A.L.A. Headquarters Library. For a summary, see his "Personnel Rating in American Libraries." *Journal of Cataloging and Classification.* 7: 14-16. Winter 1951. Also Philip E. Hagerty. "Evaluation of Personnel." In Wayne S. Yenawine, ed. *Library Evaluation.* Syracuse University Press, 1959. p. 21-29. For evolution of Enoch Pratt Free Library's Employee Progress Report from, see A.L.A. Board on Personnel Administration. *B.P.A. Notes.* Nov. 1956. par. 2-6.

30. Robert Hoppock, "Ground Rules for Appraisal Interviewers." *Personnel.* 38: 31-34. May-June, 1961. And in *Supervisory Management.* 6: 52-54. Aug. 1961.

31. See James R. Morris, "Job Rotation." In *Journal of Business., 29: 268-273. Oct. 1956. A study on the value of this training measure.*

32. Two which are still continued are those at Providence (R.I.) and Dayton (Ohio).

33. Edward M. Ryan, "Criticizing and Correcting Subordinates," *American Business.* 29: 28-29, 37-38. July 1959. Good advice and a valuable "Check List for Following Up a Reprimand." Also Samuel B. Kutash and Lydia Strong, "The Problems People Bring to the Job." *Management Review, 50: 4.13. Sept. 1961.*

    For library applications see Alfred L. Brophy and George M. Gazda, "Handling the Problem Staff Member," *Illinois Libraries,* 43: 750-763. Dec. 1961. A helpful summary of points in Bryan's *The Public Librarian,* and Douglass' Ph.D. thesis on *The Personality of the Librarian.*

34. Melvin Ansken, "Are They Hanging Hammocks at Their Desks?" *Think, 29:* 2-5. Feb. 1960.

35. Louis Cassels, "Promotion Paths Clogged? Try This," *Nation's Business* 45: 38-39, 86-87. Jan 1957.

36. See David G. Moore and Robert K. Burns, "How Good Is Good Morale?" *Factory Management and Maintenance,* 114: 130-136. Feb. 1956.

37. *A.L.A. Bulletin for February* 1939, p. 128-30.

38. "Democratic Administration," a bibliography. *News Notes of California Libraries.* 50: 572-576. Oct. 1955. Also Edwin Castagna,

"Democratic Administration." *Library Journal.* 50: 3138-3144. Dec. 15, 1957.

39. Thomas J. Luck, *Personnel Audit and Appraisal,* 317 p. 1955. McGraw-Hill. Also *Evaluating Your Personnel Management.* Personnel Management Series. No. 6. 88 p. 1954. U.S. Civil Service Commission.
40. For an example of such a document, see Enoch Pratt Free Library. *Personnel Procedures and Regulations., 35 p. Mimeo. 1949. Baltimore. See also Ruth M. White, (ed.) Public Library Policies–General and Specific.* The *Public Library Reporter,* No. 9. 1960. A.L.A. p. 33-73.
41. See labor turnover tables in "Current Labor Statistics" section of each issue of *Monthly Labor Review.* U.S. Bureau of Labor Statistics.
42. See P. 82 of the U.S. Civil Service Commission. *Annual Report:* 1953/54. 181 p. 1954.
43. Herbert Goldhor, "Personnel Turnover in Libraries." *Ohio Library Association Bulletin,* 28: 9-10. April 1958. In 1957-58, public school teacher turnover was 17% for separations and 21% for additions, in a national sample of about 1,400 school districts; see Ward S. Mason and R.K. Bain, *Teacher Turnover in the Public Schools.* 1957-58. U.S. Office of Education. Circular No. 608; 1959. p. 10, 21. "The normal annual turnover rate of all salaried employees (of the TVA) appears to be in the order of 16%." Harry L. Case, *Personnel Policy in a Public Agency: The TVA Experience.* 176 p. 1955. Harper, p. 30.
44. Frederick Gaudet, *Labor Turnover: Calculation and Cost. Research Study No. 39.* 111 p. 1960. American Management Association.
45. U.S. Civil Service Commission, *Exit Interviews in the U.S. Civil Service Commission,* 13. p. 1956.

5

The Organization for Personnel Administration

PERSONNEL administration is concerned with finding the best available people to do the jobs which are deemed necessary, and then with helping them make their maximum contribution to the library service programme. Because ability and devotion of the staff largely determine the success of that programme, personnel work is highly important to the library, to each employee and to the public. It involves many unexpected problems and questions, for which definitive answers are not possible, since circumstances are always changing. We attempt only to summarize the major relevant considerations and actual experience, including that from business, industry and government, and to present recommendations in the light of current conditions.[1-8]

The high percentage of public library expenditures devoted to salaries, the steady increase over the years in the number of public library employees, an expanding economy and the demand for more educated and trained personnel in every field make library personnel problems acute in the 1960s.[9] The A.L.A. standards of 1956 recommended that two thirds of total public library expenditures go for salaries (other than for janitors), and data on current actual expenditures agree. Anything which can improve the utilization of the personal services so secured by public libraries is important. It is an old saying that the building may represent 5 per cent of successful library service, and the book collection 20 per cent, but staff represents 75 per cent of what it takes to make a good library.

RESPONSIBILITY FOR PERSONNEL ADMINISTRATION

Individuals each have their own special backgrounds, abilities, interests and personalities. A staff of outstanding persons, with notable leadership and morale, can work wonders under conditions and with materials that would floor the weak-hearted, the mediocre and the uninterested who may so easily creep into any library. The responsibility for securing an outstanding staff is squarely that of the chief librarian. No matter how he delegates various aspects of personnel administration, he is the one person finally answerable to the trustees for the quality of the staff, its progress and development, its morale, its fair treatment and reward, its happy interrelationships, and the esteem in which it is held by readers and by the community at large. Local government officials in particular need to be better informed than they are at present on the personnel situation of the library and on the qualifications and duties of the professional staff. How well this has or has not been done is reflected in whether the library is included in local government employee welfare programmes, fringe benefits and across-the-board pay raises.

Role of the Library Board

In personnel administration it is peculiarly true that the board should restrict itself to general policies and not concern itself with their specific applications or with specific positions or persons, other than the choice of the chief librarian. Policy statements should be adopted by the trustees on recommendation of the chief librarian, after consultation by him with his colleagues, on such topics as eligibility for employment of relatives of present staff or board members, the salary schedule and the position classification plan (and the rules for their use and application), sick leave paid vacations, holidays, the employment of substitute or temporary staff, promotions, retirement, leave of absence and many others.[10] Such general policy statements free the librarian from the need of securing a decision in each individual case. It is desirable to give him reasonable discretion in applying the policy to individual cases, and to provide for possible exceptions (e.g., by their being reported as such, or at least upon specific approval in each case by the board).

Another board function is to protect the librarian from pressure for the appointment of poorly qualified persons who may have political connections, or who present claims unrelated to merit. Individual trustees usually refrain from recommending persons for employment. If a trustee proposes an applicant, he should be accorded the courtesy of consideration; and in times of labour shortage conscientious trustees may be helpful in finding good clerical and building staff. When an inferior candidate is recommended by a trustee, the latter will feel he has done his part by having made the introduction, and will not press for an undesirable appointment. If he perseveres and the matter comes up to the board, and if the board as a whole directs or requests the appointment, promotion or separation of a specific individual without or against the recommendation of the chief librarian, it is likely to be a clear case of board interference in internal management and of lack of confidence in the administrator. In several such cases good librarians have resigned rather than submit to pressure they think is harmful to the library.

Usually the appointment of a new staff member is legal and official only when approved by the board of trustees, since by law the board is the library. In practice many new employees have begun work and even received their first salary check before the meeting of the board at which their appointment is proposed. In such a case the administrator should inform the board or at least its president, in advance of appointments to key positions. The post of assistant chief librarian, for example, is of obvious concern to the board. Similarly it is usually required and desirable that promotions be approved by or least reported to the board. The natural desire on the part of the librarian to steer his board away from internal management should not lead him to withhold information from the trustees, either as to what is planned or what has been done by way of personnel actions; they as well as the librarian have to be prepared to justify these decisions in the face of possible criticism. These actions can be summarized briefly in the written agenda for each board meeting.

Role of the Librarian

Subject to the general policies so established by the trustees, the librarian in public libraries other than the largest typically is and desirably should be the person chiefly responsible for personnel administration. The McDiarmids found this to be so in 86 per cent of the 212 libraries in cities of over 30,000 population.[11] The smaller the library, the more nearly will the librarian perform all the functions discussed below or give them his immediate supervision. The larger the library, the less he will be able to do himself, and the more nearly he must restrict himself to key appointments, major policies, general goals and overall supervision. Since typically appointments of new staff member are made by the board on the recommendation of the chief librarian,[12] he would do well in as many cases as possible to make those recommendations only after he has clear and adequate ground for the exercise of his best judgment, including personal interviews with the candidates, a review of the information available on each and the opinions of those other selected members of the library staff who have interviewed them. Even in large libraries the responsibility for making the final decision on selection of a new employee should be delegated only to those supervisors in whose judgment the chief has confidence, and it is well for him to examine the paper and to retain a veto before the final appointment is made. Not for nothing is it said that an institution is the lengthened shadow of a man.

General personnel policies, such as were discussed above as the main contribution of the trustees to personnel administration, may be drafted or even initiated by others, e.g., staff committees, but are submitted to the board only with the approval of the librarian. Specific personnel policies are often avoided by boards and remain a matter of tradition or oral agreement. Even more common, formal acceptance or specific consideration has not usually been given to broader and more general policies, such as the principle of merit, democratic administration, the improvement of working conditions and the development of individual staff members. On these general objectives the librarian can get many things clarified if he will consider and formulate a clear and practical statement.[13] No such policy statement will be enforced and applied up and down the line unless it is clear that it has the support of the librarian and that he will not countenance violations.

The librarian will delegate as much as possible of the detail and preliminary steps, but he will keep adequate supervision over them to get the best results. Personnel work demands good judgment. This applies no where more than in deciding whether and to whom the crucial aspects of the personnel function shall be delegated, e.g., in choosing those to screen applicants and select the best for appointment. The formal tools of supervision are applicable here, such as reports, compilation and analysis of meaningful statistics, screening of top applicants by department head committees, regular meetings for the review of current progress and problems, etc. The chief librarian is paid in large part for proper supervision of the rest of the staff, and to a lesser degree for his technical knowledge all ability. It is unlikely that a library staff will be improving in competence and performance in the face of poor personnel administration. If it is obviously on the downgrade, a likely cause is the organization for personnel administration and specifically the unwise delegation of that function to others.

Role of the Assistant Librarian

The usual persons to whom a librarian will delegate any major part of his authority in personnel administration are (a) the assistant librarian, and the department heads and other supervisors; and (b) a specifically designated personnel officer. The delegation of a considerable part of the personnel job to the general manager type of assistant librarian, in addition to other duties, is a normal development as a given library grows in size and the chief administrator needs help. Frequently the assistant librarian takes over the personnel records and the application of policy to non-professional personnel, and does the preliminary work leading to the decisions which the librarian must make. He will thereby develop his own ability to evaluate candidates. In 10 per cent of the 212 public libraries surveyed by the McDiarmids,[14] the assistant librarian served in this fashion. At the same time in the growth of the library or even earlier, the heads of the large departments and branches will tend to become involved in the personnel function, by formulating policies, interviewing candidates, recommending action, etc. The necessity for the librarian to retain the major voice in personnel matters does not conflict with the desirability of having the time-consuming preliminary work done for him by other; the top supervisors in the library are thereby strengthened and developed in their role as managers.

Role of the Personnel Officer

More difficult questions appear when the library grows to such a size that a special personnel officer is needed. The McDiarmids recommend this for a library of about 150 staff members.[15] The 1956

A.L.A. standards suggest 75 as the cutting point,[16] but general surveys have shown the average ratio is one full-time personnel worker for every 125 employees.[17] For government agencies alone, the median ratio is one personnel worker for every 143 employees; for all firms with less than 500 employees each the ratio is one to 109 employees. A public library with 125 or more employees is likely to benefit from the investment in a full-time personnel officer, especially with the present turnover rate.

At just what level a personnel officer is appointed is less important than what he is assigned to do.[18] Even in a library with a staff of twenty-five, the paper routines performed in selecting new employees and in fixing their conditions of work, by whomever done, come to an impressive total, but much of this can be handled by an intelligent clerical aid. Where a public library has a hundred employees for more, the designation of a personnel officer is meaningless if he is simply to concentrate only the routines which were previously dispersed. If he is to make a significant contribution to the work of the library, he needs the qualities of a staff officer; most essential is his ability to evaluate persons' abilities. Even then he may not be the best person in the library to visit library schools and talk to high school and college groups for recruiting. Though this position carries no power of command over other, it does involve close relations with the numerous department heads who have to leave part of their fate in the personnel officer's hands. Presumably he has technical skills to bring to bear on personnel problems of the library and to carry out its personnel policies, but special techniques by no means assure wisdom and judgment in evaluating people, and that is the crux of good personnel work.

The number of such personnel officers in public libraries is still not large, but it can be expected to increase at a slow but steady rate in the future as it has in the past.[19] Almost without exception, library personnel officers were professional librarians originally, and only a very few have added to this any formal training or other experience in personnel work. though the knowledge and skills required of a personnel officer are as technical and as difficult as those of a librarian. Two main reasons why library personnel officers have been professional librarians and not professional personnel men are (a) the natural desire to have in this position someone intimately acquainted with the problems and circumstances of librarianship and even of the individual institution; and (b) the importance of having as personnel officer someone in whose judgment the chief librarian has confidence; this is more easily done by choosing him from the immediate staff or from the library profession than from an outside group. Nor, of course, is it by any mean true that every trained personnel worker is thereby fitted or adequate.

Civil Service

Library personnel administration depends vitally on whether the library is under a legal system of civil service.[20] It is estimated that only a tenth are,[21] and there appears no trend to increased the number. Library administrators in general believe in employment for merit only, but they are opposed to civil service because of the many serious limitations it introduces. Most public library employees who have actually worked under civil service are satisfied if not actively in favour of it,[22] not because it assures quality of staff but because it tends to bring fringe benefits, higher pay and greater job security. Unfortunately it also makes the dismissal of incompetents more difficult.

Civil service introduces other difficulties: (a) it restricts the geographical area from which selection may be made; (b) its tests of competence and of personality are of dubious validity, especially for trained librarians; (c) it takes a long time to hold an examination, score the papers, and certify candidates; and (d) it tends to be inflexible in these and other way. In many instances, delays in discovering applicants and in setting, preparing and rating examinations discourage the best candidates, especially for professional positions. In view of the long-term shortage of librarians, civil service methods of employee selection are more nearly appropriate to clerical and building maintenance positions. Libraries which have to operate under the traditional civil service practices are greatly handicapped, but the best civil service jurisdictions have improved their procedures, e.g., the "continuously open" examination of the TVA and of the United States Civil Service Commission and the practice in several cities of having the librarian participate in recruiting, of scheduling more frequent and prompt examination, and of having the candidates interviewed by a library representative. It is to the credit of civil service commissions that they have pioneered in position classification, salary schedules, service ratings, formal probationary period and other desirable personnel practices.

All of the these practices are also available to non-civil service public libraries, but many such libraries have not utilized them. In some cases they have even violated the elementary principle of employment on merit, and rarely have the tests of fitness used by non-civil service public libraries been subjected to analysis of reliability and validity. However the best of the non-civil service public libraries have made a great contribution in staff development and library service by a high type of personnel administration, and several of them have assembled staffs of greater distinction than any civil service library. In general the presence or absence of civil service is less determining than the interest and care of the chief librarian in the library's personnel work.

DEFINING THE NUMBER AND KINDS OF POSITIONS

Organization for personnel administration in a given library inevitably leads to the need for some statement of the number and kinds of positions to filled, and for a definition of their constituent tasks. A position consists of a group of duties and responsibilities assigned by competent authority to be performed by one person. It may be full-time or part-time, temporary or permanent, and can be considered separately from the person who happens to fill it at any one time. That is, a position exists even when it is not filled. Above all, a position is not a static thing; in the course of time it will change by reason of altered circumstances if not indeed by administrative decision. The qualifications and abilities of the person assigned to a given position constitute the greatest single force making for changes in it.

Someone has to decide for every library how many positions will be allowed at any given time, and their distribution by agency and grade level. In the case of those libraries with line-by-line budgets this is all spelled out for the year and can be changed only with the approval of the library board and the appropriating authority, an inflexible situation at best. In most public libraries the appropriation for salaries is in one or a few large groupings (e.g., custodial employees' salaries separate from those of all other staff members). Within each grouping the librarian is usually free, or at most with the approval of the board, to vary the number of positions in different grades or in different agencies, to substitute two part-time positions for one full-time (or vice versa), to alter the duties constituting individual positions and to make other such changes, as long as the library's total salary appropriation limit is observed. Such authority, to alter the number and kinds of positions in the library, is needed to meet changes in the service programme of the library and to cope with changing labour market.

Schedules of Staff Quotas

In a library serving less than 25,000 people the librarian can undoubtedly keep in his head the complete picture of the number and kind of positions in the library. But any library with more than a dozen employees needs a table of authorized positions, revised from time to time, as in Table 5.1.

TABLE 5.1.
Possible Table of Authorized Positions, for a Library Serving 25,000 Population: in Full-Time Equivalents

Department	*Library aide*	Senior *Library aide*	*Professional librarian*	*Custodian*	*Total*
Adult	3	1	1.5	—	5.5
Children's	1	1	1	—	3
Technical services	.5	1	.5	—	2
Custodian	—	—	—	1	1
Library office	1	—	1	—	2
Total	5.5	3	4	1	13.5

One of the more important decisions involved at this point concerns the nature of the duties to be assigned to library aides. There is no difficulty in separating out custodial jobs, or in identifying purely clerical positions, such as typists. The difficulty comes usually in distinguishing those duties which require professional training and experience from those which are in fact or might be performed adequately if not also effectively by persons with lesser qualifications. The line of distinction is not a hard and fast one which can be drawn once and never altered. It will depend for example on the relatives supply of trained librarians, and on the quality of the individual library aides. In general, any duty which can be transferred to a person of less experience and training should be so assigned, both to free the time of the better-qualified persons for even more difficult and responsible assignments and to reduce the salary cost of the work done. This transfer of duties has a long record in librarianship and in other professions; in medicine, for example, more and more jobs formerly the exclusive province of the doctor are being shared with or turned over to nurses, and nurses' traditional duties are increasingly being shifted to nurses aides. The criterion of any such reassignment is whether the less well-qualified employee is able to perform the duties in question satisfactorily in a non-emergency situation.

At various points in this book, reference is made to jobs which might well be handled by non-professional staff members but which have not always been so assigned. The frequency of non-professional or clerical tasks probably runs somewhat as follows: in technical services, help in ordering and receipt of books, typing of cards, physical preparation of books, accessioning, preliminary filing of cards and shelf listing; in circulation routines, charging and discharging, handling overdues and reserves, filing, shelving and statistics; in the reference department, checking and filing periodicals, handling pamphlets and clippings, assisting with exhibits, preparing books for bindery, mending and checking documents. Almost any clerical job consists partly of steps which are mechanical and require little judgment or discretion; so far as possible these should be separated out and assigned to non-professional assistants. Furthermore, the temptation is always to underestimate the ability of intelligent—perhaps even college-trained—library aides to learn new, more varied and more difficult tasks. Sometimes professional librarians resist this process because they fear that there will be nothing left for them to do. It is a proper test of the viability of a profession that new, important and more difficult tasks are always ahead for those who have the theoretical training and the practical experience, and this is certainly true of librarianship in general and of public librarians in particular.

POSITION CLASSIFICATION

The description and analysis of the duties of positions is usually called job evaluation, and in industry the point system and factor-comparison methods are the ones most often used. In government generally and in public libraries specifically the technique almost always employed is that of position classification.[23] In broad outline this consists of three main steps: (1) job analysis or the recording of the duties of all existing positions; (2) the comparison and grouping of the resultant job descriptions into more or less homogeneous classes of positions; and (3) the writing of specifications for each such class in order to state its particular attributes and to distinguish it from its neighbours.

Job Analysis

Job analysis is generally done by means of a position-description questionnaire,[24] and this can be made to serve well enough without employing more expensive techniques. Each employee on the payroll is asked to fill out such a questionnaire, desirably after some explanation of it and of the total project and after a chance to keep a work diary for a week at least. If the position is a new one or is otherwise vacant, the immediate supervisor answers the questionnaire. Precision in stating one's duties (and regard to such factors as extent of review by others, responsibility for error and scope of freedom for exercise of discretion) is not easy, as anyone can testify who has ever filled out a position-description questionnaire. The resulting statement should be reviewed by the employee's immediate supervisor to secure his comments and opinions without changing the individual employee's words. One of the desirable by-products of job analysis is the clarification of people's ideas as to what they are or are not supposed to be doing. The complete position description questionnaire is a snapshot picture of the duties and responsibilities of the employee in question.

Classes, Grades and Services

Once the position description questionnaires are all completed and reviewed, they are read and reread by some one person, the personnel officer in the large public library or the librarian in the small or medium-sized library. This person makes a series of judgments as to the ways in which the various positions, described by the questionnaires, related to each other. For one thing the questionnaires can be grouped by main type of work performed, viz., professional, library aides and custodial, in most libraries. These are called services and are vertical groupings in the schematic representation of the resultant position classification plan (see Table 5.2).

TABLE 5.2.
Possible Outline of Classes, Grades and Services in a Public Library Serving 100,000 Population

Grade	*Service*		
	Professional	*Library aides*	*Custodial*
1.	—	Junior library aide (20)	—
2.	—	Library aide (8)	Custodian (6)
3.	—	Senior library aide (5)	Senior Custodian (1)
4.	Librarian (8)	Principal library aide (2)	Supt. of buildings and grounds (1)
5.	Senior librarian (4)	—	—
6.	Department head (3)	—	—
7.	Assistant chief Librarian (1)	—	—
8.	Chief librarian (1)	—	—
	Total No. of positions : (17)	(35)	(8)

The horizontal division in any one service consists of those positions which are considered to have duties sufficiently similar in level of difficulty and of responsibility to justify their being grouped together in the same class and treated alike for personnel purposes. One criterion for deciding when to put two positions in the same or in different classes is the applicability of the same tests of fitness for selection or promotion. A position is assigned to a class according to its actual duties, and not according to the qualifications of the person who happens to be performing those duties. If a registered nurse is serving as a typist, to pick an absurd example, the position is grouped with other typists' positions; similarly a position consisting of clerical duties but performed by a library school graduate should be grouped with other clerical positions and not with the professional positions. All classes of positions, in different services, which are deemed to consist of duties of approximately the same level of difficulty and responsibility are said to be in the same grade.

Class Specifications

The third main step of position classification is to prepare a written statement describing the attributes of each class of positions. Class specifications may be longer or shorter, but reasonable limits are from a half to a full page per class. Such class specifications consist of the class title, the distinguishing characteristics of the work constituting positions assigned to the class, examples of specific duties appropriate to such positions, and the qualifications deemed necessary for successful performance of the work of positions in the class. In this last regard, the modern trend is to list only those personal character traits which are peculiarly important to positions in this class, and to state the necessary qualifications in terms of knowledge and skills clearly needed for successful performance rather than it terms of levels of academic achievement alone.[25] Class specifications are of little value in themselves, save to assign properly a new or revised position, but are useful and desirable in other personnel process (such as selection, promotion, salary administration, transfer). A possible class specification for senior librarian (see Table 5.2) is shown below. Position classification plans of libraries are easily available and are useful for suggestions; they should not be copied directly or followed blindly because they should reflect the circumstances of the one library in which the job analysis was made.

Class Specification for Senior Librarian

Distinguishing Characteristics of Work: Supervision over other employees; responsibility for the service of a branch or other agency; constant dealings with readers, the contents of books and library tools and methods.

Some Specific Duties: Supervision and training assistants, answering reference questions, selecting books for purchase, recommending changes in policies.

Qualifications Needed: Background, poise and ability to supervise other staff members and to deal effectively with patrons, as demonstrated by successful professional experience; subject knowledge and of books and library techniques such as is likely to be achieved by successful completion of an undergraduate college programme of study and of a fifth year of study in a graduate library school.

The rules for the administration of the position classification plan are next in importance only to the class specifications; they should include definitions of terms, provision for the reclassification of individual positions and for resurveys of all positions (every five years or so), an explanation of the class specifications, the procedure for the classification of a new position etc. A number of individual and corporate consultants will for a fee prepare a position classification plan for a library. But it is not difficult to prepare such a plan, and the librarian who does it himself will learn more and appreciate its value and limitations better than in any other way. Though the grouping of position description questionnaires and the writing of class specifications are necessarily done by one person (or at most a small committee), the results should be conveyed to all the employees of the library before the position classification plan is officially adopted by the trustees. The usual procedure is to make available the proposed class specifications and to certify to each employee the class, grade and service to which his position is being assigned. Within a certain time period, he may ask for a review of the allocation of his position. In addition, the plan in its entirety should be reviewed by the librarian and the department heads. After submission to the trustees and upon their adoption it becomes effective.

This in brief is the process of library job evaluation. The value of a position classification plan is that it enables the librarian to deal intelligently with relatively few groups of homogeneous positions, and not with each of a larger group of individual positions. Like other methods of job evaluation, a position classification plan rests on individual judgments at certain crucial points and thus cannot be absolutely impartial and accurate. It needs therefore to be kept reasonably flexible and fluid, so that errors already incorporated in it may be corrected when detected and so that changes deemed necessary in the service programme of the library will not be hampered by it. In other words, the dominant consideration is that the plan expedite the administrative needs of the institution, and not freeze existing work assignments or prevent reassignments. Finally, job evaluation by itself does not guarantee good personnel administration, but it does provide a good base for most other aspects of personnel work. Position classification, for example, is necessary for a sound salary plan, but one may have position classification without a sound salary plan and at least some sort of a salary plan without position classification. All the organization for personnel administration is preparation for effective day-to-day operation, especially the selection of new employees; and all the machinery and techniques are of little consequence if those who make these selections come up with only mediocre appointments.

NOTES & REFERENCES

1. Dale Yoder, *Personnel Management and Industrial Relations.* 4th ed. 941 p. 1956. Prentice Hall.
2. William E. Mosher, J.D. Kingsley, and O.G. Stahl. *Public Personnel Administration.* 4th ed. 656 p. 1956. Harper.
3. Institute for Training in Municipal Administration, *Municipal Personnel Administration.* 6th ed. 414 p. 1960. International City Managers Association.
4. Frances Torbert. *Personnel Management in Small Companies.* 102 p. 1951. Institute of Industrial Relations. Univ of California, Los Angeles.
5. Lowell Martin, (ed.) *Personnel Administration in Libraries.* 168 p. 1946. Univ. of Chicago Press.
6. Alice I Bryan. *The Public Librarian.* 474 p. 1952. Columbia Univ. Press.
7. Bernard Van Horne, ed. *Current Trends in Personnel Administration. Library Trends.* 3: 194. July 1954.
8. Kathleen B. Stebbins. *Personnel Administration in Libraries.* 304 p.

1958. Scarecrow Press.

9. Some current personnel problems found in many libraries are noted in a statement of the Los Angeles Public Library director to the trustees and later to the city council, viz., 'the higher salaries received by school and special librarians, the national shortage of librarians making it difficult to compete under the best of conditions, lack of promotional opportunities in some areas of work, low beginning salaries in LAPL, lack of sufficient staff with resulting irregular schedules and stress, necessity for evening and Saturday work and for work in outlying areas, and lack of monetary recognition for subject specialization and book knowledge. Los Angeles Public Library, *Operation LAPL.* Jan. 31, 1961. p. 3

10. Ruth M. White, (ed.) *Public Library Policies—General and Specific. (Public Library Reporter.* no. 9). 116 p. 1960. A.L.A. p. 33-73.

11. Errett W. and John McDiarmid, *The Administration of the American Public Library.* 1943. A.L.A. p. 168.

12. By Indiana law, the board can appoint only those persons recommended by the chief librarian; Burns' *Annotated Indiana Statutes.* 41-915 (1).

13. See the staff manuals of various public libraries such as those of Charlotte, N.C. 44 p. 1958; Knoxville, Tenn. 32 p. 1960; Summit, N.J. 12 p. 1960; and Tampa, Fla. 60 p. 1957.

14. McDiarmid. *op. cit.* p. 168.

15. *Ibid.* p. 170.

16. *Public Library Service: A Guide to Evaluation with Minimum Standards.* 1956. A.L.A. p. 41.

17. Dale Yoder. *op. cit.* p. 18-19.

18. Phyllis Osteen. "The Personnel Office and the Personnel Officer," in Bernard Van Horne, ed. *Current Trends in Personnel Administration. Library Trends.* 3: 59-66. July 1954.

9. The McDiarmids reported only two full-time personnel officers in 212 public libraries, each serving over 30,000 population in 1940. *op cit.* p. 169. In 1961, of 42 public libraries each serving over 30,000 population, 20 had personnel officers, in 6 others this function was assigned to the assistant librarian. None of these 26 libraries had less than 140 employees. *See Salary Statistics for Large Public Libraries for 1961. op. cit.*

20. John B. Kaiser. "Civil Service in Libraries," in Bernard Van Horne, ed. *Current Trends in Personnel Administration. Library Trends.* 3: 80-94. July 1954.

21. Of 4,089 libraries reporting on this in 1956, less than 400 were under civil service, and over half of these were in only three states. Vainstein. *op. cit.* p. 36, 88-89.
22. Alice I. Bryan. *op. cit.* p. 173-80.
23. Kenneth Byers, et al. *Elements of Position Classification in Local Government.* Civil Service Assembly. Personnel Report No. 554. 50 p. 1955. Also, A.L.A. Board of Personnel Administration. *Position Classification and Salary Administration in Libraries.* 81 p. 1951. A.L.A. Also North Carolina Library Association. *North Carolina Public Library Personnel Manual.* 1959. University of North Carolina Institute of Government. p. 7-11, 22-44.
24. Samples of such a form may be readily found in some of the books in the "General References," noted above.
25. About 30 years of so ago, many large public libraries had what was called a "graded scheme of service." This was a grouping of library positions by the education and experience of their incumbents. Even today most colleges and public schools have a similar or comparable grading of faculty, by their academic achievements and years of experience. But all such persons are performing essentially the same duties, those of a teacher, and therefore some other device must be found to separate them into sub-groups for salary purposes. Public libraries which are under school boards tend to use this same pattern for the definition of their positions or as a modification of the position classification plan described in the text here, at least in part because it enables them to tie in with the school teachers' salary schedule. See Clarence A. Weber, *Personnel Problems of School Administrators.* 1954. McGraw-Hill, p. 260.

6

Administration of the Book Collection

WE COME now to the librarian's stock in trade, the materials with which he deals. One of the public library's major responsibilities has always been the development of a stock of books, each worthy in its own right and potentially useful to the community. This involves policy, planning and management as preface to selection and procurement. It likewise includes the custody and safekeeping of the collections, the repair and rebinding of books and eventually their withdrawal and discard. This chapter deals with five administrative aspects to book selection: (1) objectives and policies; (2) budgeting for book selection; (3) assigning the parts of the selection process; (4) special problems and non-book materials; and (5) custody, weeding and evaluation.[1-4]

The processes of book selection, acquisition and cataloguing can be viewed as involving a "circle of interest."[5] Those who select books, primarily on the basis of reader needs, should find these various steps so organized that the original interest in getting the book will continue until these same staff members can see each book go into use by the public. Breaks in this continuity and failure by the selector and by the others involved, to "see the book through" into actual use are deterrents to full public use of each book, for which money has been spent. The process begins when a new title comes to the attention of the selector. It proceed through the stages by which the title is evaluated and selected, to the cataloguing and classification stage. The circle is completed when the book is placed in the hands of its readers. Book selection is an art, involving personal knowledge of many factors and professional judgment. Cataloguing and classification are also matters of judgment and in part are arts and in part techniques, to implement and express the selection judgments. The book collection should be built and made ready for the use of the library's total public, and not to fit some theoretical pattern.

OBJECTIVES AND POLICIES

Objectives of Book Selection

The public library enables people to have access to a larger collection of materials than each would have if he were limited to his own books. This was why the early association-type libraries were organized. As public libraries grew larger and their patronage more diversified, it became less clear what kinds of books should be collected and kept. An individual finds it easy to decide what books he wants to buy and keep, and library organized to serve a homogeneous group of people likewise has little difficulty in deciding what items to secure. But a general public library serving a heterogeneous population has wide range of possible choices and minimum of reliable guidance for those choices.

The matter is complicated both by the increasing number of books available and by the wide variety of forms of material, printed and non-printed. Yet this flood of materials, so characteristic of our age, makes the public library ever more important and useful as the mediator between the individual and the bewildering mass of print. Citizens should find a collection carefully chosen for its intrinsic worth, its timeliness and its potential usefulness in the community. The effectiveness of the public library depends as much on the wisdom of the choice of materials as any other factor. Two major responsibilities of a librarian are to build up an excellent collection of materials, and to see that the inflow of new books is prompt and continuous.

Book selection should proceed not by chance or the personal interest of individual staff members but by written objectives and policies. These should be based on the best thinking of staff and trustees, as limited by funds, on such policy decisions as total size; distribution between adult and juvenile books, fiction and non-fiction; relative emphasis on promptness of acquiring new books and of discarding old ones; and types of materials to be included and not included.

To build a collection most vital and useful to its community a library needs prompt acquisition of new books and elimination of worn-out and dated materials. If it is interested in the serious needs of adult readers, it will have relatively more subject periodicals, reference and adult no-fiction books and fewer adult novels. Decisions on such basic matters are influenced by the special strengths and ready public accessibility of the collections in other local libraries. Still to be developed are regional or state-wide cooperative acquisition programme; in most areas of the country they are badly needed.[6]

A statement of objectives for a public library book collection should deal with the types of materials to be included and not to be included. Generally, most public libraries do not purchase rare books, books used as texts in local schools, genealogies, medical texts or law books. This should not discourage getting textbooks of high quality which many adult readers prefer to more popular works that do not have as much substance and often are not so well written. And larger libraries do have state statutes and the best standard texts on at least the major aspects of the law. For printed nonbook materials there should be a statement as to what is acceptable as a gift or what will be purchased, e.g., magazines, newspapers, pamphlets, flat pictures, photographs, prints, maps and clippings. Manuscripts should be accepted in the typical library only if they deal with local history; the large city libraries are increasingly used for specialized reference materials. Non-print materials, such as phonograph records, 16-mm motion pictures, filmstrips, microfilm and framed pictures have won a place in modern public libraries.

Policies of Book Selection

After decisions are made on objectives and inclusiveness of the collection, book selection policies should be written, reviewed by the staff and approved by the board.[7] Such policy statements guide the day-by-day decisions of those who select materials. Their usefulness will be increased by the extent to which they provide specific guidance for selection in all main subject areas, including such issues as controversial political questions, sex and ephemeral recreational fiction.

The public library seeks to have books on all sides of a controversial issue. There are citizens who oppose this. They believe the public library should not circulate books critical of the economic and political system of this country. They fear such books will weaken readers' support of this country's system of private property and democratic government. Not only is this precisely the stand taken by dictatorships with regard to their public libraries, but it is contrary to the guarantees of freedom in our own Constitution.

Librarians believe, with Milton, that truth will prevail in the open market of competitive ideas. If the claims of censorship and suppression are recognized as valid for one cause, it increases the difficulty of denying them for others. Libraries in our country today are subjected to relatively little pressure from censors, probably because they have acted as self censors and refrained from purchasing controversial books. When censorship has been attempted, however, librarians and trustees who maintained their position have won community support.[8]

More difficulty is likely to arise with books dealing frankly with sex than with those concerning political issues. Here again a policy statement should be worked out in advance of an incident and be tested for adequacy and soundness. Non-fiction books are usually easy to judge. Studies like the Kinsey reports and authoritative books on sex instruction are important titles for public libraries. The problem usually arises in creative composition, especially modern novels.

Everyone draws the line at some point as to what is objectionable. The public library draw it at that point of greatest freedom combined with creative value, which is supported by at least a substantial minority of the community. In time this will become the position of the majority. Recent court decisions have established the rule that a book should be judged in its entirety and not by passages taken out of context, and by its likely effect on an average adult and not on a susceptible youngster.[9] Sex frankness in a novel by itself is no recommendation, naturally. To be acquired by a public library, the book should be well written and possess a reasonable degree of artistic integrity. Many librarians, devoted to freedom of opinion, especially as to social and economic issues, and reluctant to see any form of censorship, are conscientiously concerned over the increasing proportion of sex and depravity in current novels. They recognize that writers of literary ability but prurient minds may produce books of sensational and profitable popular appeal, which are socially destructive, and they consider that a public library has as much obligation to be concerned over ethical as over "literary" values. They are supported by their communities as often and as fully as their more liberal colleagues.

Books of recreational fiction are controversial to librarians, not because they are objected to, but because they are so inconsequential and yet so popular with certain groups of readers. Disproportionate funds go for light love stories, westerns, mysteries and science fiction, when no public library has enough money to buy all the substantial informational books needed and asked for.

While no other source of reference and non-fiction books exists in the average community for the general public, recreational fiction is found in paper-covered books, magazines, the movies, television and radio. The rise of mass media and paperback books has greatly reduced the demand for recreational fiction in libraries. It has correspondingly increased the library's obligation to provide a fair number of copies of perhaps two hundred of the best fiction titles each year. The library should neither downgrade nor neglect its fiction service; too many novels are powerful, constructive and appealing portrayals of character and of life.

The book selection policy should set some minimum level of quality for acceptable titles, and a quantity limit as to the proportion of book budget to be spent on adult fiction. The demand for fiction can be partly met by a pay-duplicate or rental collection by the transfer of recreational fiction from one agency to another instead of purchasing multiple copies, by eliminating their cataloguing, and by the use of paper covered copies.[10]

These problems need to be resolved in advance, if possible by a written policy statement, tested by experience, approved by the board and subject to review. A number of libraries have such a statement.[11] It should be written in terms of the local situation and not merely copied from that of other libraries or from some general pronouncement. It should contain as much detail as necessary; the more general the statement the less helpful it will be in screening titles for purchase. The existence of an established, published policy, well thought out, available to staff and public, and operating satisfactorily, will help to deter attempts at censorship, and provide a systematic procedure for hearing complaints and for reviewing individual titles.

BUDGETING FOR BOOK SELECTION

Budgeting

Book selection policies are greatly influenced by the book budget. Small libraries, for example, will be tempted to buy a larger proportion of "popular" books than will large libraries. A good library will bend every energy to enlarge its book fund. The book funds of most public libraries have steadily decreased as a percentage of total expenditures and in many cases in actual purchasing power as the average cost of books has risen. Thus the total known public library expenditures for books, magazines and audio-visual materials dropped from 18 per cent of total current operating expenditures in 1939 to 15.7 per cent in 1956 and to 14.2 per cent in 1960. Although the actual amount spent for materials multiplied almost five times between 1939 and 1960 (from $8,784,000 to $26,818,000 in 1956 and to $42,533,000 in 1960), the total expenditures of public libraries rose more than six times (from $48,832,000 to $170,223,000 in 1956 and to $298,263,000 in 1960).[12] The prices of books and magazines likely to be bought by public libraries, on the other hand, rose almost 50 per cent from 1947-49 to 1960.[13]

It is the responsibility of the librarian and trustees as a first decision affecting the book budget to see that pressures for higher salaries and from increasing costs are not met by reducing the book fund. To the contrary, a concerted effort is overdue to restore budgets for books and other materials, and binding, to 18 or 20 per cent of total budgets. Book funds can be used more efficiently by: (1) securing maximum discounts; (2) making books easily available by interchange between agencies; (3) encouraging gifts; and (4) utilizing paper-covered books when possible. These methods are necessary, but they cannot be expected to take the place of additional dollars in the book fund.

A.L.A. standards call for 4,000 to 5,000 titles a year to be added to each library system with a basic book stock of at least 100,000 volumes, and for at least a fifth of a volume per capita to be added annually for a system serving less than 100,000 people.[14] But only 270 libraries in 1956 had as many as 100,000 volumes each and the average annual accessions of all reporting libraries serving less than 100,000 people was less than one-tenth volume per capita.[15] What constitutes a desirable book fund for a public library cannot easily be stated in general terms, since much depends on such factors as the present state of the book collection, and the relative emphasis to be given expensive technical books and less expensive fiction.

As a rule of thumb, based on current average, the fund for books and other materials should be about 15 to 18 per cent of the total budget, which would mean about 50 cents per capita, if the library budget were about $3.50 per capita. The strength of a library's book collection lies first in its quality and second in its size, and the strength of the library's service depends on the strength of its book collection, second only to the ability of its staff because an able staff builds an excellent collection. It is often possible to document the need for book funds more dramatically than for other items,[16] and citizens quickly express appreciation for the benefits of an increasing number of new books, promptly acquired.

The second main decision involving the book budget concerns the allotment of available funds by categories, by agencies and by time, with a monthly statement on the status of the funds. Percentages appropriate to any given library as between juvenile books, adult fiction and adult nonfiction can hardly be set up here; they depend on the present state of local collections and on plans for their development. But it is recommended that 25 per cent of total book funds be used for juvenile books, 25 per cent for adult fiction and 50 per cent for adult nonfiction (including reference book and periodicals). This may be aided by limiting fiction to about 300 new titles per year, carefully selected and duplicated.[17]

Another usual allotment is by branches and departments, and such apportioning needs annual review and adjustment. No formula can be offered for distribution of funds by agency. To distribute book funds according to circulation totals puts a premium on recreational fiction and best sellers, and penalizes informational reading and study. Attempts to combine data as to adult nonfiction circulation, reference questions and other factors, as a guide to book fund allotments, have not produced a satisfactory solution. Allotments are a matter of policy, objectives and emphasis, to be decided by the librarian and professional staff. A reserve fund should be kept for special needs. Allotments are often made for special types of materials, such as encyclopedias, periodicals or replacements. Agency expenditures may be limited also to a monthly or quarterly per cent of the year's funds to keep expenditures running evenly, adjusting them for special circumstances.

ASSIGNING THE PARTS OF THE SELECTING PROCESS

Organization for Book Selection

Book selection should be the function of the entire professional staff. In early days, the trustees usually selected the books; sometimes they knew more about books than the librarian.[18] Today, except in the smallest libraries, the role of the trustees in book selection is either nominal, as in giving routine approval to lists of new books submitted by the librarian, or policy making, and as the agency of final decision on controversial or borderline titles. It is the librarian who organizes the book selection machinery; thereby, in effect, he manages, the resulting book collection. In small libraries he makes all the decisions, but in even medium-sized libraries he neither can nor should, for he will have trained assistants who work daily with readers and will be aware of reader needs. The "circle of interest" referred to earlier begins when a staff member recognizes in the announcement of a new book a desirable addition, in the light of what he knows of reader requests, community interests and the titles in the collection.

Book selecting follows no set pattern. In smaller libraries there is often an informal arrangement. Staff members read reviewing journals assigned to them and check promising titles. The librarian, his assistant or designated department heads then make the final decisions, and the titles are ordered. Usually the reference head and the children's head choose for their special fields.

In larger libraries, this informal, decentralized process is found on a larger scale, with more specialized assignments. With a number of branches and departments in the system, coordination of purchases for all agencies is necessary but delays must be avoided. Lists of books selected for purchase by subject departments, the children's department, and other central agencies may be mimeographed and distributed to all other units concerned. Enough copies of reviews and other information should be distributed so that checkings can all be received in the order department within three or four days. In large libraries these lists, often annotated and with items starred for first purchase, become part of a system of current and retrospective book selection.

In some larger libraries today staff committees review all recommendations from individual librarians, and decide on the number of copies to order, or designate titles approved for purchase, with the final choice to be made by agency heads. Usually there are separate committees for adult and for juvenile books,[19] perhaps one for pamphlets. In any of these patterns the selectors need written statements of selection policy in all subject fields.

The mechanics of book selection are less important than the achievement of certain goals. If all copies of new title can be ordered at the same time, costs can be cut by cataloguing and processing them together. The system used must prevent unintentional duplication of orders for the same title. But books should be secured promptly and made ready to circulate while they are being reviewed, discussed and requested; more specifically, when readers see current reviews and advertisements of new books, these books should have been already bought, cataloged and on the library shelves. The process of book selection must be current and brief. Sometimes these goals conflict. Thus, if the central library, in order that all the branches can make up their minds, must slow down order and receipt of its copies so long that they cannot be ready for the reader shelves by publishers' official release dates, then central's copies should be ordered immediately, i.e., "blocking" orders should not thwart promptness in getting books to readers.

A proper basis for deciding how to select a new book must also be established. At the one extreme are those who advocate that every new book be read and reviewed by a staff member. This delays purchase decisions and imposes an impossible work load. Only in the largest libraries is it practical to get approval copies of all new books, or even all new novels, for staff members to read before making decisions. Granted that it is generally desirable to read a book before selecting it, many if not most books bought by public libraries do not require such treatment. Experienced staff members who read proposed new books before purchase are almost as uniformly favourable in their judgments as the usual book-reviewing journals, and libraries which use published reviews buy essentially the same titles as do those which use staff reviews.[20]

At the other extreme there is the danger that the wholesale purchase of all new current trade books of certain publisher, advocated for very large libraries and sometimes called the Greenaway Plan,[21] will result in the acceptance of titles which are substandard, or not essential, simply because they are at hand, already paid for, and cannot be returned, and though they can be omitted they are likely to be added. Similarly it is unwise for a library to join any cooperative book ordering and cataloguing project which reduces its freedom of book selection.

Current Services for Evaluation

Most libraries select on the basis of reviews in the leading journals. *The Virginia Kirkus Service, Inc.*, is the most prompt, its judgments are perceptive of library needs and are based on galley proofs read before publication, and the annotations are extremely well done. There are many others—*The New York Times Book Review,* the New York Herald Tribune's *The Lively Arts and Book Review,* the *Saturday Review,* etc. The *A.L.A. Booklist and Subscription Books Bulletin* contains critical reviews of reference books and titles for the smaller library. Baker and Taylor's *Book Buyers' Guide* gives prompt short evaluations. On several thousand new books a year *Library Journal* has brief usually excellent notes written by practicing librarians; these are also available on cards. For children's books there are, in addition, the *Bulletin of the Center for Children's Books,* of the University of Chicago, the *Horn Book* and the MB Nubook Cards (P.O. Box 585, Oak Park, Ill), which index reviews of all new children's books in eight important journals. Children's books are more often read by librarians before being purchased than are adult books, even though reviews of children's books are often more critical than those of adult books.

For titles being considered after enough time has elapsed for their reviews to be listed in the *Book Review Digest,* numerous scholarly journals may be consulted.[22] The *Technical Book Review Index* is invaluable in its field, as are other special tools too numerous to mention here. The remarkable thing is the width of the net which must be cast for references to all the important new books and other materials.

However, waiting for publication date and reviews will retard service. Advance announcements from the major trade publishers and their advertisements in *Publishers' Weekly* provide the first notice and description of substantial titles which comprise a large proportion of main-time new adult non-fiction. If the author and subject and the quality of the publisher indicate that the book will be a worthy one and in demand, it is possible to make good decisions on these factors plus the judgment of most experienced and exacting staff members.

In most cases a competent professional librarian can fairly assess the worth of a new book in a short time, based on information ranging from an entry in the "Weekly Record" of *Publishers' Weekly* to one or more full-length reviews. A competent librarian knows whether it is six weeks or six years since a good book has appeared on a given subject. In larger libraries it is as much a matter of rejecting the irrelevant or unessential as of determining precisely what is to be added. Mistakes will be made, but they can also be made after prolonged analysis. Shorter average time and lower unit cost of a brief selection procedure are important factors.

Evaluation of the book collection, is an important, continual and usually discouraging aspect of book selection. When a doubtful or controversial title does appear, provision should be made for it to be read and reviewed by several staff members, and if necessary by the librarian or some of the trustees. Competent specialists in the community are excellent sources of opinion on the value of books in their fields. They should also be cultivated information about desirable titles for the library.

A reader's request should receive prompt consideration. If the title is ordered, he should be notified when it is available. It is important that there by a systematic accumulation of titles for which replacement copies are desired, and for their review and approval by a competent authority. Sometimes a replacement list of approved titles can then be issued to all agencies for an indication of orders; block replacements are usually ordered in the summer when the flow of new trade books has slackened.

Branch libraries complicate the process of book selection, for their collections should be tailored to the needs and interests of their communities, subject to system-wide observance of minimum standards. The subject specialists at the main library should suggest titles for branch consideration. It may not always be wise for a branch to be restricted to tiles available in central, as central may choose one of two equally good cookbooks and a branch library may want the other; and many persons of a foreign nationality may live near a branch library and need books in their own tongue. Such points should be resolved and incorporated in the statement of book selection policy.

SPECIAL PROBLEMS

Duplication of Titles

To what extent shall duplicate copies be purchased of any one title? If as many copies of a best seller were purchased as would satisfy all reader requests at the peak of its popularity, many would stand unused on the shelves for years afterward. Some libraries buy another copy for every five or so unfilled reserve requests. A rental collection, paper-covered copies, provision for a free flow of books between agencies for temporary or indefinite use help to meet the problem. Purchasing multiple copies in anticipation of demand is not recommended, for needed copies can be obtained fast enough to make unnecessary an investment of funds on a gamble. Children's books are usually duplicated more heavily than adult.

Pay-Duplicate Collection

From its regular budget no library can afford enough copies of worthy new novels in heaviest demand. Many progressive libraries maintain an extra-budgetary "pay-duplicate collection," whereby rentals of a few cents per day finance these extra copies. Some libraries include important new nonfiction. A Rhode Island court ruling pointed out that both those who wish free copies and those who prefer to pay rent for copies without having to wait so long get better service.[23] It is not desirable that a commercial concern install a rental collection in public library, control the selection of books, and reap the profit from their use; the library's own pay-duplicate collection is self-financing and it owns the books. Four requirements set up by the Rhode Island court ruling form the sensible basis on which a library can manage rental collection to the satisfaction of all. (1) There shall be at least one free copy of any title. (2) All receipts for rental books shall be expended for other rental books, and not used for other books or other purpose. (3) the library shall make no profit. (4) All books shall be transferred to the free shelves upon paying for themselves. Most libraries interpret the two last provisions as allowing the library to make up what it would lose on some slow-moving title by charging slightly more than the net cost of some other titles, otherwise the revolving fund would be depleted.

Receipts and purchases of rental books are accounted for in a separate extra-budgetary revolving fund. To turn the receipts over to the local municipality, on the ground that all cash receipts should be covered into the city's general fund, destroys the incentive to build up a large, fast-moving and efficient rental collection. One sign of a good pay-duplicate collection is the number, freshness and rapid turnover of titles transferred to free shelves within six or eight months, and the general popularity of its rental collection. To achieve this requires continuous publicity, e.g., by using stickers on the front cover explaining the four principles on which the rental collection operates, and stressing the benefits to the readers who prefer to use free copies. The rental collection should be no excuse for lowering of standards in fiction choice. On the contrary, if librarians deplore the quality of novels lent by commercial rental libraries, they have a responsibility to provide the public with high-quality fiction. Fewer and better titles, and more copies, are proper objectives for a well-run pay-duplicate collection, a great builder of reader satisfaction.

Paperbacks

Paper-covered books present peculiar difficulties, such as their bibliographical identification, and securing copies of desired titles; on these points the situation is improving steadily.[24] A good policy is to secure a sample copy of each paper-covered book considered. Many of these books do not hold up physically for more than a few circulations, though there are now several series of paperback books using good paper, good binding, and enough margins to allow for rebinding in hard covers. Increasingly more titles are appearing in paper covers only. With the current increase in book prices, public libraries are likely to use paper-covered books more instead of less, especially as several companies are now "rebinding" or treating them so that they can circulate forty or fifty times. To fill the demand for recreational fiction they can be given minimum processing and remain uncatalogued.

Gifts

A public library is sometimes offered books and materials on a special subject, or the library may initiate and develop such a collection for local reasons. Special gifts are important in research libraries, and highly desirable in large city libraries, but in the typical public library they may represent subjects not in the main stream of community interest. As they are seldom given with funds for staffing, they tend to be static and unused. If a collection must be kept separate and not allowed to circulate, it is doubly unfortunate. Special collections are desirable in such fields as local history, but the book selection policy statement should spell out the circumstances under which special collections will be accepted or be allowed to develop in the individual library. A metropolitan library will wish to encourage them for certain planned objectives; nothing said here is intended as unappreciative of special collections accessible through adequate staffs to scholars who will use them.[25]

Gifts of money to purchase books are often made by local groups, e.g., accountants, insurance men, stamp collectors, garden clubs, and by individual donors by memorial volumes. The library should promote such gifts; often the books are notable acquisitions otherwise impossible. There should be a policy statement on the library's acceptance and use of gift books generally, viz., that they be accepted only if there is no condition imposed on their use, location, rebinding or disposal. Procedures should be established for prompt and orderly review of gift books. In general, less than a third of the usual run of gift books will be useful; the library should be free to dispose of the rest. Much time can be wasted in trying to give books away, but there are hundreds of poor libraries in backward areas which should get good duplicate and withdrawn copies now being destroyed. Doubtless some state or regional system will be created "to stop this pitiful waste" of material which can be used.

Periodicals

Next to books in importance are periodicals, for both reading and reference help.[26] Since their number is increasing constantly and the quality of individual magazines changes, there should be an annual review of a library's magazine subscriptions. Inclusion of a title in a standard index of periodicals is a major consideration, since that greatly increase its usefulness.

Periodical subscriptions are best handled by blanket order through one or another of several leading agencies. Many valuable periodicals are available free, such as house organs of business and industrial firms. Small public libraries usually bind only those likely to be needed often or over a long period of time, including (in libraries of over 10,000 population) most of those indexed in *Abridged Reader's Guide*. Unbound back issues of magazines are often preferred because they can be loaned. A useful device is a collection of duplicate unbound back issues of ten or twelve magazines, e.g., *Time,* most often used for reference, for replacement and for circulation; gift copies, two or three days old, can be solicited. Several large libraries keep duplicate unbound files of several hundred magazines to lend for home and office reference use.

Newspapers

Most public libraries receive and keep all local general newspapers, important papers of nearby larger cities, and a few of regional and national importance, at least the *New York Times,* which is indexed. An age-old problem of public libraries is how to handle the type of patron who comes in only to read the current day's paper because he seeks a comfortable idling place. Solutions have ranged from stand-up reading racks to not making a newspaper available until it is a day old!

Modern newspaper stock usually crumbles after twenty-five years. Small libraries should try to get the state library to film local papers as the chief source for local history. In large cities, the solution is to microfilm the papers, thus saving space, eliminating mutilation, and lessening loss by fire or theft (rolls of film have been stolen) since the master negative is usually kept elsewhere. The negative can be used to print full-size copies of individual articles, and microfilm reading machines are in use now which can produce a readable copy of what is seen on the screen. Often the publisher of the local paper may be persuaded to give a microfilm print to the library. If not, the library should arrange to help finance its microfilming; if prints can be sold to the publisher and to other libraries this may cost no more than it would to bind. It is unusual for a newspaper to publish any index. Many public libraries, especially those with several branches, have a staff member scan an extra copy of each day's issue and clip articles for the local history collection or the vertical files; several copies can be processed at one time and sent out for branch filing.

Local History

Every public library has an obligation to collect materials on the history of its own locale. These materials sometimes are integrated with the main book collection, especially if a museum or local history society has most of the nonprint items. But in many instances the public library has the major collection, perhaps the only files of local history, especially of more recent years, including not only books, newspapers, pamphlets, maps, pictures, posters and other print, but also letters, diaries, typewritten manuscripts, official archives of local societies and institutions and other records. These tend to become a separately organized collection, and to attract gifts of additional materials as it grows and is used. Embarking on this path requires administrative decisions, financial support and a programme of constant publicity and solicitation of materials. But it can lead to an ever more valuable and unique collection, aided by local volunteer enthusiasts.

Pamphlets and the Vertical File

A vertical file in a public library means a collection of pamphlets, clippings, magazine article reprints or tear sheets, and perhaps maps and pictures. Generally these are too thin to stand by themselves and must be kept in folders in standard file drawers, arranged alphabetically by subject.[27] They are available for loan and have a relatively short useful life. Such files are of great value in all public service agencies, especially in meeting the demands from school assignments. The file should be weeded regularly and a flow of the best current materials should be maintained.

More and better pamphlets are being published today than ever before. Many sources of information about them are available,[28] and a member of the staff, or a committee for the branches, should be responsible for screening and selecting. Often they are free or so inexpensive that it costs less to order a number of copies than to spend time and money deciding how many to get in each case separately. Just as it is desirable to obtain all needed copies of a vertical file item at one time, so it is to be preferred that all copies be processed centrally and distributed to branches, subject-headed and ready for use. Thicker and more expensive pamphlets are treated like books for selection purposes, and many are catalogued and bound. Others may stand on the shelves alone or in pamphlet boxes or Princeton files. But the vertical file is the favourite method.

Maps, Pictures, Catalogues and Music

Maps are sometimes included in vertical file. The larger public libraries have separate collections of maps, including state road maps, road atlases, the U. S. Topographic Survey sheets, picture maps and other items. Many are available free or at small cost. The Cello-Clip device—heavy punched tabs mounted at the upper corners of the map and then hanging it from two or three heavy rods, somewhat like an inverted vertical file—is an efficient inexpensive way to handle sheet maps. The public is increasingly map-minded and a library should have a battery of loose maps as well as bound atlases.[29]

Similarly, flat pictures, preferably mounted on cardboard, are valuable. Art prints and informational pictures on a wide variety of subjects can be purchased or clipped from magazines or gift books not otherwise needed. If desired, they may be mounted by using the Seal electric press, which bonds them to a poster board, making them more useful to artists, teachers, students and children. Most libraries keep clipped pictures simply in folders or envelopes. Some large libraries have hundreds of thousands of items, but every public library should have at least some.[30]

Every library of over 10,000 population needs a collection of current catalogues of major colleges and universities in the region, and score of those most famous nationally. These are available free but must be requested individually each year. There are also mail order and other catalogues. Sheet music is a type of material which only a large public library can be expected to collect. Musical scores for established operas and for well-known songs should be available in many more libraries in hardcover books. Music in the form of phonograph records is available in several hundred libraries. The selection of both language, literary and musical records and tapes and films are important factors to be considered and should be the special responsibility of those staff members who service their use. These items should be covered by the selection policy statement of the library.

Government Documents

Many documents are of prime importance in answering readers' questions.[32] Libraries that are depositories for government publications receive automatically one free copy of all titles in requested series. The disadvantage to this arrangement is that such libraries are required to keep forever the publications received on depository privilege. The Superintendent of Documents has permitted depository libraries in Wisconsin and New York to transfer documents no longer needed to statewide collections. Extension of this system of one or two permanent reservoir collections in each state awaits approval by Congress. Nondepository libraries can often secure free copies of new publications from issuing agencies or from their Congressmen, as can depository libraries which want extra copies or separate items in series not originally requested. Federal government publications cost little when purchased, and paper work on orders to the Government Printing Office may be cut by buying coupons to be sent with later orders.

The *Monthly Catalog of U.S. Government Publications* is the current comprehensive listing of these materials, and it is a formidable task merely to scan each issue. There are also the subject price lists of the Government Printing Office, the bi-weekly list of *Selected United States Government Publications* (probably the best service for smaller libraries), and the lists of publications of the various individual agencies. No one of these sources can be relied on for all the items useful to public libraries. Even depository libraries have this problem, since they receive automatically only those series they have requested and agreed to keep, and often other individual titles are desired. Other tools and listings are available, and each library must work out its own pattern of selection and procurement. Unquestionably public libraries receive and use too few Federal publications and have not found short cuts to publicize and use them.

The Superintendent of Documents does not require or recommend any one method of arranging government documents. Most depository libraries shelve them in separate collection arranged according to the GPO classification number, which appears in the *Monthly Catalog,* and depend on the author, title and subject indexes of the *Monthly Catalog.* Nondepository libraries often catalogue Federal Government publications or put them in the vertical file depending on their size and importance. Many depository libraries catalogue and classify important documents too, such as decennial census reports and the *Statistical Abstract,* and regularly secure extra copies of them.

Some larger libraries file such Federal periodicals as *Monthly Labor Review* and *School Life* with the regular magazines, and put many other items in the vertical files. Selected hard cover books or thick paper-covered items and important bulletin series, such as Office of Education *Bulletins,* are often catalogued and placed on the regular shelves. All other items could remain in a special documents collection, arranged by the Superintendent of Document's code number. Those items treated specially are then so indicated on the cards of the check-in file. The practices of larger libraries are summarized in print.[31] A guide to the handling, promotion and use of documents in libraries serving less than 75,000 population is much needed. Federal documents will never be extensively utilized until Uncle Sam publishes a monthly or quarterly subject index, of the same practical character as the Wilson indexes, to the detailed contents of at least the most generally useful half of its current publications. Until then few libraries can afford time required to find the material on a given subject, except as suggested above.

Unlike Federal documents, state government publications are not well listed, indexed or distributed. The Library of Congress' *Monthly Checklist of State Publications* lists many, and many states issue a frequent compilation of new publications. Local government publications are even more elusive, but every public library should maintain a file of them. The publication and distribution of United Nations documents are well organized, but relatively few are essential except in very large libraries. Libraries can popularize document use by making them more available, by displays and by publicizing them in the newspapers. Federal publications in depository as well as nondepository libraries may be loaned for home use. Some libraries sell GPO coupons to patrons who wish to purchase their own copies of documents. Others sell directly copies of particularly useful documents.

CUSTODY OF THE COLLECTION

Access to the Collection

All public libraries are concerned with custody of their collections. Small and medium-sized public libraries tend to have all their books on open shelves to which the public has access. Such books must be put in order as often as once a day for heavily used sections. Large libraries in addition to their open shelves have closed stack collections, usually of older books; these too must be kept in order and made available to patrons. Requests are usually presented in the form of call slips and are handled by young assistants, called pages; the extra work and resultant reader frustrations have resulted in having most of the book stock on open shelves in public rooms of the modern library.

Pages also read the shelves, get materials needed by the profession staff, charge out materials on loan and discharge them when returned, check in current issues of magazines, and perform many other functions.

Theft and Mutilation

Theft and mutilation are baffling problem.[32] A determined thief cannot be absolutely prevented from making off with a book. In all except very large libraries, the use of guards at the library entrance costs more money and good will than the value of the lost books. Yet there are precautions, such as placing the loan desk next to or across the entrance and requiring a signature and address for the use within the building of expensive technical books, which need to be taken.

Two methods to reduce mutilation are to remove the temptation by substituting microfilm for bound newspapers, and to persuade the local school staff not to require or encourage illustrated notebooks on subjects where text and pictures are found mainly in library books and magazines. Staff members should glance over reading rooms to detect defacers. Loan desk assistants should be trained to riffle through the pages of each returned book, partly to spot mutilations. The library should have an established scale of charges for such damages, and provision by law by penalties for the most serious cases. Readers of all ages need to be reminded from time to time how to care for books.

Restricted Use

Some restrictions are necessary, such as keeping in locked cases or on closed shelves those books which are expensive or likely to be stolen. This is justifiable. But when books are controversial or deal frankly with sex, the use of restricted shelves is a form of censorship. Libraries must choose what books to buy but those acquire should be available to all. On the other hand some librarians do not believe that books for married persons should necessarily be on open shelves for high school students. Other types of justifiable restrictions include reserve shelves of book assigned to students or in great demand for short periods. Children are usually denied access to library motion picture films and phonograph records, to avoid excessive damage.

Inventory

Up to thirty years ago it was common practice to inventory the entire book collection every two or three years by comparing the shelf list with the books on the shelves and with the ''out'' book cards in circulation trays. Books found missing in two inventories were considered lost and the catalogue cards removed. Today few public libraries take regular, complete inventories, because experience has shown that loss rates are low—less than 1 per cent of the book stock per year—and the cost of a complete inventory of a large or medium-sized library is high. With some of the modern circulation methods it is possible but not easy to check books which are on loan.[35] Individual titles which are sought and not found over several months may be considered lost. They should either be replaced or their catalogue cards withdrawn. Books in greatest demand disappear soonest. The routine of reserving books affords the promptest way to discover that a book is missing, and it should be replaced promptly.

WEEDING AND EVALUATING THE COLLECTION

Weeding

As book selection is continuous so should be weeding the collection of outdated and wornout materials. Definite standards and policies should be formulated.[34] In the case of most public libraries it is far better to have a smaller collection of live and currently useful materials than a larger but less useful one. It definitely costs money just to house books; many libraries crying for book-space additions would do better to discard outdated books. Large university, research and state libraries keep materials and can be called on for interlibrary loans. Most public libraries find it economical to discard books more than thirty years old, many libraries would say twenty years, which have not been used once in the last ten years, some say five years, and which appear to have no further use, save perhaps for historical interest; they can be borrowed from a research library when needed.

In many subjects books are quickly outdated and should be discarded even sooner. Evidently the use of library material drops off rapidly the older it becomes, even in college libraries. Of 10,000 circulations of books in the field of personal health from the Evansville

(Ind.) Public Library published between 1918 and 1958, 52 per cent were of books in the first five years after their acquisition.[35] In a 1949 study at Stanford University and a 1953 study at the University of Chicago only 1 per cent and 3 per cent of books borrowed had been published more than thirty years.[36-37]

Just as the entire professional staff should share in selection so should they participate in weeding, assigning each member an approximately equal part of the collection but according to subject competence and interests, with a goal to re-evaluate all books about once every five years—whether to repair or replace by a new edition or a new copy, dispose of duplicates or get new copies of standards, reclassify or withdraw.

Preliminary weeding, according to definite standards of age, frequency of recent circulation, listing in the *Standard Catalog for Public Libraries* or other such bibliography, etc., can be done by experienced non-professional personnel, especially in branch libraries, for review later by a trained librarian who knows books. The judgment of experienced staff members who work directly with books is remarkably accurate in estimating circulations and reference value. The actual circulation of a book is so useful in weeding the collection that the number of recorded loans should be summarized, when a date due slip or book card is used up and replaced, and recorded on the new slip or card. With transaction card charging an equivalent record can be secured by making a stroke on the date due slip by year, each time the book is borrowed or returned. This is not to say that only these books should be acquired which are sure to circulate often, for the library should include important books likely to be borrowed only a few times but not otherwise conveniently available. But after fifteen or twenty years their future value should be reassessed in the light of actual use.

Mistakes in weeding just as in selecting are inevitable. Weeding cannot be infallible. In a collection of 100,000 volumes about 5,000 volumes should be withdrawn each year. This rate, recommended in the A.L.A. Standards,[38] is a fair average of actual practice. In weeding large quantities of books, undoubtedly some will be withdrawn which may be asked for later, but they can be had through inter-library loan. Mistakes in not withdrawing books are even more frequent, but are less likely to be noticed. They result in clogging the shelves (and the card catalogue) and in wasting funds for their continued custody. They can be a positive disservice, as in the case of a twenty year old book on cancer giving a less favourable prognosis than modern medicine allows.

The basic guidelines for weeding the collection should be laid down in the statement of book selection policy, by indicating those subject fields in which greater emphasis or depth will be sought and accepted. In most cases a second revision should verify the judgment of the first; considering whether the book is "live" enough for some other agency of the library. Nonbook materials should likewise be reviewed at intervals for possible discard.

After decision to withdraw, the cataloguing department corrects all necessary records and handles final disposition of the volume. The paperwork on this should be as simple as possible. Few books withdrawn from a public library will fetch any money return. But occasionally a withdrawn volume has a monetary value or is out of print and needed by university or research libraries, and a knowledgeable person should scan the books just before scrapping them.[39] The bulk of withdrawn books have no value except to give to institutions in depressed parts of the country. Some may be useful for their pictures or may be offered for sale to students and others at a nominal price. A set pattern of possibilities should be specified for quick disposition of withdrawn volumes; that is, they should not linger around the building more than five or six months. No librarian likes to see a book destroyed if it can still be used.

Evaluating the Book Collection

Every good librarian senses the worth of his library's book collection and constantly asks himself and his colleagues questions that lead to its improvement. This comes from working with books. Objective measures of the value of the collection are needed, partly as a check on the validity of the selection policy with reference to the various subject fields, and partly to identify titles which should be added or discarded. Checking *The Standard Catalog for Public Libraries,* or other appropriate bibliography or combination of lists, against the card catalogue, is the favourite test. This shows up titles not in the collection which should at least be considered. The Wilson Company lists are mainly the results of the pooled judgments of practicing librarians rather than subject experts, and reflect pretty well the probable demands on public library users. Seldom does a library hold all the titles on any such selected and comprehensive list; usually it holds considerably more of the titles listed in certain fields that in others. No such list is perfect, nor does it fulfill the objectives of every library. An alternative method of evaluation is to check the cards for books in the collection against several retrospective, selective and evaluative bibliographies. Titles held but not found in any of these lists should be considered for withdrawal; this also shows up older titles which are not held and which worth considering.

There are other measures of the value of a collection. Subject specialists in the local community usually are willing to examine the books in their fields, to discard some and suggest important new items. Older titles requested by readers and titles borrowed on inter-library loan may be important enough for purchase, depending on how long they have been published. Information is available on various quantitative aspects of book collections of other libraries and their rating by a given checklist of titles.[40] Evaluation can also result from in-serving training programmes for the professional staff on book selection policy, the criteria for weeding and the strength and weaknesses of the collection. Establishing any precise basis, formula or method either to select, discard or evaluate a book collection is not likely to become a reality; these are intangibles. Evaluation of the book collection should be done regularly. If a library has only "good" books on a given subject, only good books can borrowed. But there is evidence to indicate that readers do not distinguish to any significant degree between "good" books and "bad" ones, but borrow each according to their ratio in a library's collection. All the greater is the obligation that the library choose excellent books.

NOTES & REFERENCES

1. Helen E. Haines, *Living with Books: The Art of Book Selection,* 2nd ed. 514 p. 1950. Columbia Univ. Press. A useful classic, illustrating principles by commentary on important titles.

2. Mary D. Carter and Wallace J. Bonk. *Building Library Collection.* 259 p. 1959. Scarecrow Press. $6. The most substantial practical guide to the handing of book selection for all main types of libraries. Includes Evaluating, p. 117-121; Weeding, p. 121-125; Order work, p. 177-194 (though mostly in college libraries); A.L.A. Bill of Rights and Freedom to Read, p. 195-201; Policy Statements, p. 212-239.
3. Ruth M. White, ed. *Public Library Policies—General and Specific. (Public Library Reporter.* no. 9.) 116 p. Paper. 1960. A.L.A. Includes the 1953 statement of "The Freedom to Read," the 1948 A.L.A. "Library Bill of Rights" (p. 2-8) and excerpts of policy statements on book selection (p. 12-18, gift books (p. 25-30) and rental collections (p. 103-04); the latter ignores the majority sentiment in favor of rental collections.
4. Kenneth R. Shaffer. *The Book Collection: Policy Case Studies in Public and Academic Libraries.* 200 p. 1961. Shoe String Press. $4.75.

FOOTNOTES AND SPECIAL MATERIAL

5. Joseph L. Wheeler. "Methods for Making Known to Inexperienced Readers the Resources and Facilities Offered by American Public Libraries." *Library Quarterly. 5:* 391-394. Oct. 1935:
6. A recent study of 3 groups of California public libraries found that they acquired from 22% to 34% of all new books published in 1957 (with duplication of titles between them ranging from 48% to 69%). And of the titles not acquired by any library in the sample, two thirds were not available from the state library either. See Donald W. Koepp. *Titles Added to a Group of California Public Libraries* (Report no. 2 of California, Public Library Commission) 32 p. 1959. Univ. of California Library.
7. Dorothy Bendix. *Some Problems in Book Selection Policies in Medium-Sized Public Libraries.* Univ. of Illinois Library School, *Occasional Papers* no. 55. 37 p. May 1959. Concludes that a written statement of book selection policy is avoided because it would bring into the open the conflict between librarians' professed goals of quality and their actual sensitiveness to public demand.
8. In the field of censorship, reference to only a few titles must suffice: Robert B. Downs, ed. *The First Freedom.* 484 p. 1960. A.L.A. Compilation of major writings on censorship. Also Walter M. Daniels. *The Censorship of Books.* (The Reference Shelf Vol. 26, no. 5). 202 p. 1954. H.W. Wilson Co. A digest of many recent articles. Also Paul

Blanshard. *The Right to Read: The Battle Against Censorship.* 339 p. 1955. Beacon Press. A spirited analysis of the whole subject. Also Marjorie Fiske. *Book Selection and Censorship.* 145 p. 1959. Univ. of California Press. Uncovers practices used by school and public librarians to avoid controversy. Also Dan Lacy. "Obscenity and Censorship." *Christian Century.* 77: 540-43. May 4, 1960. For current censorship efforts, see the A.L.A. *Newsletter on Intellectual Freedom.*

9. Robert W. Haney. *Comstockery in America: Patterns of Censorship and Control,* 1960. Beacon Press. p. 26-50.
10. The extent to which public libraries should provide recreational fiction has been under considerable debate in England. For example see Peter G. New. "The Public Provision of Light Literature. " *Library Association Record.* 57: 149-153. Apr. 1955 and "Function and Fiction." *Library World.* 59: 115-17. Feb. 1958.
11. Enoch Pratt Free Library. *Reorganization of a Large Public Library: Ten Year Report of the Enoch Pratt Free Library.* 1935. p. 10-23, 40-75. For more recent book selection policy statements, see Dayton public library. *Book Selection Policy.* 17 p. 1960. Also Cleveland Public Library. *Report of the Committee on Reference Collections and Charts of Major Subject Fields with Ratings and Future Acquisition policy.* 45 p. 1949; Also Enoch Pratt Free Library (Baltimore). *Book Selection Policies.* 2d ed. 45 p. 1961. Also Buffalo Public Library. *Book Selection Policy* . . . 12 p. 1952; Also Los Angles Public Library. *Book Selection Policy.* 3 p. 1956. There are many others.
12. Rose Vainstein, *Statistics of Public Libraries:* 1955-56. *op. cit.* p. 14, 16. Also *Library Journal.* 85: 1407. Apr. 1, 1960.
13. Frank L. Schick and William H. Kurth *The Cost of Library Materials: Price Trends of Publications* 20 p. U.S. Office of Education Library Services Branch. Library Statistics Series OE-15029A. October 1961. p. 8.
14. *Public Library Service: A Guide to Evaluation with Minimum Standards. 1956,* A.L.A. p. 36.
15. Vainstein. *op. cit.* p. 23, 96.
16. Dallas (Tex.) Public Library. *The Dallas Public Library Needs More Books.* 38 p. n.d. 1956?
17. Carnegie Library of Pittsburgh. *Annual Report: 1953.* p. 7.8.
18. Book selection by trustees is still to be found in small libraries and for this same reason: see Dorothy Canfield Fisher. "Library in Our Town." *Atlantic Monthly.* 178: 127-130. Oct. 1946. But few trustees

known as much about books as Mrs. Fisher did.

19. For individual libraries' methods of book selection, see Morton Coburn. "Book Selection and Purchasing at the Edmonton Public Library." Edmonton (Alberta, Can.) Public Library. *News Notes.* Feb. 1961. p. 12-14 (Book selection by committee.) Also Lester L. Stoffel. "Book Selection by Staff Committee." (Oak Park, Ill.) *Illinois Libraries.* 41: 319-321. May 1959. Also Lionel R. McColvin. "Some Administrative Aspects of Book provision." (Westminster, Eng., Public Library.) *Librarian and Book World.* 45: 21-29, Feb. 1956. (Book selection by the chief librarian.) Also "Adult assistants' Meeting." Enoch Pratt Free Library *Staff Reporter*. Feb. 15, 1961. p. 7-8. Adult fiction selection by staff review; about half of all new fiction titles are reviewed and about two thirds of these are purchased.
20. Kenneth S. Tisdel. "Staff Reviewing in Library Book Selection." In LeRoy C. Merritt. *et al. Reviews in Library Book Selection.* 1958. Wayne State Univ. Press P. 174-178.
21. "The 'Get-em-all' Theory of Book Buying." *Library Journal.* 85: 3387-91. Oct. 1, 1960.
22. Victoria E. Hargrave. "A Comparison of Reviews of Books in the Social Sciences in General and in Scholarly Periodicals."*Library Quarterly.* 18: 206-217. July 1948. Found that reviews in the latter were not markedly different or better than in the former. This might not be true in other fields, e.g., technology, art.
23. Rhode Island Supreme Court. 46 (1924) 284. Also "Duplicate Pay Collections." Library Journal 49: 580. 1924.
24. "Paperbacks and Public Library Policies." *Library Journal* 86: 1831-39. May 15, 1961.
25. Emerson Greenway. "Rare Books in the Public Library." *Library Journal.* 81: 2135-40. Oct. 1, 1956. Also Nathan Van Pattern. "The University Library and the Book Collector." *PNLA Quarterly.* 14: 69-71. Jan. 1950. Viewpoints appropriate also in large city libraries.
26. Andrew D. Osborn. *Serial Publications: Their Place and Treatment in Libraries 309* p. 1955. A.L.A., the most important discussion on magazines in large libraries.
27. Norma O. Ireland. *The Pamphlet File in School, College and Public Library.* 2d ed. 220 p. (Useful Reference Series no. 84) 1954 Faxon. Also Ruth B. Ferguson and Elizabeth Ferguson. "Keeping Up with Pamphlets." *Junior Libraries:* 7: 6-7. Apr. 1961. Good up-to-date instructions on short-cut handling.

28. *Free and Inexpensive Learning Materials,* published by the George Peabody College for Teachers, Nashville, Tenn. 252 p. $1.50. The 1960 edition lists over 3,600 items, none costing over 50¢. See also the H.W. Wilson Company's *Vertical File Index,* published monthly with annual cumulations. Since Mar. 1961. Informational Pamphlet Distributors, Inc. (381 Park Ave., South, N.Y. 16) has been offering a monthly kit of 20 to 30 "published at a price" pamphlets at $6 a month.
29. George L. Williams. *Maps in the Library.* (Kent State University Department of Library Science. *Aspects of Librarianship.* No. 1.) 9 p. May 1952. Good introduction with detailed suggestions. Also, for larger collection, Clara E. LeGear. *Maps: their Care, Repair and Preservation.* rev. ed. 75 p. 1956. Library of Congress . o.p.
30. Norma O. Ireland. *The Picture File in School, College and Public Libraries.* rev. ed. 136 p. (Useful Reference Series no. 81.) 1952. Faxon.
31. Ellen P. Jackson. *A. Manual for the Administration of the Federal Documents Collection in Libraries.* 108 p. 1955. A.L.A.
32. English librarians have usually been more concerned that Americans about book losses from theft and about mutilation of books. See Ernest J. Savage. "Buy, Borrow or Steal." *Library World. 59:* 47-52. Oct. 1957. and "Buy, Borrow or Steal: Thieves Methods." *Library World.* 60:3-6.July 1958. For current U.S. problems see Lee Zimmerman. "Pilfering and Mutilating Library Books." *Library Journal.* 86: 3437-3440. Oct. 15, 1961.
33. William A. Webster. "Book Inventories with Transaction Charging." *Wilson Library Bulletin.* 36: 302-305. Dec. 1961.
34. Wisconsin Free Library Commission, *Weeding the Library: Suggestions for the Small Libraries.* rev. ed. 11 p. 1949. Madison, Wis. Also "Weeding Your Library." *Iowa Library Quarterly.* 16: 138-141. Apr. 1951. Two general practical discussions, with many examples.
35. Herbert Goldhor. "Are the Best Books the Most Read ?" *Library Quarterly.* 29: 251-255. Oct. 1959.
36. Elmer M. Grieder. "The Effect of Book Storage on Circulation Service." *College and Research Libraries.* 11: 374-376. Oct. 1950.
37. Gilbert E. Donahue. "The Library of the Cowles Commission for Research in Economics." *Illinois Libraries.* 37: 89- 94. March 1955.
38. *Public Library Service, op. cit.* p. 35.
39. American Book Prices Current. (annually). And Merle Johnson's

American First Editions. 4th ed. 553 p. 1942. Bowker.

40. LeRoy C. Merritt. *The Good Books in American Public Libraries: A Summary*. Univ. of Illinois Library School Occasional Papers. no. 60. 6 p. Dec. 1960. See also the sections on book collections, in various survey reports which can be borrowed from A.L.A. Headquarters Library.

7

Administration of Larger-Area Systems

ONE OF the main goals of American public librarianship has been to provide local public library service to all. Legal provision for public libraries is now more than a century old, yet 15 to 20 per cent of the people still do not have access to a public library organized to serve the area where they live. And over half of the population have local library service which is limited, inadequate and substandard. Nor is this from want of trying. Librarians and friends of libraries have made great efforts to provide complete coverage with at least reasonably good service.[1,2,3,4] Their efforts have had some measure of success and have provided a valuable fund of experience. Based on this experience greater efforts that ever are being made today to reach the goal.[5] This brief chapter can only sketch the outline of the problem and of the experience with the major solutions.

The matter is complicated by the wide variations in the geographic size of local government units, in the distribution of population and of wealth, in the legal structure for public libraries in the different states, and in the traditional role of cities and counties in various parts of the country. These variations explain why it is that one pattern, such as county libraries, may be acceptable and successful in California, where counties are large, populous and wealthy, and be unknown in New England, where the county unit of government is weak and little used. The southeastern states have more multi-county libraries than any other part of the country, precisely because there were so few independent local libraries whose interests had to be considered. The result is that no one national pattern has evolved of library service for larger than local unit.

There are however a few main patterns which can be outlined and their comparative merits and limitations described. First will be discussed a national programme of library systems, then the state-wide library systems, the county and multi-county units, and finally the use of such devices as federation, contract service and cooperative arrangements. The chapter closes with a brief comparison of certain administrative aspects of the main types of larger units of library service.

A NATIONAL PROGRAMME OF LIBRARY SYSTEMS

The Nature of the Problem

Variations in two main factors make difficult the provision to all Americans of access to local public library service of at least reasonable quality; one is sparseness of population, and the other is the cost of library operation. With relatively few people scattered over a wide territory, as in rural areas, the assessed valuation tends to be low and also therefore the tax support of the library. In addition such sparseness of population means that there will be relatively few patrons of the library and insufficient use of its resources and services to justify more than a bare minimum of development. On the other hand, a library has a relatively high overhead cost for physical quarters and book stock and a relatively high minimum current operating cost if it attempts to provide what might be called service of even reasonable quality. Such overhead and operating costs are more nearly justified as the volume of use goes up and as the total expenditures of the library increase, until the unit cost of library service becomes very small indeed, per unit of use of per person served or per dollar of assessed valuation.

Public libraries were started first in cities, and they still have their main strength there. In the late nineteenth and early twentieth centuries, the state library extension agencies systematically developed and helped organize libraries in every municipality of any size. In many cases libraries were started in communities too small and too poor to support them at all or at a level to produce reasonably good service. The laws necessary to establish libraries in every possible community are still on the books and now plague us by setting no minimum standards in regard to population or financial support. It soon became evident to librarians that rural areas could never organize municipal-type libraries and that many towns were too small to secure adequate library service by independent action. The next obvious step then was to secure laws authorizing county public libraries, and for the last fifty years efforts have continued to organize such. Out of 3,050 counties in this country, there are now about a thousand county or city-county libraries,[6] and many of them are small, poor and inadequate. There are still some 200 rural counties in which there is no local public library.[7]

The latest main approach and a logical next development, dating roughly from about 1935, has been the creation of multi-county libraries, of which there are now about 200, serving about 500 counties. Though theoretically able to include enough people and enough taxable wealth to justify a public library, a multi-county unit by the same token has to cope with the problems of giving service over a large area and to many small groups of people. Furthermore, because the county and multi-county library are one step removed from the local community, it has been difficult to persuade voters to approve the organization of such libraries or to provide anything more than minimum tax support. One method of overcoming this difficulty has been to use state aid or other funds for a demonstration for a year or more of what county or multi-county library could do in a given area, and then to seek continuance of the library by local support.[8] Not only were such demonstrations never needed to form municipal libraries, but the resulting elections on county and multi-county libraries have been far from uniformly favourable. A much more successful technique for the creation of multi-county libraries has been to secure substantial amounts of state aid for this purpose.

Major Current Needs

Between the use of multi-county libraries with state aid, it is at least possible to see how local access to public library service can be provided to all the people of this country. But how to secure reasonably good library service to all is more difficult and will take longer. Yet a third important problem, and one increasing in scope and complexity, is that of securing coordination and of reducing duplication and overlapping between the various independent libraries in the metropolitan centers.[9] For some years, the great growth of population has been not in the cities themselves but in their suburbs, which typically resist consolidation with each other or with the central city. Indeed one can envisage in time a megalopolis stretching from Massachusetts to North Carolina, and embracing hundreds of different public libraries. While this is a large problem for government generally to solve, and for other functions of government as well as for libraries, it brings out the need for public library service to be planned and coordinated, if not also administered, at a level above that of the smallest political unit.

Thus, for example, students and others with a serious interest in books will go to the best and largest library in the metropolitan area, sometimes to such an extent as to militate against the organization of a library in their own particular community.[10] Non-resident cards are typically inexpensive, and their availability has helped persuade rural people to defeat more than one proposal for a county or multi-county library. Clearly, what is needed is some general plan which will suggest approaches by which to cope with the problems of providing all citizens with library coverage within easy driving distance, of upgrading the quality of library service where it is now below standard, and of securing effective coordination of public library service in metropolitan areas. The outlines of such a plan are now evident.

Those concerned with library development and support must henceforward think of library service in terms of getting materials into the hands of individuals, and not in terms of little library buildings in communities too small to warrant them, whether these are independent local libraries or too-small branches of a larger system. With present-day auto travel and shopping habits there are few citizens who do not visit frequently towns of over 5,000 population. Except in sparsely populated areas, the creation of any new independent library in a town of smaller size should be not only discouraged but prevented if possible, provided there is a larger unit of library service available. And it is a great question whether even a larger system should establish a branch library in a community of less than 5,000 people; the cost of such a branch is not likely to be matched by the amount and quality of the service it can ever give.

A National Plan for Public Libraries

In various studies over the last twenty years, largely the work of American Library Association committees, a national plan for public libraries has been evolved, with three main concepts—that of library systems, the active participation of the state and federal agencies, and the use of state and federal funds to stimulate and strengthen local library service. Of these, the most important is the idea of library systems.[11] A library system may be a single municipal library, or a single county or regional library; it may also be a group of two or more public libraries of any sizes and types working together on a purely voluntary basis, by a formal contract or by federation. The concept of a library system avoids the difficulty of naming a minimum population size for public library; estimates of such in recent years have ranged from 25,000[12] to 100,000,[13] but no one figure can be justified as both necessary and practical. Certainly a library system serving less than 25,000 people would have a hard task; a population nearer to 50,000 would appear to be a desirable minimum in most cases, and closer to 100,000 for optimum results.

The concept of a library system presupposes a number of local outlets and one or only a few places of greater strength in book collections, specialized personnel and the resources and services. Just so, there are a need and place for one or only a few places in each state of even greater reserve strength in books and services with which to back up the local library systems. These would include the state university library, the state library and one or more of the largest municipal libraries, which might be reimbursed by the state for service to the libraries in its area. Not only is the state to be responsible for providing this second reserve in depth for existing libraries, but the state library agency clearly is the one available institution which could effectively move to provide local library service in those areas without libraries of their own and too poor or too sparsely populated to organize them. This might be done by operating a branch of the state library in the area if it can be proved profitable, or by using state aid combined with local funds to support a library system, or by encouraging nearby systems to extend their areas of service, backed with some form of financial assistance.

The Federal Government too has a role in this evolving national plan for public libraries. It has developed and maintains some of the largest and most specialized libraries in the country, and their materials are available to serious readers anywhere, by loan to their local library or by photo duplication. Among its other activities of benefit to public libraries, the Federal Government supports and maintains one of the largest systems of catalogue card provision in the world, a remarkable and comprehensive apparatus for national bibliography, an impressively large and efficient system of distribution to local public libraries of its own publications, specialized service of "reading" material for the blind and an increasingly prolific and effective system for the collection and publication of library statistics. Its WPA library projects and TVA library service contracts were milestones in the history of the American public library. Since 1956 the Federal Government has expended up to $7,500,000 a year in a programme of aid to libraries in communities of less than 10,000 population, under the Library Services Act. This programme has been without doubt the single most powerful incentive to the extension of library service, the formation of library systems and the stimulation of state library agencies.[14]

Practical Implications

The significance of this evolving national plan for public libraries, to the head of any individual library, is simply that he recognizes its existence and importance and that he seek to find his appropriate place in it. This plan for libraries, like the whole American system of government, minimizes compulsion and uniformity and emphasizes flexibility and adaptation to local circumstances, as witness the diversity in the state plans approved under the Library Services Act.[15] And there have been enough successes of various types of library systems to demonstrate the soundness of this approach. The best way for a librarian to protect the interests of the citizens in his tax support area is by considering with an open mind, and indeed seeking out and initiating, proposals for cooperation with other libraries, for joint service with other units of local government and for the organization of a library system in his area to give more, more varied and better library service to more people. No existing library of any reasonable size should be replaced or closed down, and no community library need lose its identity, or within broad limits its own choice of books, upon joining a library system, though it is all too clear that *new* small libraries should not be created. There is a parallel situation in the school field; the consolidation of the school district administrative units does not mean the abandonment or consolidation of the individual school buildings if they are even reasonably efficient. Individual trustees or librarians who are unalterably opposed to any change in existing arrangements should be left unopposed. There are too many opportunities for cooperative extension and improvement of library service to waste time in convincing such people where their own best interest lie. They will in time see plentiful proof of the benefits to be secured from joining larger system.

STATE-WIDE LIBRARY SYSTEMS

Library Systems Organized by the State Government

Because the provision and control of public library service is a responsibility of the states and not of the Federal Government, the state government is in each case the most important unit by far in the overall plan for the extension and improvement of public library service, and specifically for the organization and operation of regional library systems. The functions and powers of the state library agency are defined by law. State laws are necessary even to organize a tax-supported public library in any local government unit and such legislation can do much to shape the quality and average size of public libraries. Thus, in Ohio, where the main support of public libraries is by county-wide tax on stocks and bonds, every library receiving any proceeds of this tax is required to give free service to any citizen of the county. State legislation is similarly needed to authorize county and multi-county libraries and to permit them to enter into contracts for library service and to perform other activities, since it is a well-recognized principle of law that local government agencies can do only that which is specifically authorized or clearly implied by statute. It has long been debated whether public library service is a function which is and by right belongs intrinsically to the local government alone, or whether it is a responsibility of the state, which may or may not be performed by the local government but in which the state has an interest and a right to set standards and establish controls. Court cases of the past can be cited on both sides,[16] but it is clear that the state government is taking ever more interest and more active role in organization, operation and support of local public library service. The Library Services Act provided that the funds involved were to be handled by the state library agencies; the intent of the act was that the Federal funds would stimulate the states to greater activity in this field.

Inevitably, in some states at least, there will be one system of public libraries. This has been suggested by others, especially for small and sparsely populated states[17] but for large and populous one too.[18] More likely to be achieved are the plans to reshape the pattern of public libraries in each of several states to secure an integrated state-wide system, based on coordination between independent libraries and larger units, with local library service to all and at a reasonably good level of quality.[19] In New York State such a plan has been approved by the legislature and has been put into effect, stimulated by state aid.[20] In all such actual and proposed systems of libraries organized or planned at the state level of government, there are three essential ingredients, viz., regional systems operated in cooperation with the state library agency, state aid to local libraries, and an over-all plan of the end result which is desired.

Regional branches of the state library agency, or library systems serving as such, appear to be necessary components of a successful state-wide plan. They may serve to extend local library service to hitherto unserved and sparsely populated areas. They may serve as demonstrations of the value of multi-county libraries, as has been done with success by several states using Federal funds, or of the value to existing but independent libraries of cooperative action, as in the case of the Watertown (New York) regional library.[21] They may serve as regional centres of specialized materials and reference services, as in the Ohio and Pennsylvania plans,[22] as in the use of Denver Public Library to give reference service to the libraries of four near-by counties, and the Enoch Pratt Free Library of Baltimore and of the Boston Public Library to serve the other libraries of their respective states.[23] The obvious advantage of such a unit is that its service is not restricted to one particular local government area, since its funds (or that part of its funds for this purpose) come from the state. An equally obvious caution is that whenever possible the state library agency regional branch should operate through existing local libraries and seek to strengthen them and not to compete with or displace them. It is likely that there will be ever more use of this device in the future; and there is much to be said for centralizing at the state level (or in regional branches of the state library) the ordering and cataloguing of books, the provision of specialized reference service and other such functions for all the public libraries of the state.

State Aid

State financial aid to local public libraries goes back to the nineteenth century, and today about half the states have such programmemes of aid. In half of these states today, and in all cases up to about 1930, no large sums have been involved. But in about a dozen states in the last thirty years substantial and continuing programmes of state aid to local public libraries have been in effect.[24] From this experience two main lessons emerge. One is that the distribution formula recognize the differences between areas both in their taxable wealth and also in the effort made to raise funds locally for a specified level of quantity and quality of library service. That is, a state aid programme would not be advisable which allocated available funds of a strict percapita basis or in proportion to present revenues of local libraries or simply to equalize the money spent on libraries in all parts of the state. State aid is best used to effect a balance between resources available in the various areas, and to stimulate local effort.

The second lesson to be learned is that state aid should not be given simply to increase funds available from local sources, but to represent the interests of the larger community in the reshaping of local programmes, as in securing interlibrary cooperation in metropolitan areas. State aid is most effective when it is used to implement other programmes, as in the form of establishment grants for new multi-county libraries. If state aid is used to buy books, centralized cataloguing could be required; or if state aid is used to pay salaries, certification requirements should be set up and observed. The importance of state aid to stimulate services can hardly be over estimated, especially as the increased tax load on real property forces libraries in more and more states to seek other sources of revenue. One administrative consideration to be remembered with state or Federal aid is that is necessarily and inevitably involves reporting by the local unit on the expenditure of the funds so provided and the results secured. This is a far cry from state or Federal control, but grants-in-aid will always entail such reporting and the enforcement or observance of standards and broad policies deemed desirable. Reporting and standards are wholesome requirements.

The third essential in a programme of public library service organized at the state level is a plan, a document, which incorporates the best thinking of all interested parties. Such a plan is required by the terms of the Library Services Act. For best results this plan should take account among other things of the political and social realities of the state, as in regard to trading areas. It should inventory the library resources already available, including those of schools, colleges and universities, and even special libraries, and provide for their fullest possible utilization in the future. Finally it should include a programme or series of steps for getting from where the state is now in the provision of public library service to where it is thought it should desirably be. This is largely a matter of considering alternatives and fashioning a programme likely to be effective and therefore realistic. The state library agency is desirably the agency to coordinate this planning, utilizing the technical skills of experts of various disciplines. The state library association should be heavily involved since the librarians themselves are the ones most affected by any such plan. In some states, such as New York, Pennsylvania and New Jersey, it has been found wise and expedient to get the governor or the legislature to be associated in the development of the plans, so as to secure their support in the necessary legislation and financing. A plan by itself will not bring results, but the right kind of result are not likely to be secured without a plan.

Practical Implications

By a state-wide system is meant complete coverage of library service of reasonable depth and quality, and effective coordination between all public libraries in the state. From the practical point of view, what this means to the library administrator is simply that the state library agency will have a much more important role in the future than it has had in the past. And while the Public Library Inquiry found in 1949 that most of its sample of 58 libraries had nothing at all to do with their state library agency,[25] such is not likely to be the case now or ever again in the future. In a sense it is a sign of the coming to maturity of the American public library. But it will require a change in attitude of the local librarian and an understanding on his part of why he can no longer be so complacently independent as he has been.

COUNTY AND MULTI-COUNTY LIBRARY SYSTEMS

If the activities of the Federal Government and possibly even those of the state government it regard to public libraries seem far away to the individual citizen or even the individual librarian, a county or multi-county library is something which affects him more immediately and directly. At present half of all American counties are so served, but the truth is that many of them are still too small and too weak to have library service of even reasonable quality. Of 1,058 county, city-county, and multi-county public libraries in 1956, the average population served was about 41,500 and the average annual expenditures \$44,000.[26] This is too small an operation to achieve efficiency or economy. On the other hand the 148 county and multi-county libraries which in 1956 served over 50,000 people each had an average population of 117,000 and average annual expenditures of about \$110,000.[27] These larger county and multi-county libraries, especially in the metropolitan areas, compare favourably in general with the municipal libraries of the same population size.

The great advantage which the county or multi-county library offers is the possibility of maximizing available resources for the common good of a larger population than that of any one community. Thus of 880 book-mobiles operated by public libraries in 1956, two-thirds were in county, city-county, and regional libraries.[28] Technical processes can be better handled once by a small county library than separately by several small independent libraries, but better yet in a large county or multi-county library. The great disadvantage of the county or multi-county library is that even librarians expected it automatically to be able to give good quality library service, when often the wide area and sparse population actually increases the cost. The county or multi-county library can be counted on to reach previously unserved areas with minimum library service but not necessarily to give quality service, such as reference work or skilled guidance to readers in their choice of books. This is particularly true when the county or multi-county library has no large central agency or when the one large city in the county or region has remained independent. One peculiar weakness of many county libraries is that by law it is usually possible and easy for any incorporated community so served to leave the county system if it wishes to set up its own independent library. As a matter of fact there is as much diversity in county libraries themselves as between county libraries and other types of larger units of library service. County libraries may serve all of a country or only that part not already served by local libraries; they may be united with the public library of the major city in the county or be operated by contract with that or some other library; they may be supported in full by a general tax or appropriation or in part by revenues or services from the various communities covered so that the situation almost approaches that of a federation of libraries.

What any county or multi-county library can depend on is that it will have a relatively dispersed population to serve over a relatively large area. This has typically meant many small service points, unlike the trend in other fields to have people come to larger installations, as the consolidated school, the supermarket and the hospital. This scattering of small, weak distributing points will probably have to give way to branches restricted to those focus towns of over 2,500 or 3,000 or even 5,000 population, unless they are more than 20 or 25 miles from people's homes.[29] The county and multi-county library thus has unusual administrative problems of staffing, training and coordinating field service personnel. Furthermore county and multi-county libraries have traditionally emphasized service to children and to schools. Once begun this is hard to abandon, but rarely has it led successfully to the development of adult service. So these libraries have failed to grow to their full potential. In short the county and multi-county library has tended to emphasize what it could do best, service to children and ready availability of popular reading, but it has typically been unable to add to these the provision of specialized books and related materials, reference information, adult reading guidance and other technical and professional services. We are only just beginning to see county and multi-county libraries emphasize the intensive development of library service in depth as well as or even more than its extension in terms of local availability.

Practical Implications

The chief librarian of a county or multi-county library should seek to have his library serve at least 50,000 people, with enough revenue from local taxes and state and federal aid to provide service of reasonable quality.[30] He should strive to unite to his library any existing independent libraries by emphasizing to their staff and trustees how membership in the larger unit will improve both their administration and their public services. He would do well to include or affiliate with a library of 100,000 volumes or more, or to develop such a collection himself, and to emphasize adult use of non-fiction books and library reference service which in the long run will be more important to the average taxpayer than service to schools and ready availability of best sellers.

FEDERATED SYSTEMS, CONTRACT SERVICE AND COOPERATIVE ARRANGEMENTS

The time may come when some one pattern of organization for library systems will be demonstrably superior to all others. But for the foreseeable future it would appear that it will be necessary to find various ways by which existing libraries can come together both to help each other and their patrons and to extend the benefits of library service to others. The main ways by which such action can be secured are by federation of existing libraries, by contractual arrangements and by cooperation. The main characteristics of all three are first that they are voluntary, and second that the parties to them are equals and usually retain their independence of action.

Federated Systems

The great difference between the usual type of county or multi-county library and a federated system is that the latter does not involve the complete merger of one library into larger unit, and thereby the extinction of the former. Federated systems can obviously vary too in the degree to which the individual units retain freedom of action, but usually they control their own service programme (however poor it may be) and keep their own name, their own hoard of trustees, their own librarian and library staff and their own selection of books. This sort of arrangement is obviously more palatable than is a completely integrated library system, as demonstrated in New York, where the success of the state programme has been due even more to the flexibility allowed federated and cooperative systems than to the generous amounts of state aid. As with county and multi-county libraries, a federated system depends for its full development on the existence or creation of at least one large central library. Similarly a federated system allows member libraries to serve all residents of the area without regard to boundary lines of local government units; as such it is likely to be particularly effective in metropolitan areas.[31] Federation also permits flexibility in the choice of functions to be centralized and for changes in them in the course of time. Federation should be considered as a trial step and halfway measure to more concerted action. In a federated system, the librarian plays a dual role. He is a line officer in direct charge of his own library and of the headquarters of the system, but in relation to the trustees and personnel of the member libraries he is a staff officer, giving advisory and consultative services.

Contract Service

Contracts are used for a wide variety of public library purposes.[32] At the one extreme, this device can encompass the complete provision of library service to the citizens of one taxing unit by an established library of another. At the other extreme, it can represent nothing more than an agreement between two independent libraries to honour each other's borrowers' cards. Again, as with federated systems, contract service overlaps some of the earlier categories; in fact, federation itself is usually accomplished by contract,[33] as are some multi-county libraries. But contract service is usually thought of as an arrangement with a limited life, subject as it is to periodic renewal and review. Furthermore, it usually embraces one or only a few designated functions and is thus a notch or two less comprehensive than federation. Finally, contract service is usually characterized by a money payment for the service in question.

Contract service is chiefly noteworthy for its flexibility in scope of service, in arrangements between two or more parties, in readjustment to changing conditions and in other ways. Contracts have often been made between large libraries and nearby smaller libraries or communities. The usual experience in such cases is that the remuneration for the service given is less than its cost; in other words the larger library tends to subsidize the smaller one. This is a general truism in the relations of libraries of unequal size, and is one of the reasons why state aid is essential to insure fairer distribution of the burden while securing the strength of the large libraries for the sake and benefit of the small ones. Contract service was more popular in earlier years than it is now; it still has its proper use under appropriate circumstances, as in the formation of regional processing centres and of film circuits.

Cooperative Arrangements

Informal cooperation without official commitment has been a characteristic of American librarianship for years, embracing such great schemes as cooperative indexing of periodicals, cooperative cataloguing and union lists and catalogues, and such local items as interchange of books and magazines and joint discussions of new books for selection. Today there is a whole new set of possibilities to explore, such as regional cooperation in the provision of specialized books and reference service.[34] In recent years there has been a rise of regional groups of public library administrators who meet several times a year simply to discuss common problems, to exchange experiences and to know each other better. Such groups tend to lead in time to some cooperative action, such as a union list of periodicals in the libraries of the area or some informal arrangement for subject specialization in a few obvious fields. Cooperative arrangements are usually of limited application and duration, by virtue of the fact that they can go no further or faster than is agreeable to the most reluctant member of the group.

Practical Implications

For the library administrator, federated systems, contract service and cooperative arrangements represent possible lines of action short of complete merger into a larger unit. As such they are valuable for explorations of the validity of the idea of a larger library system, as well as the possibility of special functional uses in each case. The effectiveness of administration is increased when there are more rather than fewer alternatives, so that the most nearly appropriate one can be considered. This is especially true in an area where the pressures for action are strong but the best path ahead is not always clear.

A COMPARISON OF CERTAIN ADMINISTRATIVE ASPECTS OF THE MAIN TYPES OF LARGER UNITS

Table 7.1 presents in summary form a considered estimate for each of four main types of larger units of library service in regard to nine selected aspects of administration, especially as they affect the services and operation of the local libraries in or branches of the system. There is a wide variety of cases to be found in each of the four main types of unit, and no one should expect these judgments to be universally applicable. In the case of state-wide systems, the statements made are based on the plans so far devised rather than on any actual or extensive experience.

The main point of the table is that the county and multi-county libraries exercise more complete supervision over their local service agencies than do state-wide or federated systems, and are therefore in a better position theoretically to improve the administration of those agencies, primarily by bringing in more and more specialized personnel. Probably for these very reasons, such units are less acceptable to existing independent libraries, though some modern county and multi-county libraries seek to overcome this by taking on the characteristics of a federation of libraries. Primarily because of the limited size,

TABLE 7.1.
A Comparison of Certain Administrative Aspects of the Main Types of Larger Units of Library Service

		(a)	(b)	(c)	(d)	(e)
		Relationship of Central Headquarters to Local Service Agencies in Regard to				
	Type of Unit	*Choice of personnel*	*Book selection*	*Ordering and cataloguing*	*Reference service*	*Work with young adults and children*
1.	State-wide system	None if certification standards are met	Advisory	Desirably centralized	Advisory	Advisory
2.	Federated system	Advisory	Technical assistance provided	Centralized	Technical assistance provided	Technical assistance provided
3.	Multi-county unit	Supervisory	Supervisory	Centralized	Supervisory	Supervisory

Contd.

Type of Unit	(f) Acceptability of plan to independent local library	(g) Ability to provide effective reference service to all residents	(h) Ability to reduce unit costs of operation	(i) possibilities for administrative improvement of the local libraries
1. State-wide	High	Hard to say	High	Average
system		High	High	Average
2. Federated system	High	Average to high	Average to high	High
3. Multi-county	Low	Low	Average to low	High
4. County library	Low			

population and wealth of most American counties, the county library is in general the least likely of the four types to provide good information service to most residents of the area or to be especially economical in operation.

NOTES & REFERENCES

1. Gretchen K. Schenk, *County and Regional Library Service.* 1954 263 p. A.L.A.
2. John D. Henderson, "County and Regional Libraries." In Frank L. Schick, ed. *Future of Library: Demographic Aspects and Implications. Library Trends.* v. 10. no. 1. Oct. 1961, p. 104-119.
3. "Proceedings of an Institute on Multi-County and Regional Library Service." *Minnesota Libraries.* 19: 147-174. June 1959.
4. Harold S. Hacker and others, A *Federated Library System in Action: The Pioneer Library System in New York State.* Rochester Public Library. 12 p. 1959. Also in condensed form in *News Notes of California Libraries* 55: 261-66. Summer 1960. And in *Wilson Library Bulletin.* 34: 345-50, 354-56. Jan. 1960.
5. Wilfred L. Morin and Nathan M. Cohen. *State Library Extension Services: A Survey of Resources and Activities of State Library Administrative Agencies: 1955-56.* Misc. Pub. no. 37. 1960. U.S. Office of Education. p. 3-4, 23.
6. *Ibid.*
7. John G. Lorenz, "The Library Services Act and the States." In James R. Bowman, ed. *Proceedings of the Second Assembly of State Librarians,* 1961. U.S. Library of Congress. p. 49.
8. Sallie J. Farrell, "Louisiana Demonstrates Library Service." *Wilson Library Bulletin.* 23: 611-614. Apr. 1949. Also Hawthorne Daniel. *Public Libraries for Everyone.* 192 p. 1961. Doubleday. p. 52-56, 114-15.
9. Harold L. Hamill, "The Metropolitan Area and the Library." *Library Quarterly.* 31: 13-24. Jan. 1961. Also Amy Winslow. "Library Coordination and Consolidation in Metropolitan Areas," In Carleton B. Joeckel, ed. *Library Extension: Problems and Solutions.* 1944. Univ. of Chicago Press. p. 140-159.
10. See James E. Bryan, "The Christmas Holiday Jam: Student Use of Metropolitan Library." *A.L.A. Bulletin:* 55: 526-530. June 1961.
11. *Public Library Service: A Guide to Evaluation, with Minimum Standards.* 1956. A.L.A. p. 6-9.

12. Carleton B. Joeckel, *The Government of the American Public Library.* 1935. Univ. of Chicago Press. p. 317.
13. Robert D. Leigh, *The Public Library in the United States: The General Report of the Public Library Inquiry.* 272 p. 1950. Columbia Univ. Press. p. 154, 228.
14. Hawthorne Daniel, *Public Libraries for Everyone.* 192 p. 1961. Doubleday. This whole book discusses the Library Service Act and its results.
15. *State Plans Under the Library Services Act: Supplement* 2. 123 p. Bulletin 1960, no. 27. U.S. Office of Education.
16. Joeckel, *op. cit.,* p. 42-48.
17. *Ibid.* p. 296-297.
18. Walter T. Brahm, "Library Science in Ohio: 2050 AD." *Library Journal* 83: 1013-1016. Apr. 1, 1958.
19. Ohio State Library. *The Plan's the Thing: A Proposal for Extending Library Service in Ohio.* Annual Report, Part One: 1959. p. 21-31. Also Lowell A. Martin, *Library Service in Pennsylvania: Present and Proposed.* 2 v. 177 p. 1958. Pennsylvania State Library. Also "A State Wide Library Plan Proposed for Michigan." *Library Journal.* 85: 2884-87. Sept. 1, 1960. Also Walker T. Brahm. "State Libraries. p. 87-103. In Frank L. Schick, ed. *Future of Library Service. Library Trends.* v. 10. no. 2. Oct. 1961. Reviews progress and probabilities in state leadership and intensive service to local areas.
20. *Report of the Commissioner of Education's Committee on Public Library Service: 1957.* 196 p. New York State Education Department. Also *Public Systems in New York State.* 16 p. 1960. New York State Library Extension Division.
21. Charles M. Armstrong, "The New York State Experiment in Regional Library Service." *Library Quarterly.* 21: 79-93. Apr. 1951.
22. Ohio State Library, *op. cit.* and Martin. *op. cit.*
23. Katherine Laich, comp. "Regional Reference Library Service: An Outline of Cooperative Services, Existing or Proposed," *News Notes of California Libraries.* 56: 254-256. Spring 1961, Part 2. Also Enoch Pratt Free Library. *Annual Report: 1960.* p. 16-17.
24. For a summary of the status of state aid to libraries, as of a few years ago, see Wilfred C. Morin and Nathan M. Cohen, *State Library Extension Services: A Survey of Resources and Activities of State Library Administrative Agencies: 1955-56* (U.S. Office of Education Misc. no. 37. 1960) p. 5-7, 24. Also, more recently, S. Janice Kee, ed. *State Aid*

to Public Libraries. Library Trends. 9: 1-128. July 1960.

25. Oliver Garceau, *The Public Library in the Political Process.* (A Report of the Public Library Inquiry.) 254 p. 1949. Columbia University Press. p. 218-21.
26. Rose Vainstein. *Statistics of Public Libraries: 1955-56.* p. 95.
27. *Statistics of County and Regional Library Systems Populations of 50,000 or More: Fiscal Year 1956* (Circular no. 506. 1957.) U.S. Office of Education. p. 4.
28. Vainstein, *op. cit.,* p. 76.
29. Lowell A. Martin, "County and Regional Libraries: Hope and Reality." *Minnesota Libraries.* 19: 147:154. June 1959. Also Eleanor H. Morgan. "The County Library." In Joeckel, *op. cit.* p. 59-74. When in 1955 the California State Library adopted a minimum definition of a branch (open 5 days a week, with 7,000 volumes, and at least one professional and one non-professional assistant), the drop in the number of branches in county libraries was much greater than in municipal libraries. The number of county libraries with branches, by this definition, fell from 43 to 8, and the number of their branches from 552 to 23. See Grace Murray, "Branches' Is a Dirty Word." *New Notes of California Libraries.* 50: 538-40. Oct. 1955. In Wisconsin it has been suggested that communities under 8,000 be required to file with the state library agency an application of intention to create of library, so that alternate methods may be considered.
30. Some administrative aspects of multi-county or regional system are seen in the example of Washington North Central Regional Library, organized in 1961-62 as a result of the Columbia River Regional Library 5-year demonstration. It serves 5 counties, with 131,000 population scattered over 15,000 square miles (twice as large as Massachusetts). Headquarters at Wenatchee, 17,000 population, plus two secondary offices 45 and 75 miles away, serve 14 community libraries, 10 stations and branches and three bookmobiles. The books are regionally owned; each community asks for what it needs. Instruction is given to local mostly untrained staff as to methods and service. When reference questions cannot be answered locally they are mailed overnight to headquarters. HQ catalogues all the system books by IBM and supplies a printed book catalogue to each service point, which includes the total holdings of the region. The HQ extension librarian, children's, reference and youth specialists visit all points and give leadership guidance and personnel development.

31. For example, the Nassau Library System (Long Island, N.Y.) *Sum and Substance,* May 1960. Also Joseph Klimberger. "Cooperative Reference Service." *Library Journal.* 85: 1525-1527. Apr. 15, 1960.
32. Lura G. Currier. comp. *Contracts and Agreements for Public Library Service. P.L.D. Reporter* No. 6. 49 p. 1958. A.L.A.
33. The North Bay (Calif.) Cooperative Library System is in effect a federation by contract of 16 independent libraries; it now has centralized cataloguing, a system-wide coordinator of children's work, closed-circuit teletype, film circuit and subject specialization. The terminology used for various larger units of service is not always precise or consistent.
34. Rezia Gaunt, ed. *Cooperative Practices Among Libraries. P.L.D. Reporter,* No. 5. 70 p. 1956. A.L.A.

8

Running a Small Library

THIS CHAPTER is a summary of administrative aspects of operating small libraries. The A.L.A's Small Libraries Project was initiated in 1958 and financed by a grant from the Council on Library Resources, for and got underway May 1, 1961. It should produce a badly needed series of detailed informational leaflets, 250 to 300 pages, for the 6,000 libraries of under 10,000 population.[1]

Two facts have become clear. Independently the small individual libraries can never achieve such full, varied, efficient and economical service to the public, even when given advisory and book services by their state commissions, as they could be joining larger regional units. As integral parts of a large system they can have closer access to materials far beyond their own potential means; many processes can be centrally managed more economically and efficiently, releasing valuable time for direct local service to readers; each little library can draw more frequently and fully than at present on the strength which comes only from a corps of full-time trained specialists. By frequent visits the latter can pay attention to administration, organization, supervision, book selection, preparation, reference work, work with children, young people and adults, and the whole array of techniques.

The other clear point: responsibility for internal good management has always to continue inside the small local library, as in the branches of a large city system. The small library cannot profitably go it alone, but it may constantly grow more efficient. There is great satisfaction in working with a small clientele in a small community or neighborhood; acquaintance and understanding between staff and readers can be close indeed. The ineffectiveness of small libraries stems largely from failure to search for and appoint the most competent person available, as total local budgets below $6,000 do not permit a full-time trained librarian unless the time and salary can be divided among two or three towns. Good appointments are more likely under central direction from a regional head.

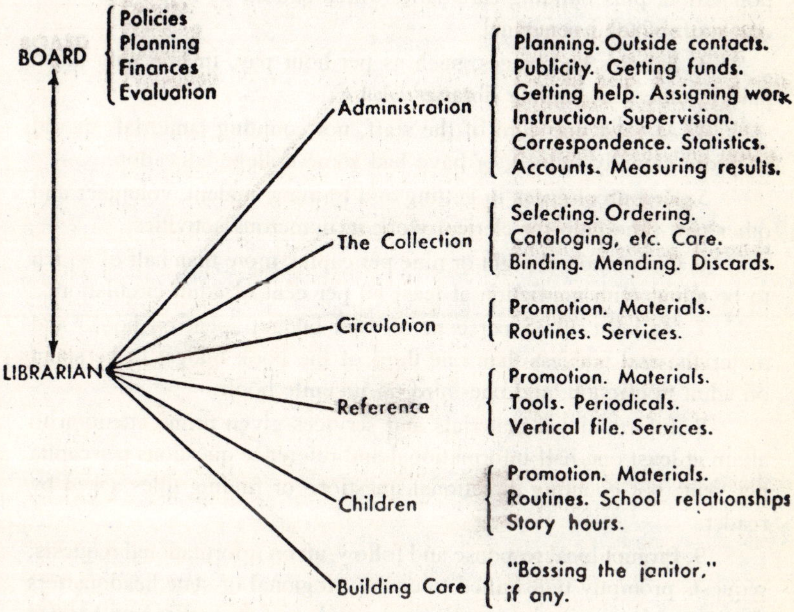

Fig. 1. The Administrative Function in the One-Person Library

POLICIES

Librarian and board in a small community have to conceive of their library as a dynamic agency for spreading the use of print into every home, making each citizen aware of the ways in which printed information can serve him. The library should lead and not be led in interpreting its role in the community, as an agent of enlightenment and a counter-influence against social, racial, religious and economic prejudices and intolerance. More small libraries need to draw more adults into the circle of users, especially to promote non-fiction use, including how to books in many fields. Some notable increases in adult nonfiction use have resulted from the librarian's stressing it.[2]

Library heads in communities of less than 10,000 have to arrive at decisions as to what they shall try to do, and how to achieve such goals and standards are the following:

1. Attaining $3 to $5 per capita minimum support, or the local share of that support as member of a regional system.

2. A staff of at least one full-time (or equivalent) per 2,000 population, plus building care staff, which should be kept at not over one-sixth of total personnel.

3. Salaries and wages, such as per-hour pay, in line with those paid in other outstanding libraries.

4. At least one-third of the staff, not counting janitorial, should be professionally trained, or have had some college education.

5. Resourcefulness in getting and training student, volunteer and other part-time help for clerical work in numerous activities.

6. Circulation of eight or nine per capita, more than half of which to be adult, with nonfiction at least 50 per cent of adult circulation.

7. At least 30-35 per cent of total budget spent on books and materials, and not less than one-third of the book budget to be spent on adult nonfiction, and one-third on juvenile books.

8. Informational materials and services given prime attention to attain at least one-half informational and reference questions per capita per year (not counting directional questions or finding titles asked by readers.

9. Prompt local response and follow-up on informational requests; requests promptly transmitted to county, regional or state headquarters for materials not in the local library, and readers notified or handed their material within five or six days of requesting it.

10. Continuing program of public relations and publicity to keep the library story always in the public mind, and to encourage greater use by individuals.

11. Constant attention to economy; (a) not starting new activities unless essential and profitable to the library's main purpose; (b) omitting, reducing or simplifying all possible routines and paperwork; making every hour count in each person's daily work.

THE LIBRARY BOARD

The librarian in a small town will wish that the board be as effective as possible. Working through the chairman, he should keep the group promptly informed at monthly meetings as to developments — not only statistics as to number of books lent in the three major categories, and number of questions looked up, but on all aspects of library organization and staff, collections, services, expenditures; the problems, trends, public reactions.

The librarian will encourage full attendance at board meetings. Many libraries would profit by a decrease in the number of trustees, from unwieldy groups such as fifteen or more to a workable active five or seven, and then capitalizing on the special interests and abilities of each trustee to further some aspect of library progress.

Trustees and librarian will formulate a statement of library policies, covering as many aspects of the work as possible, including the points just recited above and the question of joining a regional system; also, points on which public misunderstanding may be foreseen.[3] Because many small libraries cannot afford a full-time trained librarian, some trustees may, as volunteers, be drawn into the internal routines and services; their responsibilities as related to the librarian's should be discussed and defined in memoranda prepared each year when there is a change in personnel.

Officially responsible for financing, trustees should be continually devising means to secure public supports increasing to $3 per capita or more. They should promote circulation and reference service. They have to evaluate the year's progress, the effectiveness of the librarian. They will support the librarian in seeing that each staff member is developed and the staff strengthened each year. This means dropping ineffectual workers. The A.L.A. Standards are a great help in planning and measuring library operations.

THE LIBRARIAN'S VARIED WORK[4]

Planning what shall be attempted for the coming year, the coming month, the day ahead puts the librarian in control of library development in contrast to letting things run along as they have run, day by day. It signifies weak administration to permit circumstances and various persons to push the library around, or dictate policies, decision, appointments. If the librarian, whether trained or untrained, is not a pusher, not even a hard worker, but only a job holder, a new librarian should be found. A good education and knowledge of subjects and books underlie god service.

Citizens are glad to cooperate in publicity, e.g., lending store window space for exhibits that can be prepared by high school students or volunteers. News stories can often be delegated to others to prepare if the librarian will choose the subject, outline the story and have the data ready. The librarian's contacts with trustees and leading citizens should, among other things, lead to their active help in getting better library financing.[5,6]

The librarian, in consultation with the trustees, will see that each employee is chosen for merit only, choosing between two or three promising candidates. Resourceful librarians can attract intelligent, interested part-time students and volunteers to help on a variety of clerical routines and special tasks. e.g., arranging magazines and books, gathering, clipping and arranging news items, articles and pamphlets on local history, telling stories.[7]

The librarian has to give instruction to each worker, as teacher and supervisor. The supervisory function is vital for good results.

Statistics and accounts should be kept at a minimum. Statistics suggested: juvenile, adult fiction, adult non-fiction circulation; number of reference questions looked up; and number of book added. withdrawn and in the collection.

The Collection Materials

A trained librarian will take major responsibility for book selection, referring debatable questions to the trustees, but using knowledge of the staff in checking and discussing. Book orders should be placed at least once a month with a reliable library jobber who can give one-third discount, and with prompt deliveries. Readers should get their new books simplified cataloguing and classifying, possibly by use of Wilson printed cards (Library of Congress cards generally require changes and are too full of detail for small libraries and involve delay as well as cost) should be planned and laid out, possibly on a movable work board, so it can be interrupted without having to put away and get out materials and equipment. Even little village libraries need a good typewriter, perhaps a rebuilt at $50 or so. A binding allotment should be set, and books sent to a certified library bindery quarterly. An adept volunteer may do mending, following instructions available from library supply companies.

Circulation

Promotion is a always essential for circulating nonfiction. Fiction should be limited to worthy titles. Paperbacks may relieve demands for mysteries and westerns, and many libraries ask their readers to donate their read copies. An active rental collection of duplicate copies helps many libraries to meet demands for current fiction. The small library does not find expensive charging system, an improvement on the old-fashioned book-card system, with self-charging, i.e., the reader write his name and address on the book card and borrower's card if one is used; an identification card may be sufficient.

Reference Service

Even the small library needs to update its high school and its adult encyclopedias every four or five years, alternating their purchase, sticking to the two which most librarians find most useful for everyday reference work—the World Book and *Collier's Encyclopedia*. At least the *Abridged Reader's Guide* should be available, the key to 40 to 50 magazines sub-scribed to in a town of 2,000. In towns of 7,500 to 10,000 the library will take 100 to 125 magazines (using the full *Reader's Guide*). A file of pamphlets, bulletins, clippings on topics in demand, including local history and activities, should be kept up; an intelligent volunteer with some instruction and occasional newspaper recognition may find this a worthwhile interesting community activity. Each reference question should be followed through; sometimes a local citizen can give help or clues to the information, otherwise a larger library or the state commission. This aspect of local and regional or state cooperation is likely to undergo great improvement in the near future.

Service to Children

Someone on the staff needs to have special interest in and knowledge of chilldren's books. Perhaps someone, such as a mother who has reared a family of readers, may be discovered who can lead in this, or serve as story-teller. Somehow any library has to find the way to develop understanding competent help for this important age group. Numerous printed aids and selected booklists are available. Other persons are much concerned that similar special attention be given young adults — the fourteen to twenty year group, who use adult books primarily and unfortunately are left to their own devices in most small libraries. Most of all, small libraries. Most of all, small libraries need to develop their services to adult readers.

Building Care

In many libraries the janitor is paid as much as the librarian. Trustees should realize that the building is of less importance than the services given in it. In a one person library, maintenance should be cut to an hour or two a day for the days open, using oil, gas or electric heat, choosing a rapid, conscientious worker, perhaps a completent neighbour.

Debatable Activities

Because few small libraries receive $3 per capita support, it is held by some that funds accomplish more with more workers available during fewer hours open to the public, than with fewer workers to cover a longer open schedule. Group and audio-visual programmes possible in a large library can be offered in the small library only by diverting time and money from reading and informational services. Few libraries of under 10,000 population feel that they can conscientiously undertake these time and money consuming activities.

NOTES & REFERENCES

1. Numerically, 70% of the 8,190 public libraries identified by the U.S. Office of Education in 1960 served fewer than 10,000 people each. Frank L. Schick and Doris Holladay, *Systems Serving Populations of 100,000 or More: Fiscal Year 1960.* 24 p. U.S. Office of Education. OE-15-033. Nov. 1961. p. 4.
2. Jerome Cushman, "Adult Services in the Small Public Library." *Minnesota Libraries.* 1960. 19: 87-88. Sept.1958.
3. North Carolina Library Association, *Suggested Policies for Public Libraries.* 26 p. mimeo. 1960. North Carolina State Library.
4. *Public Library Service: A Guide to Evaluation, with Minimum Standards.* 98 p. 1956. A.L.A. *Also Costs of Public Library Service in 1959; a Supplement* (to foregoing). 15 p. 1960. A.L.A.
5. Pearl Frankenfield. "No Money Publicity Campaign." *Library Journal.* 81 : 2156. Oct. 1, 1956. Also Harriet S. Hawley. "Country Library Are Perking Up." *Wilson Library Bulletin,* 31: 393-394. Jan. 1957.

6. Beatrice S. Russell, "Small Library Spectacular." *Library Journal.* 85 : *1340-1342.* April 1, 1960. Unusual story of notable accomplishment in attracting 85% of the population to use the library, getting greatly increased funds a new building.
7. Katherine S. Diehl, *One Librarian.* 165 p. 1956. Scarecrow Press. New Brunswick, N.J. Through dealing with a small college library, the problems of managing and supervising, including green student assistants, fall on one trained person, and the book is full of practical parallels, helpful in administration of the small public library.

9

Library Public Relations

WE NEED to explain vividly about library public relation (PR) and library community relations (CR). By 1982 PR had become a loaded expression, and other terms were being used in its place, such as *community information,* or simply *information* or *marketing*. The term *PR* is so often subjected to attack as being vague, woolly, and more appropriate to commercial and business activity than to public service. Why not, then, sweep the concept of PR out of the library vocabulary?

It may be said that it is totally unimportant what an activity is called, so long as something actually is done. It is easy to get lost in the jungle of confused ideas and terms.

The following exposition is based on a belief in the value of keeping the term *public relations* as the umbrella term for the many activities the expression implies, such as advertising, bulletin bards, community information, library-community relations publicity, and library promotion.

HISTORY

The term *public relations* has its origin well back in history. In many books about PR the term is traced back to president Thomas Jefferson and his speech to the Congress in 1807. But public relations as an idea seems to have its roots in the earliest days of human society. Any person, group, or institution is involved in some relations, good or bad, with other persons, institutions, and "the public." According to Howard Stephenson the term *public relations* in its present connotation was first used in the *Yearbook of Railway Literature* in 1897.[1]

Beginnings of Library PR: Public Libraries

Library public relations were practised before the concept of library PR was fully identified and named. In 1876, when Samuel S. Green, librarian of the Worchester Free Public Library, wrote about personal relations between librarian and readers, he undoubtedly advocated improved relations with a public he called "modest men in humbler walks of life".[2] Twenty years later, at the 1896 ALA Conference, Miss Lutie Stearns of the Milwaukee Public Library gave a talk on advertising a library. The works of Green, Stearns, and other American public relations pioneers in the library world are described by Janis Joann Blair in her master's thesis. "From Advertising to Library Interpretation: The Development of Public Relations in the American Public Library".[3]

European librarians visiting the United States early in the century returned with new ideas, especially on how to "advertise" the libraries. For example: The Swedish library pioneer Greta Linder went to the United States in 1916, at the height of World War I. After her homecoming she presented a paper at the third Swedish library conference, 1917. She named her contribution *Biblioteksreklam* ("library advertising"). She introduced a variety of methods to use for spreading information about public library service. All her examples were from American libraries, and she was especially intrigued by the campaign in the Waco Public Library and its motto: "Get the library habit"[4].

When Joseph L.Wheeler wrote his famous *The Library and the Community* in 1924, he stated the objectives of publicity as being "to tell the public things which will benefit them to know. There is no motive involved in this other than the desire to make the library's service as widely known and used as possible".[5]

In the German library world, activities covered by *Leserwerbung* ("reader enlistment"; sometimes just *Werbung*) were comparable to some of the modern PR activities, even though they took place in the 1920s. In 1927 Lionel McColvin, the then time chief librarian of the English borough of Ipswich, stated in *Library Extension Work and Publicity:* "Thus it will be seen that we are dealing with more than just 'advertising'".[6]

McColvin's books could just as well have been named *Library Public Relations*, but that term did not enter the library world before the 1930s. In 1935 the *Wilson Library Bulletin* started the column

"The Crow's Nest," which was supposed to serve as a forum for library public relations. The same year an American librarian, Gilbert O. Ward, wrote the book *Publicity for Public Libraries.* He presented a number of reasons for pursuing publicity, but the main reason was: "In the long run, a public library usually depends for its prosperity and usefulness on what the public thinks of it. What the public thinks of it depends in turn not only on the character of the books and the service, but also on what the library does to make its books and service known".[7]

"Public relations" appears as a separate subject heading in the cumulative volume of *Readers Guide to Periodical Literature* (1932-1935), but *Library Literature* used the heading "Libraries and the Public" until the cumulative volume, when "Public Relations of Libraries" also appeared (1949-1951). In 1939 the American Library Public Relations Council was formed. In the early 1940s E.W.Mc-Diarmid and John McDiarmid reported public relations carried through in public libraries. In their book *The Administration of the American Public Library,* they expressed the opinion that "public relations involves every contact which an organization makes with any part or individual of the public".[8]

These examples may be enough to give the historical background to Alice Norton's article "Library Public Relations" where she states that public relations "has been primarily a post-World War II American development." As has been noted, however, the idea behind *library public relations* was not a post-World War II concept, neither in the United States nor in Europe: it had, in fact, come into being much earlier. Use of the term *public relations,* however, entered the European library vocabulary at a later date. In British and Scandinavian library literature it appeared during the 1950s. Harold Joliffe gives an appropriate background of the pre-PR period in his *Public Library Extension Activities*[9].

Library Public Relations and the Research Libraries

In the 1950s the concept of public relations was brought into the academic and special library world, and in 1958 *Library Trends* devoted a whole issue to the theme "Aspects of Library Public Relations" (issue ed., L. Arnold: October 1958). To read that issue in the 1980s is to be introduced to aspects of the importance of public relations for research libraries that are still rare today. For example, Irene M. Strieby's "Checklist of Media and Techniques for Public Relations Activities in Special Libraries" can easily be adapted to the library world of today[10]. It took time, however, before the function of public relations became seriously discussed in wider circles of professional research librarians.

In 1964 the German Librarian Martha Höhl wrote her small but comprehensive booklet *Büchereiwerbung*[11]. The book gave ideas to be used in all types libraries, but it was, as its title indicates, oriented toward the public libraries, as *Die Bücherei and Die Volksbücherei* have that meaning.

In the 1970s library public relations was introduced as part of the strategy of running special libraries in Britain. In *Aslib Proceedings* volumes many writers have brought up the subject, notably Haygarth Jackson[12] and Hoey[13].

Public Relations in the 'Vocabularium Bibliothecarii'?

Public relations is not included in the indispensable *Vocabularium Bibliothecarii*[14]. And in 1980 there were suggestions that the word should be deleted from the unofficial "librarian's vocabulary." Such a change is hardly practicable, now that the term *library public relations* and the concept behind it have a fairly good footing in all types of libraries. Why then change the word again? Commonly terminology facilitates the internationalization of research and education—which is necessary if libraries are to occupy a central place in society. Common words pave the way for cooperation between types of libraries and between countries. In the era of computerized literature searching, librarians ought to make it easy for each other to find out what is going on in their profession, to find new knowledge, search for ideas, and seek tools for evaluating library services.*Community relations* (CR) is not an international term, but *public relations* (PR) is.

LIBRARY PUBLIC RELATIONS IN ITS MODERN CONCEPT

Definition of PR

How then do we define *library public relations?*. The definition coined by the Public Relations Society of America is rather similar to the one adopted by the British Institute of Public Relations, which

Usherwood describes as "PR is the deliberate, planned and sustained effort to establish and maintain mutual understanding between an organization and its public".[15] But, as Usherwood later writes, "it is in fact easier to describe the practice of PR than to define it ".[16] The Swedish Public Relations Association stresses the many public sectors, the "individuals and groups inside and outside the organization".[17]

In an attempt to clarify the aims of different PR activities and to distinguish between marketing (including advertising) and public relations, the Swedish Public Relations Association once presented the model of the concept that is shown in Figure 9.1. The difference between public relations and marketing lies mainly in the differing primary objectives. The PR input intends to influence *relations:* Whether people but or do not buy, use or do not use, is immaterial. Marking input aims at an immediate sale effect. However, both these primary intentions have secondary effects, especially if the offerings promoted are good.

This model of the concept show that there is bound to be some degree of confusion among the different terms used for very similar activities. It would not be incorrect to talk about "marketing of library services"[18,19], but when using that term, one loses the essential meaning of PR, and the internal PR aspect easily becomes neglected.

The PR/CR function is an administrative function in all types of libraries. Whether PR or CR is the umbrella term used in planning PR is of no importance. Yet, even if one talks about different "communities" when defining the "publics" of academic, research, and special libraries, the CR concept gears one's associations toward public libraries.

Whatever term is used, PR or CR, the work starts within the library, with the staff. The resistance and the negative attitudes which still exist toward library public relations surely would have been overcome long ago if the main function of PR, namely *information,* had been accepted as absolutely necessary to all library planning. Also, that information should be directed internally as well as externally.

This is well illustrated in the case study, presented in *Problems in Library Public Relations*[20], where positive steps taken failed on account of the staff member who, having shown due regard to the other requisites, neglected the main function of PR, namely the information function: "The courtesy of keeping people informed is often one of the most difficult communication factors simply because it always seems to take so much time and never seems to be a priority item.

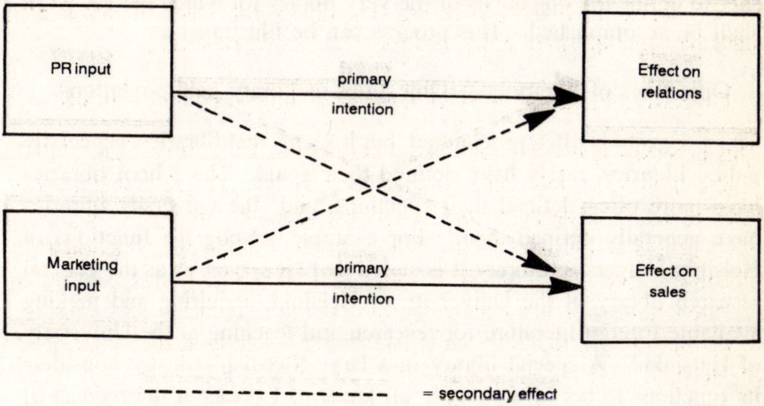

Fig. 9.1 Model showing the distinction between marketing and public rela-

This lack of understanding of the importance of planning CR, information, or PR (or whatever one likes to call the efforts to widen the library clientele) is brought up in most articles and books referred to in this discussion. Whichever term is used, it is necessary to make a clear definition and form that definition plan the work.

In the following presentation on how to plan library public relation, the Swedish definition of PR is used: "The primary purpose of public relations is to create and maintain good relationship with individuals and groups inside and outside the corporation (organization, authority, etc). This requires both analysis of the client's situation, and various types of action, mainly of an informative nature. Public relations covers subsidiary functions relating to investigation, policy-making and information, and as an overall concept, it is one aspect of the total activity of the corporation (organization, authority, etc.)".

Need of Library Public Relations

Among the reasons that we need library public relations are the following: Libraries of all types can be used by many more people than they are now. Public knowledge of library services is limited, and library users are still inadequately informed as to what the various types of libraries can provide. Many nonusers have negative attitudes toward libraries.

Before the objectives of a library's PR can be defined, it is necessary to define the objectives of the very library for which the PR work shall be accomplished. This process can be illustrated as

Objectives of library ⟶ Objectives of library public relations.

This necessity is often proclaimed, but it seems that libraries, especially public libraries, rarely have defined their goals. The school libraries have more often defined their functions, and the university libraries have generally defined them. For example, among the functions of Helsinki University Library it is stated that "it serves. . . as the general research library of the University of Helsinki, acquiring and making available foreign literature for research and teaching at the University of Helsinki." A special library in a large Swedish industry considers its functions to be: (a) to supply all kinds of I books at the request of the employees, (b) to keep a topical special library within the area of the factory's interest, (c) to spread news through periodicals. (d) to work for rational use of the literature in the industry.(e) to follow developments in its field, and (f) to contribute to high information consciousness in the industry.

The goals mentioned can never be reached without library public relations. There are academic libraries which justify their intensive library public relations work with the declaration: The cost of printed information about the library is less than the annual subscription to one of the most important scientific journals. If there were no library PR, fewer people would come in contact with that scientific journal in the library.

The public libraries are bound to have broader goals. Also, they are under constant pressure from the inhabitants of the community. But if public libraries declare that their duty is to give people what they as for, one may ask; why then do we need library public relations? Is the public library to become just another link in the giant glut of sex, sadism and shotguns, romances, wild westerns, mysteries, and light fiction cynically marketed by publishers, T.V, and other commercial agencies?

If librarians, on the other hand, define the public library as the information centre of the community, which has to provide media enabling people to become conscious about themselves and society, and if they hold that the public library must be able to offer the alternatives between which users may choose, then library public relations is a necessity. But to be able to attain those goals, the library must have official statements, approved by the local authority. It is difficult to formulate these goals in a meaningful way. Jones, in this "Criteria for the Evaluation of Public Library Services"[21], has tried to identity the objectives of public library service. Some of these are listed here, which the present author believes ought to have universal applications:

- To provide, on open shelves or in reserve, books and other materials in anticipation of likely demands, and also to provide a range and depth of material of which potential users might not otherwise be aware. . . .
- To assist inquirers to find the books and information they need. . . .
- To stimulate awareness of the facilities available so that they may be of maximum value to the community.

Public libraries all over the world have to be on their guard against commercial forces, and they should use the same means and methods as in the commercial world but with other goals in mind. The "UNESCO Public Library Manifesto" is a useful foundation when defining public library objectives[22]. Nothing can be called a "free choice" until one knows the alternatives available. Without library public relations many people will never even hear about the alternatives available. Thus the objectives of library public relations work are determined by and serve the library's goals and functions. An attempt to illustrate this is given in Figure 9.2.

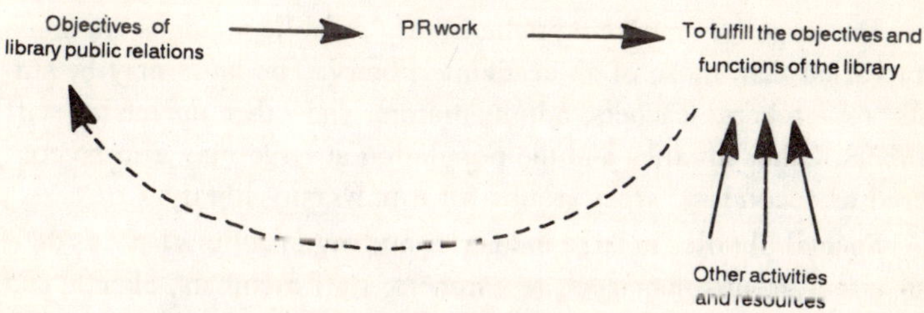

Fig. 9.2. PR in relation to the library's goals

OBJECTIVES FOR LIBRARY PUBLIC RELATIONS

Even though the different types of libraries have varied goals and functions, their public relations objectives have much in common: to spread knowledge of the media and services offered by the library. In order to reach those objectives, the staff has to be informed and service minded. Other objectives for library public relations common to all types of libraries are those intended to change and influence attitudes towards libraries as a whole.

Having defined the overall objectives for library public relations, subordinate aims must be identified, normally in terms of particular target groups. How can the library reach "all students" or "all researchers," "all employees" or "all inhabitants"? It is necessary to personalize the subgoals.

Library public relations must have *realistic* objectives, and those objectives have to be *measurable*. Measuring the immeasurable is a much debated subject in the library world.[23,24]

Target Groups for Library Public Relations Work

The inhabitants of a community can be split up into many different target groups. Employees in the industries, organizations and institutions, children, women, parents, newcomers, the handicapped, jazz fans, the aged, shut-ins, and the sick—these are just some target groups to which public libraries should relate their information provision. The population can also be divided by residential area or specialized interest (e.g., those using the bingo hall or sportsfield). People can also be grouped according to some common (sometimes temporary) interest (e.g., mothers who have their children in the same nursery). Moreover: Never forget the politicians!

The target groups for a public library's public relations are much more varied than those of an academic library. The latter may be students, researchers, teachers, administrators, and other university staff members. Other libraries and the population at large may also be considered as secondary target groups for a university library.

Special libraries in large industries and organizations have as their main target groups managers, researchers, staff members, clients, and sometimes other libraries. According to the manual *Scientific and Technical Libraries*, the "complex public" of a corporation can be grouped in the following main divisions: "employees, stockholders, suppliers, consumers, government, the company of which the organization is a part—sometimes referred to as the 'grass-roots' public'".[25]

School libraries have pupils and teachers as main target groups, but they have others as well (e.g., students in evening classes).

When the person responsible for the library public relations has identified as many target groups as possible, the next problem must be faced. Which target groups shall have priority? How do you find the potential users? Which groups need the most information? Which groups are the most neglected?

Even so, clearly formulated objectives and subordinate goals and target groups will have significance only if they are incorporated in a plan designed to reach the goals. Before this plan is designed, and examination and assessment of resources and methods to be used must be made.

Resources for Library Public Relations

The effect of library public relations can be measured only after the resources have been acquired and used. Resources included staff, signs, printing premises, notices, and money.

The importance of a flow of information between members of the staff cannot be stressed enough. External library public relations must be built on good internal staff relations. Ways of informing staff are staff meetings, staff bulletins, and written information provided to the library switchboard operator—to say nothing of "the invisible college".

Every press release, flyer, leaflet, or other information sheet for external use must also be sent to all staff members. The larger the library system, the more important it is to look after internal library public relations.

In-service training in how to answer the telephone and how to treat a client so that she or he does not feel neglected or inferior seems to be necessary in most library systems. User surveys gives evidence that nonusers often feel that the library atmosphere is cold, that the librarians make library visitors uncomfortable, and that the library building seems grim and looks like a cross between a church and a prison.

The staff is more important than the money. With little money, however, it is difficult to plan library public relations. Wheeler and Goldhor suggested in the early1960s that 1% to 2% of the library budget be used for PR.[26] An allocation of 2% to 5% of a library's total budget is now recommended in the United States.

Few libraries seem to reach this recommendation. If all libraries used at least 1% of their budgets (staff excluded) for the expenses of library PR, much would be accomplished.

The development of new communities or the expansion of existing ones increases the use of libraries. Yet library authorities sigh over the wasted capital. The public libraries often are not open when the users can come. The periodicals in the academic libraries may be sited in lovely surroundings in a place where they go unnoticed. Sometimes there is no sign in the street or on the campus indicating where the library is situated. The library may be hidden away in an obscure part of a factory or a school. Just to have a modern, new library is not good enough either. People must know that there is a library, where it is situated, and what it can do for them.

Many libraries have their own printing facilities. If a library does not, the PR planner must find out whether the community has its own printing facilities or make contact with a printer who can work fast and take jobs on short notice.

A single member of the staff must be responsible for the library PR. It is essential that *one* person coordinates all library information, internal as well as external, to avoid confusion and to give the whole picture of library activities. It is also necessary that all hired specialists (such as prints, advertising firms, etc.) have *one* contact in the library system, even though library PR can be looked upon as a responsibility of all staff members.

Library Public Relations Methods

The different PR methods to be used in libraries can be grouped in the following categories:

1. The spoken word;
2. Contact with news media;
3. Displays and exhibits;
4. Printed material;
5. Audiovisual materials; and
6. Other methods, such as pencils, balloons, T shirts, and similar "gimmick items".

None of these methods can be used alone. The different methods must be woven together in a network. In most countries libraries send out some odd booklists, a few bulk mail information sheets, and some placards and flyers—all these activities somewhat unmethodical and aimlessly undertaken. Library information seems to have reached only the already well informed. There is thus a need, before presenting the different methods and how to use them, to define the message to be sent out.

THE LIBRARY MESSAGE

When librarians have defined the objectives of their library for which a library public relations plan is to serve, they have to decide on what information should be distributed. An inventory of target groups and resources and methods to use should precede the formulation of the message. Then a systematic analysis must be made of all possible messages to send through the most suitable channel for a certain target group. Marshall McLuhan's expression "the medium is the message" ought to be taken into consideration when one chooses suitable messages.

Historically, librarians have sent out the message that they consider to be the most important. Librarians have seldom placed themselves in the situation of receivers of the library message. Public libraries, for example, have stubbornly told people that there are "good books" in the libraries and that it is "useful" to read. How many library nonuser think that "good" books are the same as "dull" books? It might be of value to provide some sort of "association test" in this respect, for as long as many people have no desire to read, one cannot entice them with "good" books.

Too many pointers have been used by librarians: "Read, Learn, Live"—Is this what nonusers want? "Read and Grow"—Not everyone wants to grow and perhaps become taller and heavier. The writer of such messages was certainly thinking of some intellectual and spiritual growth, but the sentiment does not necessarily commend itself to the user.

"Visit the Library" and "Welcome to the Library" are common exhortations in library information material. "Why?" the nonuser may ask. "Does the library want to improve its statistics?. That is not my concern!". Such messages, once misunderstood, are not easily erased from the minds of the recipients.

In connection with a nationwide library survey in Sweden in 1968 a large billboard in an underground station in Stockholm proclaimed the message "Of course, you have no time to go to the library today either." That message has been severely criticized by librarians because it had too many hidden pointers. But the text was deliberately provocative, taking into consideration the target groups for whom it was meant: people who always say that they never have time to go to the library or read books. This large poster certainly irritated people, and the fact that many were annoyed showed that they recognized the message.

In 1979 Toronto Public Library bent the famous TV tower on the Toronto skyline into a question mark on its large subway posters proclaiming "This city has a million questions." It is clear enough that the poster was eye-catching. Many inhabitants of the city wanted to buy the poster! If library public relations is to be effective, librarians have to give up using such peremptory messages as "Come to the library" what does that tell the person ignorant of a library's purpose?.

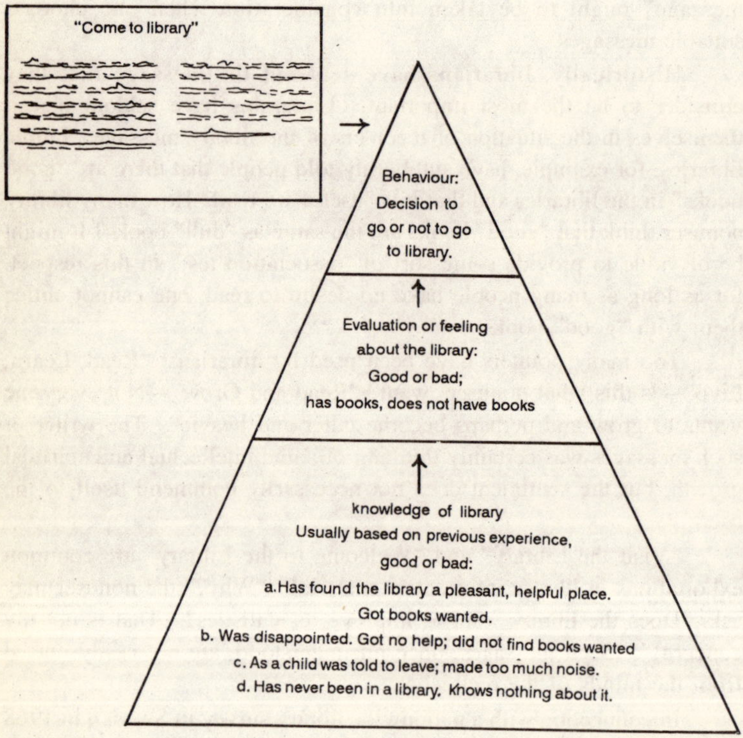

Fig. 9.3. Processes involved in the decision to go or not to go to the library

No one really knows exactly how message should be formulated in order to give maximum effect. Have library people given enough consideration to all the factors which make a person decide to go or not go to a library? With such an expression as "Come to the library" one attacks a behaviour without having thoroughly reasoned why people react in particular ways to particular kinds of suggestions.

The knowledge a person has (the cognitive component) of a library is used to form affective evaluations (the affective component). The person bases his or her behaviour on these feelings—to go or not to go to a library. This is illustrated in Figure 9.3.[27]

THE SPOKEN WORD

In most public relations textbooks the spoken word is mentioned as one of the most effective public relations tools. In the library world the spoken word has been used as a PR medium for library tours, library user education, library talks, and books talks.

The concept of the book talk originated in the United States, where book talks have been used extensively in school libraries and public libraries. In *A Long Way to Tipperary* one of the book talk pioneers, Margaret A. Edwards, traces the history of the book talk back to the early 1940s.[28] Eleanor Phinney advocated book talks and book discussions in her book *Library Adult Education in Action*.[29]

Librarians from other parts of the world have studied the teaching of book talks and book talk techniques in the United States and have brought the knowledge back to their own countries. In that way, the concept of the book talk reached the Scandinavian countries in the late 1950s.[30,31]

Definition of Book Talk

In her course about reader services at the Graduate School of Library Science, Rutgers State University. Margaret E. Monroe defined book talks with for statements, the first two of which have the following formulation:

> A "book talk" has become formalized as a presentation by a librarian to a group of potential readers of the books talked about. The "Book talk" is closely related in *content* to the comments made about books to individual readers in an informal fashion in "floor work."[32]

Historically, book talks have been associated with public libraries and school libraries. It is, however, easy to change the expression "book talk" to "library talk," and to slightly revise the foregoing definition in order to focus interest on the library rather than just the books. Speaking about catalogues and sources of information and literature searching to help the user help himself and to master the sources—-that is an art and can certainly be an effective PR method, far more effective than any printed material.

The Art of Book Talking

Many writers have advocated use of the spoken word Loizeaux says, "the library itself is a fascinating theme for any number of talks".[33] Yet, the spoken word has not been seriously analyzed in the same way as other PR methods used in the library world. Ideas for "Public speaking" are presented in various useful "how to do it" books that are published more or less continuously.[16,34,35] In *Booktalk* Joni Bodart gives some hints on how to write and give book talks for schoolchildren.[36]

The art of book talking and its techniques, however, are not covered sufficiently in library literature. It may be considered that it is easier to talk about the joy of reading and the fount of knowledge provided by library than it is to explain how to use the catalogue or to guide a library tour. Informality and the personal touch are all important. No matter what the talk is about, if it does not inspire people to read or use the library, it is useless. But if it is to give inspiration and carry conviction to the uninitiated, it is absolutely necessary that the person giving the talk should have a deep personal experience in reading and be thoroughly familiar with the books, media, and services mentioned. Moreover, the talk must derive from and carry with it the personality of the speaker. Preconceived notions based on other people's ideas and methods are almost useless, as are words and phrases written and spoken by others. This point is fundamental: An audience demands authenticity, and it repudiates the secondhand. Commitment, however, is not enough. The speaker has to learn to keep nervous habits under control, see that all the listeners are within earshot, and avoid abbreviations such as mon.,per.,and ref. It is absolutely necessary to have a personal checklist of all these small but (for the effect of the talk) extremely essential details.

Any library talk or book talk needs preparation. Preparing a talk is sometimes more time consuming than other PR methods, a fact that often seems neglected. The planning of book talks and library talks can be part of a librarian's daily routine if the habit is developed of making notes about books, sentences, ideas, and thoughts which can be used in connection with passing on information about library services. These notes can conveniently be written on ordinary catalogue cards and collected in a card index. When preparing a talk these cards will be useful as "thumbnotes" to follow during the presentation.

Finally, a library talk or a book talk must be short. It cannot be stressed often enough that too short a talk is better than one that is too long, especially when the audience is made up of people who are not used to listening. When informing nonusers, the spoken word will be the most effective PR method. If a talk is short but interesting, it makes the audience wish that there had been more information, and the speaker has gained the desired goal. On the other hand, if the audience is waiting impatiently for the talk to tend, even a potentially enthusiastic reader may become shy of books and libraries.

The following is a suggested checklist for preparing and presenting a book talk.

1. *Preparations:*
   a. Acquire knowledge about the target group.
   b. Name and address of contact person?
   c. Choose theme, Collect material.
   d. Note the key points for the presentation.
   e. Calculate the time taken for each part of the talk.
   f. Prepare book display, Booklists, and handouts.
2. *Bring to the talk:*
   a. The key points, "thumbnotes" for the talk.
   b. Books mentioned and books for the display.
   c. Other likely requisites: films, tape-slides, overhead transparency etc.
   d. Printed information about the library.
   e. Booklists, subject lists etc.
3. *In the meeting place:*
   a. Arrive in good time, irrespective of whether the talk is to take place inside or outside the library.

b. Arrange a book display near the entrance.
c. Check technical aids, such as projector.
d. If there are chairs, arrange them in a half-circle for informality.
e. Chat with audience as they assemble.

4. During the talk:
   a. Introduce yourself if no one else does.
   b. Speak clearly.
   c. Look at the listeners.
   d. Do not read from notes.
   e. Be sensitive to the reaction of the audience.
   f. Avoid sounds like "er" and irritating gestures.
   g. Show illustrative material in such a way that the audience can see it properly and has time to do so.
   h. Keep to the time limits.
5. *After the talk:*
   a. Leave adequate time for questions.
   b. Give the audience time to look at the books and the library.
   c. Arrange "buzz sessions" to formulate questions or to give answers to questions.
   d. Distribute informational material and booklists.
   e. Analyze the reception of the talk.
   f. Criticize your own performance.
   g. Follow-up and evaluation.

Such a checklist is a useful tool. Checklists will differ depending on the type of library and according to whether the talk is given in the library or some other place. Bob Usherwood gives many useful hints for public speaking: preparation, presentation, question time, and even how to face a microphone.[16]

CONTACT WITH THE NEWS MEDIA

All types of library ought to be able to build up good contacts with the news media: press, radio, and TV. The news media have different working rules in different countries. Harrison[37] presents the view of British librarians with regard to relations with news media, and Rice[38] takes up the problem of communicating through mass media in the United States. Despite its early date, the *Publicity Primer* still gives many suggestions and useful hints[33]. Many other books dealing with these subjects can easily be found[39,40] and consequently only principles and working hypotheses are discussed here.

In the long run it is essential that the news media have confidence in fact sheets, press releases, and other information emanating from libraries. Sensation journalism is short sighted and must be avoided.

What is News?

What then is news? Books or other media purchased by the library? Annual statistics? Visitors to the library? New staff members? A new building inaugurated or a new service? Programmes, exhibits, and other special events? News can be roughly divided into three categories:

1. *Real news:* Examples are—The library burns down. The Nobel Prize winner visits the library. The library extends to new localities. The floor at the university library collapses under the weight of its books. A bookmobile makes its first tour.
2. *Routine news:* This includes annual statistical reports, programmes and exhibits in the coming month, opening hours, and new additions to the book collection.
3. *Manufactured news:* One may call this pseudonews—"Miss Library," pony riding in the children's department, or wedding in the library.

Libraries are never short of real news. It is only a question of digging up the right aspects of library service and activities and of the knowledge to be found in the library. For many readers and listeners, this is news; perhaps it is news even for the journalist.

Examination of publicity records in libraries in different countries and study of press clippings seem to verify the following working hypotheses: Librarians chat happily about their libraries: articles on programmes and special events outnumber real news; public libraries have more contact with news media than academic libraries.

It is only too clear that library problems—-such as inadequate buildings, under-staffing, lack of books, the need for new services—are not common themes in information sent out.

How to Transmit Library News

What picture of a library does a reader of a daily paper receive from annual reports with lots of figures but nothing to provide comparisons? How can a list of newly purchases books—with no comments—attract new readers? In spite of all the writing about the importance of making information from libraries readable, inspiring, and dynamic, the image of libraries—and librarians—is too often dull, gray, and uncomfortable.

Common methods for contacting the news media are : (a) press conferences; (b) press releases, sometimes called "weekly letter" or "fact sheet", and (c) personal information, by letter or telephone.

Another question often discussed is whether the contact with news media should be on an informal, personal basis (by telephone mostly) or written. There can be no doubt that a well-written press release or just a simple, but thorough, fact sheet always makes it easier for the journalist.

When written or spoken information is transmitted to the news media, the sender—the library—cannot complain if some of the information does not get published, or perhaps is misinterpreted or given a partial presentation. The initiator of the information must present the facts in such a way that few mistakes can arise, but it also must be understood that journalists—as well as authors—defend their independence and integrity.

The Press Release

When contacting the news media the written word has many advantages over the spoken word. The sender can select the words and weigh them against each other to create implications that are easily lost in a telephone call. The telephone call may reach the journalist in a hectic and inconvenient situation. The written message assures the sender as well as the receiver that names of people, places, programmes, and services are correctly spelled; and that dates, figures, and other facts are correct. The written message does not demand an immediate response, as does the telephone call. It leaves the receiver the choice as to what shall be done with the message. On the other hand, there is the danger that the information will be ignored because it is easier to commit a bit of paper to the trash can than to disregard a person.

In the flood of press releases sent to the mass media people of today, it is of utmost consequence that any particular press release shall at least be looked at. Newspapers are sent to print earlier and earlier, and they also cover larger and larger areas. A written press release is easy for the newspaper staff to rewrite and then save for the appropriate edition and page.

The Art of News Media Release Writing

The way in which press releases are written many times decides whether they will be read or thrown away. Writing a press release so that it will be read is indeed an art. Different countries have varied techniques and customs to consider when reporting to the news media. Usherwood.[16] Coplan and Castagna[28], Loizeaux[33], Garvey[40], and Schumacher[41] offer many suggestions for libraries, such as using only one side of the paper, following a standard format, and typing double space. However, rules such as these are universal, and the person responsible for library public relations ought to know them and how they are applied in his or her country.

The press release writer must consider that the person who first receives the release, the journalist, may not know much about libraries. Therefore, the message must immediately arouse his or her interest. The words must be made to come alive, so they stand out from the routine releases. A message such as "new branch library in Forest Hill" may not be of interest to the journalist, who may not live in "Forest Hill" and may have no interest in libraries.

Two target groups must be reached by the press release: first the journalist and then the readers listeners, and viewers of news media. But if the first target group is not interested, the second will not be reached. Good journalists are generally tuned to the readers of their paper or the audience of their radio or TV station.

There are many such details to take into consideration when writing a press release, and none should be considered too simple or naive for consideration. It seems, however, that librarians have not taken the art of press release writing seriously enough. It must be remembered that anything written about libraries may have repercussions throughout all the world.

Writing a readable press release is not only difficult but also takes time. However, if the information function is taken into consideration in the early stage of planning new services, purchasing new media, or inaugurating a building, etc, the press release does not need to become a hurried effort that risks anonymity among a flood of papers.

If the event report is included in the first sentences and the vital information is presented in such a way that the journalist can decide at a glance whether or not the message is of interest to readers (listeners, viewers), then there is a good chance that the newspaper (radio, TV station) will contact the library.

Recurrent Weekly Columns and Radio and TV Programmes

If all the good ideas that Sarah Leslie Wallace suggested in *Promotion Ideas for Public Libraries* had developed along the lines she envisaged, people's awareness of libraries would have grown.[42] Her ideas for newspaper columns and radio programmes easily can be adapted by other types of libraries, and indeed there are several such recurrent columns and programmes, especially in the United States and Canada. Marian Edsall gives newer ideas on how to start a newspaper column.[39]

A library's weekly column sought to be considered for the house organs of manufacturing firms and research stations as well as for universities and schools. Staff journals, community information fact sheets, and tourist information newspapers are other examples of news media that can be used to tell "the library story."

Even company personnel will be made more aware of their organization's library if the PR director of the company takes the library into account when contacting outside newspapers.[43]

Advertising

If library people decide that certain items of information absolutely must be inserted in the news media, they must buy space or spot announcements. In some countries such official institutions as libraries are not allowed to use tax money for advertising, and in others it is impossible to buy announcement spots. Practices are clearly varied.

Local advertisement papers and newsletters from commercial shops can also be used for library advertisements. "Sandwich men" can be hired and outdoor bulletin boards used.

When dealing with newspapers there should be no connection between the attitude of editors and journalists toward the library and the amount of advertisement the library pays for. No true journalist would ever insist that mention in the paper would be based on purchase of an advertisement.

In addition to the considerations mentioned earlier about the message to send out, the advertisement in itself is also a message. The manuscript or proofsheet may look very attractive, but on the advertising pages it may "disappear" among the other ads. Where should it be placed? Can a certain page be chosen? Cultural events may be more easily noticed if they are placed between prices of vegetables and sports announcements, rather than alongside literature reviews. An evening in the library dealing with dogs is surely more effective if placed among amusements ads rather than in the weekly library column.

Advertisements are an effective PR method for public libraries if they give the reader an impulse to do something at once. Therefore ads ought to be used for library programmes and exhibits, but seldom for anything else. Ads about bookmobile stops, opening hours, and general information seldom have this effect.

But to have impact, the event, not the library, must be the focus. An advertisement must always include the library's telephone number and address. That gives the ad a spin-off value. Some people may call and ask: "Does the library have books about dogs? I never knew that!"

Letters to the Editor

Another way of "getting into print" is use the "letters to the editor" column. The library can frequently provide an answer to or a comment on a letter. Sometimes the library itself is the subject of a critical letter to the editor. Naturally, this is a splendid opportunity for the library to give informative, polite answer—aggression has never been a good long-term policy.

DISPLAYS AND EXHIBITS

Book displays seem to have been used in all types of libraries as long as libraries have been in existence. Why are these displays arranged? And how? Surely, lots of books in an anonymous row cannot attract new readers!

An article in a 1934 issue of *Library World, "The Guff Called Book Display," questioned the method. At that time book displays seem to have aroused the same uncertain attitudes as the so called PR gimmicks of today. Ernest A. Savage looked upon the concept of library displays in another way. When he wrote his famous Manual of Book Classification and Display,* he stated in the introduction: "A classed library is an exhibition. I decline to look upon it as anything else." Harold Joliffe advocated library displays as a very essential part of library extension work. In his book *Public Library Extension Activities* he says that the topic is so essential that it ought to be treated as a subject of study in its own right.

Definitions

Borgwardt distinguishes between the library itself as a *display* and all the small *exhibits,* which are intended to draw the attention of visitors to the books and other media in the library. Rice uses the word *display* for "a collection (large small) of related items or of items related to a theme which is assembled in one of the glass enclosed cases commonly found in libraries." In her vocabulary an *exhibit* is "a showing of paintings, sculpture, photography, or similar works of art in the meeting room or gallery area of a public library".[38] Rice gears her books toward public libraries. Other writers—for example, Garvey[40]— point out the value of displays in all types of library. For Garvey, an exhibit "is bigger and more comprehensive form of display."[40]

Here both terms are used. The concept of a library display implies that it is related to one specific theme. A display used as a PR method is wholly related to the library, its services and media.

The Purposes and Objectives of Library Displays

When Kate Coplan in the 1920s pioneered using store windows in Baltimore for library displays, they undoubtedly served as PR methods, but the concept of library public relations had not entered into the library world. And, according to Marie Loizeaux: "Everything that applies to any other type of exhibit applies to a window display, only more so. It *must* be appealing. It *must* be attractive. It must be effective."[33]

Borgwardt presents a useful list of objectives and purposes for library displays. It could be used as a checklist in all types of libraries:

1. To reveal the resources of the library;
2. To ensure maximum use of each book;
3. To bring together books separated by the classification scheme;
4. To bring together books separated by size or form;
5. To show that books relate to all aspects of life;
6. To build up public goodwill;
7. To aid students;
8. To impart information;
9. To express and idea;
10. To foster international goodwill;
11. To increase circulation;
12. To show the library's interest in the activities of the community;
13. To elevate reading standards; and
14. To provide colour and variety.

The Library Exhibit: PR Method or Special Event?

It is clear that most library exhibits also have the objectives mentioned in the preceding section. Concerts, films, lectures, programmes, and other events can sometime also be looked at as PR methods. Rice suggests that "a special event is valid only if it attracts a new segment of population to the library or rewards a faithful group of patrons"[38]

In earlier library literature about publicity[6] and about library extension activities[9] lectures, programmes, and other special events were undoubtedly looked upon as methods of making people aware of the library, as well as proving the library's worth. As the concept of public relations entered the library world, writers such as Harrison,[37] Rice[38], and Edsall[39] included exhibits and special events under the umbrella of library public relations.

Public libraries, however, have taken on the character of general cultural arenas, with various activities going on continually: concerts, debates, films, theatre productions, and other events. These may take place in the lending department or in the library auditorium, if there is one. A person responsible for library public relations can easily become submerged in working with cultural events if the boundary between the responsibilities is not defined.

Moreover, if the library's public relations activities are to aim at specific objectives, it is vital that the choice of exhibits and programmes relates to the policy for selecting and buying media space or time. Nowadays, when such events often deal with things other than the library itself another question must always be asked by the person responsible nor library public relations: Should each exhibit and programme be furnished with a booklist and a book display? Such work is very time consuming, but the results may later prove to be useful tools in a difficult selection situation. The existence of well-defined standards or norms for all events (e.g. on booklists and displays) with help the library to say no to some offers, and thus avoid swamping the PR officer in too many exhibits and programmes.

All these cultural activities have been rather common also in large university and national libraries in many countries. Their objectives, naturally, have been to exploit the library resources, to reveal the endless possibilities hidden in the bookstacks. The development, however, has been similar to that in the public libraries. From their original connection with books and authors, special events in research libraries have developed into activities used as public relations methods: "Lunchtime bluegrass at the Library of Congress? Well, why not if it makes the institution seem more open, less forbidding?".

The truth is that the borderline between exhibits and special events used as PR methods and the same things done for their own sake is nearly impossible to draw.

Techniques for Library Displays

The techniques of arranging library displays (and exhibits) are presented in depth in *Library Displays: Their Purpose, Construction and Use.* Also, Borgwardt gives a comprehensive presentation of "practical aspects". Kate Coplan's two books, *Effective Library Exhibits and Poster Ideas and Bulletin Board Techniques*, are still useful works of reference. Kohn and Tepper have useful checklists for making displays, exhibits, and bulletin boards. In most countries books have been published on the techniques used by commercial firms. These should not be neglected by library people.

Libraries have been brought out into the village squares and onto the beaches since the 1950s. The ALA Young Adult Services Division in 1959 published a leaflet called "Blueprint of a Book Show," which mentions measurements and materials to use. The small handbook *Display for Librarians,* written by Hunter, may be regarded as an enlarged and modernized British version of the ALA leaflet.

Library Display as a PR Method

A display telling the library story is an effective public relations method, but it requires a great deal of week: Who will write the text? Who will find or take the pictures? How does one find boards and booths? Who will arrange the display once all the materials are collected? Who will compile the booklist? Or the information brochure? What about costs and time schedule? Every library that uses displays must work with a checklist.

The display can be put outside the library as well as inside. Public libraries have arranged displays at agricultural show, flower shows, trade fairs, etc. Rural libraries have had mobile displays that moved from the community centre to a large store or the sports hall, then to a factory, and from there perhaps back to the community center. Banks, shops, bingo halls, and theatres are also useful places to set up a library display.

Academic libraries have used displays to spread information about their services and have placed them in student cafeterias entrances to the campus, corridors between lecture rooms, student dorms, and lecture halls.

If the library display contains books, it must be easy for people to borrow the books that are shown. A display must arouse an immediate desire to borrow a certain book. If this impulse is just as quickly frustrated, then the library display may not achieve any effect. Preparation of a library display must include arrangements for satisfying the requests that arise from the display. On-the spot loans are easily arranged if the display is outside the library. Informative, short, printed handouts add to its effectiveness.

PRINTED MATERIAL

Printed material is the most commonly used library public relations method. The techniques are so well-known and books presenting ideas for library printed materials and dealing with the graphic arts are so numerous that only examples of literature devoted to academic and special libraries are given there. For example, in lengthy chapters in *Libraries in Higher Education,* Denis Heathcote presents useful hints for library guides, floor plans, and other library publications; and Strauss, Shreve, and Brown suggest ideas for printed materials useful in scientific and technical libraries[25].

Printed material is most effective when used in connection with other methods, but the library literature often suggests that printed matter be distributed by direct mail and bulk mail. Such printed material, sent out once or twice, seldom reaches new users, even though it may inform the people already aware of the library. Nevertheless, libraries seldom can afford the constant flow of advertising that is so common in the commercial world, when it is recognized as a basic part of sales procedures. In general, utilizing the mails to distribute printed matters as library PR material must be regarded as a doubtful approach. One of the few pieces of research on this point is that of Blaise Cronin.

Examples of printed material used as library PR methods are annual reports, booklists, bookmarks, brochures, flyers, library guides, maps, picture postcards, posters, and throwaways. Advertising on commercial outdoor billboards and posters put up in taxicabs, buses, and subway trains are other print forms that are sometimes used.

The Printing Procedure

Photo-offset is the main printing technique used today. Libraries as well as local authorities often have their own printing facilities.

Are colours more effective than just black and white? Several surveys have been done about making type readable. In most ranking lists, black on white is said to give the most readable text. Black on yellow (used commonly on traffic signs) is considered by many researchers to be the best combination for readability at a distance.

It is cheaper to order a large number of copies at one time than to print a second edition later. Generally it is wise to print a large edition, larger than the first estimates may suggest, at the first printing. The product may well be used more than was estimated.

A manuscript for offset reproduction must be carefully read and perfectly finished for printing, before being sent to the printing office. Flyers and throwaways are prepared on an ordinary typewriter with carbon ribbon. Placard letters are useful for headings. Printed material need not be fancy to become effective when handed out after a book talk, or when giving a tour of the library, or when placed next to an exit.

Checklist for Manuscript Preparation

The following list can serve as the basis of a checklist. It would have to be adapted to different routines and norms in different countries.

1. Typewritten manuscript copy to be kept in the library.
2. Left margin at least 6 cm.
3. Type roughly 60 letters per line and 30 lines per page.
4. Use a standard-sized paper.
5. Type only on one side of the paper. Double space.
6. Number the pages. State name of person ordering the matter and the library name (on each page).
7. Spaced-out type is difficult to read. Underline those words which are to be printed in italics.
8. If pictures are to be used, do not write with a ballpoint pen on the reverse as it makes indentations that ruin the picture for reproduction. For the same reason; No Paper-clips on pictures! State whether the pictures should be returned and to whom (name and address).
9. Ask for galley proofs. Have a proof corrections guide at hand.
10. If changes have been made since the first galley proof, read the whole text in the second galley proof. Errors not noticed the first time may now be seen. New errors may have arisen when the first errors were corrected.

Question to Ask

If it is decided to use printed material as a library public relations method, there are many questions to ask, and answer, before the idea is transformed into printed material. For example: Is a single-sheet map of the library more effective than a map in an expensive but more comprehensive library guide? For the same amount of money it may be possible to mass produce a one-page map or print a restricted edition of a library guide. What to choose?

Branches, divisions, and departments ask for posters. Often semi-finished posters will be the best and cheapest solution as the name of the nearest local library easily can be added to the poster, by typing, writing, or some other method.

Other questions include: Are the books mentioned in the booklist easy to buy? The objective of the library public relations activities is to make people aware of the library's resources and also to stimulate an interest in reading. Naturally the library must make it easy for people to decide whether they want to borrow or buy the books.

A bookmark is an inexpensive method for giving information about new books about a certain subject, opening hours, computerized literature searching, bookmobile stops, and other library services. When ordering bookmarks for use in a hospital library there is a further question to be asked: Should the bookmarks be made of plastic so as to be more durable, resistant to stains, etc.?

Problems Concerning Copyright

Nearly all countries have laws of copyright. There are differences in details between countries, but the basic concepts are the same. They imply that authors, artists, etc., have an exclusive right to control the use of their works during a certain period. There are some exceptions to this exclusive right—for instance, as regards coping for personal use and so forth.

Copyright questions are very important in the context of library public relations. People responsible for public relations work should be aware of the provisions on copyright so that they do not use without proper permission works that are protected by copyright. Such use might entail both penalties and claims for compensation.

Those responsible for library public relations should also try to secure copyright on the material produced in this context. In most countries copyright protection is granted without any formalities. In order to obtain protection in the United States and some other countries, however, it is necessary to include a copyright notice in all published copies of a work. The notice consists of three parts, the letter *c* in a circle ©, the year of first publication of the work, and the name of the owner of the copyright.

Files of Library Printed Material

It is wise to keep a permanent file of all printed material issued by a library. In the future these items serve as a source for research and writing or as a catalyst for ideas.

AUDIO-VISUAL MATERIALS AND OTHER PR METHODS

Films and filmstrip productions are used extensively as introductions to a library and in connection with library user education.

The message to be used and the writing of the synopsis (on which the AV production is based) follow the same rules as those already mentioned in connection with "the message," library displays, and the manuscript for printed material. How then can the vitality inherent in a film be best exploited? Too many boring films and filmstrip productions have been used as library information. Unfortunately, little research is done to measure their effects. But AV are very expensive to produce, and therefore extra care has to be taken in planning and producing these materials.

Various other PR items are tried and then discarded. For example, giveaways such as balloons, pencils, etc., are numerous and need no further elaboration.

PLANNING LIBRARY PUBLIC RELATIONS

Library public relations must be a planned performance—this is often said and seldom put into practice. "There is no *lack* of public relations," But "what is actually decried in the literature is the lack of good, positive public relations, the lack of effective, planned communication which can generate understanding and appreciation of good and useful performance."

The universality of the need for planned library public relations is illustrated in an article by Nigerian university librarian Oyeniyi Osundia, who wrote "without well planned and sound public relations, all efforts made in the workrooms are hopelessly fruitless."

Different "battle plans" for library public relations are presented in the library literature—for example, the design of a public relations campaign by McGovern and the "Public Relations Problem Solving Model" developed by Osborn and Meyers. In order to be able to implement such models, all those responsible for any library service must include the information function in their planning at all levels. Thus, when a library is to inaugurate a new branch or division, or buy a data terminal, or transform the catalogue into microfiche, the person responsible for public relations—or the "exploitation department"—ought to be present at the planning meeting.

The consequence of *one* person coordinating all or some of the

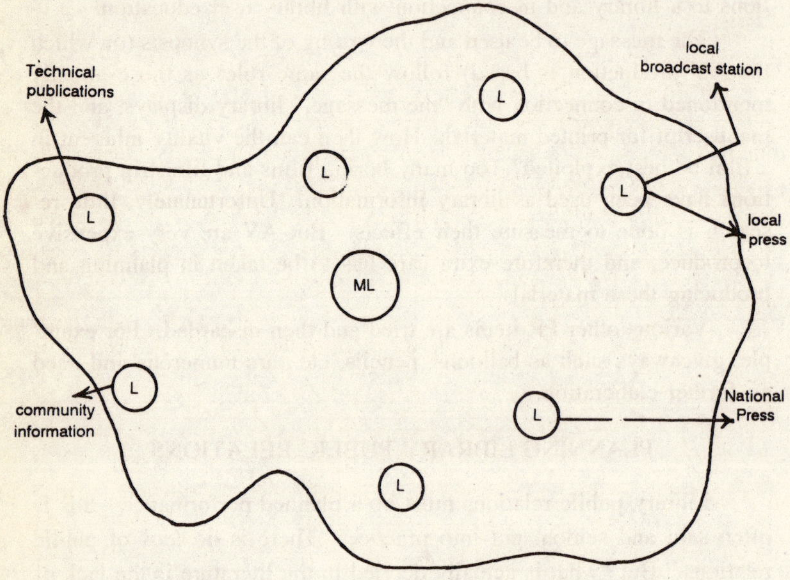

Fig. 9.4. In this model the main library, ML. is rather isolated from other libraries in the same system. Various Libraries (divisions, branches). L, have built up their own mass media contacts, but none contacts the press agencies.

library PR is best illustrated in a model, where the population can be the inhabitants of a community, the users, or the potential users of an academic, special, or school library. Figure 9.4 shows a library system's contact with the news media.

We can thus see that libraries have often utilized library PR but without having one person responsible for it and for coordinating the information function. If someone in the library system in Figure 4 is given the responsibility for library PR (in this case the contacts with the news media), a new model will be created, which is illustrated in Figure 9.5.

Library Public Relations Plans

A PR plan can be both a long-term plan and a short-term plan; it can be implemented on a national or a local basis. There must be a budget plan to serve as the platform for all decisions. The PR plan must also include a control function, and its objectives have to be measurable. Budget planning and fund raising vary from country to country.

The methods mentioned here should each have its individual pro-

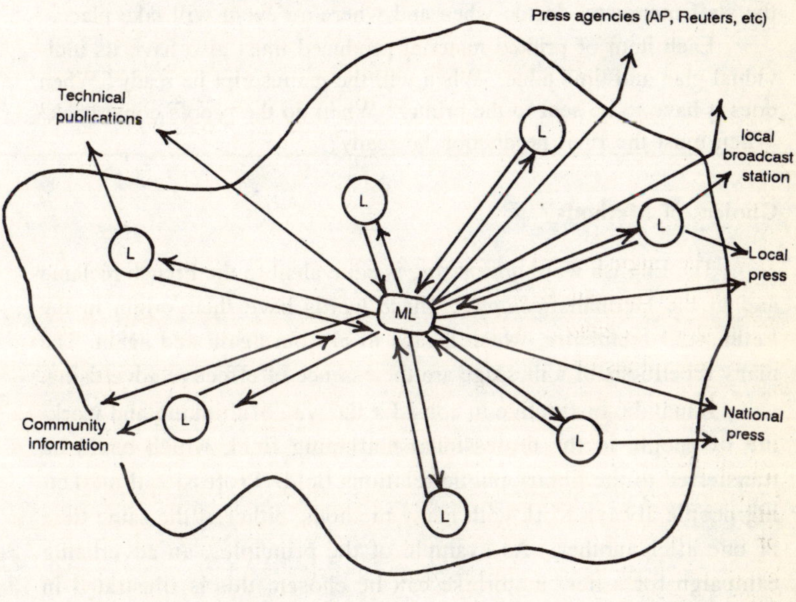

Fig. 9.5. Model with a central PR coordinator. The libraries that earlier had contacts with news media are not prevented from making these contacts, but they send information to the coordinator about their PR work. The coordinator then collects information from the whole system and sends it out again after processing.

duction plan; these and other PR methods used together form the total PR plan. One press release does not make many (if any) new readers.

It is even possible to prepare a rough plan for press releases to be sent out during the forthcoming year. If a library has nothing "new" planned, there are always services and media about which to inform the public. "Old" knowledge is news to many people. Edsall presents many themes useful for publicity[39].

Library talks and library tours can also be a part of a planned activity and spread over the year and between the staff members. As shown in Figure 9.5, the person responsible for library PR should act as a shunting station. The PR programme cannot produce good results if such a coordinator also has to make all the displays and guide all the tours. Every member of a library staff must be able to demonstrate the library and talk about it, but a coordinator should survey the public's interest in talks and tours, and after discussing the matter with the staff members, decide when and where an event will take place.

Each item of printed material produced must also have its individual plan and time table. When will the manuscript be ready? When does it have to be sent to the printer? When do the proofs come back? When must the final production be ready?

Choices of Methods

The English word *advertising* is equivalent to the French réclame and to the German *Reklame*. These words have their origin in the Latin word *reclamare,* which means to cry out again and again. The many repetitions of a message are the essence of effective advertising.

It may be instructive to consider the way of thinking and working of people in the professional marketing field, which could be transferred to the library public relations field. Professional marketing people always work with many methods, either at the same time or one after another. As example of the principles, an advertising campaign for a new motorbike can be chosen; this is illustrated in Figure 9.6.

When the manufacturer wants to promote a new motorbike model, the main target group is people who already own a motorbike. This population (i.e. motorbike owners) consists mainly of men and especially young men. When looking at the number of men and women together, motorbike owners are to be found mainly among the younger people.

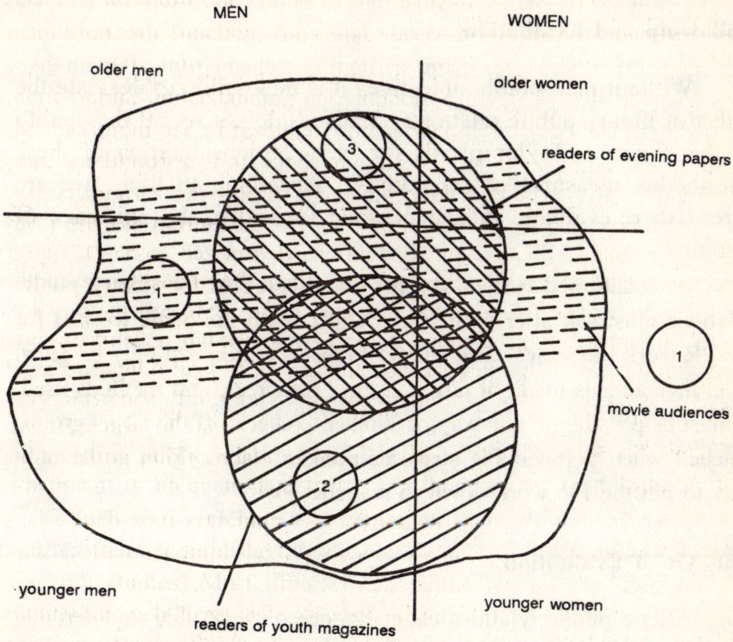

Fig. 9.6 *. Analysis of attempts to reach a potential target group. In this case the target is potential motorbike owners, but this could also be nonusers of the*

Figure 9.6 shows clearly that with each method, the manufacturer contacts new people. The figure also shows that when three methods are used, there are quite a number of people who have been reached by all three methods. Marketing people know that the largest chance that a person will buy a product that they advertise occurs when a person has been contacted many times and with different methods and approaches.

The approach may be cynical, but libraries are to reach their goal of providing alternatives to the commercial world, they must use the same principles and methods, but with other goals in mind. When looking at Figure 9.6 a librarian ought to be able to visualize how, for example, book talks (1) displays (2), and printed material (3) could reach a certain target group, and which people would most probably also become new library users.

Follow-up and Evaluation

Without measurable objectives it is impossible to evaluate the effect of library public relations. Statistics do not reveal the quality of the service. Taylor pleads for "serious consideration of these unorthodox measures of serendipity." According to him, "we are forced to re-evaluate, indeed possible to justify, the existence of libraries".

As mentioned earlier, the person responsible for library public relations must ask after each year: "Did I reach the goals we had for the PR work last year?" The answer to that question can only be given if an inventory is made of target groups, resources, and methods used. It must be possible in one way or another to check off the target groups reached when planned PR steps have taken place. This is the only way to pin the PR work down to realistic goals.

The Art of Evaluation

After a public relations campaign one must be able to determine if the campaign has had some effect. Let us assume that it appears that the PR activities have failed to introduce any new user to the library. What was the reason for the failure? The evaluation process has to consider:

1. *The situation:* What was the problem? Was the aim relevant? For example: The library has informed people about opening hours and where the library is situated. Perhaps the whole population which could use the library knew these facts but had not the faintest idea about what was in the library.
2. *The input:* Which methods were used for the information? What quantity? How was it distributed? For example: The library sent a leaflet to all households. Can the library hope to measure an effect after one direct mailing? Perhaps one book talk would have been a more effective method.
3. *The techniques:* Are there reasons for adjustments or change? For example: What if the printed material used all the old well-known symbols such as the owl of wisdom, the tree of knowledge, and a slogan about how good it is to read books. If people reached by that method have negative attitudes toward libraries, they will not even look at the message.

4. *The result*: What conclusions can be drawn? Even if input and techniques are changed, there may be no effect. Methods may be changed, but still with no effect. Then the person responsible for public relations must go through the checklist again and again until some effect can be shown.

The approach used may have been wrong. Instead of utilizing printed material, perhaps one should go out and talk to people about the library. If that does not give any effect, one must consider: Was the method itself wrong, or was it an uninteresting book talk? Thus, if one can evaluate the book talk as a good one, perhaps the problem was not well enough defined. Perhaps all the books talked about had already been read.

As soon as a campaign is shown to lack the desired result, one must begin a review. Were the techniques right? Was the input appropriate? Was the aim relevant? Somewhere along the line something was not well planned or implemented. This may seem a very unscientific approach, but there are many researchers who could verify the value of this subjective approach to evaluation, and could verify that it gives some trends about the effect of unmeasurable factors. Life is filled with such evaluations, more or less thoroughly considered. People evaluate people. Listeners evaluate lectures. Readers evaluate books. There is more value in this kind of evaluation than is often recognized.

In the commercial world there are a number of mnemonic rules for evaluating a method for advertising —for example, the AIDA formula:

A stands for Attention;
I stands for Interest;
D stands for Desire; and
A stands for Action.

A later formula has added *S*. for Satisfaction.

Few tests have been made of the effectiveness of library public relations methods, and they certainly are needed. It is not sufficient that people have seen a leaflet, or listened to a talk, or joined a library walk. Did the people involved also do something: visit the library, use it, read a book?

Some minor surveys reported in master's research theses and similar works have tried to measure the *attention value* of a given item of information and its memory value; that is, whether people have remembered the information. There have also been minor surveys measuring the success of various methods in bringing new users to the library.

There is a great need of more knowledge about the evaluation of different library PR methods, so that they can be used more efficiently. In fact, the overall goal—a more thorough exploitation of library resources—is still nearly as far away as at the time that Ranganathn's Five Laws of Library Science were formulated.

One of the many reasons that this situation is still so bad in most countries seems to be that the persons responsible for library public relations seldom have sufficient time or support from the chief librarian, committee, or board to carry out a programme of planning, evaluation, and follow-up.

TASKS FOR THE PERSONS RESPONSIBLE FOR LIBRARY PUBLIC RELATIONS

It is not enough to budget for library public relations and hire a PR office, as is sometimes done in large library systems. The library board or committee must give the public relations person the chance to fulfill his or her task. No matter who is directly responsible for public relations, it is important that the member of the staff should also be allowed to attend board or committee meetings.

The job expectations of a full-time or part-time public relations director have been suggested already in *Local Public Library Administration.* Fontaine has registered some "specific public relations concerns cited by most directors and public relations/community relations officers" in the United States. This article closes with an attempt to summarize the tasks included in the PR function, based on empirical experiences:

1. Take responsibility for the PR budget;
2. Analyze moods in the library and attitudes toward the library;
3. Plan and coordinate external and internal information;
4. Maintain contact with news media;
5. Take responsibility for the library's printed materials;
6. Plan and coordinate study visits and library tours;
7. Edit the staff bulletin;
8. Inspire members of the staff to plan and give book talks;
9. Function as consultant for the library displays;

10. Suggest ideas and seek new ideas for developing suitable communication channels, both from the staff to the library management and to the staff from that management;
11. Initiate and promote research and development work relating to PR; and
12. Promote understanding of the role of the information function in the library organization.

REFERENCES

1. Howard Stephenson, *Handbook of Public Relations.* McGraw-Hill. New York, 1990.
2. Samuel S. Green, "Personal Relations between Librarian and Readers." *Am. Lib., J.* 1. 74-81, November 30, 1876.
3. Janis Joann Blair, "From Advertising to Library Interpretation: The Development of Public Relations in the American Public Library." Unpublished master's thesis. Kent State University. 1966.
4. Greta Linder, "Biblioteksreklam." *Bibliotekshladt* 4-5 242-257 (1917).
5. Joseph L. Wheeler, The *Library and the Community.* American Library Association. Chiago, 1924.
6. Lionel McColvin, *Library Extension Work and Publicity*. Grafton, London,1927.
7. Gilbert O. Ward, *Publicity for Public Libraries,* 2nd ed. H. W. Wilson, New York, 1935.
8. E.W. McDiarmid and John McDoarmid, *The Administration of the American Public Library*. American Library Association and University of Ilinois Press, Chicago, 1943.
9. Harold Joliffe, *Public Library Extension Activities*. The Library Association, London, 1962.
10. Irene M. Strieby, "Checklist of Media and Techniques for Public Relations Activities in special Libraries." *Lib Trends* 7(2), 290-297 (October 1958).
11. Martha Höhl. *Buchereiwerbung*. Druckschriften der Arbeitstelle für des Buchereiwesen 4, Deutscher Büchereiverhand. Berlin 1964.
12. A.R. Haygarth Jackson, "Publicity or Selling the Information service." *Aslib Proc.* 25, 385-388 (1973).
13. P.O.N. Hoey, "Public Relations; The Soft Sell," *Aslib Proc.* 25, 375-380 (1973).
14. Anthony Thompson, *Vocubularium Bibliothecarii*, 2nd UNESCO,

Bruges, Belgium, 1962.

15. Bob Usherwood, "Library Public Relations: An Introduction," in *Studies in Library Management*, Clive Bingley, London, 1972-1974. Vol. 2, pp. 115-133.
16. Bob Usherwood, *The Visible Library*. The Library Association, London, 1981.
17. Greta Renborg, "Public Relations Activities for the Stockholm City Library," *Scand Public Lib. Q.* 1, 1-13 (1970).
18. Christine Oldman, "Marketing Library and Information Services" *Eur J. Marketing*, 11(6), 460-474 (1977).
19. D.A. Yorke, *Marketing the Library Service*, The Library Association, London, 1977 (pamphlet).
20. Cosette Kies, *Problems in Library Public Relations*. R.R. Bowker, New York, London, 1974, 179 pp.
21. Arthur Jones, "Criteria for the Evaluation of Public Library Services" *J. Librarianship*, 2(4), 228 (October 1970).
22. "Unesco Public Library Manifesto," in *Standards for Public Libraries*, IFLA Publication 9, Verlag Dokumentation, Munich,1977, pp 13-16.
23. *Approaches to Measuring Library Effectiveness: A Symposium: School of Library Science* (Allan F. Heersfield and Morell D. Boone, eds.), Frontiers of Librarianship 14, University of Syracuse Press. Syracuse, N.Y., 1972.
24. P.H. Sewell, "The Evaluation of Library Services in Depth," *UNESCO Bull. Lib.* 22(6) 274- (November-December 1968).
25. Lucille J. Strauss, Irene M. Shreve, and Alberta L. Brown, *Scientific and Technical Libraries: Their Organization and Administration*. 2nd ed. Becker and Hays, New York, 1972.
26. Joseph L. Wheeler and H. Goldhor, *Practical Administration of Public Libraries*, Harper and Row, New York, 1962.
27. Greta Renborg, *Bibliotekens PR-och knotaktarbete*, Biblioteksjänst, Lund, 1977.
28. Kate Coplan and Edwın Castagna, The Library Raáches Out. Oceana Publications, New York, 1965.
29. Eleanor Phinney, *Library Adult Education in Action*. American Library Association, Chicago, 1956.
30. Brita Olsson, "Bogpraesentation." *Bogens Verden* 4. 169-174 (1960).
31. Greta Renborg. *Det uppsökande biblioteket. Biblioteksjänst.* Lund. 1963
32. Margaret E. Monoroe, comp., *Course outline for L.S 610:578 Reader*

Services, Graduate School of Library Science, Rutgers State University.

33. Marie Loizeaux, *The Publicity Primer,* 4th ed. H.W Wilson, New York, 1959: reprinted 1967.

34. Virginia Baeckler, *PR for Pepnnies: Low-cost Library Public Relations,* Sources, Hopewell, N.J. 1978.

35. Vivienne Ellis, *Lively Libraries*, Australian Library Promotion Council, Melbourne, 1975.

36. Joni Bodart, *Booktalk*! H.W. Wilson, New York, 1980.

37. Kenneth Cecil Harrison, *Public Relations for Librarians,* Andre Deutsch. A Grafton Book, London, 1973.

38. Betty Rice, *Public Relations for Public Libraries*, H.W.Wilson, New York, 1972.

39. Marian S. Edsall, *Library Promotion Handbook*. Oryx Press, Phoenix Ariz Mansell, London, 1980.

40. Mona Garvey, *Library Public Relations,* H.W Wilson, New York, 1980.

41. Roy E. Schumacher, *Public Information and the Library*. Missouri State Library, Jefferson City, n.d.

42. Sarah Leslie Wallace *Promotion Ideas for Public Libraries*, American Library Association, Chicago, 1953.

10

Public Relations Beginnings in Britain

"PUBLIC relations in British Libraries (like the British law code) is largely instinctive and hardly visible." It seems appropriate to begin with a quotation, an article in which so much of the thinking is borrowed from other people. The initial comment is from a letter by R.J. Collison, librarian of the British Broadcasting Company; the article as a whole stands on a framework of facts (but not necessarily opinions) taken from L.R. McColvin's *The Chance to Read.*[1] For the rest, there will be some acknowledgments in the next and others remembered though not mentioned, excepting Eric Moon, now librarian of Newfoundland, who has helped with this article in more ways than self-esteem will permit remembering.

Great Britain would fit comfortably—or at least, easily— into the state of Oregon. The territory is small, the population relatively homogeneous, and the tendency to read well-established in a country which publishes close to twenty thousand titles a years. These circumstances do much to explain the principal sources of pride in the British public library service—for example, the completeness of coverage. Some kind of public library service reaches everyone in Great Britain, except the 30,000 people who live in a Welsh town called Mountain Ash and enjoy a peculiarly Welsh kind of anachronism called a miner's institute.

The total circulation of books from all British public libraries in a given year is roughly the same as in the United States, with less than a third of America's population. Moreover, the circulation of the average city library in England has risen by about a quarter since 1939, and the over-all increase is 56 per cent; in American cities, the increase over the same nine years has been about 5 per cent.

It would be foolish and invidious to suggest that the happier aspects of British librarianship are the products solely of territorial and social conditions, but certainly they have been achieved less painfully than they will be in America. This is particularly true of the national inter-loan scheme. Through the use of union catalogues in regional bureaus, the National Central Library for Science and Technology, something like half a million books a year are mailed from libraries that have them to libraries that need them for individual readers. Almost all public and many non-public libraries cooperate in this scheme, making their book collections available to people all over the country and even overseas. This will come in America; it has already been proposed,[2] but it cannot come easily.

All public libraries in England are supported by local taxation. They are administered by committees appointed from their own number by local government authorities. The local government authority is the town or country council, which is an elected body. There is at the time of writing (March 1958) no intervention and no financial aid from the national government. However, the minister of education has appointed a committee to study the service and some kind of national government support is a possible but unlikely outcome.

To American librarians, the majority of whom work inside the same kind of administrative structure, and who in general realize that the value and indeed, the existence of a library depends on public interest and support, it must seem criminally wrong that in England public relations is "hardly visible." It is, but there are extenuating circumstances.

The British have been called reserved, phlegmatic, shy, and much else more frankly disagreeable. They are people like any other and generalizations fit them no more comfortably. It is a fact however that individualism dies hard in England, and the British for this reason or through arrogance resent attempts to organize and improve them. This may be a factor in the failure of librarians there to use extensively the techniques of persuasion. If that is so, it is likely to be a temporary factor. Richard Hoggart has charted the spread of mass mediocracy in his gloomy and fascinating book *The Uses of Literacy*.[3]

A better excuse for the near-invisibility of public relations in British libraries can be found in the combination of elements produced by library staffing patterns and library education. British libraries are hopelessly understaffed. In terms of statistics, each staff member is responsible for the circulation of about twice as many books as his American counterpart. This is particularly obvious at administrative an professional levels, where totally inadequate staffing budgets have created an artificial surplus of qualified librarians. Since clerks and pages are not generally employed, the surplus of qualified librarians is absorbed in work which would be done as successfully by an intelligent horse. Under such pressures, the long-term advantages of a public relations programme calculated to ease these conditions are easily overlooked.

Professional education in England does little more to encourage the kind of social awareness that is a prerequisite of the public relations sense. The School of Librarianship at London University provides a postgraduate course similar in intention to the standard American professional education. For the nongraduate majority. the progression is this: bookish children from the kind of high schools dedicated to the humanities, untouched by the world, eyes turned unwaveringly inward, creep chrysaloid into a predicament where people are an inescapable fact. After some months, if they have not given up, they change one night into little librarians. Before their wings are dry, they are persuaded to abandon their evenings to study.

After a year or so, they sit fir the Library Association's First Professional Examination, which investigates their potential and acts as a warning. If and when they are successful in this, they are confronted with the Registration Examination. This, together with three years approved library experience, brings the title Associate of the Library Association and election to the register of qualified librarians.

Study for the Registration Examination may be undertaken as a sort of hobby at evening classes or by correspondence courses, or with lick after only a year's study at one of the nine full-time library schools which have opened since the last war. In all professional examinations the Library Association, not the school, is the examining body.

Seven subjects are studied for the Registration Examination.[4] One of them is English literary history, or the literature of science or of sociology. All the rest are concerned with techniques: cataloguing, classification, administrative processes, library law, reader guidance, and what have you.

The librarian is now, in theory, ready for anything the profession has to offer. In fact, he is likely to be a first assistant or branch librarian, earning between $1500 and $2000 a year, and still liable to find himself anchored to the circulation desk or shelving books. Next, he may try for the Library Association Fellowship.

The Final or Fellowship Examination is generally required of applicants for senior positions. It covers roughly the same ground as the Registration Examination, but digs deeper.[5] The subjects involved are bibliography and book selection; library organization and administration; the literature and librarianship of a special subject; and one of a motley collection of possibilities, including work with children, advanced cataloguing, and the literature, God save us all, of Wales.

Exhibit work, the production of book lists and bulletins, and being nice to readers are appearing more frequently in various interstices of the syllabus. The full-time library schools go further, transcending the syllabus to preach a senses of professional direction. But at this breaking instant the L.A. examinations are doing little more to expose British librarians to the public relations idea than the *London Times* does to introduce its readers to sex.

The British public library service may be conservatively described as one of the finest in the world; it would be perverse not to acknowledge this but complacent to overlook the fact that it remains seriously inadequate. Having suggested reasons for the retarded emergence of public relations techniques, it is necessary to show that these are sorely needed.

Standards of library service vary in England from the excellent to the appalling. The inadequacy of staffing patterns has already been mentioned, and this is reflected most clearly where relations with the public are the least satisfactory. Building are almost universally inadequate, and too many country towns conceal in some forgotten back street a mouldering librarian guarding a mouldering book collection in dubious tribute to Andrew Carnegie. The over-burdened national interloan scheme, described above as a source of pride, offers from another point of view a commentary on the weakness of local provision. The public will never regard a library service as satisfactory until it can provide all but the most esoteric material from stock and immediately; sooner or later librarians will have to acknowledge the justice of these demands.

Where there is poor library service there is either a poor Librarian or not enough money. Moreover, poor librarians beget poor budgets and vice versa. Of the 577 independent British library systems, 167 spend less than $15,000 a year and 45 spend less than $3,000. A partial answer is legislation to insure that areas served are big enough to support an adequate public library, and the minister of education's committee is likely to be especially concerned with this possibility.

However, irrespective of the size of the community served, so long as the extent of public library financial support is a matter for local decision, the only final solution is to show that good library service is essential.

It would be unfair to leave the impression that the evangelical necessity has been totally disregarded. It is, as Collison says, "largely instinctive" and "hardly visible" but it is not negligible.

Annual reports, book lists, bulletins, and exhibits are produced which both in quality and proportionate quantity stand comparison with the American output. Generally, in spite of circumstances and horrible examples to the contrary, library staffs are tolerably well-mannered. These are the things which are, or are becoming, "largely instinctive." On the other hand, very little attempt is made to reach people who are not library users, and virtually nothing is done on a national scale to promote public esteem for libraries and librarians.

"There's nothing sensational about sound librarianship—not a thing, indeed, that's newsworthy." This quotation from S.C. Holliday's *The Reader and the Bookish Manner*[6] is a fair summary of the British librarian's approach to his work. Where a library has progressed past this point, its librarian is ahead of his time. Such men exist, and notably W. Best Harris, Librarian of Plymouth.

Plymouth is a city in western England, with a population of about a quarter of a million. For many years, it was chiefly notable for spending less on its library services than any other authority of comparable standing. During the bombing in 1941, its central Library and one branch were destroyed. In an address to a branch of the L.A., Harris described the public relations programme he devised to meet this unpromising situation when he went to Plymouth in 1946. This programme is revolutionary by British standards, and embodies features which are far from commonplace in America. An example is the great stress placed on public relations work directed at members of the local Council.

In a personal interview with, or letter to, each new City Councillor, the library's facilities are put at his disposal to help in the preparation of speeches. Photographs, slides, and film-strips illustrating the work of all city departments are prepared along with descriptive notes and used extensively by city officials and politicians. Harris makes it his business to know personally every member of the Council, and uses the constant publicity which the library receives to attract the most able Councillors onto the Library Committee.

More conventional public relations tactics used in Plymouth include exhibits in local factories and the headquarters of social, professional, and political groups, talks to these groups, and book lists devoted to their special subjects. Conversely, such organizations are encouraged to visit the Central Library for talks on its use. Harris has spoken on the B.B.C. twenty-four times in five years, which must be the British record for that medium, and a western regional television programme has been devoted to the work of the library. It is understood that Plymouth's relations with the press have reached a point where local journalists present themselves at the librarian's office for a weekly conference.

Since 1946, Plymouth has built a superb new central library, and its annual expenditure on libraries has risen from $36,000 to $240,000. In a letter, Harris says: "I attribute this story of increase entirely to Public Relations."

While it is certain that no other British public library has developed a public relation programme along such classic lines or (Liverpool perhaps excepted) with such effect, Plymouth is not along. Many public libraries are experimenting with some aspects of public relations work, as, for example, in the field of special services to business and industry. Several of the major industrial cities provide such services and the L.A. is organizing a number of cooperative schemes, beginning with one to be based on Newcastle, in which public and nonpublic libraries will offer a joint information service to these special publics. A similar project, CICRIS, is already functioning in West London.

Children form another special public which is, rather remarkable, receiving special attention. In theory, children have for a long time been recognized as "the readers of the future", but they do not pay taxes and in England, seldom bully librarians or threaten Council members. It is possible for this reason that, with so much to do and so little to do it with, work with children has been neglected by library administrators, and work with teen-agers as such ignored. A common arrangement is for a single qualified but underpaid children's librarian to supervise the central library's junior collection and to guide by remote control the junior assistants placed in charge of branch collections. In general, it has been in spite of administrative disinterest that a tradition has begun to grow of story-hours, children's book weeks, library visits by and to school classes, and related forms of collaboration with teacher-librarians. Moreover, the children's librarians have come to exert more influence than any other members of the professions on publishers, authors, educators and through PTA's and similar groups, society at large.

This achievement can be explained only in terms of the extraordinary devotion of those who work with children, but a contributing factor has been suggested by Joan Butler, organizer of work with young people in Hertfordshire County. Miss Butler points out in a letter that, while there is no shortage of authorities on adult literature, children's librarians on adult literature, children's librarians are virtually the only people qualified to assess the literary and other merits of juvenile books, a fact which is recognized by the book trade, the press, and the public. The value placed by authors and publishers on the Library Association's Carnegie and Kate Greenaway awards is an obvious example of the book trade's general concern with the professional judgment of children's librarians.

It was noted above that the over-all circulation of British public libraries has increased by 56 per cent since 1939, but by only 26 per cent in city libraries. Before considering nonpublic libraries, some comment should be made on the rural library service, the rapid growth of which explains these statistics. The county libraries which serve the rural areas were not established until 1920. To the usual geographic problems of this kind of library provision was added the historical disadvantage of late development, and until about ten years ago, the county libraries deserved their reputation as poor relations of the municipal systems. Acknowledging exceptions, this is no longer true, and it is an interesting possibility that the growth and vitality of the county libraries can be attributed to a kind of unconscious public relations process. Miss Butler, already quoted on a different theme, says this:

"The counties . . . were given few staff and fewer buildings and were told to introduce books into the villages of the country through the schools, church groups, clubs, Women's Institutes and other such organizations with the active help and co-operation of the local people . . . these early planners planned more wisely than they knew or then a later generation is always prepared to give them credit for, for the seed of infinite growth was in that instruction to serve the community through those organizations which were an accepted part of its life or which had been formed by the people themselves.8 "Instinctive" or merely accidental, this blueprint for a library service also describes a public relations process.

Very little has appeared in print about public relations in non-public libraries. The comments that follow are therefore based for the most part on correspondence with librarians in the non-public fields. Nothing emerged more clearly from this correspondence than the inadvisability of generalizations.

The librarian of the Bodleian Library pointed out that his library's academic reputation attracts scholars from all over the world. "The problem is . . . to make sure that its working space is not filled up by those not qualified to use it. . . ." On the other hand, an organization called the Friends of the Bolderian has been in existence for over thirty years, and there are already six hundred members of a more recent group, Bodley's American Friends. The primarily economic value of such bodies, obvious to American librarians, has still not been recognized in British public libraries.

Nor would it be recognized by the librarian of London University's Institute of Education, D.J Foskett. "The public library. . . has to convince people that its existence is necessary. . . . The situation is different from that in America, where the salesman is the national hero, and, if you have only ideas to sell instead of objects, you sometimes call your salesman public relations officers . . . the university and special library does not really have to do much to advertise itself, since it is established to provide something that people want. "However, Foskett goes on to mention as fairly common practice the routing of fugitive material to its pursuers, the related technique of abstracting, the use of exhibits, and introductory tours of the library.

Recent developments in British school libraries, as in the county libraries, owe a great deal to studies fostered by the Carnegie United Kingdom Trust, which led in the middle 1930's to the establishment of specialized professional associations and part-time training for teacher-librarians. Fresh impetus was provided in the 1944 Education Act, and, by 1950, the Ministry of Education recognized that "The library should be the centre of the intellectual life of the school, available at all times reference, for study and for private reading."[9]

Private institutions excepted, schools and their libraries are provided by county authorities rather than by individual municipalities. The libraries are generally supervised by teachers, but in some cases by professional librarians. School and public librarians obviously have much to offer each other, and it is in the development of cooperation between them that public relations most usefully serves school librarians. This is widely recognized, and implicit in the various forms of collaboration already mentioned in terms of public library work with children. Again, most of what has already been said about the influence of children's librarians on publishing standards applies equally to school librarians, whose expanding budgets provide an important market not only for text books but for entertainment and background reading. How much the increased use of school libraries is attributable to increased provision and a changing educational philosophy, and how much to internal public relations, the present writer is not qualified to judge. However, it seems clear that where internal public relations are practiced, it is a matter of personal decision on the part of the librarian, rather than a developed policy of the county education authority. It seems relevant here to quote the case of the London County Council, which three years ago raised its annual grant to school libraries from an average $42,000 to $390,000. S. Richards, the Council's press officer, attributes this remarkable increase not to a public relations programme, but to a general realization on the part of Council members, taxpayers, and teachers that books are important. In his latter he adds, however, "that the democratic method of local government administration . . . could (and in my personal view undoubtedly should) itself be regarded as a piece of public relations machinery."

The status of the public relations idea in British special libraries varies as wildly as it does in the public libraries and is complicated by differences in the organizational structure and terms of reference of individual special libraries. The subject demands a separate article.

Two kinds of government library can be distinguished. The British Museum, the National Libraries of Scotland and Wales, the Science Library, and the Patent Office are in approximately the position of the Bodleian—the problem is not how to attract readers to them, but how to impose reasonable limits on their use. (This is in itself a public relations problem, through it may not be recognized as such by the guardians of these institutions). The government libraries attached to individual ministries are a different case, existing almost entirely for the benefit of government officials. According to K.A. Mallaber, librarian of the Board of Trade, internal public relations are practised in such libraries. He specifically refers to the circulation of bibliographies, recent additions lists and guides to the service, and to introductory and refresher courses on library use. In these courses, individual attention is given to those officials who constitute a cadet corps and will eventually form an administrative elite. Mallaber adds that good library service is the most effective form of public relations, a truism which bears repeating.

Preceding articles in this issue examine various aspects of American library public relations in sequence; this essay has attempted to provide a microcosmic view of British practice in the same sequence. Perseverance in this policy brings it unwillingly to a consideration of the position of the L.A., a body which it is hard to view as anything but the villain of this particular piece.

The L.A., was founded in 1877 and received its Royal Charter in 1898. It provides for the examination and registration of qualified librarians, it "holds meetings and conferences, collects and publishes information on library services, maintains an information bureau and library, organizes research into various fields of library study, and generally affords machinery for united action when this is desirable and for the exchange of ideas."[10] Regional interests are represented on the L.A. Council by the branches, as: London and Home Counties Branch, Northern Branch, Welsh Branch, etc. Different kinds of libraries are represented on the Council by the sections, as: Youth Section, County Libraries Section, Reference and Special Libraries Section. There is at present no sectional representation of municipal public libraries. The largest and most influential section is the Association of Assistant Librarians, which represents a kind of librarian rather than a kind of library, and is regarded by some as an unfortunate example of cross-classification.

Among its officers, the L.A. enjoys the services of a publications officer, an education officer, and a librarian and information officer. None of these men is or could be considered a public relations practitioner. This is a pity, since for the majority of its members the L.A. lacks charm, and for the outside world it lacks a voice.

The Association of Assistant Librarians represents the younger and/or livelier members of the profession. Through its meetings and its literature it has, for the past five years or so, persistently campaigned against the parent body's public nonrelative. In 1956, it submitted to the L.A. Council a memorandum written by Eric Moon, its secretary at that time, on the need for a public relations officer. The body of the memorandum was concerned with illustrations of the L.A.'s "superbly inadequate" communication with members, and its nearly complete disregard of the outside world. Indeed, the deliberations of the Council have seemed on occasion, such as immediately before an annual general meeting, to have been wrapped in a Gothic twilight, from which emerges, as it were, a manifesto nailed flapping to the church door at midnight. This is not satisfactory, and the L.A.'s external public relations are worse. There is unhappily not space here to quote all the inefficacious listed in Moon's memorandum, but two examples will serve.

Some years ago, F. Wertham's *Seduction of the Innocent*[11] roused parents to the dangers of "horror-comics." Educators, psychologists, and parents publicly stated and repeated that the provision of good reading was the surest defense. The L.A. maintained a dignified silence.

In 1955, a large-scale newspaper strike sent people back to books; library membership and use soared. Finding the L.A. puzzled and inert in the face of media interest in this phenomenon, it was suggested a modest public relations programme to exploit the situation. The answer was that "this kind of opportunism was not considered desirable."

The L.A. still does not have a public relations officer, but the Association of Assistant Librarian, memorandum precipitated a L.A. sub-committee for what might be called passive public relations. That is, it is supposed to meet criticism but has no authority to institute an active campaign. To the difficulties inherent in a committee approach to the problem is added the fact that this particular committee has hardly ever met. So far it has accomplished nothing whatsoever. A more positive development was the institution of the monthly *Liaison,* under Moon's editorship, as an enclosure of the *Library Association Record* to carry professional news. There is already some discussion of publishing the Association's official announcements in a fortnightly

"Liaison" and relegating the *Record* to the position of a scholarly quarterly.

The L.A.'s familiar ostrich position is both vulnerable and inelegant, and the A.A.L. has not been alone in its attacks or in its more constructive suggestions for improvement. Some of the most valuable national level public relations projects have been instigated and, in most cases, carried through by the London and Home Counties Branch under its secretary, Norman Tomlinson, librarian of Gillingham. Most public librarians are members of the National Association of Local Government Officers, and Tomlinson has been active in promoting the union's interest in librarians and vice versa. He, moreover, is having increasing success in persuading publishers to reprint unavailable but important books, by measuring and guaranteeing their potential market with library purchasers. Finally, the London and Home Counties Branch has suggested that the L.A.'s Annual Conference should be made the occasion of a National Library Week. It is understood that this project is under consideration for a first attempt next year.

Distressing as it is that this kind of development is never initiated by the L.A. Council itself, the activity of some of its branches and sections seems to offer grounds for optimism. Moreover, the lack of any clear distinction between professional and clerical duties is under attack; the eventual separation of these functions will give librarians more time for librarianship and a gradual increase in the status of the profession. Finally, the full-time library school are providing, materials for a philosophy of librarianship.

Any significant change in professional direction emerges first as a *fait accompli* in the work of a few individuals. Professional discussion becomes obsessed with it. It is opposed by an old guard but, where there is enlightened teaching, it is absorbed as an article of faith by the student body. As this group achieves maturity and authority, the idea passes from discussion into general practice. The public relations idea in British librarianship is already developing past discussion, and it is difficult to see how the process could be reversed. It will change the face of library work in England as completely as did that other American import, open access, fifty years ago.

REFERENCES

1. L.R. McColvin, *The Chance to Read: Public Libraries in the World Today*. London, Phoenix House, 1956.

2. American Library Association, *Public Library Service: A Guide to Evaluation, with Minimum Standards.* Chicago, The Association, 1956, p. 19.
3. R. Hoggart, *The Uses of Literacy.* London, Chatto and Windus, 1957.
4. The Library Association, *Year Book.* London, The Association, 1957, pp. 11-13.
5. *Ibid.,* pp. 13-26.
6. S.C. Holliday, *The Reader and the Bookish Manner.* London, Association of Assistant Librarians, 1953, p. 51.
7. W.B. Harris, Public Relations. *The Librarian and Book World,* 46: 61-65, April 1957.
8. Joan Butler, Public Library Provision for Children . . . County Libraries. *In*: The Library Association. *Education, Libraries and the Use of Books,* Callingham, England, The Association, 1957, p. 15.
9. H.R. Mainwood, School Libraries. *In*: The Library Association, *ibid.,* p. 5.
10. McColvin, *op. cit.,* p. 50.
11. F. Wertham, *Seduction of the Innocent.* New York, Rinehart, 1952.

11

Library Objectives and Community Needs

THE MANY statements of public library objectives, of a general nature or related to a specific library, are variations or extensions of Leigh's statement in *The Public Library in the United States,* that the objective of public library development is "to serve the community as a general center of reliable information and to provide opportunity and encouragement for people of all ages to educate themselves continuously."[1] Margaret Monroe, studying three library systems that had long maintained vigorous programmes of library adult education, found that the "thread of philosophy which ran through the thinking about library adult education for this period of thirty-five years [1920-1955] was that public librarianship had a responsibility to stimulate and guide the community to use of the library's materials for the best growth of individual in terms of his needs and interests and for the well-being of society as a whole."[2]

"Stimulate and guide" is only another way of expressing Leigh's "provide opportunity and encouragement," but Monroe states two ideas that Leigh at best implies, that of individual growth concerned with individual needs and interests, and that of the welfare of society, both being seen as purposes for the use of library materials. Such bold concepts involving value judgments (in the case of the second one presumably made by librarian) might have been expected to rouse controversy, but they have been little questioned. Those members of the profession who look with suspicion on such goals have rarely objected in print.

Librarians have interpreted these purposes differently through the years, however, Robert E. Lee has noted that "The most common educational services provided by public libraries between 1850 and 1964 were direct toward five specific educational goals. Two of these goals, civic enlightenment and personal development, remain constant throughout this period. Moral betterment was a goal from around 1850 to 1890, vocational improvement a major goal during the years between 1930 and 1950, and community development of major concern from 1957 to 1964."[3]

Determining the needs and interests of individual library users in order to guide and stimulate them to their "best growth" is an inherent function of every situation in which the librarian deals with the patron. Lee points out, however, that concern for the potential user developed before the turn of the century.[4] To determine the needs and interests of people unknown to the librarian, and to select materials and plan services with community development as the goal, clearly require community study.

A guide to such community study as the basis for the development of adult education activities in public libraries was developed as part of the American Library Association's Library-Community Project, 1955-60.[5] In response to an inquiry[6] sent in 1967 to seventy-two public libraries, to which fifty-one responded, the majority of the respondents, from libraries of varying sizes and wide geographic distribution, indicated the existence since 1954 of a turned in their libraries from "sketchy knowledge of the community to systematic study of the library's relationship to the community." An explanatory note defined this as "the need to know more precisely what the educational needs of the community are. There is a trend toward making a systematic study of the community to find out needs, interests, and resources."

In order to determine the validity of the assumption that public librarians accept the responsibilities stated in the goals and purposes quoted above, and base their materials selection and services on a knowledge of their communities, it would be necessary to study every aspect of their services, especially services to adults whose needs and interests are so varied and difficult to determine. An examination, admittedly limited, of services to groups can indicate only the degree to which these activities seem to be based on generally accepted library objectives.

An overwhelming majority of librarians who responded to the questionnaire[6] sent out by several authors of papers in an issue of *Library Trends* reported that they identified and planned to meet the needs of community groups through assistance in programme planning, library representation on coordinating councils, contacts with community coordinators, and staff membership in organizations. A smaller but significant member reported seeking advice of representatives of various socio-economic groups, and using direct mailings.

The most frequently reported services regularly provided for community agencies and organizations were compilation of booklists, provision of meeting room facilities, assistance in programme planning, and exhibition of materials. Also reported by well over half of the respondents were compilation of a directory of clubs and organizations, cosponsorship of programmes with community organizations, and provision for film previewing.[6]

The most frequently reported activity offered as part of the library's own programming was the presentation of book reviews and book talks, followed by instruction in use of the library, discussion groups on special subjects or issues, film discussion groups, and listening groups (music, poetry, drama, etc.).

Many of the respondents accompanied their replies with brochures, announcements, programmes, evaluative reports and materials lists prepared for use in group activities. Although material covering the last five years was asked for, most of that sent was dated 1966-67. Without question such materials reflect only a portion of each library's service to groups.

A survey of the literature from 1955 to 1965 yields very little description of public library service to groups to use as an indication of possible changes or trends in the goals such activities serve. World affairs discussion groups, programme planning institutes, a few programmes based on labour materials, and a large (in 1955) but diminishing number of activities for or concerned with the aging constitute the bulk of the roster. Therefore, the materials available for this chapter are as useful a source of information as is available.

Examination of them indicates that libraries are concerned with excellence. The selection of materials used in these activities is clearly based on high standards of quality. The day of the noon-day review of the latest joke-studded autobiography or action-packed romance seems to be over. The travel films of the "into-the-sunset" variety have been superseded by more significant materials. Librarians are taking seriously their responsibility for value, as they see it.

Three different bases for developing group activities are discernible. One is the material itself, another national or world-wide concerns, and the third the special needs and interests of the individual community.

The use of material as a base is the most prevalent. From one end of the county to the other the same titles of books and films appear. In library after library a group has toured the Louvre with Charles Boyer[7] and shared the problems of people of Latin America in *Child of Darkness, Child of Light.*[8] Bishop Pike's *You and the New Morality*[9] has appeared on lists, been reviewed, and been discussed by a group in the library, at an organization meeting, or on radio or TV. Fiction rarely seems to be considered an adequate base for such programming.

Usually where these current materials are used in a series of talks or discussions, no connecting thread among the sessions is evident. Obviously, the series is based on available materials that the librarian considers important. The goal, evidently, is to acquaint people with the best of the current output, and in some cases may simply be to entertain, or to bring people to the library. One library labels its film showings ''Informative Film Entertainment.''

To guide and stimulate people to consider matters of national or world-wide significance is a goal that is reflected in a somewhat smaller number of activities. Lists of materials, prepared for general distribution or often for the use of a community organization, are on such topics as peace, the United Nations, Latin America, Africa, the presidential election, modern art, and conservation. Conspicuous by their rarity are lists on Vietnam or other aspects of foreign policy; on such aspects of civil liberties as race riots, black power, illegal detention and wire tapping; on drug addiction; on the continuing Near East crises: or on religion and Federal aid to schools. No doubt many more such lists than were available for examination have been prepared and activities developed around them, but the available evidence indicates that the grittier topics do not constitute a major source of activity development, except when a current book or film happens to deal with one or another of them. Continuing world affairs and Great Book discussion programmes, so well-entrenched that they are seldom reported any more, do, of course, deal with such topics, and without question, library materials collections include them.

Activities based on specific community needs are reported frequently by a few libraries, and rarely, or not at all, by most of the libraries. Some such activities are related to needs that are inevitable in any community. Family finances, including stocks, estates, real estate and income tax, are the subjects of lecture series in some libraries, illustrated occasionally by films, and accompanied by materials lists. Family living and parent education, mental health, community beautification, the arts, problems of the mature woman, preparation for retirement, and problems of the aging are the subjects of a variety of activities.

The programme activities geared to the aging require some explanation. They are prevalent, usually as a once-in-two weeks or once-a-month group meeting. Some of them are materials-based, with reviews and showings of a variety of materials with no discernible relation to each other or to any particular audience. Other are geared to some of the interests that are generally ascribed to older people, such as travel, history, hobbies, and books on holidays. A few are designed to deal with the problems of the aging, such as health and nutrition, living with relatives, developing interests, and managing limited funds. These latter programmes are usually related to the specific community, since representatives of community agencies serving the aging are often involved.

A second group of community-inspired programme activities is determined by geography. Films, recordings, and books on a city, state, or region are presented to groups. Definitely community-based, these programmes deal largely with the history, ecology, recreational facilities and, occasionally, the economy of the area. Although they may be designed to give information to the newcomer, or, as in the case of the nine-year summer series in the library in one of the most beautiful states of the union, to the tourist, they are no doubt enjoyed as nostalgic entertainment by many other citizens.

Activities geared specifically to current, pressing community needs are usually characterized by library cooperation with one or more agencies or organizations in the community. An urban affairs forum at the library may be co-sponsored by Citizens Advisory Committee; a three meeting series on the school drop-out co-sponsored by the Better Schools Committee; a session on emergency psychological services by the Family Service Association and the Mental Health Association; a programme on the water resources of the area by the League of Women Voters; or a continuing series on local issues co-sponsored by the Community Association and a branch library of a large city. Whether the library initiates the process that determines the need or whether the lead is taken by another group is not indicated, and is not important as long as the library maintains sufficient awareness of the community to judge whether the areas dealt with are of true significance and that no gaps are left.

In the field of service to the disadvantaged, cooperation with other agencies and organizations continues to be the rule. Working with the city's Anti-poverty Action Committee, one library sponsors a consumer education series, covering food stamps, credit buying, what food to buy and how to prepare it; another prepares lists for volunteer aides for study centers, in cooperation with the Community Leadership School; another cooperates with the YWCA on training volunteers to man a career referral office, stressing the use of materials; another develops a parents' programme with the Head Start staff. Activities in support of community literacy programmes are prevalent.

A traditional way of determining major community problems and extending the library's ability to contribute to their solution is the programme planners' institute for representatives of clubs and organizations. Several libraries reported that such an institute is an annual event; one library holds a number of such institutes in its branches. Where the emphasis is on programme techniques and problems, and sources of material and information, a constructive but rather limited goal may be achieved. Only two libraries reported that planning was done with a citizen's group, and that community issues were identified as suggested programme content. Programme methodology and the use of materials were demonstrated and introduced in the context of the subject areas identified. Such an institute is designed to meet the highest objectives of the library, and is based on a legitimate analysis of community needs.

An overview of all the activities indicates that most of the libraries reporting probably subscribe to the objective of continuing education, but in such a limited way that their commitment to the objective may be questioned. A series of unrelated film showings, or book reviews, or material-based discussions does not meet the definition of library adult education agreed upon in 1954 at the Allerton Park conference on training needs of librarians doing adult education work in libraries. Lester Asheim reported that the consensus of the group assembled was that adult education, for the purpose of the conference, could be defined as,

> those library activities for adult individuals and groups which form a part of the total educational process and which are marked by a defined goal, derived from an analysis of needs

> or interests. These activities aim at a continuing cumulative educational experience for those who participate, require special planning and organization, and may be originated by the library or by a request from the individuals or groups concerned.[10]

The great bulk of the activities reported is neither purposeful nor continuing and cumulative. At best it is a cafeteria offering of materials characterized, fortunately, by excellence, but contributing only incidentally to the continuing education of those who form a passive audience, or even take part in a question or discussion period.

The topic-based programmes developed to meet the needs of specific segments of the community meet the objectives of continuing education. The activities that are based on a knowledge of the specific community and developed in cooperation with other community organizations and agencies fulfill the objectives at the highest level. The staffs of a relatively small proportion of libraries seem to accept the objectives fully, or to understand how to develop activities to achieve them.

In letters accompanying some of the responses, the reasons given for a limited programme of services to groups were the familiar and legitimate ones of lack of staff and time. In some instances, however, the number of random activities was large. The staff need to develop and carry out these activities could have spent their time on activities that would more specifically serve the generally accepted educational objectives of the library.

Lee points out that the educational work of the library is based for the most part on unexamined assumptions, and recommends analytical study of the ideas upon which the provision of educational services and programmes of public libraries is based. The apparent tenuousness of the relationship between accepted objectives and many of the activities intended to carry them out supports his recommendation, and suggests that the matter is one of some urgency, deserving of a high priority in programmes of library research.

THE SEARCH FOR INFORMATION ABOUT COMMUNITY NEEDS

The availability of information about community needs is a growing concern for many professions and public agencies. It is the purpose of this section to examine the approaches to community needs being advanced by various disciplines and to relate them to the philosophy and the practices of the library profession. The examination is used on the identification of the needs of the organized and the unorganized segments of society and on the community search for leaders.

Publications from the many fields concerned with social goals and public welfare give evidence of a widespread acknowledgment of the urgency for reassessment of both human needs and human resources. There is a concern for breadth and depth in citizen understanding of community problems. There is an awareness that solutions must be based upon productive insights into and use of the competencies of all citizens. These are conclusions that service professions, tax-supported and private, recognize and reflect in their literature. The search for new directions has created a climate for professional and civic intercommunication and for approaches which have been variously reported as forms of "interdisciplinary planning." "popular participation," "community interaction," "social dialogues," "group processes" and "shared experience."

Behind all of these words are two basic concepts of the library profession: involvement and commitment.

These concepts hold that the library is at the centre of community involvement. It is, in many parts of the country, the initiator of involvement. By the very nature of its function it can be no less than a participant. Knowing the community and purposefully sharing in its efforts at self-understanding is a fundamental tenet of the profession.

It is a conviction confirmed by the Public Library Standards, which state that "Continuous as well as periodic study of the community should be made through knowledge obtained by participation in governmental planning, through study and coordination of surveys already made by other agencies, through cooperation with other organizations in new studies, or by a library-initiated community analysis."[11]

These concepts further hold that the participation of the library in community fact-finding and in its analysis and implementation is a total commitment. It involves all library personnel and the understanding and support of library boards. It constitutes a continuing learning situation which is grounded in the concept of community development not merely as a technique or a process but as an adult education function.[12]

The library's first responsibility as a resource for information on community needs is the acquisition and use of a materials collection dealing with local affairs and local people. Nevertheless, it has become increasingly evident that the traditional in community information collection building is not adequate to provide an understanding of the pressures and problems that prevail in all areas of corporate life. It has been pointed out that social sciences are "data-starved." So are communities. As a consequence the literature of the 1960's probes into more effective use of technological advances for information analysis and into the values of social laboratories for the identification of need and the answers to human problems.[13]

People in organized groups have been examined by sociologists, adult educators and others from innumerable angles ranging from studies of function to correlations of status to civic effectiveness.[14]

Time-tested aids used by many agencies, including libraries, in the recognition of the needs of organized groups include: (1) community studies; (2) discussion groups and town meetings; (3) clearing-house files of data on organizations, their objectives and programmes; (4) affiliation with coordinating councils; (5) cooperation with and use of area communication media: newspapers, TV, and radio stations; (6) programme planning institutes and leadership training courses; (7) staff participation in diversity of organizations; (8) assignment of staff as institutional and group resource people; and (9) involvement in adult education programming. The library profession's latest contribution to this list is the accumulating experience record of the library community consultant and the neighbourhood coordinator programme as initiated by the Brooklyn Public Library.

Discovering the needs of the unorganized takes the personnel of all service agencies into person-to-person relationships. This is one of the most satisfying of techniques for the identification of needs. Nevertheless, it has its limitations and public service institutions in recent years have turned to new allies for more comprehensive insights into the needs of the unorganized. These allies include: (1) the articulate and responsible leaders of socio-economic groups; (2) the workers in Head Start, adult literacy projects, and other anti-poverty programmes; (3) the specialists in varying disciplines who work together through reciprocal referrals; (4) the leaders in adult and young adult continuing education activities of churches, schools and other community agencies; (5) neighbourhood coordinators; (6) credit and consumer cooperatives;

(7) union councils; (8) government field representatives; (9) area committees of human resources; (10) lay advisory committees for mental health and special education movements; (11) senior citizens organizations; (12) visiting nurses and rural extension agents; and (13) university extension instructors and advisors.

Efforts to develop skills in identification of the needs of individuals and groups have underscored the importance of finding leaders at the grass roots level to work on these needs. The most significant result of the search for community leaders is a change in attitude on the part of many agencies toward the involvement of people. Post-mid-century thinking supports a pluralistic approach to community problems as evidenced by efforts to involve human beings from all environments and all age groups, to coordinate the contributions of representatives of all types of organizations, to experiment with leadership recruitment and training patterns initiated by differing disciplines, and to plan ahead in terms of large units of service involving not only greater opportunities but a broad network for leadership potential.

The claim cannot be made that all approaches to leadership development are new, but there may be innovative elements in their implementation. Some represent practices that are taken for granted by workers in one field but have only recently been adapted to the programme of other specialist. Still others represent ideas that have been buried in print for decades and have been given new life by the demands of the 1960's. The following are samples of the approaches to the identification and the training of leaders:

1. The emergence of a concept of a "participative leadership" as applied to the community planning mechanism, i.e., the involvement of representatives of the people immediately affected by a problem in the total process of examining needs, exploring ways to meet these needs, and in the setting of priorities.[15]
2. The enlistment of individuals from groups to be served for training as expediters to bridge the gap between the professionals and the people in the implementation of a programme.[16]
3. A shift from the "human relations" theories to the "human resources" concept of motivating volunteers, co-workers, or employees to greater initiative, responsibility, creativity, and leadership.[17]

4. Examination of changes required to promote active citizen interest in a dynamic group democracy.[8]
5. Consideration of ways to counter the fallacy of the "one big brain" theory and the "they" concept of responsibility in decision processes.[9]
6. A recognition of the importance of building an indigenous leadership core supported by but not directed by experts.[20]

The public service professions have experimented in the 1960's with programmes designed to strengthen sources of community knowledge, to reduce communication barriers between professionals and individuals, and to sharpen the techniques for meeting community needs. The following are representative of the types of programmes which have been advanced by a number of professions in the 1960's:

1. Training for community action through group discussion of case histories of successful and unsuccessful techniques in finding leaders and sorting out the real needs of individuals and communities.
2. Emphasizing through medical education development of skills to answer the question. *"Are there ways we can discover the kinds of strength people have, and then build on them?"*[21]
3. Structuring in-service training for isolated social workers to take advantage of informed community awareness.[22]
4. Experimenting with the temporary relocation of college students and faculty units from the parent campus into selected communities, to do research and to guide specific changes.[23]
5. Creating interdisciplinary departments in universities for unified approach to controlled investigation and practical action in urban areas.[24]
6. Employing graduates of varying disciplines to support the work of specialists as in the case of social workers and other non-medical consultant serving as working members of medical teams.[25]
7. Exploring a system of qualitative social accounting with indices to measure the quality of life on all levels.[26]
8. Advancing the "futurism theory"—the concept that long-term problem-solving may be predicted and achieved within a foreseeable period of time through the use of sound information, sharp criteria, well-defined goals, coordinated work of specialists, periodic assessments, and persuasion.[27]

The library profession on a national level has kept pace with other disciplines in the effort to point to directions for effective community service. It has produced standards which clearly define the library's responsibility to the total community. It has published materials regarded as precision tools for getting at community information. Various divisions of ALA and some of the state libraries and library schools have conducted institutes whose proceedings and reports have laid a foundation for a literature of guidelines for leadership training and for action in diagnosing and meeting needs of people.

Library literature reflects contradictory opinions on the scope and the methods of the identification-of-needs process. There are those who insist that libraries should be aggressive agencies for social change.[28] This point of view is supported by challenging descriptions of direct action programmes designed to reach the unserved in their own surroundings.[29] At the same time there are voices which counsel limiting priorities to the long-established service patterns organized for the public which voluntarily seeks out the library. Librarians at each end of the spectrum of opinion are faced with the same insistent demand for reliable data on which to base judgments. George Beaton has said, "It is difficult to predict what kind of library service is needed until you are definite about what the requirements of your users will be."[30]

The innovations in the library field which have strengthened the library as a community resource centre in the 1960's are primarily those which were developed through community action in which the library was partner in coordinated studies of social issues and human needs. In most instances the projects with the most striking innovative styles were those financed through Federal funds. The innovations include the use of such personnel as community coordinators, field workers, and itinerant materials specialists. Innovations also led to the establishment of informal library neighbourhood centres, to audiomobile units and other side walk services, to sustained and coordinated project development with allied agencies, and to the machinery for special surveys for analyzing needs of groups and individuals within a given area. Undoubtedly these innovations cumulatively increase the library's body of knowledge of organized and unorganized group needs.

One obstacle to the acceptance of the ideas of the change-seekers in the library profession seems to have come about through confusion in communication. Critics point out that some of the devices and techniques have social welfare implications. Nevertheless, the stated objective of the proponents of out-in-the-community projects is to fulfill the library's long established educational goals for all segments of the community from the elite to the illiterate. The library innovator's major concern is still with materials, but with an emphasis on a deliberate and purposeful search for people who need those materials.[31] The involvement of staff in the processes of identification of needs is basic to current innovative projects. The practice of assigning staff to identify the needs of the unorganized is also slowly spreading into libraries with traditional programmes.

One area of recent experimentation for other disciplines, but which is established library practice, is the employment of representatives of varying culture and economic backgrounds. Reports of special library services for the disadvantaged document the continued spread of the employment of the indigenous.[32] However, there is little data on ways in which the average library has used people of differing ethnic backgrounds in determining or interpreting local needs. A few libraries have reached into the ranks of other professions, such as adult education, for specialists to strengthen their programmes for reaching people. Others make use of volunteers from the ranks of the retired or from service clubs for personal contacts.

Libraries operating without the stimulus of Federal funds have moved at a slower pace in experimenting with new methods to reveal the needs of the non-user. Library literature does include reports of many activities which resulted from identification of social need such as service to the homebound. In large part such activities are extensions of existing services. However, they are not unique results of new methodology. Genuine innovations are limited. Eleanor Smith has pointed out that what is needed in creating resourceful library approaches to community needs is "a commitment from librarians to experiment."[33]

The fact remains that the objectives and services of library are distinct from those of any other public agency. A corollary fact is that the needs of large proportions of the organized and unorganized in all communities are still to be recognized and met. The widespread awareness of the gap between these two facts has led many librarians to the examination of needs through direct collaboration with representatives of socio-economic groups and other potential consumers. The unserved have a prime spot on the agenda for planning in individual libraries, in systems, and on the state and Federal levels.

Foresighted leaders in the library world are beginning to debate the possible realignment of library services to meet the demands of the urban-metropolitan dominated society of the immediate future. Research into the characteristics and requirements of the user and the non-user of public libraries has been recognized as imperative for intelligent action. A "Libraries 2000 Committee," proposed by the ALA for mobilization of librarians for "shaping the future of American librarianship," complements the ranks of the nation's long-range planners. These are the signs that the library profession will keep pace with other service organizations in identifying and meeting the needs of people at all levels.

REFERENCES

1. Robert D. Leigh, *The Public Library in the United States.* New York, Columbia University Press, 1950, p. 223.
2. Margaret E. Monroe, *Library Adult Education; the Biography of an Idea.* New York, The Scarecrow Press, 1963, pp. 443-444.
3. Robert Ellis. Lee, *Continuing Education for Adults through the American Public Library, 1833-1964.* Chicago, ALA, 1966, p. 114.
4. *Ibid.*, p. 18.
5. Library-Community Project Headquarters Staff. *Studying the Community: A Basis for Planning Library Adult Education Services.* Chicago, ALA, 1960.
6. "Survey of Trends in Group Services in Public Libraries." August, 1967. Responses on file at the Adult Services Division, American Library Association.
7. *The Louvre.* Motion picture. National Broadcasting Company. Released by Encyclopaedia Britannica Educational Corporation. 44 min., sound, color, 16 mm.
8. *Child of Darkness, Child of Light.* Motion picture. Foster Parents Plan, 1966. Made by Wilding, Inc. 25 min., sound, color, 16 mm.
9. James A. Pike, *You and the New Morality.* New York, Harper, 1967.
10. Lester Asheim, *Training Needs of Librarians Doing Adult Education Work.* Chicago, ALA, 1955, pp. 8-9.
11. Standards Committee. . . of the Public Library Association. American Library Association. *Minimum Standards for Public Library Systems, 1966.* Chicago, ALA, 1967, p. 29.

12. Bertis L. Jones, "A Philosophical View of Community Development as an Adult Education Function," *Adult Leadership,* 13:240-241, Feb. 1965.

13. Harold D. Lasswell, "Do We Need Social Observatories?" *Saturday Review,* 50:49-52, Aug. 5, 1967.

14. Ruth C. Young, and Olaf F. Larson, "The Contribution of Voluntary Organizations to Community Structure," *The American Journal of Sociology,* 71: 178-186, Sept. 1965.

15. Leopold Lippman, "A State Plans for Its Mentally Retarded," *Children,* 12: 171-177, Sept.-Oct. 1965.

16. Robert Reiff, and Riessman, Frank. *The Indigenous Nonprofessional* (Community Mental Health Journal. Monograph Series, No. 1) Lexington, Mass., Community Mental Health Journal, 1965.

17. Miles, Raymond E. "The Affluent Organization," *Harvard Business Review,* 44: 106-114, May-June 1966.

18. Ronald Lippitt, "Training for Participation," *Adult Leadership,* 41:42-44+, June 1965.

19 Pearson Hunt, "Fallacy of the One Big Brain." *Harvard Business Review,* 44:84-90, July-Aug. 1966.

20. Clarence King, *Working with People in Community Action: An International Casebook for Trained Community Workers and Volunteer Community Leaders.* New York, Association Press, 1965.

21. Pauline G. Stitt, "Helping Medical Students Find the Strength in People," *Children,* 13:104, May-June 1966.

22. Donald Brieland, "The Efficient Use of Child Welfare Personnel," *Children,* 12:91-96, May-June 1965.

23. "Tinkering-Around U [Ideas at Ten-College Union for Research and Experimentation in Higher Education Meeting]," *Newsweek,* 69:47, Jan. 2, 1967.

24. Paulson, Belden. "Research, Training, and Action in Milwaukee's Inner Core. A Case Study about Process," *Adult Leadership,* 15:361-362+, April 1967.

25. "You Could Die Waiting [New Centers Supported by O.E.O.]," *Newsweek,* 68:76, Dec. 12, 1966.

26. "Social Goals and Indicators for American Society," Vols. I and II, *Annals of the American Academy of Political and Social Science,* 371:1-177, May 1967; 371:1-218, Sept. 1967.

27. Andrew Kopkind, "The Future-Planners," *New Republic,* 156:19-23,

Feb. 25, 1967.

28. Henry Drennan, "Little Miracle on Chapel Street," *American Education,* 2:1-5, July-Aug. 1966.
29. Evelyn Levy, "Library Service in the Inner City," *Wilson Library Bulletin,* 41:471-477, Jan. 1967.
30. "The Metropolitan Public Library," *Wilson Library Bulletin,* 40:922, June 1966.
31. Peter Hiatt, and Henry Drennan, eds. *Public Library Service for the Functionally Illiterate.* Chicago, ALA, Public Library Association, Committee on Services to the Functionally Illiterate, 1967, p. 19.
32. *Ibid.,* pp. 43-44.
33. Conference on Library Service to the Undereducated. Drexel Institute of Technology, 1965. *Library Service for the Undereducated* (Drexel Library School Series, No. 15). Philadelphia, Drexel Press, 1966, p. 10.

12

Public Relations of the Public Library

ONE OF the imponderables of human relations is the many faces each of us as individuals presents to our several worlds. A man may be a hero to his children, a martinet to his office, an apple polisher to his employer, a boy wonder to his mother, an aging failure to his neighbour. Behind these faces hides the man he is. An institutional personality, on the other hand, is built by forming from the many individuals within it, one face to present to the world. This face which the world sees is reflected in the mirror of every act. Lucky the library which has inherited such a face, formed by years of tradition and ever young with the fire of faithfulness to an ideal.

An institutional face is molded carefully, each feature related definitely to the body as a whole—its abilities, its potentials, and its needs. Is the library to face the world as a community friend, a comfortable, gregarious person with a hand stretched forth to everyone? Is it to be the reserved scholar attracting the intellectual? Should it be a conservative? a progressive? a radical? Is it insular in its outlook? Is it cosmopolitan?

Once molded, this the face which must be made familiar to the world. This must be the picture painted with every stroke of policy, every shade of service, every line of contact. In P.R. parlance this is the theme of the institution, represented by symbols chosen to fit the time, the group, and the need. The picture of the library presented to the public should be based not only on the aims and ideals of those who shape the policy but also on the hard rock of possible achievement. Every promise on the face must be honoured in the service delivered by body.

A good public relations programme is a planned one, which can be divided first into two branches, internal and external. Internally, board, administrators, and staff are the sculptors who mold the institutional face. Externally, that face is brought to the community as a living, breathing thing.

Because one of its prime functions is interpretation of the community to the library and of the library to the community, the library board should be the first link in the chain of public relations. Here is formed the policy on which service is based and which, siphoned down to the library consumer, forms his opinion of that service. Situations differ, a board may be floundering for want of P.R. skills; or it may count among its members a professional public relations man. If, on the other hand, a board has placed a P.R. director on the library payroll, it should give ear to his advice, and call on him for the help he can give. He can assist the board (1) in knowing the library. Election or appointment to the board presupposes an interest; it does not, however, insure knowledge of library organization, methods, background, long range aims or immediate needs. As an example, introductory tours of the library system give an on-the-spot introduction to particular situations, services and staff, helping to fix a defined picture in the trustee's mind which will stand him in good stead during his term of office. (2) P.R. communication skills can be used in presentation of information for board consideration and action. (3) Such skills are also valuable in presentation of board matters to other bodies. Instances are budget and bond requests, building programmes, legislative programmes and the like. (4) The P.R. counsel can offer profitable guidance on dealing with the press and other news media. Trustees have, after all, the ultimate responsibility for library service and the impression they make as individuals and as a body are the seed from which the public opinion of the library grows.

Policy set by the board must be transmitted both to the public and to the staff. Since the employees are the ones who will implement the policy or be directly affected by it, they must not only be informed clearly and fully with the reasons and the thinking behind the decision, but the matter must be so presented as to win the widest possible acceptance.

Corporations have even discovered that the P.R. chief, given his proper place in the organization, can be effective in the labour- management relations of board-administrator-staff.

A librarian, who is not his own P.R. director, can find in the one he hires many of the same helps the board does. A P.R. counsel can provide guidance on the skillful presentation of programme and policy, both upward and downward; he can interpret the reactions of others to a plan; he can suggest approaches designed to win readers' acceptance; he can advise against ideas which will not prove popular, because of their form, the timing, or existing conditions; he will enlist every talent and effort to place the institution and its chief in the best light to both public and staff. Finally, the P.R. chief should act as a weather forecaster, knowing the prevailing climate of staff opinion so well that the librarian can avoid squalls.

No able librarian wants a brow smoother. No able P.R. a director wishes to act as one. Rather, the two work together to present the whole picture, the "face" of the institution to both staff and public, the one supplementing his knowledge and ability with the skills and techniques of the other.

To gain full benefit from P.R. skills, the librarian and the board must appoint a person who they trust, and then proceed to trust him. The P.R. chief should be made familiar with the aims, the hopes, and dreams which his chief holds close; he must know the problems, the sore sports and the dangers which he fears. He must be close enough to the mind of the librarian to be able to speak with his words and to see a problem with his eyes. This relationship requires stature on both sides. The one must be big enough to share his personality without fear; the other to recognize the bounds within which he uses the knowledge confided to him.

Because the burden of carrying on the day-to-day relationships with the library's present and immediate public falls upon the staff, it follows that any P.R.-conscious library will choose intelligent, capable, and personable employees. Granted that all who are hired meet these requirements, it must be recognized that building good public relations continues after the hiring date. High in priority is the maintenance of good and stable staff morale. Assuming that the employee has found the salary and benefits agreeable to him when he accepted the job, the first step in making him a satisfied and a satisfactory employee is his orientation. Here the P.R. director can work with the personnel office. Four things can be recognized at once as necessary: (1) The staff member must become acquainted with his fellows and they with him; (2) He must become familiar with the rules and regulations governing both staff and service; (3) He must know the library's history, tradition, and background, its aims and general policies; and (4) If a newcomer, he must be introduced to the city, to its advantages, customs, and history.

All of this represents not only an introductory but also a continuing policy. It is a problem which both business and institutions have recognized, and are trying to meet, with none claiming a completely satisfactory solution. One-the-job training can teach skills, even some rules and regulations. Meeting, lectures, panels, and films are usable methods. Readable pamphlets and news sheets are others. Some libraries have tried skits, role playing, and buzz sessions as indoctrination devices.

Use of a sponsor, a big brother or big sister, is an excellent method of making the newcomer to a large staff feel at home. A sponsor provides the answers to the questions a new man is hesitant about bringing to his superior, and provides the friendly hand which opens the door to staff organizations and social functions in that lonely period before one forms one's own friends. In a small group, easily met and recognized, the sponsor is too formal a device.

Once oriented to his surroundings the employee cannot be left unnoticed by the library which employs him. A supervisory training programme run concurrently with the orientation programme will assure good and stimulating supervision, the kind of supervision which will develop future supervisors. The P.R. officer will foster other factors contributing to good morale: management's encouragement of employees suggestions; awareness of employees as individuals; recognition of achievement. Nothing is more prized than the word from the head, the feeling that the employee is a person to the man at the top rather than a body filling a vacancy. All good public relations take time. Once unwilling to take that time cannot complain of a public's failure to accept him.

Many a company has recognized that the best salesman for its programmes and its products are its own employees. They have found that the off-the-job utterances, the over-the-fence report of company policies, the family's opinion of the employee's firm, often play a larger part in the building of public opinion than all the billboards in the world.

Knowing this, large companies have begun a studies programme of wooing employee support. Libraries may not go as far in the pater familias role but they should be able to match industry in the most important factor of all in building employee goodwill—effective communication. The man who knows what and especially why will give a better picture of his firm than the uninformed speculator.

Communication has a high priority in good staff relations but also on the list of administrative headaches. Regular channels should be set up in order that release of information to the staff is prompt, official, and complete. Regular patterns of communication likewise have the advantage of preventing unintentional breaks in the management-to-staff line.

Careful planning of timing for release of news has long been a policy of government, business, and science. It can be equality useful in intra-library matters. Staff officers should feel free to call for P.R. counsel on timing as well as on P.R. skills in communication in order to win staff recognition of an administrative policy of free exchange of information. Exchange is an apt term, for effective communication is two way.

Over-the-desk relations are the product of good morale, good attitudes between divisions, and constant training in human relations. The latter is taught by example, by print by speech, by supervision, by film, by meetings, by panels, by discussion and interview, and by recognition of success. Always, always, it must be recognized that librarians as well as publics are individuals; they react differently; they learn differently. No wise library will put all its training eggs in one basket. It will use as many media of communication as it can effectively produce in order to reach and affect the minds it wishes to influence.

External public relations can be subdivided at once into two obvious groups: those with present library users, and those with potential users, presently affected only indirectly by library benefits. The first know from firsthand experience what the library is, what they like about it, and what they do not. They may be more critical because of the experience; or, like good friends, they may be ready to excuse and explain away. This acquaintance with the library does not mean that they can be ruled out of P.R. plainning or that they will not be affected by new policies and programmes. Any approach to them, however, must take into account their present knowledge. The nonusers must be reached also. They, to , must find growing in their minds a picture of the face of the community library.

Staff members should also be encouraged to take part in community affairs. Membership on boards and committees, in civic and social clubs, participation in drives and projects help to humanize librarians and, therefore, the library in the public mind.

Every public can be subdivided into common interest groupings. The divisions are flexible and can be multiplied into as many as an active imagination can find practical. Common interests can form the bridge over which the library crosses to the individuals in the community. Using then, as many media of communication as he can employ effectively with the talent, budget, and staff at his command, the P.R. director builds acquaintance with the library, its policy, its service, and its aims. Methods found useful by business and industry as well as institutions include:

1. *Press:* In addition to the daily press in the area, important outlets are the neighbourhood shopping papers, the foreign press, newspapers of racial and religious groups, weeklies and monthlies, house organs, bulletins, and the library professionals press. Here it is important to know what is news, what the various organs use, and when they want it.

2. *Radio and television:* One of the most cooperative areas of communication as far as libraries go, both media reach a vast audience. Competition for the eye and ear of that audience is keen, however, and libraries should give thought to what they can present through these channels which cannot be presented better by others. In building his programme the wise public relations officer will remember that the press, radio, and television agencies of his community form one of the publics he wants to reach, a public which must be given the same picture of the library as the other publics. To weave a smooth fabric of relations, he will make it easy for them to get information about the library; he will see to it that the information is accurate, timely, and easy to use; he will help them in securing materials on non-library stories; he will honest; he will make sure that the news he gives them is real news; he will learn as much as he can about their methods, problems, and techniques in order to fit as well as possible into their scheme of operations; and he will never fail to express appreciation for a job well done by any of these media.

3. *Visual aids:* Use of posters, billboards, car and bus cards, and the like have one serious drawback for libraries. Competition for the public's attention is so keen today that unskilled attempts are worse than futile. They can become dangerous. This field is one in which

successful competition costs money, frequently more than a budget provided by public funds can stand.

4. *Films:* Growing in favour with libraries as means of presenting their story, this media is low enough in cost per viewer if the audiences are large. Production cost as a whole, however, is a large one, especially since sound and colour have made other films seem drab. Cooperation from private and civic groups in the production of library films has eased the budget strain in some places.

5. *Exhibits:* Important in all public relations projects consideration of the particular public to be reached is especially important in display. Materials shown, techniques of presentation, and message to be delivered must all be studied in the light of the group for whom the exhibit is intended.

6. *Printed matter:* Reports, brochures, lists, flyer—each has a place with particular groups for particular aims. No one piece can be expected to influence every reader. Here, too, both copy and layout should be considered with the consumer in mind. An annual report prepared for the man in the street is a different thing from one prepared for a group of librarians.

7. *Direct mail:* While in some cases this seems the only answer to a specific need, the need should be thought out carefully. The vast amount of second and third class mail received daily by both business and individuals has so conditioned the receiver that he pays little attention to much of it. With postal rates raised and receiver interest lowered, the expense involved in both time and money should be well considered.

8. *Talks:* Here is one of the most effective ways of reaching an audience if the speaker is good. Sincerity, simplicity, ability to turn a phase, and skill in painting colourful word pictures make a popular speaker.

9. *Special events:* Open houses, anniversaries, weeks, fairs—these are the vehicles which bring people in and get the story out. Any unusual event can be a springboard for good publicity.

10. *Groups:* Within every community are great resources of talent, enthusiasm, and ability in the many civic minded lay people who give uncounted hours to causes which need their aid. Libraries, as well as the community chest, the schools, the Red Cross, and other organized public projects, have a claim on that talent, enthusiasm, and

ability. To develop the claim means hard work. The initial approach may be through an already functioning group—the Jaycees, and the women's clubs of the nation are two good examples of organizations which have turned a listening ear to libraries—or through the formation of an organized Friends of the Library. Old or young, great or small, from Scouts and Campfire Girls to senior citizen groups—every organization can make a vital contribution to the library's programme.

In any case, the librarian or his P.R. officer must present to the group a definite need or immediate project. Naturally, the plan will have in mind the needs of the library. It must also take into account the purpose, ability, and policy of the organization to which it is presented. To win acceptance it must carry appeal to the imagination and the heart of the layman. Most important of all, it must be flexible enough to stand alteration by the ideas and opinions of the group's members. Finally, the library must be prepared, in working with groups, to see the original plan go out the window and an entirely new one, proposed by the group, take its place.

In some instances, many organizations are joined in a common project. Most of the ideas mentioned in nine above could well be community-wide projects; national Library Week is another good example.

Let no librarian think that by lining up a complement of hard-working organizations, he can then sit back and relax. Quite the opposite. In many cases it is more difficult than doing the job one's self without outside help. Enlisting the aid of qualified groups, keeping their interest alive, channeling their services to the library's best advantage, and handling the relations between the professional staff and the volunteer helpers is a delicate and challenging task. The clearance of authority, the coordination of assorted outside workers, the accompanying multiplication of human problems, credits to be given and received—all add to headache which seems a necessary accompaniment to any big programme. In recompense, however, the library reaps the benefit of many fresh ideas from non-library brains and the talent and know-how of other professions on the one hand. On the other, by bringing in lay people on a working basis, the library gives them an intimate understanding of its own problems and a brotherly sympathy for its aims and needs. If the P.R. aspect has been skillfully handled, the group will be inflamed with the library ideal and because of the strange thing called human nature, the more its members do for the library the more they will love it and want to help it.

Building the library picture in the community is a continuing job and a important one. Public libraries are so varied in size, in budget, and in area of service it is not easy to give any set formula for the handling of public relations in libraries generally. It is a function of administration and, whether the librarian does it himself or delegates it, the P.R. activity should always be kept on the administrative level. If the activity is delegated, it follows that the librarian must choose a person of integrity, creativity, ability, and common sense, a person in whom he can place complete confidence. The duties and responsibilities of a public relations officer should be understood by the librarian as well as by the officer. Public relations is one job; publicity is another. To call a job by the first and assign to it only the functions of the second is inept, confusing to the public, embrassing and frustrating to the titleholder.

Here the head of the small public library is probably muttering that all this talk of public relations officers, advertising, publicity, and such are all right for the big institution but altogether unreal for the rest. But does the small library fail to buy art books because it has no "art department"? Does it fail to catalogue books because it has no "catalog department"? No, the librarian and the staff, small though it may be, are the art department, the catalogue department, the reference department, and the public relations department along with all the rest. The staff is smaller, it is true, but the scale of operation is smaller also. The job is heart-breaking, it looms so large; but remember, it is in the large library, too. No matter what the size—of the building, the staff, the budget, the collection—each is always too small for the potential area of service.

Smallness has its compensations as well as its drawbacks. There is possible in a smaller community far more personal acquaintance and firsthand knowledge than there is in the larger. The librarian may do most of the work himself, including the public relations job; but the newspaper editor and the radio station owner or manager are also far more likely to do the same. Therefore, the jobs that in a larger community are handled by second or third level staff members are done on the top level in the smaller town. The small town librarian knows the majority, if not all, of the community leaders personally. In a larger city, the librarian knows some but must rely on his trustees, his P.R. officer, and his staff for liaison with the others.

Also, in a smaller library the librarian has firsthand knowledge of how his P.R. directions are carried out. He teachers public relations by example as well as by direction; but he is also on the spot to see how both example and direction are followed by his staff. He need not filter policy, practice, and results up and down through a chain of command. Therefore, in the preceding discussion, the small town librarian can read his own name for both librarian and P.R. officer and prepare to do the work of both. He may lean more heavily on the help of trustees, Friends, and other public spirited citizens in building his public relations programme but how well the challenge has been met is shown by the excellent records libraries have made throughout the nation.

In almost every case, the job of public relations grows from a single person with responsibility for one area—publicity, advertising or the like, until—in most organizations—the public relations director supervises publicity, display, communication, research, advertising, and related fields. To carry out a good programme, a good and adequate staff and good equipment are essential.

A public relations director should be aware and informed of everything that impinges on that field. This can range from board to building staff, from budget to books, from neighbourhood group to chamber of commerce. The public relations officer should be one who recognizes the boundaries of his operations, however. He offers his abilities in communication, in human relations, in influence of behaviour to the ones working directly in any phase of library activity. He does not take over the specific job. He offers counsel as it affects or is affected by human behaviour.

No perfect public relations director was ever created nor has the perfect public relations programme been planned. The qualities one should possess are endless. Nevertheless, the man who has respect for his institution and the goals it has set, for the people who work in it, and for the public it serves; who sees both—his fellow workers and the public—not as a mass but as individuals, has gone a long way toward the building of a firm and lasting programme of effective human relations.

REFERENCES

1. J.C., Aspley, and L.F., Van Houten, (eds.) *The Dartnell Public Relations Handbook.* Chicago and London, The Dartnell Corporation, 1956.

2. E.L. Bernays, *Public Relations.* Norman, University of Oklahoma Press, 1952, pp. 169-180.
3. Benjamin Fine Planning. In: E.L., Bernays, ed.: *The Engineering of Consent.* Norman, University of Oklahoma Press, 1955, pp. 185-213.
4. Doris E. Fleischman, and H. W. Cutler, Themes and Symbols. In: Bernays, E. L. ed.: *The Engineering of Consent.* Norman. University of Oklahoma Press, 1955, pp. 138-155.

13

Public Relations of Academic Libraries

WITH increasing numbers of young people clamouring for admittance to colleges and universities, the attention of educators has turned toward the improvement of the intellectual climate of the campus, and toward relating the purposes of formal education to a changing world. Academic libraries, therefore, are challenged, as never before, to scrutinize their resources, their facilities and their services, and to reappraise the role of the library in higher education.

There is evidence of increased interest in public relations on all fronts as it is requested to have more descriptive information about the public relations of academic libraries.[1] However, college and university administrators (with exemplary exceptions) are still too prone to ignore the techniques of business and industry, and to reiterate the dusty cliches about the library as "the heart of the college" or "the core of the curriculum." It must be recognized, as C.D. MacDougall points out,[2] that ". . . sound public relations means the daily application of common sense, common courtesy and common decency in accordance with a continuous programme of enlightened self-interest. . . ." While a constant preoccupation with public relations may lead to undue self-consciousness,[3] nonetheless, a decent respect for the rights and needs of students, faculty, and administration must be coupled with a sensitive concern for the good name of the institution which the librarian, or janitor, or student assistant may for the moment represent.

Citizens are discovering Education, and are being urged to face up to the acute teacher shortage and lack of classrooms. But how much attention is being directed to the increased need for materials and resources of our academic libraries? In terms of higher education, the astute librarian must perceive the role of libraries in the total educational process and determine their function in relation to the whole. Speaking of "the social function" of libraries, B. Landheer reminds us that everything in contemporary society can be seen from the aspect of the producer, the consumer, and the general public.[4] For librarianship, authors and publishers represent producers; librarians are more like distributors; the reading public our consumers. The outside world (our related publics) constitutes the general public insofar as it is indirectly affected by the integrated activities of the first three groups.

Any institution is secure only as long as it commands the fullest measure of public understanding and support. Therefore, higher education in the United States has been taking a serious, second look at itself. Academic libraries, as part of higher education, must awaken to the need for increased understanding and support. For too long, academic libraries have been content to plod, forgetting that every service they offer (or do not offer) has overtones affecting public attitudes. The role of the library, and the status of the librarian, on any given campus reflects, to a large degree, the academic vitality of the institution.

Where athletics, beauty queens, and military balls dominate the publicity, the library is usually on the fringe of campus life rather than at its centre. On the other hand, when one of the nation's top liberal arts colleges deliberately concentrates on raising intellectual standards, the library becomes the focal point of the learning process, and receives commensurate support.[5]

In the scramble for new dormitories, student unions, and gymnasia—all of which may be vital to higher education—administrators must be made to recognize the need for new or expanded library facilities. Dormitories and student unions are self-liquidating, athletic and social events always newsworthy, but activities of an intellectual or cultural nature relating to the curriculum or to library services are conspicuous by their absence from most news releases. In the light of such obvious neglect or indifference on many campuses, how can any academic librarian sit back and claim that public relations are of no concern to him? It is the public which makes possible the existence and the operation of our institutions, as both MacDougall and R.B. Harwell have indicated, and librarians must realize that one of their primary responsibilities is cultivating the goodwill, understanding, and support of the various publics they serve.

While it is easy to agree with Harwell that relations within an organization are as important as those external to the organization, it is not agreed that staff relations are necessarily a part of *public* relations. As applied to the academic library, public relations may best be defined as "... the sum of the library's external relations with students, with faculty, with administrative officers, and with the community at large; and generally in that order of importance, depending upon the library's size and circumstances."[6] It is true that you cannot proclaim one thing and practice something different; to this extent, of course, library staff is involved in public relations. Basic to a good public relations programme is a competent and informed staff that understands the underlying policies of good service.

Two prerequisites are necessary before embarking upon any programme, of public relations in academic libraries: (1) Librarians need a knowledge and awareness of the policies and programme of the college or university of which they are a part, and (2) they must be convinced of the necessity for continuous motivation of the library's clientele relative to resources, facilities, and services.[7]

"When in doubt, give attention to the needs of students."[8] Nothing should take priority over the best interests of those for whom higher education is designed; sometimes this means listening to student suggestions, and sometimes it means initiating policies or programmes that are in the student's best interest. While most students are in college to get an education, many of them wish to acquire it painlessly. Whether or not the faculty coddle or spoonfeed, or encourage independent study, the library's responsibility is to stimulate intellectual curiosity and inspire appreciation of the accumulated wisdom of the ages. The most salient means the librarian has for achieving good relations with students is to make himself available. Librarians, whether in reference or circulation, in technical processes, or any other phase of library operation, have a responsibility to assist students when they seek help or obviously need it. For this very reason, one university librarian has two offices: one that is always open to students, faculty, and visitors; the other, his private hideaway for accomplishing a serious project. In the small college environment, the many opportunities for contact with student may prove beneficial to the library as well as the student. As Harwell suggests, good will is one of the priceless ingredients of an effective public relations programme.

A second, and oft-debated technique, for building sound relations with students is the handbook or guide to the library and its resources.

New methods and processes in the field of printing and publishing are making their impact upon library publications, and some form of printed introduction to the academic library is welcomes by students. Another means of building good student relations, and one that is almost necessary today in competing with other campus activities, is in the area of exhibits, book sales, and other special events. Several college libraries have displays of inexpensive prints which students may buy; at least one new university library building includes a fully-equipped art gallery. Paperback bookshops, initiated several years ago at Hamilton and Beloit colleges, pay dividends in goodwill. Whatever is done will take imagination, time, and effort on the part of some member of the library staff.

Librarians should participate, as much as possible, in campus activities including student-sponsored events and organizations. Such manifestations of interest help dispel the stereotypes still held by students who seldom see or talk with a librarian. As an adviser, or member of the Union Board, or faculty representative on a committee, librarians are enabled to implement their public relations policies, and to do a great deal to break down the barriers between students and library staff. To cultivate students is to built goodwill; to build goodwill is one of the primary functions of effective public relations.

It would seem axiomatic that the cultivation of good relations with one's colleagues on the faculty helps the academic library and its staff. Universities, and many colleges, are made up of worlds within worlds. The specialist in one field is flattered by the colleague who makes an effort to lean something in his area of learning. Manifesting a friendly interest in various departments of the college or university can stimulate or revive a colleague's interest in services offered by the library. There are certain other techniques, certainly none of them unique, by which the academic librarian can aid his public relations programme with faculty: (1) Get out of the library and join his colleagues for lunch occasionally, or meet them at the Union for coffee; (2) Attend departmental, divisional, and faculty meetings, insofar as time allows; (3) Support lectures, concerts, and other events in which other colleagues are interested; (4) Stand ready, at all times, to give extra help in a crisis situation. This may be ordering a book by telegram, securing a needed item through interlibrary loan, or providing a periodical, film, or recording on short notice. It is in the day-to-day contacts with faculty that capsules of goodwill are stored.

At the same time that librarians are "extending" themselves beyond their own four walls, they must be prepared to answer the questions and criticisms based upon misunderstanding or campus gossip. To do so tactfully is to mend fences are they are broken, and contributes to professional esprit de corps. In some institutions a library committee helps the librarian in interpreting policies and services; however, it is beyond the scope of this chapter to argue the pros and cons of such committees.[9] Another means of communication beyond the library is through various non-verbal techniques. While there is no unanimity on the type of publication which most effectively serves the faculty, current acquisitions lists and faculty bulletins are two examples widely used. These may vary from occasional mimeographed or multilithed publications to the highly professional, printed quarterlies published by some of the larger university libraries.[10] Competition for the reading time of faculty members should convince library administrators that their publications must be attractive yet functional, present information accurately yet concisely.

Various departments, or individual staff members, can help in this area of faculty public relations by routine techniques that are often effective stimulants to better relations. In the matter of new acquisitions, faculty should expect to be kept informed about books which they have requested. Reference librarians can often bring current articles from periodicals to the attention of a faculty member. An efficient, smooth-functioning, inter-library loan service is one obvious means of winning faculty goodwill. The busy faculty member, working on his advanced degree, or preparing a book or article for publication, depends upon the library for assistance in securing materials that cannot be obtained locally. The generous loan policies of larger academic libraries make possible loans to even the smallest institutions.

College and university librarians are quick to recognize the importance of the president, the vice-president, or academic dean in their relations with the administration, but how often do they know their lesser administrative officers such as the director of admissions, the alumni secretary, the registrar, or the person who is responsible for development or public relations? Recently a new development director was appointed at one midwestern college. During his first months of orientation, the librarian was able to sit down with the new colleague and informally brief him on library problems and needs. The exchange of ideas and information will undoubtedly prove beneficial whenever the expansion of library facilities are considered in the over-all development programme of this institution.

The administration officers frequently need reference materials which the library can provide, and prompt and courteous attention to such requests is an important responsibility of the library staff. Administrative personnel should be included in the distribution of library publications, such as a faculty bulletin or newsletter; the appropriate personnel should receive at least one written report a year from the librarian regarding the year's accomplishments and future plans.

Harried administrators, who are susceptible to departmental and divisional pressures, will never be aware of library needs unless kept informed and up-to-date. While being sensitive to the problems and responsibilities of the various administrative personnel, the librarian must take the initiative in any two-way communication that exists. Some librarians have become so adept at working with administrative personnel that they have been invited to assume responsibility in certain areas of college or university administration. Everett McDiarmid at Minnesota, B.L. Johnson at Stephens College, Eugene Wilson at Colorado, are examples of librarians turned administrators.

The significance of the library on a given campus may well be due to the professional enthusiasm of the librarian, and how effectively this enthusiasm is reflected through administrative personnel from the president on down. If librarians are not aggressive propagandists, why should we expect others to recognize the role of the library in higher education?

Currently, many institutions, large and small, are re-examining their programmes of "continuing education," and genuinely seeing the best means of serving their alumni and friends who are interested in expanding their knowledge or keeping abreast of current events. One measure of the vitality of an institution is how well it keeps in touch with its alumni and friends, and as all colleges and universities know this is one of the most fruitful areas of public relations. It is an area that can be rewarding for academic libraries, too. A successful alumni reading programme has been conducted by the University of Michigan for a number of years; Dartmouth[11] and the University of North Carolina are examples of institutions that have well-developed Friends of the Library groups; many schools make library resources available to graduates whose local library offering may be limited.

With a few enthusiastic sponsors, any college library can develop a Friends' group, and thereby expand its public relations potential outside the campus. Collections that would otherwise be without distinction have become valuable and interesting because of the financial support and active interest of alumni and friends. Support from such sources is especially necessary at the time of a new building programme. A number of small colleges have acquired modern library buildings that would have been beyond their means without the interest of devoted friends and alumni. The Sandburg Collection at the University of Illinois, said to be valued at over $30,000, was made possible by the contributions of alumni. One of the best small collections of Russian literature in the United States was acquired two years ago by Beloit College through the interest of an aluminus studying in central Europe. Alumni "weekends," summer conferences, and institutes, are typical techniques for building goodwill, and the library should assume its share of responsibility in promoting such activities.

Town and gown rapport is exceedingly important in the college or university community, and the library can contribute its share in building good relations in the local community. Cooperation with other libraries, issuing "privilege cards" to community residents, and personal contact with key leaders of the community, can be of mutual benefit with little effort and almost no expense. An exchange of current periodical lists, avoiding duplication of certain expensive titles, and the co-ordination of reference services, are obvious techniques that can multiply library service in any community. A further extension of this idea is being carried out by a group of New England colleges situated within a fifty-mile radius of one another.[12] Students may now have access to the resources of five libraries instead of one. Some academic librarians have found it profitable to participate in civic organizations and other community projects that cannot help but have public relations value to their institutions. While primarily for students and faculty, the academic library should welcome the serious-minded citizen who also wishes to make use of its resources.

The cumulative effect of public relations is the reputation or prestige gained by an individual, institution, or organization in the community served. As C.A. Schoenfeld reminds us: "Public relations, in the proper sense of the term, is primarily a matter of institutional conduct and only secondarily a matter of publicity."[13] We cannot avoid having public relationships, but we can, by building and maintaining sound and productive relations, control the results. In recent years colleges and universities have gone beyond the printed page to bring information to its various publics. First radio, now television, the picture- brochure, and a dozen other methods and media are now used to stimulate public sympathy and support. Since libraries are basic to the purposes of higher education, the librarian of the future will go beyond commonly accepted media and strive, through technological and communicative innovations, to bring together the right material, the right person, at the right moment. The Center for Documentation and Communication Research at Western Reserve University, established at the School of Library Science in 1955, is evidence that the profession is alert to its responsibilities in the exploration of new horizons. One of its major objectives: "To conduct research programmes for the definition of techniques and principles underlying the organization of recorded information . . .",[14] and a second, "To improve the accessibility of recorded information . . ." can have a yet unrealized effect upon library public relations.

Since our very future survival depends upon our capacity to understand one another, and since knowledge is necessary in the process, education remains the cornerstone of progress. The academic librarian must do everything possible to know the resources of his own library, to eliminate misunderstanding, to create and build positive relations, and to streamline and improve library services, so that he may make his maximum contribution to survival through learning.

REFERENCES

1. R.W. Orr, Public Relations for College and University Libraries. *Library Trends,* 1:123-135, July 1952.
2. C.D. MacDougall, "A Working Concept of Public Relations." *Library Trends,* 7:239-247, Oct. 1958.
3. W.F. Reck, *Public Relations: A Programme for Colleges and Universities.* New York, Harpers, 1946, p. x.
4. D. Landheer, *The Social Function of Libraries.* New York, Scarecrow Press, 1957, p. 6.
5. Archibald MacLeish, Tower That Will Not Yield. *A.L.A. Bulletin,* 50:649 654, Nov. 1956.
6. D.W. Heron, The Public Relations of Academic Libraries. *College and Research Libraries,* 16:144, April 1955.

7. H.V. Deale, The Fourth "R". Library Journal, 81:1641-1644, July 1956.
8. E.D. Whittlesey, *The Faculty and Public Relations.* Nashville, Tern., The Methodist Church, Board of Education, n.d.
9. Public Relations of Libraries. See listing in *Library Literature.*
10. American Library Association, Library Periodicals Round Table. *A Directory of Library Periodicals.* Pittsburg, Kansas, State College Library, 1957.
11. Dartmouth College Library, *Friends.* Hanover; N. II.
12. Hampshire Inter-Library Center, *Massachusetts Library Association Bulletin,* 44:59, July 1954.
13. C.A. Schoenfeld, *The University and Its Publics: Approaches to a Public Relations Programme for Colleges and Universities.* New York, Harpers, 1954, p. 2.
14. *Bulletin of Western Reserve University.* New Series, vol. 59, no. 8. Cleveland, The University, May 29, 1956, p. 5.

14

Public Relations of the School Library

"TO HAVE or not to have" is *not* the question when it comes to public relations in the school library. The only choice open to the school librarian is between having an effective or ineffective relationship with the school library's public. Obviously, the success of the school library programme is determined by the choice the school librarian makes. It is important for the school librarian to realize the public relations is a "continuing process of keying policies, services and actions to the best interest of those individuals and groups whose confidence and goodwill a school library covets; and secondly, it is the interpretation of these policies, services and actions to assure complete understanding and appreciation of the school library."[1] Accordingly, the school librarian has a key role to play in building an effective programme of public relations.

When a school librarian begins to study the problem of public relations, immediately there comes a realization that the school library's publics are the school administrators, the teachers, the students, the parents, and the members of the whole community. Each public may deserve a special programme of interpretation in order to assure complete understanding and appreciation of the function of the school library.

If a "good school library is a collection of many materials of learning—selected, organized and administered for service to the students and faculty of the school,"[2] then the school librarian's task is that of making friends and winning confidence, approval, and material assistance from the groups which are immediately concerned with the services of the school library. Librarians have always sought to capture ways and means by which all tasks involving the bringing together of library materials and their users might be made easier and more certain. Planning these tasks will not guarantee effective use, but it will aid immeasurably in assisting the users.

School library public relations acquires its direction and meaning to a large extent from the school itself. Of necessity the over-all plan of school library operation should follow the regular administrative procedures for public relations of the particular school system. Then too, the superintendent, the principal, the teachers, and the school librarian should work together to plan the over-all public relations programme. This suggests that each member of the faculty should have whatever public relations responsibility falls within the scope of his general authority. Naturally, the school librarian should assume his responsibility for the area of interpreting school library service. The school librarian is the logical interpreter of all school library activities. He can either let his publics know the activities through an organized programme of public relations, or he can let his publics gain their impressions of the services and actions of the school library through unplanned contacts. The school librarian must take the initiative in planning and carrying out a programme which will gain support of the administrators, the faculty, the students of the school, the parents, and members of community.

Public relations efforts will be more effective when plans are made for the specific publics served. One of the librarian's responsibilities is to keep his administrative superiors informed land to get their approval for the planned activities in school library public relations. Channels of publicity that have been set up on the school must be followed. Since few courses in education prepare administrators with an adequate understanding of the nature and services of the school library, the school librarian should be aware of the need for interpreting the library to the administrative staff. When planning a programme of enlarging the administrators' understanding and recognition of the school library, the school librarian should remember that administrators are very busy people. Furthermore, when the librarian considers the heavy schedules of the superintendent and principal, he should time his approach at a period other than rush hours. The wise school librarian does not try to sell the entire school library in one afternoon. He involves the superintendent and principal in planning long-range objectives. He demonstrates to his administrators that he knows the work of the school library and does it!

It is always advisable for the school librarian to provide the superintendent and principal with information in brief form for a monthly report which may be transmitted by the administration to the board of education. This report can be factual to include the basic school library statistics, but it should also include an informal resume of exhibits, work with groups, classroom units, special features, and the like. The school librarian interprets the financial needs of the school library to the school administrators by planning a detailed budget which explains the need for and use of each item. No school board member can be expected to spend freely the taxpayers' money on the school library unless he is acquainted with the high rate of return in educational values from the tax dollars invested in a school library.

In explaining to administrators the need for increased staff, the librarian emphasizes the continuous contacts which make it possible to work directly with more groups and more departments. As a result an enlightened administration will free the librarian for full time library work and secure additional staff when needed. The librarian invites the administrators into the library to see the teaching laboratory at work, and he lets them examine the tools of learning. In addition, he keeps the administrators' office files continually supplied with pictures and slides of publicity and newspaper clippings about the activities and services of the school library. He provides his administrators with periodic write-ups of activities with various groups; e.g., the gifted child. Recorded comments of teachers, students, and parents as they attend special functions in the library, for example, a National Library Week Open House, assist the administration in understanding the many types of public relations programmes at work in the school library.

Every library needs adequate quarters, conveniently located and suitably equipped. The wise school librarian uses every public relations device available to interpret the planning of school library space for the administrator as to adequacy, comfort, attractiveness, and service. For example, the filmstrip,-"School Library Quarters," and detailed plans of recently completed school libraries with floor plans and photo graphs are available from the American Library Association's Headquarters Library. To be suitably equipped, a library needs a wide variety of instructional materials; books, films, filmstrips, maps, globes, pamphlets, periodicals, pictures, recordings, slides, and related learning materials must be provided to meet the demands of the curriculum and the capabilities of the student body. Through the school librarian's interpretation of these materials of learning, administrators will enlarge their understanding of the need for them. An Indiana Superintendent said recently: "So important is an adequate collection of appropriate books and materials for boys and girls through the twelve years of school, that such a library has become the mark of a good school and a school without this mark cannot be judged a good one."[3]

To insure continuous communication between the library and the classroom in the use of materials, the school librarian will assist administrators in understanding the need for the school librarian to serve on committees for curriculum development and for the improvement of the over-all programme of instruction. In turn, the school librarian appreciates his administrators and gives them credit for their contributions.

One of the school library's most important publics is the faculty. The success or failure of the school library programme will be determined, in a large part, by the quality and amount of library use by the classroom teacher. As a working member of the instructional staff, and as a part of the school library's public relations programme, the school librarian keeps the contribution of the school library to the teaching programme constantly before the faculty. Generally, the school librarian is a fully trained teacher who knows and understands the school, its objectives and goals, and the school curriculum. As the librarian works with courses of study, with teachers and with students in completing assignments, becomes to understand the teaching methods of each member of the faculty his point of view and his special interests. At departmental meetings the school librarian makes suggestions and recommendations and receives requests from fellow teachers. He prepares bibliographies and arranges for a constant flow of curriculum materials to and from the classroom. The new teacher sees the librarian as a co-worker ready to help him and his students, and the alert librarian offers to have a session in the library for new teachers in the school, showing them around and answering their questions.

As it is important for the school librarian to know and understand the work of the teacher, similarly it is essential that the faculty know the duties and responsibilities of the school librarian—selecting, organizing, and servicing an up-to-date materials collection, working with classes, working with individuals in free reading and reading guidance, and giving ready reference or informational services. Sometimes the school librarian may be resented by other teachers who assume, because the librarian does not teach five periods a day, that he has a very light schedule of work. This misunderstanding will not happen if the school librarian attends and participates in in-service training programmes, faculty meetings, professional meetings, and parent-teacher meetings and if he has other opportunities to work with his colleagues. Involving all members of the faculty in the selection of materials, getting the teachers' assistance in discarding materials, and sending to the teachers lists of new books, magazines, films, filmstrips, and other purchases in their teaching areas are good public relations practices. The librarian's daily contacts should invite teachers to come in to read or to browse, to talk with students or other faculty, or to chat with the librarian.

The stereotype concept of a school librarian is too often that of a person who is aloof, snobbish, unworldly—who is standing guard over the books and materials with little or no regard for the individual, whether he is a student or a member of the faculty. The frequent appearance of the librarian in the classroom as a helping teacher and a tactful, friendly person directing the services of the library will erase such stereotypes. Perhaps, too, as a result of these contacts in the classroom the school librarian will be more effective in the informal teaching done in the library. The school librarian should also be present for the social events and school-sponsored activities to demonstrate that he is interested in the success of every part of the school.

The school librarian assists the faculty in their efforts to be informed about the latest developments and trends in their respective fields of teaching. Every school library should have an educational or professional collection which provides materials on curriculum, teaching, evaluation, counseling, and current social trends and as file of important professional magazine. Fortunate is the teacher who has the resources of a good school library, and equally fortunate is the school librarian who as a member of a faculty that is aware of the services offered by a good school library. B.L. Johnson said, Teaching is a creative activity; librarian participation in teaching can and must be creative in the highest sense of the word.

The students of the school are another important public. Satisfied students are the best publicity agents for the school library programme. The school librarian is in a strategic position to learn much about student interests, attitudes, and problems. From this information he guides the students to find books and materials suited to their interests and abilities and to solve their problems. Effective public relations with students will be strengthened through the appropriate use of displays, exhibits, discussion groups, story hours, assembly programmes, and book talks. Through browsing, discussing, and sharing, students learn to discriminate and develop judgment in the evaluation of materials. The librarian provides students with lists and other bibliographic services, encourages students to help in the selection and discarding of materials for the library and invites students to assist in formulating library policy.

Some librarians have found that student library committees provide opportunities to express opinions concerning policies and procedures in the school library. Through library participation students learn responsibility for use of public property and social responsibility in group situations. Students learn how to plan and work together effectively. One activity which has public relations merit as well as educational value for the student is the student library assistant programme. The best training comes from actually doing a variety of tasks; e.g., circulation, publicity, book lists, all under the direction of the librarian. A manual of instruction that describes the duties to be performed should be provided for each assistant. Varied assignments, arranged by planned work schedules and rotation of work, give students opportunities to develop a variety of learning skills and also to be a part of the public relations programme of the school library.

The school librarian, through a planned programme in teaching the use of the library, has an opportunity to improve public relations with students by teaching students to locate, organize, and use the library and all its resources. While teachers frequently share in giving various kinds of library instruction, the school librarian must assume the major responsibility for the programme of teaching the use of the library. An attractive library bulletin explaining library organization and different ways of using library materials will be very helpful to students. Skills in the use of the library which are learned in school will be used by the student whenever he uses libraries throughout his life. The school librarian can see that students have opportunities to become acquainted with other libraries in the community by arranging visits sponsored by the school library and by encouraging them to use the public library and other educational resources.

In furthering good public relations with students the school librarian should provide ready reference service and suitable work spaces for individual research as well as for group and committee work. The reference and research uses of the school library will depend, in a large part, upon the classroom teacher and his assignments, although hobbies and special interests of students sometimes lead to research. In our present day society there is much concern for the scientific approach to information; therefore, it is important that young people learn to use many tools in finding answers.

Other public relations techniques for implementing the students' use of the library may include assistance in planning club and co-curricular activities, publicity about the school library and its resources through a library reporter to the school newspaper, and assistance with career day activities and hobby shows. Some school librarians have used an attractive news bulletin board of current happenings about students, clubs, and sports to draw students into the school library. It should be remembered that an attractive school library is like an attractive home—students like to come to it. When pleasant surrounding are coupled with a tactful and friendly librarian, students will feel "at home." And when the librarian provides adequate materials and suitable work spaces students will make use of these.

A fourth important public to be considered in the school library's public relations programme is the members of the community. The school librarian can build stronger the public relations of the school library by knowing the community and by being an active part of it. Even though school library public relations begin within the school, much of the success which the school librarian desires will depend upon the impression created outside the school. The librarian's individual conversations and person-to-person contacts are very influential because these reflect the policies, practices, and actions of the school library. Librarians should never overlook the fact that every community has organized groups such as the P.T.A., Woman's Club, League of Women Voters, and the Junior Chamber of Commerce who have a natural interest in the school and its library programme. These groups are enthusiastic about reports on children's reading skills, the free reading programmes in the school library, provisions for the gifted child, research techniques, and the scientific approach to information. School library personnel need not be accomplished public speakers, but the librarian should know how to prepare a speech and how to deliver it. Sometimes speeches can be made more interesting by the use of student-made projects, pictures, slides, portable exhibits, and charts.

Parents are an important part of the school library's public. Through home visits the librarian assures parents of his interest in the student's welfare and invites the cooperation of parents in solving problems. Other means for making contact with parents are open houses, teas, and book talks which provide opportunities to visit the school library, to see its facilities, and to observe its services. Many school librarians have found that advisory citizen committees are important public relations contacts, since they assist in informing the public as well as in developing policies.

Some school librarians have found that a good public relations technology is to use the school library card catalogue to include cards by subject area of resource the people who live in the community and who are willing to supplement classroom discussion by talks, reports, or slides of their "first hand" experiences while living in other places and getting to know other people. The librarian should not overlook highly trained people in the scientific and technical areas, who usually are pleased to assist teachers and librarians in the teaching areas in which they are expert. Tapping the resources of community groups, such as industries, crafts and social agencies the librarian has available for loan many exhibits and displays for use in the school library. In addition, the card catalogue also may contain cards by subject area of field trips, places of historic or local interest, museums, public buildings, and shrines which are useful in enriching the teaching programme of the school. It is important that the card contain full information concerning location, hours open to the public, the person to contact for arrangements, and distance from the school.

Another community agency which can be of assistance to the school library in serving its publics and in enlarging library resources for school personnel is the public library. If a public library is located in the community, the school librarian should be well informed of its resources and should work closely with the public librarian in all areas in which coordination can make more materials more available to more young people. Much can be accomplished if the public librarian and school librarian will meet periodically to share, in a friendly and understanding manner, their common problems and the possible solutions. In addition, the school librarian can strengthen his relations with his publics by being informed about and making use of regional and state agencies and services. Advisory services are available also from state departments of education, national and state professional associations, and from nearby colleges and universities. Professional library journals often carry articles and ideas concerning public relations and publicity. A wealth of current literature is available on school public relations and can be adapted to school library public relations.

School librarians do not have to look far to discover an array of media for their use in communicating with their publics. If not in the school, somewhere in the community the librarian can find motion pictures, filmstrips, pictures, slides, exhibits, displays, bulletin boards, newspapers, magazines, radio, and television, which are at the librarian's disposal for interpreting school library service to its various publics. It is important that the school librarian select the proper medium to reach a particular public which the school library serves. Once he chooses the right medium, he will have a better opportunity for reaching a particular public and for achieving desired actions or attitudes. Whenever the school librarian considers a mass media approach to public relations, it is important that he considers the available resources, the time needed for preparation, the cost, the possible effectiveness, the subject matter presented, and the extent of influence. If the school librarian considers these factors, he is in a better position to choose the best medium to do an effective job of public relations.

The public relations minded school librarian knows that exhibits, displays, and bulletin boards are the show windows of school library service. These are splendid media for keeping students, faculty, administrators, and the general public informed of the work, assets, and services of the school library programme. The school librarian uses his ingenuity to make use of many places in addition to the school library for exhibits and displays. Some possibilities are school corridors, auditoriums, or gymnasiums; store windows; meeting rooms used by community groups; local and state fairs; and youth and teachers' conventions.

The medium of the motion picture may also be used to show the services of the school library. The visual image can inform and deliver a message which will be remembered for a long time. An excellent example of the motion picture as a public relations instrument is "A Carpet Under Every Classroom." Written and produced by Marion Hock, librarian of Manhasset, New York, High School, the film is intended to show the nature of school library work and how the library supports the school programme. It is designed for use with teachers, curriculum consultants, administrators, school boards, parents, and interested lay groups. Some librarians have found that slides and filmstrips can be just as effective as the motion picture in a public relations programme. One can also use slides on television for spot announcements or parts of a programme. If desired, sound can be added to slides or filmstrips by the use of a synchronized tape recording. However, the school librarian will be more effective by giving a running commentary because he can choose his remarks to fit the interests of the group.

Photographs are a familiar and highly valuable visual aid to public relations in and out of the school library. They are concrete and interesting and arrest attention. Even an amateur photographer—either the school librarian, a member of the faculty or a student—can take very creditable pictures with care and practice. Among the many activities for photographing are student activities, bulletin boards, exhibits, types of materials, and types of services. The school librarian should be careful that the shots taken of the library portray the story which he wishes to tell. Every school librarian should build a good picture file which shows the activities of the school library for publicity purposes. Large blow-ups can be used for posters and in display in corridors, at conventions, and in store windows.

Newspapers, radio broadcasts, and telecasts can carry news of the school library's activities to a wider public than that reached by other media. Local papers and broadcasting stations usually are cooperative because they are interested in giving the community news of local events. The formation of a library club, an unusual presentation of a film showing, an announcement of a previewing session, a speech by a locally important man to the student body concerning a library related topic, and the election of officers can all qualify as news. Sensitive to the high public interest in radio news, some school systems have developed a daily news show devoted exclusively to school news. The school librarian should see that school library activities are reported. Taped interviews add variety to the regular newscasts. If handled properly, panel discussions can be highly successful, particularly if lay citizens are panel participants. The studio classroom type of television show has been used widely and could easily show the variety of services offered by the school library.

The well-known questions of the newspaper world—the "five W's"—What, Where, Who, When, and Why, with the How as an alternative to the Why—should be used as a guide in testing each news release. It is usually easier to "rough out" a report first, then make the necessary changes. Editors appreciate copy that is typed, double-spaced, and on only one side of the paper. A margin of at least an inch should be left on each side of copy; the first sheet should have four inches of space at the top containing the subject across the middle of the space. The name and address of the writer should be placed in the upper left-hand corner. A school librarian who has learned how to write and to take good action photographs will be able to present an acceptable story.

Every school library public relations programme needs careful evaluation to appraise its work with the school and community. Methods of evaluation can range from informal observations to inventories, checklists, and special rating devices. The public relations conscious school librarian always takes inventory of what he is doing and planning. Here is a checklist of ten questions which may help in the evaluation of the school librarian's planned programme for the public relations of the school library. These questions also serve as a summary of this discussion.

1. Does the school librarian know the value of good public relations and does he recognize that he is the key to the public relations programme of the school library?

2. Does he know the interests and needs of the various publics which he serves?

3. Does he interpret the school library programme to his administrators by involving them in the planning of the programme; by reports; by preparing a budget; by explaining the need for space, staff, and materials; and by serving on committees?

4. Does he interpret the school library programme to the faculty by knowing the courses of study, teaching methods, and curriculum materials; by participating in all professional meetings; by involving the faculty in the selecting and discarding of materials and by taking part in all school activities?

5. Does he interpret the school library programme to the students by providing a wide variety of library materials which meet the needs, both curricular and co-curricular, abilities, and interests of students; by involving students in selecting and discarding materials and in formulating library policy; by directing a student library assistant programme; by teaching the use of library and by providing reference services?

6. Does the school librarian see that students know all the educational resources in their community including the public library?

7. Does the school librarian consciously consider the community in interpreting the school library programme by knowing the community and being an active part of it, by reporting to organized community groups, by using citizens of the community as resource persons, and by personal contacts?

8. Does the school librarian keep the school librarian programme before parents by visits; by open houses, teas, and talks; by advisory committees?

9. Does the school librarian use every known public relations media-pictures, motion pictures, filmstrips, slides, exhibits, displays, bulletin boards, newspapers, radio and television—to interpret the school library programme to its various publics?

10. Does the school librarian have a sense of direction, of values of appreciation, of human relations and of adventure, and does he evaluate his public relations programme?

REFERENCES

1. W.E. Reck, (Statement adapted) as quoted in Griswold, Glenn, and D.P. Griswold, *Your Public Relations*. New York, Funk, 1948, pp. 4, 22, 23.
2. Mary V. Gaver, *Every Child Needs A School Library*. Chicago, American Library Association, 1958.
3. L.A. Lockwood, Superintendent of Schools, Columbus, Indiana.
4. B.L. Johnson, and Eloise *Lindstrom, The Librarian and the Teacher in General Education: A Report of Library-Instructional Activities at Stephens College*. Chicago, American Library Association, 1948, p. 21.

15

Public Relations Activities of Special Libraries

THE SCOPE of modern public relations is sufficiently broad for the special library whether it exists as a separate entity, as do a few, or as working unit of larger organization which is generally true of the vast majority. It is only with the latter type that this chapter is concerned. For the purpose of this discussion, only public relations activities of industrial libraries will be emphasized. Although this may seem a relatively restricted frame of reference, actually their activities are not too different from those of special libraries in government agencies, in insurance companies, in banks, in publishing houses, in medical societies, and in other types of organizations; each deals with a clientele limited by some factor such as size, geographical location, or subject interest.

Formation of special libraries, as components of the types of organizations mentioned above, began to gather momentum at least a half century ago, whereas the current and generally accepted connotation of public relations is scarcely a generation old. Thus, the development and evolution of the special library's public relations antedates the present concept of the term based, as it now is, on careful attention to good will as professional goal rather than on specific techniques of reaching the goal. In the special library, public relations has been, from the beginning, a way of thinking translated into action. It continues to receive emphasis; otherwise the library would quickly lose its effectiveness.

Fortunately, the inception of the industrial library was never hampered with such traditions as are exemplified in *The Old Librarian's Almanack . . . for 1774* (Printed and sold by B. Mecom, at the Post-office in New-Haven, 1773), such as this one take from the section. Timely Advice to Librarians: "So far as your authority will permit of it, exercise great discrimination as to which persons shall be admitted to the use of the library. For the treasure house of literature is no more to be thrown open to the ravages of the unreasoning mob than is a fair garden to be laid unprotected to the mercy of a swarm of beasts." In this same source there are other examples of not just negative, but altogether bad public relations for libraries of which they have divested themselves through the years.

Any library, regardless of type, has several distinct publics but it is the nature and complexity of these publics which determine its essential activities. Each programme must be tailor-made to fit these particular publics. That much of the discussion of public relations pertains to the system of which it is a part, rather than to the tool itself, is a "take-off" point made in the opening chapter and accepted by each of the authors. It is then in the functions of special libraries, as affected by the organizations they serve, wherein one discerns differences as well as similarities in activities between them and other types of libraries.

Thus similarities as well as contrasts unit in providing the motivation for considering the subject independently. Yet at the same time one has the opportunity of equating them with the working concept of public relations. In doing this comes the realization that goodwill generated in any type of library builds goodwill for the profession as a whole and aids in attracting able persons to choose it as a career.

Since organizations vary greatly in both objectives and operations, diversification manifests itself in their libraries. It has never been possible or perhaps even desirable to follow a particular pattern. There are many special librarians who "start from scratch"—an opportunity which presents a real challenge. Even if the library has been organized previously, the special librarian, to a considerable extent, makes his own job. He can improve existing services and develop new services of values and, by anticipating trends, he can initiate the gathering of vital information in order to expedite service never before requested. Each of these factors is closely allied to good public relations.

Both the special library and its most important public, its clientele, are captive. The close personal day-to-day contacts make it possible for information to be provided for a projects and, as the project develops, 'one can see how the information fits into a pattern of usefulness and finally its part played in the total result whether the result is one of success or of failure. This opportunity to observe the end use of information redounds in rare satisfaction to those responsible for its provision. The entire process of working closely with the clientele in raising group productivity provides an excellent climate for good public relations.

Another difference lies in the area of non-conformity. It has already been pointed out that special libraries vary; they are under no legal requirements to conform in services rendered although some standardization may be desirable and not altogether impossible in the future. Every decision made by the library has a public relations aspect which keeps it in harmony with its parent organizations. Let some move be made which creates an unpopular reaction among some of its clientele and the library management soon learns about it. Immediate steps must be taken to repair the damage. On the other hand, a library which operates as an independent unit may never be made aware of the poor public relations aspects of a decision, for example, to close the library on weekends and evenings—the only time when working people can spend time there using materials for personal growth.

Related to this is the whole question of rules and their attendant inflexibility. Regardless of how many publics with diverse interests the special library has, it still has the advantage of being able to adjust its rules—always kept to a minimum—to the needs of its parents organization. Too many regulations can create bad public relations; if and when they are necessary they at least can be administered to avoid serious inconvenience. Or they can be changed. Or perhaps they can be done away with entirely. For example, if one regards a book or journal as part of the equipment for a research project, then consider the difference in attitude toward the library which allows loans for an indefinite period and one which requires return after two weeks or even a month. A project rarely ends in such a brief period.

The only sound first step in a public relations programme is to "put the house in order," according to C. D. MacDougall. R. B. Har well, whose article follows MacDougall's agrees with this point when he says that such a programme must first be properly fitted into the administrative pattern of the library. Even one of the earliest writers on the subject notes that public relations, like charity, begins at home. These thoughts all suggest that, in any discussion of the library's public relations activities, one should begin with the library staff—first by delineating the librarians's responsibility to operate the library in such a manner so as to gain understanding of the clientele, to hold to the confidence of management, to secure maximum productivity of the staff, and to gain goodwill generally—all in an atmosphere conducive to these ends.

A large number of the special libraries are of the so-called "one-man" type, wherein the librarian has complete responsibility for the entire operation. In this event, he is his own goodwill ambassador since contact with the library is solely through him. But as his organization grows, his public relations cannot always be on a personal basis even though the clientele has become accustomed to his particular touch. To keep pace with the growth of an enterprise, the library staff increases in number. Thus, it is incumbent on the librarian to develop responsibility for working within the framework of a coordinated programme and to share common goals of the enterprise with the library staff.

In choosing additional staff members, it is the librarian's task to find talent—persons with inquiring minds who are informed, articulate, and well trained in the particular work for which they are needed. This may relate to the development of an entirely new service or it may be complementary to established activities which demand extension. However, an employee's attitude and performance are governed by what he finds "on the job." One cannot employ staff endowed with enthusiasm, initiative, loyalty, and devotion for specific tasks. These qualities must be developed, both individually and collectively, since they are the *sine qua non* of good public relations. So the librarian has both an initial and continuing responsibility to give real meaning and significance to assignments to the staff may view them in terms of themselves and the clientele, in fact of the organization as whole.

Everyone in an organization, from the chairman of the board to the guard at the gates, is a potential client of the library. Although it is always a challenge to turn the random user into a constant one, the library staff members cannot focus merely on him or even on the inattentive (that is, those who never use the library); they must place the emphasis of information gathering and communicating upon the segments of the organization prepared to use services to the greatest advantage. With this as an objective, they can further aim at fostering good client relationships which are the most important factor in internal public relations, not only in establishing the free flow of information in and out of the library, but in maintaining confidence and understanding as well.

The library staff must ever be on the alert to know when special service is needed and when self-service will accomplish better results. Although, as individuals, many can be counted upon to express appreciation for aid and likewise let it be known when disgruntled, it is occasionally wise to survey objectively to learn if the clientele, as whole, is satisfied with the *status quo* and if not, do something about it. The term clientele has been used deliberately rather than patrons, which term carries a connotation of patronizing. In contrast to the latter, Webster defines client as "who employs the services of any professional man." Anything done to let the community know that a librarian is more than a mere keeper of books is good public relations for the entire profession.

Since the library exists for the benefit of the enterprise and therefore the bulk of activities are within its framework, there are also many other relationships to be taken into account, such as relations with suppliers The library is often an important spokesman for the company but more often it is a silent partner is building public relations. Not all publics can be reached directly; some are reached only through aid given intermurally but, regardless of method, the impact of library service extends beyond its own four walls and even beyond the organization it serves.

Relations with publics in combination can be illustrated by action taken on a request which came to a library staff (Lily Research Lab., Latin America) to develop an educational medium for sales service representatives in Latin America. The subject was the library service available in that organization, and whatever form was used to tell the story, it had to be small enough to carry in a brief case because of weight limitations of plane travel. A series of twenty coloured slides was made showing library staff members providing information by means of reference work, bibliographies, inter-library loans, microfilm, maps, special files, weekly abstracts, as well as routine circulation of journals. An appropriate script accompanied the slides which required a viewing time of fifteen minutes. By means of this audio-visual presentation the representative were better prepared to tell of the careful search preceding development of company product and explain to members of the health profession they contacted how their questions could be effectively handled on a referral basis.

There is still another type of an organization's public relations for which the librarian has direct responsibility. From time to time inter-library loans are negotiated, professional projects shared, or reference questions answered, all calling for an exchange of ideas or materials. Working relationships thus established through contact with other librarians must be carefully nurtured; they broaden information resources not only in the local area but scattered throughout the country as well. An important by-product is the opportunity for the library staff to play an effective part in the development of sound public attitudes toward the organization as a whole. Another benefit of professional contacts made through the exchange of facilities and talent is the impetus given to staff development and growth.

Special librarians have an obligation to cooperate in profession-wide projects within the limitations imposed by their own situations. For example, there was the occasion this year to participate in plans for National Library Week—a challenge to the entire profession to relate the programme to all types of libraries. Help in promotion was offered to the staff of Lily Research Laboratory by all Indiana State Library which cooperated with the State Citizen's Committee and the Steering Committee for the project. When concrete plans were presented, the management of the library was eager to help their staff by providing plant-wide bulletin boards space for colourful posters; special slogans for use in postage meters for out-going mail; double placards, or "tents," for use on tables in the plant cafeterias; bookmarks and flyers for items circulated both by plant libraries and the public library extension service; and space in employee publications. Thus, through concerted efforts, we were able to take part in National Library Week at a minimum of cost, time, and effort.

This discussion indicates the essentiality of goodwill as an asset of special libraries in their relations with publics—as many publics as there are distinct combinations of people with whom libraries communicate—either directly or indirectly. Since emphasis has been placed on the need for such activities rather than on the how of their execution, a classified list of media and techniques is appended. Regardless of methodology it would be difficult to convince a special librarian that there is any substitute for effective communications, excellent service, correct information, and unusual initiative in building a sound public relations programme; nor would many admit that there is any thing particularly new in the field. If indeed there is, it is the recognition that special librarians are becoming increasingly aware of their responsibilities to the profession as a whole; they are experimenting with development of personal qualitative standards for librarians; urging improvement in library education, and cooperating in recruitment on a nation-wide basis—all strong elements in good public relations.

Checklist of Media and Techniques for Public Relations Activities in Special Libraries

I. Numerous media exist, in addition to the usual communications in persons by telephone, and in memoranda, which can be used effectively such as:

Weekly library bulletins,
Feature articles in house organs,
Use of plant-wide bulletin boards,
Moving pictures of library operations,
Tours of library for all new employees,
Bookmarks to announce new employees,
Bookmarks to announce new materials,
Effective brochure introducing the library,
Library corner or column in company newspaper,
Attractive formats for bibliographical compilations,
Pictorial posters showing information centre in action,
"Reading as a Hobby" exhibit at annual hobby shows,
Information section in handbook for new company employees,
Explanation of library service in organization procedure manual.

II. Some techniques are:

a. *With clientele who depend on the library*

Attention to specific interests,
Bibliographies on any subject,
Assistance with editorial problems,
Display of company news releases,
Cheerful consideration of criticisms,
Careful consideration of recommendations,
"Extra touch" such as a comfortable chair,
Aid in acquisition of personal library items,
Suggestions for binding of personal periodicals,
Presentation of library service at a research seminar,
Duplicating and/or copying machines available in library,
Suggest classification schemes for personal information files,
Reproduction of tables of contents of important current journals.

b. *With management*
Material for talks,
Daily intelligence digest,
Indexing company publications,
Annual reports summarized to one page,
Provision for employee's recreation reading,
Participation in company's educational programme,
Preservation and organization of company archives,
Advice in classification of personal book collections,
Cooperation in the plant-wide public relations programme,
Good working relationships with library committee members.

c. *With the library staff*
In-service training,
Staff manual kept up-to-date,
Cooperation with management,
Handle exhibits as staff projects,
Communicate effectively and clearly,
Invite ideas for library bulletin boards,
Staff participation in employee activities,
Staff meetings in which members participate,
Encourage additional educational preparation,
Bulletin board for exclusive use of library staff,
Suggest contributions for professional periodicals,
Man the station library maintained by local public library.

III. Media and techniques useful outside the organization are:

a. *With professional colleagues*
Exchange of duplicate material,
Attendance at professional meetings,
Adherence to rule of other libraries,
Visits to library facilities in the area,
Cooperation with professional projects,
Participation in National Library Week,
Report help gained through inter-library loan,
Arrange for professional meeting in company library,
Consultation regarding library development in the area.

b. *With potential library employees*
Library summer work-study programme,

Vocational talks to high school groups,
Acquaint library schools in the area with library,
Illustration of library in company's recruiting folder,
Annual open house for students interested in Library work,
Keep colleges informed of successful careers of their graduates.

In using this checklist it should be kept in mind (1) there are several overlapping items in the above categories; (2) not every library will find it practicable or even desirable to consider all of them; and (3) not every library will find it practicable or even desirable to consider all of them; and (3) many of the suggestions may already be incorporated not only in programmes of special libraries but in those of other types as well—school, college, and public.

16

Public Relations of State and Federal Libraries

THERE is some inconsistency, real or apparent, between the reports of surveys of citizen opinion that show that people like the library as an institution, whether they use it or not and the rather widely held conviction among librarians themselves that they are among the world's poorest publicists. Libraries undoubtedly share in the traditional respect people generally give to symbols of culture, and their own public relations and service programmes cannot be said to be alone responsible for this favourable attitude. Also, while library publicity is admittedly often of poor quality, we are coming to recognize that it is only one aspect of public relations. In the light of this recognition, and the fact that poor publicity is often worse than none, it is perhaps just as well that library publicity has generally up to the present been low in quantity. This is not to say that good publicity is not needed for all types of libraries, state and federal libraries included. However, public relations cannot be promoted by publicity alone, or, indeed, by all kinds of popular pamphlets. It remains primarily a matter of regular, face-to-face relationship with those persons who are in strategic positions to be of aid to the library and to promote its services.

Both publicity and public relations programmes have been generally associated with extroverted personalities. Alice Bryan recorded for the Public Library Inquiry in 1952 that while personality inventories showed most measured qualities of public librarians to be near the general norms for many people in similar academic and white collar service occupations, their median scores were somewhat below established norms for persons with comparable general education with regard to aggressive leadership and self-confidence. This is in terms of averages, not uniformities, and all who understand the operations of libraries know that the range of activities in a good library system has in it room for the range of personalities one would expect to find in an institution that deals with literary, scientific, and artistic materials and with people interested in such materials.

If Miss Bryans's profile of public librarians is accurate for librarians generally, it is probably true that they are not attracted to nor are they naturally adapted to public relations activities of the kinds which they may believe to be engaged in by the socially undesirable characters. There is need for recognition that the good and competent performance of many professional and other library tasks by library workers who are less extroverted—more introverted people, in other words—is in itself the soundest possible base for excellent library public relations.

The need is also acute for librarians at administrative levels to understand, accept, and act upon the fact that public relations is an important and inescapable function of library management. In short, the objectives of all libraries, local, state, and federal, require that certain library posts be filled by people having highly developed management skill including that of public relations.

For librarians to accept this more fully, and to overcome any natural distaste for public relations activities, it may be useful to emphasize MacDougall's implication, that much of the adverse criticism regarding public relations really pertains to certain increasingly discredited activities of the business and political system of which public relations and publicity have been a part, rather than to the tool itself. This does not in any way condone certain of the practices for which, according to ethical and religious concepts, some aspects of the economic and political system and the promotion that has helped these practices to flourish are properly condemned. For libraries, too, and the materials they contain, can be made to serve undesirable ends.

In discussing the assumptions with which the Public Library Inquiry began its nationwide survey, R. D. Leigh states in *The Public Library an the United States*, "If we had been living and working within a totalitarian or feudal society, some of our assumptions would have been different. We were not oblivious to the fact that the public library is in no sense a peculiarly democratic instrument. Indeed, a survey of recent public library developments throughout the world indicated the fascist and communist countries have been most active in promoting public library growth within their borders. But their libraries do not operate under assumptions such as have guided library development in democratic countries.

Even before Miss Bryan's profile of public librarians, librarians have long seemed rather firmly convinced that they lack the basic qualities regarded as necessary for carrying on public relations programmes. There is much public apathy toward libraries that leads to the belief that this is true. Yet, leading career advisers and public relations specialist state that the three essential requirements for a successful career in public relations are: knowledge of the humanities, of patterns of human behaviour, and of the techniques of communication. Most professional librarians majored for their undergraduate degrees in subjects included in the humanities. Thus, the basic formal education of many librarians has provided at least one and sometimes more of the three prerequisites. Librarians live each day amid the books that tell what is known and being discovered about patterns of human behaviour, and about techniques of communication. Book in the humanities are also easily available.

Much of what will be said here is meant to apply in general both to state and federal libraries, but with considerably more emphasis to state libraries because of the writer's greater familiarity with them.

State and federal libraries are public libraries; in fact, state libraries are, where most fully developed, and in all cases should be, the axis of the public library systems that surround them. Yet, the most fully developed of them supplement of the public and other local libraries they serve with such a broad range of the more technical, unusual, and specialized materials, information, and services that these state and federal libraries more nearly resemble large university or large special research libraries, except that they have more diversified clienteles. They serve more numerous and more different kinds of "publics" than any other type of library. Thus, their public relations are inherently more complex.

State and federal libraries serve their purposes most effectively when their relations are good with (1) the general public, (2) the state or federal government generally, but particularly including the members and staffs of Congress or the state legislature, budget and finance departments, and, in the case of departmental libraries, the special departments of which the libraries are part, (3) local libraries, particularly but not exclusively the public libraries throughout the states,

(4) state and national library associations, (5) local officials and organizations of local officials, (6) other state and federally supported libraries, (7) organizations of state or federal employees, and groups whose memberships are often made up largely of state, local, and federal government officials and employees, such as local chapters of management and public administration societies, (8) civic, professional, scientific, and business organizations, and (9) communications organizations, press, radio, and television.

As examples of the above, Foster Mohrhardt, director, U.S. Department of Agriculture Library, has pointed out that good relations with the American Medical Association are important for the National Library of Medicine, and they are equally important for the Veterans Administration Library. The Department of Agriculture Library must have good relations with associations of land grant college workers, agriculturists, biologists, and chemists. The Department of the Interior Library must have good relations with petroleum groups and geologists.

One basic difference between state and federal libraries is that in many states the state library encompasses many of the subject reference and research responsibilities which at the national level are performed by individual subject or departmental libraries.

Not only the chief state and federal librarians but the field and consultant staff members are the centres of any real public relations programmes. There is no escaping the fact that public relations are likely to occupy a great deal of time and effort in after-office hour of the chief officers of any library. This means going to many meetings and having many personal contact and professional conferences.

State and federal libraries have, as do other libraries, many individual patrons, but because they serve such wide areas and large numbers of people, it may be said that major targets of their public relations necessarily are groups, in and outside of government, and in and outside of the library profession. This in no way minimizes the importance of their relations with individuals.

Federal libraries have relations with groups which, in addition to the federal government and its particular branches the libraries are charged to serve, are the counterparts of the publics of state libraries. Several of the federal libraries have been more complex group relationships, which reach out not only to libraries and other group and individuals throughout the United States but to the libraries and cultural, educational, and scientific development of other countries. The Library of Congress, together with the National Library of Medicine and the United States Department of Agriculture Library constitute what may be called our national libraries. The National Library of Medicine acts as the world's repository of medical information and historically serves not only this country but the world. The same is true of the U.S. Department of Agriculture Library. The publications of these libraries, particularly the indexes and abstracts provided by them, indicate their international responsibilities.

Military libraries form another important and widespread category of federal libraries. W. B. Coon, Sixth U.S. Army, librarian, Presidio of San Francisco, comments regarding the public relations programms of military libraries. Coon's own library the Sixth U.S. Army Reference Library, serves as a headquarters reference resource and a reference materials supply centre for all libraries in the command, somewhat as state libraries supplement the resources of local public libraries.

Military libraries fall into three general categories: the academic specialized libraries at the major services schools such as the National War College and the Infantry School; numerous technical libraries such as the medical libraries in major hospitals and legal libraries at many posts; and, finally, the general libraries, comparable to public libraries, at all military installations. These latter may include branches, bookmobiles, and other extension outlets. The academic libraries are similar to civilian college or university libraries, and the technical libraries are similar to special libraries. Their public relations programme appear to be somewhat similar to those of their civilian counterparts.

In the military hierarchy, general libraries usually come under Special Services, or similar organizational elements such as Morale Services or Personnel Services. They have organizational equality with other activities serving the voluntary user, but they provide not only for off-duty needs of military personnel but for their job-connected needs as well. Public relations has been of much concern in these libraries. Although there is no regulation in the Army, for example, that prescribes library public relations, it is significant that over 10 per cent of the instructional portion of the Army's official Library Operational Guide is devoted to public relations and publicity. Publicity is regarded as essential for military general libraries for many reasons including the rapid rate of turn-over of military personnel at any given post, a turn-over completely unlike anything most other kinds of libraries experience. Thus, public relations and publicity are not regarded as extras but rather as part of the over-all library operation, and time is budgeted for them just as for materials selection.

Although there are no military librarians with the sole duty of public relations work, nearly all staff members participate knowingly and on scheduled time in publicity and public relations activities. Evidence of the quality of their efforts is seen in the several awards won by military libraries in the annual John Cotton Dana Library Publicity Awards Contests. The Army has for five years sponsored an annual library publicity contest of its own, which has helped to make publicity a normal activity in Army libraries. Military libraries participated actively in the recent observance of National Library Week.

Military libraries overseas have done a good job in bringing understanding and information both to military personnel and foreign nationals. This has been done despite the fact that the mission of these libraries, unlike that of United States Information Service libraries, does not specifically include dealing with foreign nationals. These military libraries have sponsored lecture programmes, travel films tours, children's programmes which included representatives from the local civilian communities, and open house to which the civilian community was invited.

Perhaps a major contribution of military libraries to library public relations in general has been their emphasis on making libraries inviting and friendly, normal places. They pioneered in dispelling the old, forbidding "hush-hush" atmosphere that kept many people out of libraries. Normal conversation and smoking are accepted as matters of fact in military libraries. These libraries have also probably played an important part in breaking down the fiction that librarians are severe and slightly sour spinsters with aversion to any sound louder than a whisper. Millions of men in uniform have seen attractive young librarians positively identified by their distinctive blue uniforms with library service patches. The ultimate effect of this kind of public relations is difficult to estimate.

United States Information Service libraries in overseas locations comprise another major segment of federal libraries. As would be inevitable in any programme so closely connected with United States foreign policy, opinion regarding the U.S.I.S. libraries varies both at home and abroad. Also, like other systems of libraries, some are stronger than others. To all who believe in the power of accurate information to improve understanding between peoples and nations of the world, and in view of the need for such understanding, these libraries perform an essential service. That their missions may at certain times, in certain places, and to certain people, seem to be that of biased propaganda, is probably escapable in the complexities and stresses of international relations. Perhaps it can be taken as a sort of tribute to the belief of people in the power of books and ideas that these libraries have occasionally been attacked and destroyed, unfortunate as these occurrences have been.

In November 1952, the *New York Times* reported on a survey of American informational activities aboard by twenty-four foreign correspondents covering forty-four nations. They were critical of most media, including the Voice of America, but hardly an ill word was uttered about any of the U.S.I.S. libraries. Numerous reports since that date stress that next to exchanges of persons between nations, overseas libraries are the strongest part of any information programme. These libraries combine the services given by public and special libraries in America. Around their basic reference collections is built a series of collections on the thinking and experience of America in fields of particular importance to the host country. Their special adaptation of library collections to user need, plus the high quality of carefully selected librarians, has made these libraries good cultural ambassadors for the United States.

The overseas libraries have provided in many countries what may be the only examples the people there have seen of libraries designed for general, free, public use, with easy access to publications, and the friendly assistance of informed librarians. Although criticized by some investigators, the inclusion in the collections of materials critical of the United States greatly enhances acceptance of the whole United States information programme, and serves to convince the people of the host country that the libraries are not there for propaganda purposes. Their very neutrality lends them authority.

American information librarians often work on committees of local librarians abroad and thus make further contributions to library development in other countries. It has been in many countries a revolutionary thing to see the libraries with open shelves and lending books without charge. Most public libraries in Germany, for instance, have charged a few pfennings (one pfenning is about 1/4 cent in U.S. currency) for each book loaned. Some shelve books by size in closed stacks to make the maximum possible use of every foot of scarce space. In some cases, the German librarians have felt that the American libraries are setting an impossibly high standard which German libraries cannot reach, causing German libraries to be compared unfavourably by the German public.

Comprehensive state libraries are probably more deeply embedded into the governmental structures of which they are integral parts, both with respect to controls and services, than other public libraries. In this respect, also, they resemble university, college, and school libraries in being integrated into the structure of their parent organizations. On the other hand, some state and federal government departmental libraries, as contrasted to central state libraries and the Library of Congress and a few other federal and state-supported libraries, often lack needed integration into the total department structure. They are at times appendages for which the department has real need but they are lost in the complexities of the organization and cannot function well because they do not have proper planning or supervision.

It is often difficult for the distant users of state and federal libraries to make their needs known directly to those who have authority for budget and policy approval. This is particularly true of libraries which serve whole states or regions composed of groups of states. Budget and policy approval rests with professional governmental administrators who are remote from the libraries and individuals who depend upon the state and federal libraries for library materials and services for which these libraries for library materials and services for which these libraries are their chief or only source. Thus, often the librarian alone, in the absence of any affective way for library users to make their needs known, proposes and defends the budget and programme of the library. For example, one large state library is still provided with a book budget that permits purchasing only one copy of any book, a policy established when the state's population was less than one million people, although the population of the state has grown to over fourteen million. This is largely due to the lack of any established means by which the supplementary book needs of the libraries of the state and the individual users can be expressed directly by the users to those with budget authority at the time decisions are being made about budget and policy.

The officials and employees of the state and federal governments form a large, important, and diversified segment, but only a segment, of the clientele of each. State and federal governments are becoming increasingly complex, and their influence on the lives of every man, woman, and child in the state and nation is great. The need of government personnel for reliable and comprehensive information is unlimited, and the provision or lack of such information is far-reaching in effect. Those needs as well as the needs of libraries and individual users at points distant from the seat of government would be better served by some means of direct expression to budget and legislative authorities, in addition to the government librarians' requests.

There are often state and federal departmental libraries on specialized subjects, but despite their existence, the central state libraries and the Library of Congress carry chief responsibilities for services to state and federal governments taken as a whole. The U.S. Department of Agriculture Library has special responsibilities for all of the land grant institutions in additions to its department-wide services. Some federal libraries have regional branches as do some state libraries but federal libraries have no direct administrative controls over state or local libraries other than their branches, just as no state library has administrative control over any local library.

The better the working relationships, that is, the greater and easier the flow of needed informational materials between federal, state, and local libraries of all types, the better the library needs of all the people can be met. These are partnership relations, and are most productive when completely free of any tinge of paternalism and of fears of controls being exercised by one level over another. Since there is no means for the libraries at either federal or state level to compel any action, both state and local libraries have all to gain and nothing to lose from the fullest possible participation in the library system. Such participation makes the total library service of the country at the same time more complete, effective, and economical.

Libraries at all levels have a long way to go before this productive participation in a nationwide library system is fully realized. Thus, none of the libraries is realizing the greatest possible benefit from a complete use of public relations possibilities. This kind of working relationship has nothing to do with direct administrative control, even where state and federal financial grants may be involved. If any library at any level chooses not to participate, it may refrain from doing so, even at the cost of the quality of its service.

Recognition of mutual interdependence, and freedom from fear of the level above is usually grater the larger and stronger the individual local or state library. Some of this feeling of security from possible encroachments of control from above, on the part of larger, stronger libraries, may stem from the fact that many state libraries have been so undernourished financially that their staff members and services have not been accorded much respect from the best local libraries. ("Miss So-and-So does the best she can with what she has, but she has never had anything with which to work.") The Library Services Act is helping to strengthen state libraries, and in such ways that local libraries, both large and small, can see the values to them of having working partnership relations with state libraries. This is because the strengthened state libraries are at the same time strengthening local libraries through programmes under the Library Services Act, helping libraries to help themselves toward modern minimum library standards.

It is probably inescapable, natural, and even wholesome, salutary, and in the American democratic tradition that smaller libraries guard their independence rather jealously, even though there is no imaginable means by which their independence could be violated against their will. When that independence takes the form of strong local pride, and includes the exercise of strong initiative for maximum local library effort, the local library can reach high effectiveness and gain in the feeling of security against encroachment from "outside." More libraries are realizing that not even the largest libraries in the country can hold in their own collections all the materials that will ever be needed by their users, and that all need to call upon the resources of other libraries, in order to meet the needs of all readers.

On the other hand, when independence is defensively asserted, and is not accompanied by sound efforts to maintain a good standard of local service, the local library users and taxpayers are the losers. The needless assertion and misdirected energies could better be channeled into improvement of the local library.

The relations of state to local libraries are sometimes impaired by the perhaps unconscious transfer of fears and resentments felt by small businesses against big business as represented by chain stores, large corporations, and the taxing and regulatory powers of state and federal government. Similar fears are said to exist among local school authorities with relation to state and federal school agencies. It is difficult to make clear that library service, voluntarily sought, and library materials presenting all points of view and advocating none, selected by library user from a cooperative system of libraries, differ greatly from the economic competition between large and small business, the taxing and regulatory powers of governments, and the system of compulsory public education. With reference to the latter; libraries at all levels sometimes suffer from being categorized with schools as educational agencies. While libraries have lifelong educational objectives, their form, functions, and methods are entirely different from those of the more formal, compulsory public school system with its necessary emphasis on classroom instruction lasting usually just through the period of human adolescence.

It would be surprising considering the traditional and ingrained wariness with which different levels of government in the United States view especially the level above, if the Library of Congress did not "lean over" to allay the fears of other government libraries that they may be "swallowed" or overshadowed. Although there are no fears on the part of state libraries, of which the writer is aware, that federal libraries will "swallow" them or usurp their functions, there is an absence of as close working relationships between federal and state libraries as could be developed with profit to both. The creation with the American Library Association, in its recent reorganization, of the new division, the American Association of State Libraries, provides a vehicle through which state and federal libraries can begin working more closely together. It would seem only natural that state libraries would have to take the initiative in seeking this closer relation, since the higher governmental level is usually acutely self-conscious that initiative on its part is often interpreted as aggressiveness meant to do some kind of usually undefined harm to the level below.

The responsibilities assigned to the Library Services Branch, U.S. Office of Education, Department of Health, Education and Welfare, by the 1956 Library Services Act have required some expansion of the Branch to enable it to work on specific library extension programmes with state library agencies. The public library extension agency of each state qualifying for federal grants receives assistance in the development and application of plans and programmes that are financed by such grants. Public relations with state libraries and the library profession as a whole are a concern of the Library Services Branch. Two recent evidences of this concern are the appointment of the Advisory Committee on the Library Services programme, and cosponsorship with the American Association of State Libraries of the Institute on State Plans under the Library Services Act on January 27, 1958.

There is one area in all government libraries where public relations could be considerably improved. This is in the relationship between federal libraries and the libraries of states, counties, and municipalities. The national libraries are said to feel that they must usually give an answer to any request from a taxpayer anywhere in the country. For example, if someone writes to the U.S. Department of Agriculture Library and wants to know the names of farm organizations in California, that Library would probably supply the individual with names of organizations. Although this is a highly desirable kind of service from the standpoint of the individual, it does bypass the local or state library in the state or locality from which the inquiry comes. If national libraries referred requests that can be handled by state or local libraries directly to those libraries it would enable them to establish continuing relationships with the individual who needs service. This practice is followed by the California State Library and several other state libraries when requests come directly to them from individuals in communities with library service. Thus, most lending outside the seat of government is done through local libraries. People living in communities without library service may, of course, receive direct service upon application to the state library. This direct service in no way substitutes for good local library service.

State libraries often have to carry water on both shoulders in relations with local libraries some of which feel that state libraries do not do enough to help them, and others which fear that the state may do too much. Even the strongest and best-supported state libraries cannot and should not do for local libraries the things which they are able to do for themselves. It is enough for state and federal libraries to perform to the fullest those services which they alone can best perform. It is not always easy to identify the things which will be done better on a permanent basis by the local library than if attempted by the state library. In general, state library services other than supplementary book and reference services, should be those of an in-service training nature, advisory and consultant work, demonstrations and experiments, and management and organization studies which will result in strengthened local services and more capable local personnel.

It will not be possible for state libraries to escape all misunderstandings and misinterpretations of motives, either for declining to give services, the local need for which will recur again and again, unless local personnel can be trained or obtained to keep them up, such as weeding, cataloguing or recataloguing of book collections, nor for seeming to promote and push programmes that would enable localities to give better services in the future, primarily by their own efforts. The latter type of programme and promotion, although needed in all states, will almost surely subject the state library to occasional charges of empire-building.

Only one report was found of a recent professional survey of the public relations practices of a state library agency, the West Virginia Library Commission, with recommendations for specific steps toward improvement. Five state libraries, those of Nevada, New Hampshire, Michigan, Mississippi, and Oregon, are reported to be using a small portion of federal funds received from Library Services Act appropriations for public relations. Many state and federal agencies are unable to employ public relations officers unless specifically authorized by their legislatures to do so.

Both state and federal libraries depend upon the quality of their services, the federal to the state and local libraries, the state to local libraries, for acceptable and effective working relationships. Therefore, the relations between federal, state, and local libraries rest, as they properly should, on cooperation and on leadership by consent.

These are some typical activities of state libraries which, because they render valued assistance, result in improved public relations for libraries generally, although not always for the state library itself, if they are well done and done in cooperation with others: planning for adequate library service for all residents of a state, including assistance in organizing and extending local library service; supplementary book, periodical, and film service; expert consultant, advisory, and survey services; institutes and workshops for local library personnel; development and establishment of library standards; administration of certification systems; administration of state and federal grants-in-aid; library demonstration and experimental programmes; collection, compilation, and publication of statistics.

State libraries will do well to keep constantly in mind that although leadership and the highest possible quality of services to local libraries are essential, statewide library programmes depend primarily for their force, vitality, and widest implementation on the strength, initiative, persistence, and professional awareness of state library associations, including associations of library trustees and friends of libraries. In fact, some of the best accomplishments of state libraries come about when others—individuals or groups—such as a long-range planning committee of a state library association, a legislative committee or legislative body, a governor, a trustees' group, after long consideration and study take up a course of action or an idea that may have originated with the state library, carry it through, receive all the credit, and the state library's part is forgotten. Although everyone and every institution enjoys receiving credit, much good can be accomplished for libraries and their public relations if no one cares especially who gets the credit.

17

Publications Exchange

THE IMPORTANCE of the governmental and institutional publications, which form the bulk of current exchange materials, has been recognized by governments as well as by research institutions. The fact that the system of barter known as exchange can secure important foreign publications for users of developed countries circumvent the soft currency problem, make these publications available to technically-backward countries, and place these publications in countries whose citizens know too little about American libraries is recognized and appreciated.

There have been a number of significant developments and trends in exchanges since the beginning of World War II. They are as follows: the increased concern of governments for the extension and improvement of international exchanges; Unesco leadership in the same field; the establishment of national book centres, such as the United States Book Exchange; the use of procurement officers; and finally, the small beginnings of multilateral exchanges.

One of the most striking trends in the exchange of current publications during the past decade has been the increased interest which governments have shown in it. World War II made painfully apparent to American government the shortage in this country of vital information about other countries. Efforts to avoid World War III have pointed up the importance of the wide distribution of publications from this country which might make for better understanding with other nations. Both of these needs are met by the single operation of exchange.

The United States government has supported exchanges for more than a century. The service of the Smithsoian Institution in shipping and in receiving publications for libraries in this country, now known as the International Exchange Service, has been in operation since 1849.

In addition, the Institution executes the federal government's exchange agreements with other nations. The feeling that this longtime programme was inadequate was evidenced by the federal government's Interdepartmental Committee on Scientific and Cultural Cooperation when it authorized in 1948 "a comprehensive report on the legislation, policies, procedure, and programme of the United States Government for carrying on exchanges of publications. . ."[1] The resulting excellent and comprehensive report by Kipp confirmed the importance of exchange as an instrument in a cultural relations programme.

Additional evidence of governmental concern is given by the two year contract by the United States Book Exchange and the Foreign Operations Administration under which fifty-three foreign countries will acquire scientific, technical, and educational literature from the Exchange. The Exchange will send publications to libraries and institutions in F.O.A. countries without handling charges in exchange for their publications. The programme is intended to build up back-issue stocks of books and periodical of F.O.A. counties, and its two-year, $10,000 budget is apportioned to various parts of the world on the basis of need. The enlargement in the foreign holdings of the Exchange will be an incidental advantage to libraries in this country.

Another development, this time in the international field, is the decision of the Organization for European Economic Cooperation to sponsor an exchange of scientific and technical documents among its members. This decision extends to the whole of Western Europe the system of pooling and distributing scientific and technical information which proved valuable during World War II. The plan went into operation on January 1, 1950, with each of the member nations agreeing to supply free to charge six copies of its pertinent official documents to each of the other fourteen members.

Much credit of the increased activity in exchanges among nations must go to the leadership of Unesco. The Unesco Clearing House for Publications is the only international publications exchange service. It promotes inter-governmental exchange agreements, encourages the establishment of national book centres, and seeks to reduce or eliminate import duties and transportation costs on publications exchanged. Unesco has published a manual on the international exchange of publications, and publishes monthly the *UNESCO Bulletin for Libraries,* which gives current information on exchange possibilities.

National book centres have been discussed frequently in library literature during the past twenty years. Some centres have been active since the Brussels' Convention of 1886; others have sprung up since World War II through the encouragement of Unesco. The range of their activities varies greatly, as do their sponsoring agencies and means of support. Some, such as the Japanese and British centres, function primarily as information agencies. Others, such as the Hungarian and East German centres, serve as transmission agencies. A third group, represented by the French and Australian centres, perform both of the above functions and in addition negotiate exchange agreements.

The exchange of duplicate materials presents quite a different problem from the exchange of current publications. In this country the significant development in the exchange of duplicates has been the formation of the United States Book Exchange. The formation of such a centre was suggested as early as 1876 by Melvil Dewey. It was his idea that such a centre would be the least expensive way of exchanging duplicates, and that an activity that could not be profitably carried on in the least expensive way should not be carried on at all. Since 1876 there has been all through library literature a thread of articles suggesting the formation of such a centre. Now there is a centre, and its progress and usefulness must be of concern to all who are interested in the exchange of duplicates.

Historically the United States Book Exchange was preceded by the Duplicate Exchange Union and by the short-lived Wilson cooperative clearinghouse. In 1937 the H. W. Wilson Company offered to serve as a clearinghouse to facilitate the completion of fragmentary serial sets among libraries. The service operated at a loss and was withdrawn after a few months trial. The Duplicated Exchange Union met with more success, perhaps because it was initiated by librarians, who felt an obligation to support it. Largely through the efforts of Neil Van Deusen, the Union was formed in 1940 as a periodically duplicate exchange. In 1944 its scope was broadened to include non-serial duplicates, and changes were made in its method of operation. The Union is still active, but it is interesting to note that the Detroit Public Library withdrew in 1949 because it felt that the United States Book Exchange would be more efficient. The reasons given were that the Exchange had a larger membership, consequently a larger stock to draw from, and that participation did not require listing of materials offered.

The United States Book Exchange succeeded the American Book Centre for War-Devastated Libraries. The fact that it grew out of a benevolent organization may have coloured some librarians thinking about it during the first years of its existence. The Exchange was formed in 1948 as a service organization to handle duplicates in one central place. Its sponsors included the leading national library associations as well as many national scholarly, educational, and research organizations. Its financial support came from a $90,000 grant made by the Rockefeller Foundation, supplemented by fees paid by participating libraries for materials obtained and by contracts with the State Department for services performed for foreign libraries. By the end of 1953 the Exchange could report 3,000,000 duplicates on hand. It offers such special services as the supplying of L.C. catalogue cards with books selected from the Exchange lists, the acceptance of orders for periodicals as well as the listing of duplicates on hand, the willingness to accept all periodicals which member libraries may wish to send, the holding of a semi-annual open house at which librarians may select from stock, and the investigation of the non-receipt of items due member libraries on regular exchanges in cases where claims have not been answered by the exchange partner.

The question of the cost of using the services of the United States Book Exchange is a basic one. The Exchange report in 1951 that during its first year and a half it had placed 100,000 foreign and domestic serial items in participating American libraries at a cost to the participating institutions of about $20,000. This is an average cost of 20 cents per item. In the October, 1951, issue of *Serial Slants* a librarian reported that for her library U.S.B.E. items had cost 34 cents each and that items received on regular exchange cost only 4 cents each.[2] Cost-per-item is not, of course, the whole story. As the U.S.B.E. collection becomes larger, it becomes potentially more useful. The elimination of the need for listing duplicates certainly saves time for libraries. However this advantage can be cancelled by the cost of transportation involved in sending duplicates to the Exchange, particularly if the library is some distance from Washington.

Inevitably the Exchange must compare its services with those of the periodical dealer. A library having a list of periodical wants may well decide to send it to a dealer, who will accept it at no charge, rather than to the Exchange, which charges 10 cents per title for considering wants. This disadvantage, of course, can be avoided by those libraries which are close to the Washington area and can economically send librarians to the Exchange's open house with their want lists in hand. A series of regional exchange centres would extend this advantage to all member libraries.

It seems unlikely that the United States Book Exchange will ever replace the exchange carried on by associations of special libraries limited to one field of interest. The oldest of these is the Medical Library Association Exchange, started in 1898. Other exchanges are operated by the American Association of Law Libraries and the American Theological Library Association. These specialized exchanges serve the same purpose in relation to periodical dealers that cooperatives do in the commercial field. In the general field the greater number of periodical dealers helps keep practices and prices reasonable.

A post-war development of potential importance to acquisitions is the use of trained procurement officers to secure hard-to-get materials. The Division of Acquisition and Distribution of the State Department has developed a successful procurement programme for obtaining European publications for the Library of Congress. John Fall, writing in the April 1954 issue of the *Library Quarterly* says, "If libraries could in some way make a working arrangement with the State Department procurement officers or with other federal agencies abroad, the acquisition of books and documents would be materially increased".[3]

A more specialized project is that of nine federal agencies working together through the Inter-Agency Foreign Map Procurement Coordination Committee on a map procurement programme. This project, which attempts systematic coverage of the world, has been serviced by six full-time geographical attaches and four temporary attaches. According to the 1953-1954 report of the Library of Congress Map Division,[4] the Division has received under the project an average of 15,500 maps per year from approximately 125 official mapping agencies located in 58 countries or dependencies. Since maps are more often official publications than not, such a programme is particularly important and productive. The programe also has implications for to the procurement of other types of material. It is a systematic, cooperative programme and shows the value of the personal contact which the procurement officer is able to set up and maintain. Certainly research libraries in this country know the value of procurement agents through the work of the Documents Expediter. Further exploration of the use of this procurement method would seem to be indicated.

The multilateral exchange of current publications as a means of converting publications in one subject field into those of another has been suggested but not thoroughly explored. The Unesco Clearing House for Publications gives multilateral exchange promotion as one of its aims. Under this programme it attempts to set up an arrangement whereby one institution gives to a second institution which gives in turn to a third which in turn gives to the first institution. The possibility of such three-way exchanges was considered by the Midwest Inter-Library Center about two years ago. A number of member libraries agreed to supply publications which could be used to obtain other publications for the centre. According to Ralph Esterquest,[5] director of MILC, the method has been used in only one instance so far because no other need for it has arisen. However, the centre still considers the method a possible one and will use it if need arises.

Serious problems remain to be solved if exchanges are to approach their full potential effectiveness. Lacks in bibliography, the economics of exchange, and inadequate coverage must be studied. The increased writing of recent years on the subject of exchanges,[6] the point of dissatisfaction with current exchange practices, and the increased concern of government about exchange all suggest that action would be taken to systematize and rationalize exchange practices. The time is ripe for a modern-day Alexander Vattemare to vitalize the world's exchange resources, but today it will take more than a single ventriloquist to accomplish all that should be done.

A serious handicap in the setting up of foreign exchanges is the lack of adequate bibliographies. One of the proposals which came out of the Conference on International Cultural, Educational, and Scientific Exchanges held at Princeton University in 1946 was that Unesco prepare a world list of periodicals which would indicate which titles were available on an exchange basis. Since this problem of bibliography is not peculiar to those engaged in exchange work, a more realistic approach to it would be the encouragement of the publication of national bibliographies which would include periodicals and exchange materials as well as the more obvious publications.

Studies of exchange costs and coverage are overdue. Figures on the cost of exchanges are so varied for different libraries that one must suspect that hidden costs are not always recognized. One library, such as Columbia University, may assess its exchange costs and conclude that it is getting nearly six times as much in returns as the expenses which it puts into its exchange programme[7] while another library may find that it is sending out more value in publications than it is receiving. Acquisition librarians need to know as a guide to everyday operations whether it costs more to request a title through exchange than it does to place an order for it. One obvious way to reduce the cost of exchange would be to give some study to the techniques involved. Uniformity of listing, the use of the least expensive shipping methods, greater selectivity of material for listing, and the use of restricted subject lists are all obvious, but often ignored, economies.

The existence of the Farmington Plan as a means of placing at least one copy of each priced non-serial, foreign publication of research value in this country points up the lack of systematic coverage in the exchange field. Form a research point of view items received through exchange are just as important as trade items. The need for over-all planning for acquisition through exchange is recognized, but so far no action has been taken. Out of the writing that has been done on this problem during the past decade a two-point programme emerges on which there is some agreement and which might be the basis for a practical plan.

Part One of the programme would extend the federal government's treaty exchanges to permit the acquisition of one or more additional sets of foreign government publications to be deposited in research libraries in this country. This would require legislative action, as the 1936 act which regulates the treaty exchanges does not allow for additional copies. Librarians would not question the value of such an addition to the government's programme. It would not seem too difficult to convince government officials also of the value of such action since such receipts add to the research resources of this country and serve its welfare.

Part Two of the programme would arrange the systematic receipt of copies of all non-governmental, non-priced foreign publications of research value. The suggestion has been made that U.S.B.E. serve as an agency for the procurement of such publications, distribution to be based on the Farmington Plan. Efforts to secure a grant to set up the plan have not been successful so far.

If the federal government and U.S.B.E. would consent to carry out the two parts of this plan, the materials thus secured could very well be distributed on the basis of the Farmington Plan assignments.

This would assure at least a second copy of foreign documents available in this country and at least one copy of non-governmental publications.

A more ambitious programme, and one which should at least be considered, is that dependent upon the existence of a system of regional libraries in this country. This plan would involve getting all of the publications in multiple copies for deposit in the regional libraries. In general the securing of a first copy of the materials which we are discussing requires cost and effort while the securing of additional copies requires little more cost and effort.

The idea that a country of this size would have more adequate library service with a system of regional libraries is not a new one. Just as country library systems bring better library service to individuals, so national regional libraries would bring better library service to libraries. It has been suggested that the Midwest Inter-Library Center might well be the first of such a series. K. D. Metcalf[8] in 1951 stated, "I think that, ultimately, there should be, in addition to the Midwest Inter-Library Center, a number of other regional libraries, one in the North-east, one near Washington in which the federal libraries should join, one somewhere in the South, and one in the far West." The deposit function of the Mid-west Inter-Library Center is the one most emphasized at present. Perhaps the member libraries of the Center should consider a change of emphasis.

A system of regional libraries has obvious advantages. Additional sets of worthwhile publications are added insurance that these publications will be available when needed. Additional sets also make the publications more readily available to students of the sciences, including the critical social sciences. Regional libraries might serve as branches of the United States Book Exchange, thus eliminating the distance problem felt by libraries west of the Alleghenies. As an alternate plan to that of the U.S.B.E. securing non-governmental foreign exchanges (Part Two of the above programme), the regional libraries could secure such materials through the use of the publications of the research libraries in their regions to exchange for the publications of foreign institutions. Close cooperation between the regional libraries in setting up exchanges and in relaying information to each other could have widespread benefits.

The cost of setting up such a system and of securing additional sets of publications for it may seem large, but it is infinitesimal compared with the arms programme. The potential good with full availability of foreign publications could do in this country cannot be overlooked. The fact that additional publications would have to be sent from this country to secure additional copies is a further advantage. The State Department has recognized the importance of a free flow of information from this country to other countries, permitting the presentation of our points of view and making available to other areas of the world needed technical information.

In 1947 R.B. Downs[9] wrote in *Science,* "The free interchange of cultural, scientific, and educational information is unquestionably one of the most critical needs of the world today. Society's progress depends upon the extent to which scholars and scientists have unrestricted access to all sources of information. Likewise, international understanding requires that the cultural records of every nation be fully available to all other nations. Finally, intelligent and informed world opinion must be based upon the wide dissemination of educational materials. These are our stakes in efforts to perfect the machinery for international exchanges." These are our stakes in all exchanges.

REFERENCES

1. L. J. Kipp, *The International Exchange of Publications.* Wakefield Mass., Murray Printing Co., 1950, p. 6.
2. Lesley M. Heathcote, Letter to the Editor, quoted in *Serial Slants,* 2:12-13. Oct. 1951.
3. John Fall Problems of American Libraries in Acquiring Foreign Publications. *Library Quarterly,* 24:109-110, April 1954.
4. W.R. Ristow, Annual Reports on Acquisitions: Maps. *Library of Congress Quarterly Journal of Current Acquisitions.* 11:239- 249, Aug. 1954.
5. R.T. Esterquest, Letter dated Oct. 18, 1954.
6. E. E. Williams, Exchanges: National and International. *Library Trends,* 2:562-572, April 1954.
7. A. H. Lane, The Economics of Exchange. *Serial Slants,* 3:19-22, July 1952.
8. K.D. Metcalf, University Libraries Face the Future. *Library Quarterly,* 22:8, Jan. 1952.
9. R. B. Downs, International Exchanges. *Science,* 105:421, April 25, 1947.

18

Professional Associations' Role in Public Relations

"PROMOTE, encourage, and foster" are words often used in expressing library association objectives. Intrinsically, these are public relations-minded concepts. When they are interpreted in terms of "good will" toward libraries, the association is assigned a definite responsibility for an "active" public relations role. This responsibility is even properly placed in the organization. Public relations, because of its indefinable limits, is regarded as a management function. In an association the officers, committees, and headquarter staff are the "management." So, by simply assuming that a library association is born public relations-conscious and has put the job in appropriate hands, the cope and direction of the public relations effort may be explored.

With even minimum study, the complexity of the scope becomes apparent. One is forced to recognize quite quickly that public relations cannot be isolated but is an integral part of the association's total operation. A wide range of existing and proposed activities will require attention. These extend from a large-scale promotion programme, through an infinite number of publicity projects, to the intangible of an attitude. In limiting such a sweeping area to a practicable plan the association "management" becomes judge, prophet, and opportunist. There are obligations to establish priorities on immediate needs, to determine the long-term aims, and to remain alert for each new opportunity which may arise.

Association public relations will stem in two directions just as it does in a business organization. One communications programme is planned for the public; and another, as the case may be, is planned for members or employees. Assuredly, the two may often be very similar but quite distinct interests are served for the basic objectives are library-minded public and a happily rewarded, public-relations-minded profession. Such objectives also demand an integrated communications pattern. The public and the librarian must understand each other to engender the coveted results of "good" public relations and mutual satisfaction.

The association only begins to fulfill its management function by developing a public relations plan. Organization, operation, and evaluation are further essential management processes. All demand serious attention if the association wishes to be aggressive rather than optimistically hopeful in carrying out its responsibility as spokesman for libraries and librarianship.

Organizing and operating the public relations programme requires that sufficient money, expert advice, and suitable materials are provided. These factors have a particular importance, for many times the public relations plan will operate through member librarians everywhere who make up the communications network. To do the job will, they must be adequately equipped. In a sense, this like furnishing a salesman with enough samples and making certain that his training includes the knowledge he will require to present his product and to answer the questions about it. Member librarians deserve no less.

Every plan, once it is in operation, is subject to evaluation. Here, the public relations programme may present problems because measurement is bound to be difficult. Costs and benefits will not always adapt themselves to a neat orderly pattern for tabulation. This circumstance should be less perplexing to those who attempt to calculate the value of library service than to many others for both are filled with intangibles which resist a dollar and cents interpretation. By the same token, anyone in the library field should have developed the ability to astutely sense the probable benefits. If the evidence and the best guess" about the public relations programme indicate that it has fallen short in bringing about the desired result, there is fair warning to find out why this programme is not hitting home, revise the sights and develop a new plan to remedy the weaknesses.

Some of the generalizations are in order before discussing the specifices involved in the association role. The public relations programme cannot be a one-time or even a sometime thing. Sporadic campaigns, no matter how energetic, with little support during the intervening periods, do not suffice. To be successful public relations is continuous and is part and parcel of every day's activity. The results of attention given to it may not be readily apparent but neglect may be dishearteningly conspicuous.

Since the librarians themselves are ultimately responsible for building the reputation of libraries and librarianship, what the association does for them becomes a foremost consideration. In essence, this amount to assisting the individual librarian to present his "best front" from the public relations point of view. A suggested minimum plan for internal communication is one which offers both training and good logistic support. It is an educational programme and a publications programme.

The public relations educational programme is conducted mainly through the media of the profession's journals, meetings, and technical manuals. It is designed to cultivate a wider appreciation of the meaning and value of public relations and to extend the knowledge of public relations' techniques and applications. For the practical mind and the "too busy" librarian more than theory must be provided. The report of a successful publicity venture in one library stimulates interest on the part of another. The straightforward suggestion on how-to-do-it may be given a trial. The value of group meetings and discussion groups should not be overlooked since speeches and demonstrations are sometimes far more effective than written words. Librarians have long been proponents of the importance of manuals or handbooks and a few on subjects akin to public relations may prove worth-while. A consultation and advisory service, on whatever scale it can be established, should find customers. And finally, the association in its relationships with members must provide the best possible public relations example.

The publications programme offers a thoughtfully developed and expertly prepared group of promotional pieces which by virtue of association sponsorship are accorded due authority. These are the material aids which the individual librarian needs to do his part of the over-all public relations job but cannot provide for himself. Their form message, and use are matters for consideration by the best talent the association can obtain. Posters, pamphlets, films, general press releases, and certain types of exhibits all fall within this category. They are the tools for recruitment campaigns, the take-home reminders of a speech, and the adopted views of the profession on legislative matters.

It is granted that the services to members which have been mentioned are not new. The associations have worked along such lines for a long time. It is also granted that public relations is just a part of the associations's job and deserves only its rightful place in the total picture. But, a more diligently pursued internal programme is needed until doubt and hesitancy about sound promotion disappear, until the individual recognizes that he must do something himself to achieve truly "good" public relations and until the whole idea of creative library public relations becomes a thoroughly natural development.

Even though top billing is given to those phases of the public relations plan which operate through the membership, association responsibility for direct action is neither minimized nor lessened. Special public relations programmes, press coverage on professional developments, and routine publicitv are equally important aspects of the total programme.

The usual publicity based on conferences, conventions, and group meetings may be too "old hat" for mention but prompts a thought about good press relations. Actually, this is nothing more than a reminder to find the time needed for interviews and to offer it graciously. Cooperation and a friendly attitude are the little things that count. They add up to the "even break" that everybody wants.

Since much conference publicity is focused on individuals, it brings to mind the news possibilities which are provided by numerous professional, or otherwise noteworthy accomplishments of members. These may reach the "press" through personal initiative or through an employer. If not, the association can fill the breach. There is a haunting thought that if more people knew more about librarians as personalities, as scholars, and as citizens the profession would hit a ten-strike.

It is just plain good business to take advantage of the public relations value of every association activity. The important thing is to develop a good watch-dog technique and not allow any public relations potential to escape notice. General association matters, committee or group projects, and headquarters services make up a fairly wide area for surveillance but alertness should pay off well in term of news releases and feature articles.

Association policies and professional developments which affect the betterment of society deserve to be made known generally. They point up the place of libraries and librarians in the world and record the attempts to forward its progress. Association concern about international affairs, education, and professional standards are basic examples.

Committee and group activities provide the subject material for a continuing publicity programme. Happenings are reported as they occur throughout the year and fill in the spaces between the "bit" events. Any association publication, unless it is completely library-centered, has reader somewhere outside the profession. The announcement of an institute on library buildings holds attraction for an architect. A salary study interests any number of non-library groups. Special services designed for schools, city government officials, or industrial organizations are used only by those who are aware of their existence. An award established for or received by a librarian adds prestige. A scholarship gains popularity when the recipient's name is familiar. Such a list could go on almost indefinitely.

Headquarters operations and services which involve relationships which the public lend a stout hand in creating a favourable view of the profession. The value of vigilantly maintained public relations at this location cannot be over-estimated for headquarters is the association's permanent representative and continuing force. It enjoys something of an impartial position through being part but not of the profession and conceivably, by virtue of this status, speaks more freely and is heard with lesser charge of prejudice. The executive secretary, the placement officer, the public relations director, and others contribute in an infinite degree to the reputation of both the association and the profession.

This is a bit like leaving the icing on the cake until last. Some of the very "best" public relations come about through cooperation with non-library groups. No matter whether these lead to events which are large or small, each will testify to the fact that the association's own public relations is "good". Effectively combining the librarians' interests with those of another profession or successfully enlisting the support of a non-library group must mean that an adequate job has been done in telling the library side of the "story."

Joint professional endeavours are a definite gain from the public relations point of view. Two or more voices are raised instead of one and the impact on public opinion increases proportionately. Such joint efforts are beneficial in other ways; through them common interests are identified, mutual regard is acknowledged, and notions of professional isolation disappear. Meetings, campaigns, or just simply working together will add "friends" to the roster. No chance of participating in a worthy effort with another professional group should be dismissed lightly for by this means the professions begin to speak for each other.

Support of the library "cause" by civic, business, and philanthropic groups in another distinct area to be cultivated. The very recent past has seen some outstanding examples of what can be accomplished. Librarianship was included in the New York Life Insurance Company's series of advertisements on careers. Its wide magazine coverage and the availability of reprints for extensive distribution informed many people of the need for librarians and the advantages of library work. National Library Week, conducted under the sponsorship of the National Book Committee in cooperation with the American Library Association, was the first national wide campaign on the behalf of reading and libraries. Through the media of print, radio, and television both a reading and listening public was contacted. "Operation Library," a project of the Junior Chamber of Commerce has spread from a state to an international programme of gaining support for individual libraries. Achieving the financial and active aid of non-library groups, as represented in these instances, is a challenge to the library association and a true indication of its public relations ability and instinct.

The whole programme of internal and external communication outlined in this chapter is a fairly large order. How much of a public relations package each association buys will depend upon its needs and ambitions in this direction. But, if widespread understanding and popularity of libraries is to materialize in the foreseeable future, an all-out library promotion plan is specified. The water will need to be tested with more than just one toe.

PUBLIC SERVICES AND PUBLIC RELATIONS

A library board faces a number of interesting but frustrating problems as it develops the public service programme of the library to serve the needs of the community and as it engages in public relations programmes directed toward improved library service. Here we will try to explore some of the legal bases for the operation public service and public relations programmes. A study of the statutes and cases shows that, in general, legislatures have granted wide authority to the library board to conduct the affairs of the library, but have not undertaken to define powers specifically. Rarely have courts have called upon to interpret the powers of the library board. Thus a library board finds itself in a position where it must act and hope that should its actions be challenged subsequently the courts would agree with the board's interpretation of its powers and duties.

As the library board plans the public service programme of the library it must determine who can use the library and what regulations are needed to make the materials of the library available to all on an equal basis. If auditorium or other meeting space is available the board must plan for its use also. Library boards have been vested with certain powers to perform these acts.

Many state legislatures have followed the early pattern of the Illinois Library Law of 1872[1] which gave the board of directors power:

1. to "make and adopt such by-laws, rules and regulations for their own guidance and for the government of the library and reading room as may be expedient,"
2. to "exclude from the use of said library and reading-room any and all persons who shall willfully violate such rules,"
3. to exercise exclusive control "of the supervision, care and custody of the grounds, rooms or buildings" set apart for the library.

This act also declared that "Every library and reading-room, established under this act, shall be forever free to the use of the inhabitants of the city where located, always subject to such reasonable rules and regulations as the library board may adopt, in order to render the use of said library and reading-room of the greatest benefit to the greatest number . . . ." In addition the board was given specific power to "extend the privileges and use of such library and reading-room to persons residing outside of such city in this state, upon such terms and conditions as said board may from time to time by its regulations prescribe."

Although this language has not been interpreted by the Illinois courts with respect to the day-to-day operation of the library, it seems reasonably clear that a library board operating under such language has sufficient power to regulate the use of the collection and of the library building itself by deciding who may borrow library materials, requiring borrowers to register, fixing the library hours, making restrictions and conditions on loans, setting fine schedules, limiting access to certain portions of the collection, inspecting briefcases, exercising general disciplinary powers to keep order, etc.

In reality, as the library board undertakes the formulation of general policy on any of these matters it encounters difficulties immediately. For example; "who may use the library?" seems a fairly simple question at first, but on closer examination many conflicts between theory and practice are revealed. Generally, library boards and personnel are persons dedicated to the premise that library service ought to be available to anyone who desires it and undoubtedly in many cases service is given without regard to the status of the patron. Certainly this is true of reference service even though it may not be true of circulation of library materials. In practice, however, the board is restricted by such provisions as found in the Illinois statute that the library "shall be forever free to the use of the inhabitants of the city where located."

The use of the term "inhabitant" has been common in many states though the political unit involved may vary and other statutes use a different classification. The Delaware statute, for example, refers to "the district" or "any person outside the district who owns real estate assessable . . ."[2] and the new Library Services Act requires that library service be made available free of charge to all residents of a community, district, county, or region.[3] Do these terms refer to one who actually resides, votes, owns property, works or is a student within the political unit and what is the effect of such language on the practice of racial segregation? The cases give little assistance in the interpretation of these words.

What issues face a library board as it undertakes to "extend the privileges and use of such library and reading-room to persons residing outside of such city in this state, upon such terms and conditions as said board may from time to time by its regulations prescribe"? Under this language it seems clear the board would have power to extend library service and it may charge a fee for such service. Under some other statutes the board may be required to make such a charge.[4] However, when considering the extension of library service to others that the "inhabitants" boards must be aware that they may encounter opposition from local taxpayers and also should bear in mind that such extension may stifle effort to secure organized library service in the unserved areas.

There are still other facets of this same "who can use" question. Today, the increased use of inter-library loans as a method of supplementing local book collections, and the demand for such things as multiple copies of current fiction, films, records, and projection equipment which can be financed only if the library can charge a fee for the use of these items present familiar problems. Yet both of these might raise the "forever free to the inhabitants" issue as pointed out in the previous chapter on financial support.

Inter-library loans have been recognized specifically in some recent statutes. The Colorado statute expressly permits "exchangers of books and other materials with any other library, either permanently or temporarily,"[5] and the Oregon statute permits exchanges of books to other libraries in Oregon.[6] Although many libraries charge rental fees for some books, films, records, equipment, etc., the Indiana Library Law of 1947[7] which provides that "residents . . . shall have the use of the facilities of such library without charge . . . except that the library board may fix, establish and collect fees and rental charges," is the only specific statutory authority found for the collection of such rental fees.

The enforcement of the library's rules and regulations involves another area where the board is given general power to act but is given little practical guidance in meeting specific fact situations as they arise. Legislatures have frequently made sanctions available to the library board for the enforcement of its rules and regulations. Statutes commonly make malicious cutting, tearing, defacing, breaking, or injuring books a misdemeanor.[8] In some states willfully detaining books beyond the loan period is a misdemeanor.[9] Other statutes give the county or municipality power to pass ordinances dealing with these problems.[10] As a purely practical matter, however, these sanctions are not used except in the case of he perpetual delinquent or where rare or valuable material is involved because court costs are too high and the potential loss of goodwill is too great.

Most states have given the library board specific power to exclude persons who willfully violate the rules from the library. This provision gives the board a general sanction for the enforcement of its regulations and may be invoked to control noise, loitering, etc. It may be that this power would permit forcible eviction, but reliance on more subtle measures and the local police authorities might be preferred.

When the library board undertakes to formulate a policy for the use of its auditorium or other meeting rooms by various groups within the community, it is presented with some serious questions involving community goodwill. Statutes such as the Illinois act grant the library board specific power to exercise exclusive control "of the supervision, care and custody of the grounds, rooms, or buildings" set apart for the library. This language is simple to read but difficult to administer when the question of use of library rooms by outside groups is raised. The Minnesota attorney general, in construing similar language found in the Minnesota statutes, has said: "Exclusive control of the rooms and building contemplates a determination by the board as to what use shall be made of such rooms. Its action must be reasonable, not arbitrary. If in conformity with such standards, the board may say who may use the room and when it may be used and who may not use the room."[11] The Library Bill of Rights adopted by the American Library Association in 1948, states: "As an institution of education for democratic living, the library should welcome the use of its meeting rooms for socially useful and cultural activities and discussion of current public questions. Such meeting places should be available on equal terms to all groups in the community regardless of the beliefs and affiliations of their members."

Although the language of the statute and of the opinion seem quite clear on first reading, and the statement of policy is excellent, none are of much assistance to the board in the resolution of practical problems still left in their hands. Certainly as a point of departure, the use made by outside groups cannot be such as would interfere with the primary purposes of the building. But beyond this point, there is little to guide the library board. What are "socially useful and cultural activities"? Should religious groups, purely social groups, political parties, etc., be permitted to use the rooms? Occasionally? For regular meetings? The Minnesota attorney general refers to a reasonable not arbitrary standard, but suggests no criteria. "Non-controversial" might be used as standard, but what is "non-controversial" and wouldn't such a judgment involve censorship of what the community should hear or do? Should a charge be made and if so, how much? Should it not, at least, cover the out-of-pocket expenses involved to the library?

Up to this point the problems relations to the provision of library service, as well as the necessary restrictions on use of library materials and meeting room were discussed. At least in the library world the concept of the public library as an "institution of education for democratic living" has developed. The recognition of the library's role in the community, the stimulation of library use by members of the community and the development of active support for the library programme have become important objectives of profession associations and recognized functions of library boards and personnel. Library boards and library administrators have found themselves in the position of competing with parks, the recreational programmes of the community and, in some instances, with the schools for support. In carrying out the public relations programmes, librarians have issued quantities of publicity in all forms, have appeared at public meetings, on television and on radio, and have prepared book displays at fairs, in store windows, as well as in the library itself. Board members and librarians have participated actively in support of legislation proposed by professional associations. All of these activities have been carried on zealously when a change in the tax levy is contemplated or a bond issue is proposed.

It is interesting that in the maze of writing on these subjects, the library and the legal literature fail to provide any discussion of the over-all legal bases for such activities, nor do they provide any consideration of the possible restrictions on the political activities of library personnel. Certainly it must be recognized that library board members and library personnel have the same right, in fact duty, as any citizen to partake in these activities. Members of professional organizations have a greater duty in this respect.

This still leaves a series of difficult questions. Can tax funds, or space, time, supplies or equipment purchased by tax funds be utilized to conduct a public relations programme? Can tax funds be used to employ a public relations director as a member of the library staff? Can such funds be used to lobby for legislation? Can they be used to stimulate support for a bond issue or an increase in the tax rate? No exact answer has been found to any of these queries. It is doubly important, therefore, that library boards be aware that they may face these issues squarely. It may be that legislation is necessary to clarify the board's powers in these areas, or it may be that the courts would find these powers to be included within the general powers of the board.

It is well recognized that political units, such as libraries, have only those powers expressly granted to them or necessarily implied or incident to the express powers granted. An examination of the library laws of many states failed to reveal any express grant of authority to conduct a public relations programme. The remaining question is then whether this power can be implied from those powers which are granted to the library board.

The heart of this question is whether the use of tax funds for a public relations programme runs counter to the concept inherent in American democracy that public funds may be used only for public purposes since to do otherwise would be to take property without due process of law. This term "public purpose" has been construed by the courts in some cases involving advertising expenditures by governmental bodies. Although there is some conflict of authority on this point, in the cases where the expenditure has been upheld, the advertising was usually the chamber of commerce variety and in some instance the statue granted power to spend funds to stimulate industrial development. It must also be pointed out that where upheld these expenditures were made by elected officials whereas library board members are usually appointed. In one New Jersey case the court held that a "municipality may lawfully publicize, at public expense, what its governing body conceives to be sound reasons, relating to the essential local welfare, for the rejection by the people of the State of proposed amendments to the Constitution."[12] In discussing this case, the *Harvard Law Review* pointed out that this case was the first in which the court made the leap from sanctioning advertisements of a chamber of commerce type to approving advertising expense in a campaign to influence the electorate.[13]

In determining to what extent a public relations programme can be treated as falling within the general powers of the library board, it is important, first, to examine the nature of such a programme. Commonly, public relations programmes are directed at three goals: (1) To inform the community of the library resources available and to stimulate use by members of the community; (2) To gain support for proposed legislation; and (3) To gain support for tax levies or bond issues. It can be agreed that library boards have an obligation to make the materials of the library available for use. In some sense all of these activities may be regarded as part of this process and therefore, such expenditures fall within the scope of the board's power. Also it has been stated that "one obligation resting upon every public institution in a democracy is that of standing ready at all times to render an account of itself to the people and to show cause why they should continue to support."[14] This reasoning may support a public relations programme. However, one does encounter an ethical if not legal question in using tax funds to raise taxes. L. M. Nourse,[15] in describing the energetic campaign conducted to raise funds for the St. Louis Public Library, recognized this question when he stated it was considered inadvisable to use public tax funds for this purpose but that fortunately special funds from gifts were available.

In studying the propriety of undertaking a public relations programme, library boards should bear in mind that time paid for by tax funds as well as the more direct expenditure of the tax dollar is involved. Since they are unsalaried, it may be in this area that the board member can make his greatest contribution to the library's programme and to the cause of library service for all without encountering the question of misuse of tax funds. Library personnel face a vague distinction between the proper and improper use of staff time.

In summary, many questions relating to the legal issues involved in the administration of the public service and public relations programmes by library boards have been raised here. Few answers have been found; some solutions have been suggested. Specifically it can be said only that the language of the statutes granting powers to library boards to conduct the affairs of the library is general. As library service has developed, library boards have been confronted with problems and have resolved them within those general powers as the necessities of the situation demanded. Although more specific direction might be desirable in some cases, the limitations coincident with the more specific language would present additional difficulties.

REFERENCES

1. Ill. Laws 1871-1872, sec. 1-11, pp. 609-611; Smith-Hurd Ill. Ann. Stats., c. 81, sec. 1-16 (at sec. 5 and 6).
2. 48 Del. Laws, c. 198, sec. 14 (1951); Del. Code Ann. Tit. 14 sec. 7142.
3. 70 [U.S.] Stat. 293 (1956); 20 U.S.C. sec. 351-358.
4. 48 Del. Laws, c. 198, sec. 15 (1951); Del. Code Ann. Tit. 14, sec. 7144.
5. Colo. Laws 1947, c. 234, sec. 18; Colo. Rev. Stat. 84-1-18 (1956)
6. Oreg. Laws 1955, c. 432, sec. 21; Oreg. Rev. Stat. sec. 357-640.
7. Ind. Acts 1947, c. 321, sec. 17; Burns' Anno. Ind. Stats. 1933, 1952 replacement, sec. 41-917.
8. California Education Code, sec. 23321.
9. Colo. Laws 1947, c. 234, sec. 19; Colo. Rev. Stat. 84-1-19 (1956).
10. N.C. Laws 1953, c. 721, sec 160-77; Cen'l Stat. of N.C. sec. 160-76 (1957 Supp.).

11. Minn. Atty. Gen. Op. 285-B, Dec. 5, 1947.
12. *City Affairs Committee of New Jersey City* v. *Board of Commissioners of Jersey City,* 134 N.J.L. 180, 46 a. 2D 425, 426 (1946).
13. Municipal Corporations. *Harvard Law Review,* 59:1172-1174, Sept. 1946.
14. American Library Association Coordinating Committee on Revision of Public Library Standards. *Public Library Service: A Guide to Evaluation with Minimum Standards.* Chicago, The Association, 1956, p. vii.
15. L.M. Nourse, A Fair Income Campaign. *Library Journal,* 78:400-403, Mar. 1. 1953.

19

Public Relations and Publicity

A LIBRARY'S programme of public relations means the concern and the activities of trustees, heads and staff members to put the library into cordial and understanding relationship with all the people of the community. It means the average citizen's image of the library and the librarians when he hears them mentioned, the extent and warmth of the community's good will toward the library, its understanding of what the library is trying to do, and its appreciation for the quality and morale of the library's staff and services. Public relations is a two-way matter, with as much the intention that all its own staff members shall understand and work with the community as that community segments and groups may understand the library and work with it. Each librarian needs a sixth sense of what public reactions will be toward whatever news and impressions issue from the library, about its objectives, policies, plans, problems, its collections and services, its organization and personnel, its finances and building needs.[1,2,3]

The part played by publicity in public relations is indicated in the following formula,[4] which shows as common denominator the Service Concept, or the Desire to Serve. Without this underlying purpose, publicity is insincere and public relations will never flourish.

$$\frac{\text{Determining Public Needs} + \text{Courteous Efficient Service} + \text{Informing Public of Services Offered (Publicity)}}{\text{The Desire to Serve}} = \text{Good Public Relations}$$

Public relations is not in itself a product; it is a series of steps to create a relationship with citizens so that library services can be improved and can reach a wider circle. Good public relations also aid in recruiting better workers and improve staff job satisfaction and morale and thereby reduces turnover. A library which the community respects and whose staff is considered of high quality and on their toes, finds it easier to attract and keep good staff members than does a mediocre library. What the public thinks of the library personnel may be the chief element in what it thinks of the library.[5]

AN ESSENTIAL PART OF ADMINISTRATION

The Public Relations Society of America's *Public Relations News* has defined P.R. as "the management function which evaluates public attitudes, identifies the policies and procedures of an individual or an organization with public interest, and executes a programme of action to earn public understanding and acceptance."[6] A slogan of the Advertising Clubs of America reads: "Advertising Lowers the Cost of Distribution." For the library this means that with the given investment in building, books and staff, volume can be increased through publicity, and the per-circulation and per-reference question costs will thereby be lowered. Those who conjure up a "quality vs. quantity" conflict, and insist that quality will be lowered if quantity is increased, those who argue that good service needs no advertising, or that if citizens really want to read they will come and use the library, or that little will be gained by efforts to attract more readers and library use—all these are ready to be convinced that library public relations and publicity are expensive and futile aspects of library administration.

As late as 1958, "exhortation, pleading and argument are [still] essential in a discussion of library public relations. . . [to overcome the notion] that they require more time, energy and budgetary provision than they are worth." But "proper public relations practice is based on objective scrutiny of every phase of library's administration and services and a continual finding out about whether they meet the real needs of people. . . putting it to the democratic, hence dangerous test . . . distressing to a library administrator whose ideas are tightly bound."[7]

The library *has* public relations, whether or not library officials realize it, or wish it, or plan it; every citizen is potentially interested in all news and impressions about the library as a public institution. The public has the right to know everything about its library. The active and resultful publicity and public relations programmes of so many progressive libraries, large and small, for many years, justify the assumption that every library has to give some time and attention to public relations as just defined, and to publicity or promotion. Budget, progress and the effective service of the library are dependent on good public relations and goodwill. Compared with many other institutions and enterprises, the library is in a favoured category; in the main it has a connotation of respectability, of idealism and helpfulness. On the other hand, a library should ask itself whether its townspeople consider it a "Morgue of Culture," aloof, superior and ultraconservative.

SOME GENERAL FACTORS

1. Everything the library can do and say to build up public belief that it is alert, active and forward looking, quickly responsive to public demands, interested in progressive methods and economy, operated by devoted and highly skilled staff, and busily engaged in helping more and more citizens in every category results in good public relations.

2. Librarians, like business executives and other groups, tend to associate and discuss with, and be influenced by, acquaintances within their own social, economic, cultural and religious circles. They may fail to understand or even seek to appreciate the general run of the population around them. This consists predominantly of wage earners, consumers, small businessmen and clerical workers, housekeepers and others whose viewpoints and philosophy of life may be different from their own. Unless the library's public relations programme, its everyday publicity, is aimed at and prepared to be understood by Tom, Dick and Harry, it will not get very far. Librarians should find deep pleasure in meeting and understanding all these strangers who in turn generally take it for granted that library representatives are friendly and helpful.

3. Library publicity is not "blowing one's own horn"; the public likes to know all about the library. The library can help build a city's pride in itself, e.g., by exhibits of new books written by local authors,

or by news stories about whatever credit may come to the library and its staff, and by being well run and a credit to its community.

4. Honesty and sincerity underlie good publicity. Some libraries hesitate to advertise their book and services because they fear the books will be out when asked for, and that they cannot make good on reference questions. But the public has sense enough to understand ordinary difficulties, will wait its turn for books, and will be patient while information is being sought from other libraries. If the library does not let the public know about books and service, it is not capitalizing on the money the taxpayers have invested in them.

5. Continuous publicity is necessary; repetition builds reputation. It takes a long time to sell facts and ideas; much publicity fails by quitting too soon. "Keep it simple; say it often; be sure it's true."

6. Publicity needs to be aimed at and to tie in with the everyday interests, motives and philosophy of the public, including citizens who don't yet use the library or read much. The attitude of friendly helpfulness to all sorts of individuals is essential. But all this is made more vital by aiming it at individuals, or at some special group, not at a vague mass of citizens. Think of a few typical non-readers as well as readers and aim the publicity at what you know they are interested in.

7. Publicity has not only to describe services and materials; it has to explain library objectives, problems, plans, projects, personnel, standards and accomplishments. It can recite cases where individuals have been helped by library materials, but also the ways in which citizens and groups have cooperated and helped the library.

8. A good library will take the public into its confidence as to policies and plans, as to methods and rules, as to problems, finances, costs and personnel, and as to criticisms however justifies. Dignified silence is not always appropriate; neither is a bad-spirited argumentative defense. If library decisions, practices and services have been carefully thought out and programmed they should give rise to good-spirited news stories which explain pros and cons.

9. It may be taken for granted that even those already using the library have little or no idea of all its services and how they are managed, e.g., indexes to periodicals and to government bulletins, which unlock materials they never thought of, even on topics of their own personal interest.

ORGANIZING THE P.R. PROGRAMME

Planning

One must consider (and weekly or fortnightly discussion is helpful) which devices will be most fruitful, e.g., radio spots or a more elaborate programme; newspaper stories or exhibits; what particular audience is to be reached; and how much time, talent, money are available. "We tend to pick up and use ideas without weighing them against our important needs" (Stibitz).

Budgeting

No statistical or cost studies were found to justify any given per cent of total budget for public relations. There are too many uncertain, informal, part-time, unreported factors, and most librarians seem agreed that results cannot be definitely measured in increased circulations. Results become evident enough when a bond issue is approved 5 to 1 by the voters, or when circulation doubles in two years. Friend[8] and Cundiff[9] evidently studied, by questionnaires, approximately the same 43 or 32 libraries, in cities of over 250,000 population, and found such varied activities, organization and staffing that no cost figure or pattern could be arrived at. While 19 of Friend's 43 libraries reported "a full time director, one had in addition, 2 assistants for display and lettering, one for writing, one photographer, one secretary and two part-time pages." But department heads and staff who initiate, guide or share in varied aspects of P.R. give much additional time. It comes down to two contending factors: how strongly the librarian believes in P.R., and how much he feels can be spent from a never adequate budget. For a rule of thumb we suggest 1 or 2 per cent of the budget, for total staff, materials, printing and outside costs.

In Large Libraries

In cities of over 150,000 a full-time qualified person will be more than busy, and the salary is justified; some libraries rate this as an urgent need, supplemented by whatever part-time assistance he can get from all departments and branches. Chief qualification is a keen understanding of library objectives, a belief in the everyday usefulness of books and printed information evidenced by his own reading, a strong desire for public service, and the ability to work with people including those who don't use the library. Numerous candidates may appear for this interesting position, but it takes also resourcefulness, a flexible outgoing mind, a solid educational background, and imagination and initiative to see, week after week, how books, can tie into the stream of community activities.

Yet another qualification is the ability to plan and organize the publicity work and to get through it without demanding too much expenditure of funds and staff help, and without absorbing too much time in overhead motion. A rapid worker is an asset, especially one who can handle many contacts by phone in such a cordial and definite way as to get results and make the participants enjoy it. If such a person can be found within the staff, well and good. But an enthusiasm, for example, for making posters, lists and exhibits is a sign of only one of the least-important qualifications needed. Often someone is brought in from newspaper work or an advertising agency, with publicity experience and well intentioned, but basically not a book user or an understanding proponent of dynamic library service. Unless such an "outsider" has always been a reader, a reference-service user, and keenly interested in library functions, there is considerable risk that his efforts will be superficial and only partly effective. A tryout on some specific story or project may help in evaluating a local person for a full or part-time position.

In Medium Size and Small Libraries

Although several cities of less than 150,000 population have full-time publicity director, cities smaller than that will have to designate an able staff member to handle as much P.R. work as possible part time, unless someone is available to come in from other employment for two or three hours a day. Here again, this person's chief practical problem is to plan activities and call on numerous other persons inside and outside the library to help on definite assignments.[10] P.R. work handled on a part-time basis will fluctuate in intensity according to the demands of the person's regular duties, but much can be done. Creating publicity in the library which has only one to five already-busy workers calls for resourcefulness indeed. Not many assistants have an awareness of public attitudes, yet some of the most interesting and effective publicity ideas have come from these small-staff libraries, as evidenced by the experience stories in frequent issues of *Wilson Library Bulletin.*[11] The smaller the library, the more resourceful it needs to be in getting citizen cooperation to help carry out various projects.

Committee Work

If committee meetings can quickly get to business, it may be profitable to call two or three or a half-dozen staff members to thresh out, plan and assign aspects of one or several projects. A 1958 Evansville staff committee session came up in ten minutes with twenty-eight suggestions on how to bring to citizens' attention the existence and location of the library, e.g., spot radio and TV announcements, street-corner signs, staff talks to clubs, letters to new residents, marquee advertising, bookmarks, picture postcards, etc. Another ten minutes produced nineteen ideas to meet the statement "I don't have time to read." Calling a group of citizens together to plan and carry out publicity for the library is a favourite method during finance or building campaigns. It probably needs cultivating as an all-year device to get more publicity without great cost; for instance, a merchant may be willing to prepare and run a series of store window exhibits, or have his show card writer do the lettering on posters and show cards.

Drawing Ideas from Departments

The person in charge of P.R. needs to be informed of everything interesting or significant that goes on in each aspect of the library, especially from the librarian and each department and branch head. All of them are busy; they often forget or overlook happenings, or news that should be played up, such as the arrival of important new reference service tools, and how they can be useful to many citizens. They may have publicity-minded assistants to initiate or remind them of promising items. The P.R. officer has to keep all these sources frequently alerted, encouraging and welcoming all that can be reported to him. He can utilize much of this for news, exhibits, circulars, etc. A library may run along smoothly in seeming routine, but in most libraries there is something newsworthy happening every week or month; in large libraries there is something new every day.

PUBLIC RELATIONS INSIDE THE LIBRARY

Each staff member from head librarian to janitor is a creator of public attitudes toward the library. It is not simply a matter of having a public relations officer, a programme and an array of bright publicity ideas. Those who fear that publicity may be insincere or inflated are right in insisting that good service and good attitudes by the library staff have to underline good library relations with the public. The way the staff looks and acts, dressing neatly, looking cheerful, meeting and serving each reader with a smile, keeping busy but alert to help reader, speaking so that voice and manner reflect an interest and intention to see that he finds what he came for, doing well each part of the job, following instructions and working to carry out the library's objectives—all these everyday attitudes build up the public belief that librarians and their library are friendly, helpful, competent.[12] Good performance has top priority. These points have special validity in the circulation department, which has the first and most frequent contacts with readers. Some librarians see to it that their most competent and personable workers are posted here, because reader impressions of the whole library organization are especially influenced by what happens in this department. A good library sees to it that minimum of staff gossip is carried outside, and that assistants refrain from talking over, within the public's hearing, their grievances and criticisms of colleagues and of the institution of which they are part.

Current library designing and equipping capitalizes on the part played by the building itself. Adequate directional signs and explanatory placards, such as how to use the card catalogue, how the building, department and bookcases are arranged—everything which will make it easier for the public to use the library—will make for goodwill. Readers should enjoy their visits to the library, and the whole staff should be called on for suggestions as to how this can be assured. Several libraries encourages friends with gardens and greenhouses to bringt in beautiful plants and flowers, the year round, to be placed on service desks, with conspicuous acknowledgement cards. The public gets pleasure from the gift and the giver.

Trustee policies, decisions and board actions, are major elements in the public concept of the library. Trustees will not be inhibited by public opinion but will take action for the public good and then inform the public, rather than assuming that what they do had better be kept quiet. Many libraries have a reporter attend board meetings. If the library has a P.R. officer, publicity from the board should be cleared through him, for it is his job to know how to say what will be of interest to the public. On possibly controversial subjects, board and librarian should work out with him the wording for news releases. A P.R. worker who does not feel quite sure of himself will go over news releases with several colleagues of good judgment to see if a story has any hidden booby traps.

PUBLIC RELATIONS OUTSIDE THE LIBRARY

Having given attention to improving services and impressions inside the library, a library is better prepared to undertake varied outside publicity. The present chapter can be only an outline, not a handbook of publicity methods. The chapter notes list such guides.[1,2,13,14]

First in importance is to realize that the librarian and agency heads have to get outside the library building, get acquainted with their community, and organize publicity aimed at all the citizens, not just those who are already coming into the library. They should find out who the local leaders are, think out what facts about library services will appeal, and try to have five- minute interviews with key persons.

House-to-House Promotion

Only a few libraries have assigned time for selected staff members to do intensive promotion, door to door, taking a few books, lists or circulars, and talking directly with householders, finding out their interests, projects and problems, and describing materials, and services they could get. This could give the staff, for the first time, a closeup of adult reactions to the idea of reading and reference help, a realistic understanding of why so many adults don't read, and what it is, if anything, that can appeal to them. A venture by the providence P.L. to call on business concerns with selected materials and explain how the library could find pertinent information did not turn out as well as hoped. This canvassing is time-consuming, involves careful preparation but may be rewarding.

Speaking to Groups

Whole groups of adults can be reached in far less time by arranging for library talks at their meetings, centering around library materials on the group's interests. There is also an opportunity to explain library objectives, methods and problems. Arrangements can be made over the telephone, but the talk should be well planned, full of incident and lively.

Friends of the Library

Organizing and enlisting the help of a large organized auxiliary group of friendly influential men and women has had notable results in spreading public knowledge of the library, enlisting support, getting funds, and passing bond issues. One wonders why it is not almost universal. Some trustees fear that the "Friends" will get so influential and active that they will tell the trustees how to run the library. A good board should be big-minded enough to work with and welcome ideas from outside. True and fortunately, Friends in some cities have boldly intervened in library situations needing correction and have insisted on and financed critical surveys. They deserve credit for getting a great number of moribund, politics-ridden and thoroughly bad library situations straightened out. A good Friends organization is considered by many progressive librarians of both small and large libraries to be their greatest public-relations asset. But, through the librarian, care should be taken that the officers chosen each year shall be not only strong, courageous leaders determined to push the library ahead, but tactful, discreet, and neither antagonize library and public officials, nor seek office to exalt themselves but to help the library in ways that the community may approve.[15]

Newspapers

For the amount of time required from the library, the variety of topics covered, and the wide diffusion of the library's message, top priority goes to the local newspaper. If there are several papers the library will treat them all alike. Everything depends on the care with which the library gets together the facts and ideas for each news story, so it will sound like news, and not merely library propaganda. The most frequent failure is in not putting the point of the story into a short opening sentence and paragraph; as a result the editor must do a large-scale rewrite that takes more time than he thinks the story is worth. Build up an understanding by editor and reporters of what the library is already doing for citizens, as well as what it hopes to do.

There are two news services to which libraries may subscribe,[16] and receive timely, competent prewritten releases on a great variety of library matters, ready to be filled in, altered and retyped by the local library to hand its newspaper. Such stories should not be accepted automatically; if a story does not seem to have real-life substance and importance to local newspaper readers, it is better to scrap it. There is also a source for illustrated informational publicity leaflets, kept up to date.[17] The A.L.A. Headquarters Library can supply or lend scrapbooks of clippings and other material for news stories.

Radio and TV

The time cost involved, even with free programme time, is so considerable that the list of large libraries which find regular radio or TV programmes profitable is constantly changing. A number of libraries, some of them in cities of only 20,000 or 30,000, prepare one-minute, half-minute or even ten second spot announcements of news, information about the library and human interest stories. These are run free by the station staff, sometimes using slides from library photos, provided each item is briefly and effectively phrased, centers around a specific subject, and sounds newsy: a new book on babies, housekeeping, child care, marriage, hobbies, current events, etc., or a change in rules or staff, or a new or modified service.[18] A quick summary on the value of books and reading, quoting two or three telling phrases from a current news or magazine story,[19] may be welcomed.

A.L.A. Public Relations Office sends out spot announcements to be adapted locally. Radio and TV book reviewing is reported in the Media page of Publishers' Weekly.

Direct Printed Publicity

In the advertising world what is called "direct mail" is printed matter distributed by mail and involving postage expense. Though much of this advertising is discarded without being opened, printed circulars and booklists of similar type showing they come from the local library are not likely to be ignored. They can be distributed by Boy Scouts, house to house, or office by office; stores, banks, city departments and many local organizations can enclose them in their mailings of bills and notices. A staff "brainstorming" session will doubtless come up with many devices for distributing library circulars "for free," under local conditions. The problem with this direct printed promotion is printing cost; mimeographing may be the only way out. Some citizen may be sufficiently interested to pay part or most of the cost to print an important message.[20]

Exhibits Inside and Outside

If the library building is located in the midst of the crowd, its front can be remodeled and opened up to exhibit inside activities. Or it can have a large exhibit window facing the sidewalk. Or, if it stands too far back, an exhibit case can be built close to the sidewalk, lighted and equipped with screened plexiglass to protect the contents. Some outside cases have not been designed to be weatherproof, or easily accessible for changing exhibits. Any library can get permission to use window space in vacant stores, or even in occupied busy stores. The range of subjects for exhibits is boundless, with pictures, collections, mementos, working models and a variety of possible materials to supplement books on the subjects.[21,22] Explanatory placards are essential. Some libraries that are adept in managing volunteer help get art classes, store decorators and other outsiders to prepare and set up window exhibits, so as to avoid expense and not use much staff time. Whatever time the library can give to exhibits should go into effective exhibits used outside the library as a promotion device, where crowds of people can see them, and they should be so eye catching that people will stop and study them. The same is true of bulletin boards,[23,24] especially outside the library, to display lists, posters, announcements and book jackets.

Special Events

Loizeaux gives a publicity calendar which suggests the birthdays of great persons, the anniversaries of great events and great books, and many other topics for publicity, from newspaper stories to exhibits.[25] Some of these events, not overlooking those of a local nature, can be the occasion for public meetings, with notable speakers and considerable fanfare. Similarly a convention in town offers a good chance for the library to publicize the services it can render on the subject in question. The annual Book Week and the highly effective National Library Week have been so effective where the library has organized real participation, often including a local book fair, that both seem almost certain to be much further developed, with profuse instructions and ideas available to help a local library.

Annual Report

Whether or not the library issues to public officials and to other libraries a somewhat detailed report of its affairs and progress, including those of individual departments and branches, some brief attractive summary report including its receipts and expenditures should also be issued and widely distributed to the general public. A six or eight-page leaflet with a few graphs and pictures, sent out with store bills, bank statements, etc., will help to bring a much clearer concept of the library to a wide circle of citizens than almost any other device, and in cities of 15,000 upward it well justifies its cost.[26] Most important is a summary, maybe one column in the local paper. A graph of increased use is profitable. A.L.A. can lend an assortment of samples for ideas and layout.

Recognition of Cultural Accomplishments

Several libraries have an exhibit and news story whenever a local resident has a book, play or musical piece published. Soon this builds up community realization that the library is a real stimulant to local cultural enterprises. The exhibit should contain photos and materials used by the author. One library has had exhibits of books that *should* be written about its city and state, by showing large cellophane dummies of these non-existing books, suitably titled and decorated to be impressive, and surrounded by similar actual books from other cities and states.

WHAT IS NEWSWORTHY?

It is hard for librarians to realize and remind themselves that almost everything the library has possible publicity value. Growth and success are always good news, e.g., an increase in circulation and in reference questions, or in any aspect of public service, phrased in terms of how much more the "readers are borrowing," rather than "library is circulating." If librarian and trustees develop a three of five-year programme it should make headlines for its news value and give a chance to explain the importance of many aspects of the work, and the reasons why.

Economies

One aspect of librarianship, often overlooked, is especially good in its effect on the public-any piece of news as to how the library is simplifying its routines, cutting red tape, and actually saving money, or more often getting greater quantity and better quality for the proportionate amount of money spent. In other words, economy. In the period between the two World Wars, it is well to recall, librarians argued heatedly over "cost per-circulation" and as to how much a library should spend to do this and that. Economy advocates were reminded that "mere circulation" was an artificial measure, that it indicated nothing about "quality," and that the matter of how to achieve economy was rather beside the point. On the contrary, if a library by dividing total circulation into total expenditure can show that its per-circulation cost is decreasing, or that more books are being processed for the salary costs in the processing department than in the preceding year, it is decidedly a matter of public interest.

Finances

Building up public realization that the library is finding economies and not simply spending all it can get makes the best background for budget requests. Constant emphasis in news stories, exhibits and other publicity on the diversified and detailed individual services rendered the public helps create the impression that library service requires skilled professional workers, and explains why most library budgets allot some 70 per cent of all funds to the salary item. A library serving less than 100,000 population, and spread out among four branches plus central, may be able to get completely favourable publicity and thereby have public support for greater funds, but when the pinch comes, or if a critical survey is made in behalf of the taxpayers, the financial unwisdom of acceding to neighbourhood pressure for unprofitable branches would become apparent, and the library would be forced to cut off its least productive enterprises. As soon as the library's budget request is presented to public officials, a news story with graphs and figures should be released to show the public why the budget items are justified. Despite the repugnance of local officials in a town where the library is underfinanced toward figures from a group of similar- size cities which are giving their libraries much more per capita, such comparative figures should be freely and widely publicized, for in the long run it is public opinion which influences the actions of appropriating bodies.[27]

Staff

Library personnel, if it has any degree of devotion, any considerable educational and professional preparation, any distinction as to character and ability, is always a matter of public interest. One problem is to overcome the reluctance of individual staff members to permit any publicity about themselves. Obviously, their appointment, promotion, resignation and retirement are news, but so is any honour, important committee appointment or other mark of distinction received. The educational background and professional career of each new person should be played up, partly to counteract the notion, widely held and often resulting in political pressure, that almost anyone can qualify for librarianship. Such stories are also justified to explain the important day-by-day accomplishments of those staff members whose planning, services, initiative and leadership mean much to the whole community. There are many routine duties performed so well by assistants, including clerical workers, that they deserve news stories, or exhibits, or other publicity, such as the display of an unusually large statistical table, skillfully laid out and so perfectly typed that it is a work of art, giving credit to the typist. Or, an exhibit of library mending or rebinding. The public enjoys and appreciates a staff whose work the library's leaders believe in keeping in the public eye.

Branch Publicity

A library with branches must be adequately financed to take proper care of each. This includes publicity in their behalf. Part of this will originate and be issued from central, both for a particular branch and for several or all branches. Centralized publicity is generally more economical and effectual than scattered efforts at several points. The branch librarian is master of his own publicity fate. He can initiate or solicit publicity for his branch, but as much of it as possible should be handled at central, such as printed circulars and lists and traveling exhibits. A branch librarian will undertake many publicity enterprises in his own neighbourhood, where he and the branch staff are acquainted, including talks at meetings, phone calls to group heads, programmes and meetings at the branch.[28] A branch librarian who fears he is inadequate on publicity should delegate it to an assistant.

Surveys

Libraries which have been critically and objectively surveyed deserve credit for shaking themselves out of lethargy. They can profitably capitalize on the survey as a public relations device. Citizens should be informed why it has been undertaken, to improve services and find economies; what the surveyor finds on first impression, provided he emphasizes devotion and efficiency of the staff, handicaps, and how much the library could do under better condition; what he finds further on these and other constructive matters, or has discovered of situations in obvious need of correction. A surveyor for tax-supported library will not indulge in theoretical discussion that larger budgets do not assure better service, but will comprehend the difficulties and library faces in getting itself financed according to A.L.A. standards, and aim for better personnel and methods that will produce a better library.

Some of the most fruitful surveys have been initiated by Friends of the Library, and by local citizen organizations, which often are aware that the library board, or the librarian, is somnolent, and wish to see the library brought up to today's concept of efficient public service. The librarian may be able to suggest such a project. Mere surveys of public opinion about the library may turn out to be much work the little result, because (a) people tend to be complimentary in remarks or answers about a library; (b) many of the persons quizzed have no real idea of what a library should be doing, how well, and at what cost; and (c) in the case of new buildings the average citizen has no idea of the basic principles of library location, design or planning, and has a mental picture of the traditional Carnegie-type building which repels rather than attracts his support. The library may handicap itself by turning up public opinion opposed to what it knows should be done. However, opinion polls sometimes discover worthwhile things if they are carefully planned. One librarian was "alarmed" when 66 per cent of the answers favoured a pay-duplicate fiction collection; she evidently had taken the academic view that a free library should not have anything on a rental basis. By tactfully handling the public relations involved, she found the League of Women Voters' survey a source of strength.[29]

Campaigns

When for any reason, generally for a bond issue for a library building, the voters have to approve some library project involving public expenditures, a large-scale concentrated campaign is essential. The whole community has not only to be thoroughly informed as to facts and reasons, but has to be made enthusiastic to rectify library conditions that in most cases have existed too long. Such factors as crowding, inconvenience of readers, obsolescence, the right of library patrons to have modern facilities, and the careful planning, the attention to economy and efficiency involved in the enterprise, have to be played up to enlist the support and cooperation of the voters. During such an enterprise it is imperative to discover incipient objections and opposition and the causes and reasoning behind them, and to issue carefully documented and argued explanations to combat them *before* the opposition can get organized. Here again good administration foresees trouble and heads off hostile pressures. Because some campaigns have not been carefully planned, with citizen committees and staff members working actively in every precinct and at every level of the population, they have failed, even for the second or third time, though in the end they have generally won. In one city, bond issues for branches and for central improvement carried two, or three, even five to one, because they were planned and managed as citizen enterprises with great numbers of persons working in the library's behalf.[30,31]

THE SATISFIED CUSTOMER

Customer satisfaction is the real test of a library's effectiveness. The perennial question is whether each reader is getting what he desires, promptly and with good spirit. Attention paid to the adventures and difficulties of the steady procession of individuals who come to the library is the chief element in good public relations.[32]

NOTES & REFERENCES

1. Marie D. Loizeaux. *Publicity Primer.* 4th ed. 122 p., 1959. H. W. Wilson Co.
2. Sarah L. Wallace. *Promotion Ideas for Public Libraries.* 88 p. ,1953. Reprinted 1958. A. L. A.
3. Len Arnold, ed. *Aspects of Library Public Relations. Library Trends.* v. 7. no. 2. Oct. 1958. p. 237-330.
4. Adapted from Miriam E. McNally, "Publicity Wonderland" in *Wilson Library Bulletin.* 18: 511-515. March 1944. Used by permission of *Public Relations Planner* from their 1960 32-p. pamphlet, The Library Image; see note 17, below.

5. Robert D. Leigh and Katherine W. Sewny, "The Popular Image of the Library and the Librarian." *Library Journal.* 85: 2089-2091. June 1, 1960. Followed by Gerhart Wiebe (public opinion psychologist) "Image; its Definition and Measurement." p. 2092-2097.

6. Richard L. Tobin, "What is P. R. Anyway?" *Saturday Review.* 43: 109-110. Nov. 12, 1960.

7. Arnold *op. cit.* Introduction, p. 237-38. Also Fred Wezeman. "Why Tell?" *A. L. A. Bulletin. 49*: 403-404. Sept. 1955.

8. David S. Friend., *Public Relations in Public Libraries: A Survey of Organization and Administration...* 90 p. typed 1955. Thesis, Graduate School of Florida State Univ.

9. Dorothy Cundiff, *Public Relations in Public Libraries. . .in Metropolitan Areas of Over 250,000. . ..* 69 p. typed. 1957. Thesis, Graduate School, Univ. of Mississippi. These two theses duplicate each other in many respects, especially enumeration and description of activities Friend's covering more aspects.

10. Anne M. Farrell, "Public Relations on Nothing a Year." *A. L. A. Bulletin.* 53: 385-388. May 1959. How San Francisco's PR head got notable results without any budget for her department. See also "Municipal Ideas That Bloom in May." *American City:* 75: 171-172, 175. May 1960.

11. *Wilson Library Bulletin.*Monthly, September to June. Nearly every issue of this periodical reports interesting publicity and promotion devices, especially for small and medium size libraries. Also the Library Publicity issue of *Illinois Libraries.* Feb. 1961.

12. Sarah L. Wallace. *Patrons Are People.* 2d ed. 48 p. 1956. A. L. A. See also Galvy Gordon. "The Library Staff Member and Public Relations." *Wilson Library Bulletin.* 34: 485-487. Mar. 1960.

13. Allen H. Center, ed. *Public Relations Ideas in Action.* 327 p. 1957. McGraw Hill. Many of the 500 tested programmes and techniques from commerce, industry, the professions and nonprofit organizations can be translated into library terms.

14. *Public Relations News.* Weekly. 375 Park Ave., N. Y. 22, N. Y. For large libraries this is full of stimulating ideas and accounts of projects, lists of materials, answers to questions, etc. Many of these large-scale projects can be shrunk and modified for library use. Other materials, including bibliographies, are issued by Public Relations Society of America, 375 Park Ave., N. Y. 22, N. Y. Its 1960-61 Public Relations Register lists 3,300 members, many connected with welfare, education-

al and governmental agencies; no doubt some of their local affiliates could be enlisted to help on library problems.

15. Sarah L. Wallace, *Friends of the Library; Organization and Activities.* 111 p. 1962. A. L. A.

16. Public Relations Planner: A Practical Service for Libraries. Monthy. P. O. Box 4132. South Denver Station. Denver? Colo. Since 1953 this competent 4-p. monthly News Letter of Ideas has given the suggested text and the impetus for news stories, exhibits and other publicity used in several hundred local libraries. Included also are booklists, circulars, e.g., on reference service, posters and other material for local use. In 1960 it issued in cooperation with Montana State Library *The Library Image, Manual of Library Interpretation.* 32 p. a valuable outline to guide any library's P.R. programme. Also *Library Publicity Clippings.* Box 753. Salinas, Calif. Monthly news letter, prepared stories and spot announcements.

17. "Your Library Card and How to Use It." 16 p. "Information Unlimited." 16 p. "How to Find Out" (Reference service) 16 p. "Librarian Wanted" (Recruiting.) 16 p. 24¢ each. Also "What's Good Library Service?" 16 p. 1960. etc. Channing L. Bete Co., Greenfield Mass. Attractive and effective booklets by a library-trustee publicity man.

18. Frances G. Nunmaker, *The Library Broadcasts.* 166 p. 1948. Wilson Co. Still the major source book for ideas on radio and TV programmes. Evelyn and Ralph Edwards, "Mighty Mike Helps the Library." *A. L. A. Bulletin.* 53: 369-373. May 1959.

19. Such as from George Gallup, in *Ladies' Home Journal,* cited in Chapter 1.

20. *Print It Right: How to Plan, Write, and Design School Public Relations Materials.* 48 p. 1953. Nat! School Public Relations Assoc'n. 201 16 St. Washington 6, D.C.

21. Kate Coplan, *Effective Library Exhibits.* 127 p. 1958. Oceana Pub. Co. Especially useful for cities of any size, where beside exhibits in the library, store window space can be borrowed. Also *Display World.* Monthly. Display Publishing Co. 407 Gilbert Ave., Cincinnati 1, Ohio.

22. Louisiana Library Assoe'n. *Quick'n Easy: 164 Library Exhibits.* 41 p. 1958. Mary G. Stewart. P.O. Box 131, Baton Rouge, See circulars-re show card machines of several sizes using various types and colors for posters, shelf cards, etc. from such concerns as Show Card Machine, 330 West Ohio St., Chicago 10 Ill.

23. Robert E. Hein and E. K. Davis. *Easy Bulletin Boards*. 49 p. 1959. Easy Bulletin Boards, Box 103, Cleveland, O. How to set up 200 illustrated examples quickly and inexpensively. Also, Kate Coplan. *Poster Ideas and Bulletin Board Techniques. . .* xxx p. 1962. Oceana. Expert suggestions and 200 illustrations, including 3-dimensional arrangements.

24. Rhyllis Weisjohn, ed. "Bulletin Board Display." *Wilson Library Bulletin.* 34: 569-583. April 1960. Valuable condensation of an M. A. thesis, full of specific ideas with diagrams of principles, arrangement, colour, assembling, lettering, illustrations, topics and captions. 37-item bibliography.

25. *Chase's Calendar of Annual Events for* 1961. Apple Tree Press. 2322 Mallery St., Flint 4, Mich. Lists 852 items, among which the library may single out the few most promising. See also Chamber of Commerce of U. S. Annual list of special days, weeks and months.

26. Four articles on coverage, preparation, printing and distribution of reports appear in *Library Journal.* 85: 3615- 3620. Oct. 15, 1960. See also Herbert Goldhor, "We Tell the Public About Our Library." *American City.* 74: 113-114. June 1959.

27. Joseph L. Wheeler, *Library and the Community.* 417 p. 1924. See Chapter 14 on publicity about organization, methods and finances.

28. Kate Coplan, "Public Relations of a Branch Community." *Wilson Library Bulletin.* 27: 525-527. March 1953.

29. Lucille Washburn, "A Survey Helped Our Library." (Indiana) *Library Occurent.* 20: 75-76, 90-93. Sept. 1960.

30. William Chait, "Library Building Campaigns." *A. L. A. Bulletin.* 50: 425-428. July 1955. Also Ruth O. Longworth, "Library That Public Relations Built." *Library Journal.* 82: 2098-9. Sept. 15, 1957. and "Second Try at the Polls." *Wilson Library Bulletin.* 32: 488.489+. March 1958. Also Howard W. Winger. "Park Forest Trics for a Public Library." *Library Journal* 80: 534-536. Mar. 1, 1955. Also "Yes Can. The Park Forest Library Election." *Illinois Libraries.* 37. 154.7. June 1955. Also John P. Streit. "Keys to Successful Library Referendum." *Illinois Libraries.* 41: 711-717. Dec. 1959. Also Arthur Kissner. "Publicity for a Building Project." *Illinois Libraries.* 43: 111-117. Feb. 1961 Valuable for details of organizing an elaborate campaign and why it failed. Also Alexander Crosby's Chapter 7, "The Trustee and Fund Raising," in Winser. *Handbook for Library Trustees.* 2d ed. 1959. p. 65-76. Also Guy G. Garrison, *Seattle Voters and Their Public*

Library. 81 p. mimeo. 1961. Illinois State Library. Analysis of Social and other population factors in each census tract as influencing bond issue vote failures in 1950 and 1952 and success in 1956, but gives no recommendations for library action to get results. The foregoing items bring to date the following 1955 bibliography:.

31. "Bond Issue Campaigns: A Selected Bibliography. . . . . " *News Notes of California Libraries.* 50: 425-8. July 1955.

32. Sarah L. Wallace, "How to Keep the Library Customer." *Library Journal. 79: 1365-1369.* August 1954. Summary of a series of staff and business executive discussions on practical details to improve service attitudes.

20

Public Services Abroad

THIS CHAPTER considers the subject as a whole in a number of western European countries whose library systems are, in point of service, comparable both among themselves and with that of the United States. In the west and south of Europe are several countries with long cultural traditions and with extremely rich libraries which are of invaluable service to the researcher, yet it is impossible to speak of a certain standard of public services in their library systems. Consequently, the limitation to a small number of countries and to certain developments in those countries will need no further explanation.

Not so very long ago R. D. Leigh[1] said of the library system in his country, "In brief, the United States has a multitude of libraries, some of them magnificent institutions, but it has no library system." This applies not only to the public libraries that were the subject of Leigh's study, but equally to research libraries where there is a growing realization that it is impossible to continue in the old way. The growth of the university libraries and the ever greater demands made on these institutions confront their leaders with whole series of problems. It is not only the financial consequences of the ever increasing accessions figures and the resulting necessity to extend the buildings, but problems such as the upkeep of the subject catalogue, maintenance of departmentalization, open shelves, and speed of service make librarians cast about for new ways and means.[2,3] These new ways and means are found in the field of cooperation, witness the Farmington Plan, Midwest Inter-Library Center, and various union catalogues.

If in the field of library cooperation—primarily on behalf of the public services—Europe can already report achievements, this is not particularly to the credit of European librarians. As a rule necessity has here accomplished what in the United States was not felt as a need. Moreover, the markedly different geographical situation made cooperation much easier in the smaller European countries. But merited or not, cooperation is a characteristic of the library system in a number of countries.

Perhaps Denmark is the most perfect example of this. "Co-operation is an outstanding feature of Danish library policy," is what the Danish librarian Knud Larsen[4] declares in an article on the cooperation of the research libraries in Copenhagen. In it he demonstrates how by a rational division of tasks and a corresponding transfer of stock these libraries have made their holdings into a single rational collection which can be made available efficiently to researchers and to the country's libraries. The latter, especially the public libraries, have profited to the fullest measure by this reorganization.

The whole Danish public library system is based on a close cooperation regulated down to the smallest details. Most of the public libraries in the country are very small and operate in communities with populations between 500 and 2,000. There are over 1.200 such village libraries—very often a collection of books housed in a school where the teacher does the librarian's work as a sideline. These parish libraries are the basis of an organization of which the 88 city libraries form the next level. Of the latter, 33 are also county libraries acting as centres for the parish libraries in a certain district. When the parish libraries cannot meet a request for reading matter, they pass it on to the county library, which is generally able to help but sometimes has to call upon the research libraries. First among these is the State Library at Aarhus, which acts as the center for the public libraries and sends nonfiction without charge to any place in Denmark outside of Copenhagen. The library at Aarhus, founded in 1902, has developed very rapidly and is now also the library of the new university founded at Aarhus. Its holdings are not, of course, as extensive or as old as those of the Copenhagen libraries, so that these must often be called on for aid.[5]

Though there are important differences between the library systems in the Scandinavian countries, there is a great deal of similarity between the Danish public libraries and those of Sweden and Norway in their methods of operation. Both these latter countries, on account of their much larger territory and very scattered population, are faced at the outset with different problems than Denmark, yet one is struck by a basic design that is often strongly reminiscent of the Danish. New library laws in the three countries have strengthened the financial position of their public libraries and have greatly improved the organization of the whole. The system of central libraries, each assisting the smaller libraries in its area in the provision of reading matter, has gained considerable popularity in Sweden and in war-stricken Norway. The book mobile service also has an important part of fill in these countries with their enormous distances. The cooperation of the research libraries in the interlibrary loans system is also found; to give only one example, Uppsala University Library alone sends out some 12,000 volumes each year to other libraries.[6-10]

It is well-known that the public library system in the Scandinavian countries has been strongly influenced in its development by the American example. Attention will now be focused on a country where receptivity to idea of the public library has indeed been fostered by what happened in America and, even more, in England, but where this idea was put into practice in a very different way, partly because of the influence of developments in Germany. In Holland the public library in the modern sense dates from beginning of this century. In contrast to what was done in the Scandinavian countries, there was no attempt made here to integrate the small popular libraries scattered up the down the country in the new system. In the Netherlands a system in which a limited number of larger libraries would be established in towns of reasonable size was preferred. Perhaps the tradition of the existing popular libraries was still being felt, for 95 per cent of Holland's public libraries have been founded and are run by societies or foundations. Under a state subsidies scheme of 1921—repeatedly amended since—these libraries are subsidized by the state if the local authority first lends its financial support. By this scheme local authorities are obliged to help financially if they wish to qualify for a state subsidy for a public library within their boundaries.

There now exist in the Netherlands over a hundred public libraries which do not leave the rural areas quite so neglected as the above might suggest. Many of them send weekly selections of books to nearby localities where they are usually looked after by the schoolmaster. Very small and remote places obtain fair-sized collections of books for the winter months from the Central Society for Traveling Libraries at Amsterdam.

However, developments have not stopped here. Since the war there has been an increasing awareness that in comparison with other countries the public libraries were lagging behind and that a radical reorganization was demanded. This reorganization is making itself felt primarily in the library systems of the smaller towns and villages, which are more and more, and with ever mounting success, being serviced regionally from a central point. Libraries in the Netherlands are now experiencing a number of changes of great interest.[11]

For works not represented in their holdings the public libraries the library centres for rural areas can approach the research libraries. They will then turn first to the Royal Library at The Hague since it is there that the union catalogues of books and periodicals, which list the holdings of 53 and 166 libraries respectively, are maintained. Besides libraries individuals living anywhere in the country can apply to the Royal Library to borrow books, provided they have an introduction from a local official. All requests which the Royal Library cannot fill are passed on to those libraries which the union catalogues shows as holding the works applied for, and these then send such works directly to the borrowers. In this way the Royal Library receives some 90,000 requests by mail a year, while an average of 25,000 works are loaned outside The Hague. The other research libraries also take part in this lending scheme, though the university libraries show lower figures for works loaned out of town than the Royal Library. The function of the Royal Library in the Netherlands can to some extent be compared to that of both the State Library at Aarhus and the Royal Library at Copenhagen in Denmark.[12]

The library situation in Great Britain is too well known to need ample discussion. The centenary of the Public Libraries Act of 1850 has already celebrated. The number of urban public libraries and branches is very large, and with few exceptions libraries are now operating in all English counties. From these, collections are regularly sent out to local library centers, of which there are now between 22,000 and 23,000 in Britain. All the county's libraries benefit from the cooperation organized by the National Central Library in London and from the regional library systems into which England has been divided. Each request that a library cannot fill is sent to the central regional bureau, which either finds a library in its region which can fill it or transmits the request to the National Central Library, where the regional union catalogues have been combined into a single national union catalogue. Moreover, N.C.L. lists the holdings of 225 so-called "outlier libraries," mostly special libraries which have agreed to loan books when special requests reach N.C.L. The number of requests thus dealt with by N.C.L. exceeded 100,000 in 1952. There is room for improvement in this system, and its benefits could be greatly increased through the participation of the largest libraries in the country.[13-15]

Variations in the forms of cooperation are found in such countries as Switzerland and Western Germany. Switzerland does not know the true public library; it has excellent research libraries, cantonal, and town libraries, but it tries to supply the want of a public library by the institution known as la Bibliothèque pour Tous. The activities of the latter are best compared with those of the travelling libraries in many of the countries dealt with above; boxes of books are sent to sundry neighbouring places from local depots, while small existing libraries are provided with supplementary material. But once again it is the National Library at Berne, with its central catalogue, and the university libraries which supply much of the reading matter.[16] The need for cooperation in Western Germany, where the libraries suffered such enormous losses and where the postwar demand for literature was larger than ever, goes without saying. With union catalogues at Cologne, Frankfurt, and Hamburg, an information service and a corresponding interlibrary loans systems have been created which, considering the difficult circumstances attending the work, are truly remarkable.[17]

Thus, for all national differences, the picture is largely the same everywhere: a system of closely cooperating libraries in which the research libraries gladly make their holdings available to the public libraries, while the intensive interlibrary loans traffic is nearly always facilitated by the presence of union catalogues. Where the latter are lacking in the form of large card catalogues—as in Denmark and Sweden—it is by yearly collective catalogues of foreign accession, published in book form, that the desired information is made available. This cooperation does not stop at national frontiers. There is very intensive loans traffic between the Scandinavian countries; Western Germany, England, and Switzerland are the countries that top the international loans list with imposing figures, and even the Netherlands, with their confined linguistic area, sent 498 volumes abroad in 1952 and borrowed 395.

All this should not, however convey the impression that the library systems of the countries are studied somewhat more closely, it becomes apparent how important the differences are. Consequently, it is far from simple to compare public services in these libraries with what is done in the United States, and what follows cannot be more than an outline picture.

A library type mentioned repeatedly above is the national library, for which tradition still retains the name Royal Library in a number of countries. Along with the Library of Congress, the great majority of these libraries are the repositories of the national production of books and periodicals. Some of them also have in common the maintenance of their countries union catalogues. But in most other respects the difference is large indeed. If these libraries are assigned a general character, it is Oslo that best fits the description, since there we have a university library acting as national library. The royal libraries at Stockholm, Copenhagen, and The Hague confine themselves to the humanities, and even in the British Museum this emphasis is found. These four libraries are distinguished by important early holdings, both of manuscripts and books, which are regularly added to. On the other hand the Swiss National Library is pre-eminently a collection of Helvetica, the importance of which lies primarily in its modern holdings.

It is clear that the service given by these national libraries must be of a strongly divergent character. They are research libraries, but they have to cater for a very heterogeneous public; the educated layman interested in science and learning will come as well as the seeker of antiquities and the university-trained researcher. If, however, the British Museum is placed alongside the National Library at Berne, we are faced with two extremes: on the one hand the Mammoth Library with its world-famed treasures, which allows access only for serious study, does not lend, and, in its traditional sphere of solid bibliographical and scholarly work, withdraws, somewhat from the dynamic tempo of the present; on the other hand, the much smaller Swiss library, founded in 1895 and now housed in one of the most modern library buildings of Europe, with a preponderantly modern stock of Helvetica, lent out in liberal fashion, while thank to the union catalogue the other inter-library loans traffic is also centralized there. Both libraries give service, but a service of a very different character, and one should not demand of either institution the type of service that naturally belongs to the other.

Occasionally it can be said that in some respects the national library does not differ very much in its function from that of the large public libraries in the United States, as in cities like New York,

Philadelphia, Boston, and Cleveland, with their special collections and rare book rooms. There are no comparable libraries on continent of Europe, though England has comparable public libraries in Birmingham, Liverpool, Manchester, and a few other cities. Scandinavia has similar libraries, such as the City Library of Stockholm and the Deichmanske Bibliotek at Oslo; but, generally speaking, in the Scandinavian countries, in England, and in the Netherlands, the public library holds, besides fiction, general educative literature and special literature for those who want to obtain further qualifications for their career or their subject. Often the city libraries have additional collections in the field of local history.

Among the services given by the public library, the first that should be mentioned is reference. In this respect the States certainly are well ahead of European countries, perhaps less where the available material is concerned than in the information and guidance of the public in its use. Undoubtedly there are public libraries in England which do striking work in this respect, but in his 1942 report Lionel McColvin declared, "Reference library work is the outstanding failure of British librarianship." It is unlikely that the situation has been brought to a satisfactory level since the end of the war. But other countries may learn much from England in this field: thus the Netherlands have a number of public libraries with good reference rooms, but the use of these and especially of the information service could be greatly intensified. Moreover, the accommodations are often so poor that the installation of real reference collection would be out of the question. In Denmark and the other Scandinavian countries the situation is definitely better. Denmark and Sweden are the happy possessors of numerous reference works; one is often astounded by the wealth of material which is awaiting use in the reference rooms of their public libraries. Good information and help, even extending to the preparation of reading lists, are assured. For the rest, it should be remembered in comparisons with the Unived States that the American library user is more inclined and better accustomed than his European counterpart of ask for information on matters for which the European libraries would direct him to other bodies.

An attractive branch of public library work is the work with children. In Denmark in particular this has been ably and minutely organized. School libraries are found in many schools, and these form an administrate whole with the junior library which accommodated in a school or at the local public library. In many cases the junior library is an independent institution. It is the junior library which looks after the school libraries, while in rural areas where the parish library is also accommodated in the school, this is often done by the county library. The latter also sends class sets (one book in a large number of copies) to the schools for use in class. School reading rooms may be attached to the schools, and where there is no other public accommodation available locally for children they are open to all school children. Here the children can do their homework, but, in some places at least, they are also instructed in the use of the library and this instruction is part of the curriculum. They learn the difference between polite literature and subject reading, learn to handle the decimal classification, and are even trained in the use of catalogues. Also they are made conversant with encyclopedias and works of reference. The result is that afterwards, when visiting the public library, they have hardly any difficulties, so that librarians are less and less asked to supply purely technical assistance and have more time left for other matters. It is superfluous in this context to expatiate on conditions in England and the other Scandinavian countries. It is sufficiently known that there, too, a great deal has been and is being achieved in the field of junior and school libraries. What is less well-known is that since the war in evident increase of interest in this field can be perceived in the Netherlands. In Amsterdam in particular a number of charming, separately housed junior libraries have been founded. There are children's libraries in other cities, and in numerous public libraries a special course of studies for children's librarians; a standing committee to study problems in the supply of children's literature has been in existence for several years; and in 1951 a Congress on Books and Youth was held which resulted in the setting up of a bureau to deal with these matters.

We can only make a random selection of the other activities of public libraries. Extension work in Europe has not reached the proportions found in the Unites States, yet work in hospitals (including mental) prisons, barracks, and on ships has become a normal task of public libraries in England and Scandinavia. In Denmark the supply of reading matter to the inmates of old-age homes has become a typically national phenomenon, and in the other countries we find similar activities. For example, we might point to the library for the blind in the public library at Amsterdam. We might also include here the cooperation found in some of the smaller towns of the Netherlands between the public library and local industry in forming a works extension. The business branch which in numerous American public libraries is a normal department—often separated from the main library—is found in a slightly different form in Europe. Here it is necessary only to refer to the commercial libraries attached to a public library in Manchester and Leeds and to the Library for Commercial Economics attached to the Amsterdam Public Library.

Finally there is the adult education. England has had a long tradition in this field, but it is only in the last twenty-five years that the public library has participated therein. Here the public library found an opportunity to become a center of local cultural activity by providing accommodations for groups or by arranging the meetings (discussion groups, lectures, gramophone recitals, concerts, etc.). That this opportunity was fully realized appears from the fact that now some 150 libraries in England possess halls for lectures, meeting rooms and occasionally even theaters. In Denmark, the classical country of the Folk High Schools, where there are also many other group movements for popular education, the study group has become a normal feature in the public library. From one to more than six rooms in the public library building are often reserved for these. Numerous textbooks for the work of these groups have been published, and it is the task of the public library to provide supplementary literature. To the end that public libraries may perform this work adequately, they are assisted by a Study Group Center at the State Library at Aarhus.

As was remarked above, adult education has a long tradition in England, the universities of Oxford, Cambridge, and London having given it a start in the period between 1873 and 1876. Besides the Extension lectures aimed at a public with general interest there are the Tutorial classes, generally for a maximum of three years, and the Sessional classes, for one year, which involve regular studies during the winter months. The university libraries play an active part in that they make available traveling libraries for the students in these several courses.

This function of some English universities is not found on the Continent, but on the other hand it is characteristic of a European university library that its doors are easily opened to those outside the university. It is also not uncommon for a university library to serve also as a city library or as (in Switzerland) a cantonal library. And the strictly university library is often more accessible than its American sister. To give one instance, there is no fee for extramural readers in the Netherlands and the regular period of loan is one month for them as well as for the students.

As we all know, there is a considerable difference between the American and the European university in that the latter does not have undergraduates. The European student comes to the university at the age of eighteen after a secondary schooling of six years. He is then better prepared for university work than is the American student beginning his studies at a liberal arts college. And the problems which the European students presents to his university library to solve are simpler than those with which the American library is confronted.

What service does the university library in Europe give to professors, students, and outsiders? In his 1951 Philadelphia disquisition on the financial difficulties threatening the university library, K. D. Metcalf mentions as one possible way out the reduction of the service to what might be called the European university library level. The service is less important than the books, and in any case the scholar will find his way. The handicap of having to wait twenty-four hours for one's book and refusal of access to the bookrack would have to be taken into the bargain.[2] Metacalf's words make clear what is the American opinion of the service in European university libraries. And it cannot be denied here that American leads Europe in several respects. But all the same some marginal notes can be made to this dictum. In the first place the waiting period of twenty-four hours is certainly an exception. The German University library does not have a very good name in this respect, and it is regrettably often that one has to reckon with a few hours' delay. But there are numerous university libraries (and also national libraries) where conditions are considerably more favourable and where the waiting time is not more than fifteen minutes. Naturally departmentalization is an adverse factor here, but this true in America as well as in Europe. The numerous departmental libraries common to the American university are also found in Europe, and one gets the impression that this development has not yet reached a standstill.

As to open shelves, this is indeed a privilege which the European library does not and cannot give its visitors. The German university libraries used to have systematic arrangements in the stacks which are of course, essential if free access to the shelves is to have any meaning. George Leyh's famous dissertation on the drawbacks of systematic arrangement caused all the leading major libraries in Germany with the exception of the Prussian State Library to change during the interwar period to the *numerous currens* system. Even after the World War II not a single research library which had to make a fresh start chose the systematic arrangement. To be quite honest it should, however, be admitted that there are some libraries in Europe, mainly in England and Scandinavia, which allow free access to the stacks or to a systematically arranged part of their holdings, yet it is perhaps no accident that such libraries are housed in relatively new buildings. Many libraries in Europe are still handicapped by old or, at least, small buildings and would be unable, if only for this reason, to adopt a systematic arrangement. If we remember, moreover, that in many American libraries all works published before 1700 are placed in the rare book rooms, it is clear that in the large research libraries of Europe this system is hardly practicable.

Considering the difference between the American and the European bookstack, it is not so surprising that libraries in the United States swear by the dictionary catalogue, while the research library in Europe uses the alphabetical author catalogue and the classed catalogue. Some tensor years ago a heated battle was fought in Germany between the supporters of the classed catalogue and those of the alphabetical subject catalogue, a battle which resulted in particular from the sorry state of the systematic catalogue in the German university library. This battle was finally left undecided; but the fact that so many libraries were giving up their classed arrangement in the bookstacks undoubtedly contributed to the retention of the classed catalogue. On the whole the classed catalogue—always accompanied by an alphabetical author catalogue, of course—preponderates in the European research libraries.

Here and there we also find an alphabetical subject catalogue, sometimes even by the side of a classed catalogue. In view of the often divergent systems underlying the latter, an alphabetical index of subject leadings to this catalogue is indeed necessary. If it can be said that the combination of alphabetical author catalogue and classed catalogue with index of subject headings forms a satisfactory apparatus, it must on the other hand be recognized that the libraries in the United States show a much greater unity in this respect. Moreover, the condition of the catalogues in many European research libraries leaves much to be desired, as the classed catalogue is out of date or sometimes absent altogether. America also has its difficulties with the dictionary catalogue when this becomes to unwieldy, yet possession of this catalogue makes for better equipment than is found in many a European research library. For the public libraries equipped with an alphabetical author catalogue and an alphabetical subject catalogue the difference is not particularly great.

The typical general reference department of the American university library is entirely wanting in Europe, but information service is given at the catalogue and in the general reading room, while member of the research staff, whether or not on duty in seminar reading rooms, can answer questions. The specialist knowledge of these staff members, who have usually completed a prolonged university training in their respective fields of study, makes it possible to give to eve highly specialized questions the attention which they deserve.

There is one other group of libraries which is continually increasing in importance and which has not yet been discussed to far, viz., the special libraries. This is a group of the most varied kinds of libraries, and it is impossible to give an idea of their service. Among them are very active libraries aiming at detailed documentation in their own fields but restricting their services largely to the institution or the business to which they belong. It is through cooperation with other libraries that the holdings of such special libraries can be made useful to a wider circle. Thus it is especially this type of library which contributes to the Netherlands Union Catalog of Periodicals, by which very important holdings of special journals are made available to research work in general.

From what precedes, it may be concluded that in principle there is not much divergence in the ideas of what service should be given, but that practical realization in America is in many respects in advance of European practice. Better accommodations, larger staffs, and ampler funds —at least for the larger libraries—are of course quite important, but what matters equally is the use that has been made of all this. We find this especially in the speed of delivery of materials, their accessibility, and the systematic arrangement of the bookstack, the excellent organization of the catalogues—advantages which are often, and notably in the university libraries, missed in Europe. The public library, too, has not reached anything like the level of its American counterpart, not even in the countries of western Europe which have made the greatest advances in this field.

On the other hand, the effort toward cooperation, which is manifesting itself more and more in American library circle, is often behind Europe in this very field of public services. Europe has a much more strongly developed inter-library loans activity, and public libraries here are much more vigorously support in their work by the holdings of the research libraries than they are in the United States. Even in a country like Germany, where the gulf between the research and the public library (the latter being considered as a popular library) has not quite disappeared, we can speak of cooperation between the two kinds of libraries.

Another remarkable feature is that the apparently vast differences between the American and the European libraries turn out, on closer inspection, to be less important than was anticipated, and they show a tendency through changes in both camps to diminish. The catalogue of the American library, on which so much pains and ingenuity have been lavished, probably cannot be maintained in the same fashion in the future in the face of the ever mounting costs. Moreover, the dictionary catalogue has already increased to such an unwieldy size that certain libraries have introduced a division into author and subject catalogue. One prominent librarian has already advocated a simple author-finding list for the large mass of holdings.

The space problem in American libraries has become so acute and the financial objections to extension or new buildings have become so large that solutions are sought along European lines. In 1902 President Eliot of Harvard defended the view that books were still accessible if delivered within twenty-four hours, and that for reasons of economy shelving in double rows according to size would be necessary. At the time, Eliot raised a storm of indignation, but he would certainly feel some satisfaction if he could see the present developments. The New England Deposit Library and the Midwest Inter-Library Center are the first instances of an evolution in which works of small demand are put into store by libraries and are thus accessible only after considerable delay. But even in the bookstacks of the libraries themselves we now see all manner of compact storage systems which clearly indicate the direction of developments. In the new library of the University of Wisconsin at Madison the books are stored in the stacks in three groups of volumes of different sizes, while in a separate section of the stack compact storage has been introduced for the more rarely used works.

The inter-library loan, which has never been very popular in the United States, is certain to develop more strongly under the new General Inter-library Loan Code of 1952, and the Farmington Plan, appointing numerous libraries as repositories for literature on a certain subject, inevitably results in an extension of inte-rlibrary loans.

If we see here an evolution toward European norms, at the same time the American example, especially since the war, has not failed to make its influence felt in Europe. Notably in Germany this isclearly perceptible. If in 1932, in his book on the Scandinavian Public Library Erwin Ackerknecht could still measure out at large his objections against open shelves, in 1952 we see Hans Hugelmann, in his work on the Volksbücherei, declare himself against the open shelves on pedagogic grounds, only to state in his preface that he has meanwhile changed his opinion. The development in Western Germany is proceedings clearly in the direction of free access to the books, and we need only look into the journal of the Verein Deutscher Volksbibliothekare, *Bücherei und Bildung,* to discover how enthusiastically the new system is supported. The loss of books in Germany has also resulted in a stronger tendency that before to amalgamate the older holdings of local research libraries with the Volksbücherei into an Einheitsbücherei thus reducing the distinction between research and popular libraries and drawing nearer to the pattern of the American public library. Developments of a kind similar to those seen in Germany are also in evidence in the Netherlands where open access to materials has been introduced in many public libraries.

REFERENCES

1. Leigh, R.D. *The Public Library in the United States.* New York, Columbia University Press, 1950, p. 74.
2. K. D. Metcalf, The Ever Expanding Demand for Materials and the Threatened Decline of Support. *In* Pennsylvania University. Library: *Changing Patterns of Scholarship and the Future of Research Libraries.* Philadelphia, University of Pennsylvania Press, 1951, pp. 27-36.
3. K. J. Brough, *Scholar's Workshop.* (Illinois Contributions to Librarianship No. 5) Urbana, University of Illinois Press, 1953.
4. Knud Larsen, Co-operation Between the Research Libraries of Copenhagen. *Journal of Documentation,* 7: 83-91, June 1951.

5. Preben Kirkegaard, *The Public Libraries in Denmark.* (Danish Information Handbooks) Copenhagen Danske Selskab, 1950.
6. Erwin Ackerknecht, *Skandinavisches Bücheriwesen* Stettin, Verlag Bücherei und Bildungspflege, 1932.
7. Arne Kildal, *Norske Folkeboksamlinger.* Oslo, H. Aschehoug and Co., 1949.
8. Hermann Tiemann, Reise durch Schwedische Bibliotheken. *Zentralblatt für Bibliothekswesen,* 63:439-456, Nov.-Dec. 1949.
9. L. R. McColvin, Scandinavian Visit. *Library Association Record,* 53:392-399, Dec. 1951.
10. Tönnes Kleberg, Some Uses of Microfilm in the Library of the University of Uppsala. *Journal of Documentation,* 7:244- 251, Dec. 1951.
11. H. E. Greve, *Geschiedenis der Leeszaalbeweging in Nederland,* s-Gravenhage, Uitgeversfonds der Bibliotheekverenigingen, 1933.
12. Leendert Brummel, The (General) Union Catalogues in the Netherlands. *Libri,* 1:201-209, 1951.
13. R. F. Vollans, *Library Co-operation in Great Britain.* London, National central Library, 1952.
14. L. R. McColvin, *The Public Library System of Great Britain,* London, Library Association, 1942.
15. National Central Library, *37th Anual Report of the Executive Committee for the Year Ending 28 February 1953.* London, The Library, 1953.
16. Association des Bibliothêcaires Suisses. Association Suisse de Documentation Bibliothèques pour Tous, 1920-1953. *Nouvelles de l'Association des Bibliothécaires Suisses et de l'Association Suisse de Documentation,* 29:187-264, 1953.
17. Rudolf Juchhoff, Der Zentralkatalog der wissenschaftlichen Bibliotheken des Landes Nordrhein-Westfalen. *Zentralblatt für Bibliotheswesen,* 63:42-47, Jan-Feb. 1949.

21

Legal Status of Public Libraries

THE LEGAL status of public libraries has been so well presented by Joeckel[1] in 1935, by Garceau[2] in 1949, and by Leigh[3] in 1950, that it would seem unnecessary here to attempt to go over much of the same ground. Because current trends may show more clearly when contrasted with the long history of library organization, however, a brief resumé, with apologies to the above authors, is in order. Aside from this, the present chapter will report events and trends of more recent years.

Our first "public libraries" were private libraries, designated variously by the general term "social," and specifically by the words "association," "partnership," or "vocational," derived from the way in which they wee organized. The association or subscription library, and the partnership or proprietary library, became the two most common legal forms of organization. Association libraries are often referred to as subscription libraries because they accepted members for a set annual fee. "Proprietary library" is also another name for the private library organized as a common-law partnership, under which the partners invested their money in shares. The association or subscription library became the more popular type, although there were combinations using both methods of securing support.[4] Names of these early libraries, often seeming to indicate the origin or purpose of the institution, have added to a certain confusion about the history of the period. "Ladies' libraries," "gentlemen's libraries," and "young men's institutes" are example.[5]

When the idea of free tax-supported public libraries arose, library organization tended to become a part of some division of government. For the sake of brevity, a somewhat arbitrary description would be that, for most of the nineteenth century, public libraries were organized as a part of the government of the community in which the library was situated. In other words, some were set up under the municipality or village, some under school districts, others under the township. The exception was the association library. It is natural that some of the older association libraries continue to exist at the present time, receiving public tax funds although privately administered. But even today new libraries, particularly small ones, are being established as association libraries. Although figures are not available this is probably more common than the library profession is aware of. As an example, Pennsylvania library laws permit the establishment of libraries by private groups, and if the library wishes to apply for tax funds it must permit two members to be appointed by the government authority which provides the funds.[6] Since association boards commonly have large membership, control still is in private hands. In Allegheny County Pennsylvania, the seat of the Carnegie library idea, there were thirty-one libraries in 1950, twenty-four being of the association type.[7]

From the standpoint of legal status, the association library represents a conflict. The public accepts it and uses it as a public library, but no unit of government has direct responsibility for its support and management. Its area of service and jurisdictional rights may be non-existent or open to contest with another library.

Library organization next turned to the county as the unit of government, and the first half of this century, particularly 1930-50, has seen great emphasis and stress on selling this type of library organization. Multicounty and regional library units of organization have also come into being in the past few years. Today it seems the public library movement is still using all the various units of government as a legal basis for new library units, much as an opportunist using the path of least resistance, and in so doing has beaten three different paths in its attempt to reach the larger unit goal: the county library, the multicounty or regional library, and the state library. As a matter of fact, the *National Plan for Public Library Service* [8] in 1948 proposed five principal types of large units for the United States, namely, (1) county libraries serving whole counties, (2) county libraries serving parts of counties, (3) regional libraries, (4) federated library groups, and (5) special state districts; but these boil down to the three mentioned just above. Federated groups represent merely a method or means for securing county, regional, or state service, as will be reported later. A look at each in the light of current happenings is desirable.

County as the library unit. Joeckel[9] listed 230 county library units in existence prior to 1935, excluding those having annual income of less that $1,000. By 1949 about one-fourth of the 3,069 counties in the United States had established county libraries of some sort.[10] This figure includes regional libraries however, and a breakdown of figures reported by the American Library Association[11] would show some 537 county libraries.

Legislative enactments of some of the states in the last few years indicate the speed of the trend toward the county unit. Maryland's public library law of 1945 set up the county as the only basis for new libraries, repealing the rights of other municipal units to establish libraries.[12] Similarly, while Ohio has supported all its libraries since 1934 from a county tax, new laws were passed in 1947 removing the right of all sub-divisions of government except the county to create public libraries. Only county or multicounty libraries may now be established in Ohio.[13] The powers of library boards regardless of the unit of government are the same, and likewise every public library in a county is free to all the residents of the county. The net result as far as the public is concerned is that only one library system exists, even though legally there may be a number of independent libraries in a county.

In 1949 Michigan amended its state aid law to facilitate the establishment and development of county and regional libraries. The same year twenty-seven counties in Arkansas passed a library tax measure, and by the date also, fifty-two of California's fifty-eight counties had county library service.[14]

Multicounty or regional library as a unit. Eighty-five "regional libraries" were listed in the 1949 *County and Regional Libraries*[11] issued by the American Library Association. The term "regional library" is a loose one, covering a wise range. It may be used because of a contract between two libraries in a single county, or at the other extreme may apply to an entire state area. The regional library now seems to represent the inspirational goal that the county library stood for some years ago, and the late legislation indicates a trend toward such organization.

The Kansas legislature enacted laws in 1951 permitting the establishment of regional libraries.[15] The same year the New Mexico legislature provided for the organization of county and multicounty library service.[16] Ohio, in 1949, passed enabling legislation for setting up regional libraries.[17] Michigan amended its state aid laws in the same year to facilitate establishment of such libraries.[14] Massachusetts, a state with many small libraries, established in 1950 a demonstration regional library which is described later in this report, this in addition to three large-area libraries already in existence.[18] The regional library seems to have taken more root in the southern part of the country than elsewhere, since Alabama, Arkansas, Georgia, Missouri, north Carolina, South Carolina, Tennessee, and Virginia display a total of forty-eight such agencies.[11]

The State as a unit of service. Because of our system of government, the legal status of libraries is determined entirely by the states, either directly through legislation or indirectly through the "home-rule" powers of municipalities. Whether library service is primarily a concern of the state or of the locality has never received a convincing answer. Up to 1935 only one state had a constitutional provision specifically affecting the library.[19] Since then Missouri has added a section to its constitution making the commonwealth responsible for library service.[20] State library legislation over the country is uniformly permissive, and there does not seem to be any inclination to make library service mandatory. Despite this, however, in actual practice executive agencies are making it more and more a concern of the state.

Several small states long have been giving direct library service, and additional ones are exploring this field of extension work. Although controversy exists on the matter, enough states are active in it to indicate a new pattern. By 1948 the Vermont Free Public Library Commission was supplying its entire area with regional service and supplementing the resources of the local libraries.[21] The New Hampshire State Library operates bookmobiles, giving supplementary aid to public and school libraries which are not open daily, covering in this manner all sections.[22] In 1949 New York State set up its $100,000 a year experimental regional library service center at Watertown, offering additional facilities to existing local libraries in three counties.[21] The Illinois State Library has devised a plan to divide the state into six districts and extend assistance to the libraries in each.[21]

Implications of unit of library service larger than the state are to be found in the report of the Committee on Library Development of the Pacific North-west Library Association, involving multistate planning.[21] Likewise a northern Great Lakes Planning Council has been created to develop a joint programme of library organization for six states in the area.[14]

Methods of obtaining larger unit of service. While a county or regional unit seems to be the common objectives of these efforts, the legal means or methods used to obtain that end vary considerably, and the resulting library organization in many instances is coming to have extra-legal status. At the risk of controversy it is this writer's firm conviction that library service, whether it be in a city, township, county, or region can only be organized legally in two ways:

1. As unit of government, i.e., a library organized as a part of government, and constituting a complete entity with a single administrative authority over the territory under its jurisdiction. Under this method the procedure in creating a county or regional library would be to combine existing libraries into one legal administration. When such consolidation takes place the number of existing units is usually decreased.

2. On a basis of contract, i.e., library service by contract, involving agreement of tone administrative library unit, or government agency, with another library. If more than two libraries are included, the arrangement today is called federation. A federation necessarily entails a contract. Likewise an association library is concerned essentially with contract service—to its members under the terms of membership, to the public in return for tax support, or by other understanding. When federation takes place, the number of units usually does not decrease but remains the same, and in some instances has increased. Since the National Plan for Library Service envisages a reduction in the number of units, federation may seem inconsistent with that.

Are the larger units of today being set up by consolidation or federation? As far as county libraries are concerned, search of library literature reveals only scattered examples in which consolidation of existing libraries into a single administrative unit, or with a larger unit, has taken place. There may be others, but they do not appear in the record. In Ohio the number of independent units has been reduced from 280 in 1948 to 271 in 1952.[23] Four small libraries in Ross County previously operating as a federation consolidated into one. Several small libraries in Cuyahoga County merged with the Cuyahoga County Library. These, together with similar mergers in other counties of the state, account for the nine eliminations. The independent libraries of Yakima City and Yakima County in the state of Washington joined into a single unit in 195, to form the Yakima Valley Regional Library.[24] The year previous the Vancouver City and Clark County libraries of the same state merged to become the Fort Vancouver Regional Library.[24]

For the most part, however, the approach to county service seems to be through the door marked "Contract or Federation." The trouble is that this door, once opened, remains open, and that those who enter federation can usually back out. A clash of personalities or an unresolved difference of opinion can dissolve the arrangement. Nevertheless, there are many interesting examples. Monroe County, New York, established in 1952 a loose combination of twelve libraries in the county, including the large Rochester Public Library, each library to continue its local financing. The federation is to provide inter-library loan service, delivery, publicity, and union catalogue.[25]

A hybrid plan, between consolidation and federation, was the interesting and unusual procedure used in 1948 to unify small and large libraries in Erie County, New York. This is the county in which some twenty small institutions, each independent, together with the Buffalo Public Library and the Grosvenor Library, became "a part" of the Erie County Public Library. The arrangement is rather complex, but the units mandatorially are a part of the county library as far as finances are concerned. They can receive funds only through the county library budget. The local boards remain in existence, however, and the administration of each library is coordinated through a contract signed by all the parties.[26]

A contract between county. officials and an existing library for service throughout a county is a familiar device.[11] This is particularly applicable where a large library is in existence, and suggests that whatever the legal organization of large existing public libraries, it has not tended to change and is not likely to do so in the near future. Preference for the status quo, with legal and taxing obstacles, may account for the situation. Notable exceptions appear in the Yakima and Vancouver, Washington, libraries mentioned above, and at Dayton, Ohio. Recent Ohio legislation facilitates the transformation of existing libraries into county units. As a result the large Dayton Public Library shifted its legal basis from the school district to the county in 1948.[27]

In setting up multicounty or regional libraries, the legal problems involved in crossing county lines have no doubt discouraged the formation of single administrative units and encouraged use of the federations now so common. Wisconsin appropriated $50,000 in 1951 to set up a bicounty or regional library demonstration. This is planned as a three year trial, with the local area matching the state grant.21 Massachusetts, a state with many small libraries, in 1940 had established a form of regional library service in three separate sections, providing bookmobile service to supplement local facilities. In 1950 a new region, the Western Massachusetts Library Federation, was set up on the strength of $36,500 from Marshall Field for a two-year demonstration. This coalition is concentrating on provision of professional service- pooling the resources of the libraries and allowing each in turn to share the services of trained library specialists, while retaining local autonomy.[18]

Finally, something new has been added. In a few instances the state agency is coming into the picture, giving erect public library service to the individual, or is on the ground as a partner doing the behind-the-scenes tasks for the local libraries. This is happening in various ways, but the final effect it will have on the legal status of the local library remains to be seen. Delaware, Illinois, Massachusetts, New Hampshire, New York, Tennessee, and Vermont are providing supplementary regional facilities in one form of another.[11] Delaware, New Hampshire, and Vermont give direct service. New York's Watertown demonstration is providing a headquarters for some fifty small libraries in a three county area, but does not serve the public directly. This plan has received national attention, and its proponents argue that it leaves the legal basis of the local library intact but is broad enough to reach unserved sections.[28] From the legal standpoint the only way such a result can be accomplished is by the creation of more independent units within the region, which would be counter to the attempt on the part of library leaders to lessen the number of libraries. Here it is of interest that "Tennessee has no regional library law but through contract has 10 regional libraries patterned after New York in general principle but less adequately financed."[29]

Garceau's report for the Public Library Inquiry looks with favour upon the New York pattern, and suggests that possibly one-half of the total library expenditures within the state should be made directly by the state agency. He contends that "Such a plan escapes the most obvious hurdles of local tax limitations and frozen real property taxes."[30] The fallacy, however, is in the assumption that while local tax limitations and frozen taxes exist, they do not occur at the state level. Prior to the upheaval which produced the appropriation for the New York regional experiment, the grant-in-aid arrangement in New York had remained frozen for many years.

The question arising is whether library service can be provided partly by a local unit and partly by a state. Can it be managed half and half, or will the state, like the camel in Arab's tent, eventually take over? It seems that this problem, and the broader aspects of the state agency's position in direct public library service, is in need of study. In this connection Leigh, in his summarizing for the Public Library Inquiry, implies that there may well be monopoly systems in library service comparable to those of public utilities.[31] The idea has merit; and ways in which the legal obstacles to consolidating all the existing units in a sample state could be overcome could be a subject of profitable study.

This chapter cannot discuss the legal aspects of the countless and different tax provisions by which libraries are supported. Potterf held that "a cardinal defect in the legal personality of many library boards lies in the narrow limits within which they can levy taxes."[32] His solution was a broadening of the base of local taxation. This is certainly to be desired, but it should be pointed out that few library boards, if any, have direct power to levy taxes. Public libraries ordinarily have been organized as parts of taxing authorities, and not themselves as taxing authorities; so that final discretion for levying taxes, even within statutory limitations, usually rests with a school board or city council, or with township trustees or county officials. It would be most difficult for library boards to obtain legislation making them direct taxing authorities, and there is not indication of such a trend. Certainly existing association libraries, which are dependent upon whatever units they have persuaded to support them, show little desire to become part of government in order to overcome their inability to levy taxes. However, one result of introducing large units of service is the broadening of the tax base, and is no doubt one of the factors encouraging the trend.

Within the last ten years there have been persistent efforts on the part of the library profession to secure federal legislation and funds to demonstrate public library service in every state. These attempts have thus far been unsuccessful, but if such legislation ever should be enacted a new pattern of library would emerge, and could conceivably lead to changes in the legal status of library organization.

Summary. The constitution of many libraries still consists of the private corporation or association of one hundred years ago. Contrary to the trend toward the large unit, small libraries are still being formed on this basis. Women's clubs and other civic groups organize as private associations to provide public library service to new communities and new residential areas. Although no actual figures are available, it is possible that more new small library units are being created today than there is consolidation of existing units.

The legal basis of many other libraries is still bound up with the time-honoured unit represented by the municipality, township, or school district. In the history of library development the county as the legal basis for service has only recently become a favourite. Multicounty or regional library organization seems to be the next step. In the creation of county and regional libraries, some are formed by consolidation of existing agencies into single administrative units; but currently a contract or federation of existing libraries, which may include the state library agency, without loss of local autonomy, seems to be the prevailing device. Lastly, with some state agencies providing facilities directly, the state itself may become a legal basis for public library service, and the largest unit of it.

REFERENCES

1. C. B. Joeckel, *The Government of the American Public Library.* (University of Chicago Studies in Library Science) Chicago, University of Chicago Press, 1935.
2. O. Garceau, *The Public Library in the Political Process.* New York, Columbia University Press, 1949.
3. R. D. Leigh, *The Public Library in the United States; General Report of the Public Library Inquiry.* New York, Columbia University Press, 1950.
4. Garceau, *op. cit.,* p. 17.
5. Joeckel, *op. cit.,* p. 3.
6. W. T. Brahm, and Mildred W. Sandoe, *Allegheny County Library Survey.* Pittsburgh, Allegheny Conference on Community Development, 1950, p. 11.
7. *Ibid.,* p. 28.
8. American Library Association, Committee on Post-War Planning, *A National Plan for Public Library Service.* (Planning for Libraries No. 3) Chicago, The Association, 1948.

9. Joeckel, *op. cit.,* pp. 321-322.
10. Leigh, *op. cit.,* p. 58.
11. American Library Association, Public Library Executive Office, *County and Regional Libraries: The United States, Its Territories and Canada; A Selected List.* (Mimeographed) Chicago, The Association, August 1949.
12. Maryland. State Department of Education. Division of Library Extension: *Public Library Laws. 1945.* Baltimore, The Department, 1946.
13. W. T. Brahm, Ohio Revises Its Library Laws to Encourage Large Units of Service. *Library Journal,* 72: 1014, July 1947.
14. Helen A. Ridgway, Library Legislation and Planning, *in Book of the States, 1950-51.* Chicago, Council of State Governments, 1950, pp. 299-303.
15. Zelia J. French, Letter dated September 26, 1952.
16. Irene S. Peck, Letter dated October 7, 1952.
17. W. H., Page, ed., *Ohio General Code Annotated; 5.* Cincinnati, W. H. Anderson Co., 1951, Supplement, pp. 45-46.
18. R. J. Sullivan, Western Massachusetts Library Federation. *Library Journal,* 76:1980-1981, Dec. 1, 1951.
19. Joeckel, *op. cit.,* p. 54.
20. C. H. Compton, Missouri's New Constitution and the Free Public Library. *Library Journal,* 70:1001-1003, 1115-1117, 1179-1181, Nov. 1. Dec. 1. Dec. 15, 1945.
21. Helen A. Ridgway, Library Legislation and Planning, *in Book of the States, 1952-53.* Chicago, Council of State Governments, 1952, pp. 265-268.
22. Mildred P. McKay, Letter dated September 29, 1952.
23. Ohio. State Library: *Directory of Ohio Libraries, 1952.* Columbus, The Library, 1952.
24. Washington. State Library: Largest Libraries in Yakima County Merg to Become yakima Valley Regional Library. *Library News Bulletin,* 18:141-142, Dec. 1950, Jan. March 1951.
25. New York Has New County Library. *Library Journal,* 77:1591, Oct, 1, 1952.
26. Erie County, New York. Public Library: *Annual Report, 1949.* Buffalo, The Library, 1949.
27. Ohio. State Library: *Directory of Ohio Libraries, 1948.* Columbus, The Library, 1948.

28. Mahoney, R. E. Experiment in Regional Library Development. *A.L.A. Bulletin,* 45:140-141, April 1951.

29. Martha Parks, Letter dated October 6, 1952.

30. Garceau, *op. cit.,* p. 230.

31. Leigh, *op. cit.,* p. 275.

32. R. M. Potterf, Library Board's Achilles Heel. *Library Journal,* 71:1163-1167, Sept. 15, 1946.

22

The Developing Patterns of Main Library Organization

ALTHOUGH there are no two public libraries totally alike in organizational structure (today there is universal acceptance in all major main public libraries of subject departmentalization as a device for effectively bringing the patron and the material together. The development of departmentalization in public libraries into three major activities divisions—public services, technical services and administrative services—came early in American library history. The account of the development of departments by function (circulation and reference), by clientele age (adult and children), by type of work (acquisitions and cataloguing), and by administrative need (business office and building maintenance) have been thoroughly covered by Metcalf[1] and the McDiarmids,[2] and recently reviewed by Overington.[3]

In the evolution of the organizational structure that is the accepted norm today in large main libraries, many names famous in the logs of library history appear—Poole, Putnam, Foster, Brett, Vitz, Perry, Wheeler. They all made their contribution but Wheeler's experiment at the Enoch Pratt Free Library had the most lasting and significant effect on library organization. The Enoch Pratt Free Library, completed in 1933, was the culmination of the gradual evolution of departmentalization in libraries which began at Cleveland in 1925 and continued at Los Angeles in 1926.

Because the public library is a practical and viable institution, the classic organization perfected by Wheeler in 1933 has been changed and is today changing further in response to new developments in society. New media such as audio-visual material, which are becoming an increasingly important segment of the resources of the library, were unknown in the library in the early 1930s. Effective management and economic strain have caused libraries to reexamine the relationship and the number of departments within the library. The development of regional responsibilities and the growing use of the library as an information centre have had lasting effects on libraries and indicated new patterns for organizational structures. Making changes in its structure, its type of service and its collections are essential if the public library is to continue its central role within the community.

Currently most large urban libraries segregate audiovisual materials into a separate department by form. A part of the basic concept of subject departmentalization groups all materials relating to a given discipline together to assure the widest possible information resource. Barton feels that this approach, assembling all materials at one place, enables the researcher and staff specialists to offer flexibility in inquiry response.[4]

Films and recordings are most frequently separated as a distinct unit from subject departments because (1) it is easier to shelve and store such specialized materials in concentrated areas; (2) it is easier to have a qualified staff to make repairs to film and check for scratches and other damage to recordings; (3) films are usually for group use and these groups are better served by a staff knowledgeable in this type of material; and (4) film selection is a great deal more involved than selection of printed materials because of the specialized technology involved such as adequate sound, filming techniques, and editing, in addition to adequate subject matter coverage.

Recordings are more and more finding their way into the subject departments, especially in the fine arts areas. With the advent of the tape cassette there is little maintenance, and the subject department staffs can easily handle the care involved. Unlike films, recordings are used both in the library and in the home for use by individuals, just as printed materials are.

Microforms whether fiche, print, card or film are a growing resource for all libraries and are handled differently in practically all libraries. The older established libraries have treated microforms as a storage method and house them in a separate unit. Overington says the care and servicing of the material and the accompanying equipment is simply a technical operation and has no place in the subject department.[5] Using this philosophy, most of the very large libraries do have separate microform sections or departments. In spite of this logical determination, the Houston Public Library in its reorganization programme plans for a new main building is planning to have microforms separated into the various subject departments with other types of materials of like subject. It is true materials must be retrieved by the subject specialist in either case; however, having them more readily available will hopefully encourage their wider use.

As printed matter and as an important segment of the current material available on all subjects, periodicals are generally field in the department in whose subject field they fall. The wisdom of this practice is obvious because of the extension value which periodicals offer to the book collection. The reader can work in one area with all material. (Microforms somehow escaped this piece of logical thought.)

Actual practice has shown that the heaviest demand for periodicals is from both high school and college students. Term papers and debate topics frequently have such currency that periodical literature is the prime source which is not restricted to any one subject department discipline. To cope with this problem, some library have changed their policy of scattering periodicals to various departments and have created special open shelf periodical collections of the most used titles such as those found in *Readers' Guide to Periodical Literature*. Queens Borough Public Library, Enoch Pratt Free Library and Memphis Public Library and Information Center have successfully followed this plan which has greatly relieved their staffs from this very routine service.

Documents are handled in widely divergent manner in the several large urban libraries of the country. Many libraries feel that because of the wealth of information available in document form, content should be emphasized instead of publisher. Many other libraries, however, fashion the collection as a separate entity or section of one subject department in which their current and popular usefulness is frequently lost or forgotten. Dallas, Denver and Louisville have had great success, however, using this technique with increasingly wider use of the material by the public. Certainly a very strong and persuasive staff is essential.

From Wheeler's classic assortment of subject departments, there has been an increasing trend toward fewer and larger departments. There are several cogent reasons for this development: (1) the library user is greatly benefited by a simpler structure; (2) with the classification system presently in use, subjects are not normally brought together in many small departments as with a consolidated scheme; (3) there are naturally fewer problems with book selection overlap; (4) the larger number of departments require a larger staff and consequently a heavy drain on the budget; (5) with fewer departments, duplication of general reference tools is not as necessary (although) some library attempt to hold duplications to minimum, others consider subject departments as special libraries and attempt to round out the collections by heavy duplications); and (6) fewer departments indicate a possibility of fewer departmental catalogues.

Gwynn has strongly stated that subject departmentalization has created a complex organization which in fact acts as a barrier for the patron in the use of the library.[6] Having a larger number of public service desks confuses and bewilders the novice library patron in finding his way in very large library. Difficulties of control and coordination often occur with a plethora of departments. In spite of these criticisms, large libraries have universally taken the subject department path. Gscheidle pointed out that departmental organization is a device used by administration in order to cope with size.[7] It actually becomes a necessity for the large library with a book collection too large to be serviced from one area. The complexity and higher cost are products of the large library rather than the system.

Demonstration of the change or progression of groupings for departments is easily shown by examining the Enoch Pratt Free Library's organizational structure through the years. In 1933 the library had six subject departments; the 1965 reorganization plan combined these into three. Further restructuring is presently being evaluated and studied. A recent staff study considered the situation under the reorganized plan which had functions in general reference, telephone reference and the public information centre unrelated, and suggested changes to smooth the relationships between functions.[8]

Table 22.1 shows that although there is no absolute agreement as to subject departmentalization, there are areas where similarity does exist and where different approaches are practised. There seems to be consensus that structure roughly would combine science and technology, art and music, literature and language, history and biography, philosophy and religion, and sociology and education. With the trend for larger units, the indication seems to be to bring science and technology and business and economics together.

There is a wide variance in what constitutes the collection for the popular library. Subject departments are geared to offer the best service to the specialist and serve the specific need. To serve the patron with a general need, the popular library, frequently referred to as a branch library within a large specialized library, was created. In some libraries, such as Dallas, the department actually houses the fiction collection alone. Pratt has a fiction and popular reading department.

TABLE 22.1

Subject Departmentalization in Selected Large Public Libraries in 1971

Libraries	*Subject Departments*
Brooklyn Public Library	Language and Literature
	History, Travel, Biography
	Social Science
	Science and Industry
	Art and Music
	Fiction
Dallas Public Library	Literature and History (includes biography)
	Science and Industry (includes business)
	Community Living (sociology, law, philosophy, religion, recreation and sports)
	Fine Arts
	General Reference
	Popular Library (actually fiction)
	Texas, Local History and Genealogy
Enoch Pratt Free Library	General Reference
	Popular Library
	Social Science, History and Education
	Business, Science and Technology
	Fine Arts
	Humanities
	Maryland
Public Library of Cincinnati and Hamilton County	History
	Literature
	Education and Religion
	Government, Law and Business

	Science and Industry Fine Arts
Public Library of the District of Columbia	Art Black Studies, Music Biography Business and Economics Fiction Foreign Languages Literature Philosophy, Psychology and Religion Sociology and Education Technology and Science Washingtonia Popular Library
Queens Borough Public Library	Art and Music Business, Science and Technology Social Science Language and Literature History, Biography and Travel Long Island Popular Library
Seattle Public Library	Literature, Language, Philosophy and Religion History, Biography and Government Education Business and Economics Science and Technology Art and Music
San Francisco Public Library	Art and Music History and Social Sciences Literature, Philosophy and Religion Periodicals Science and Technology Popular Library

Other libraries have experimented by including a teen-age collection. Some libraries which had not used the popular library have now created one in response to a definite public need. San Francisco recently established a popular library stocked principally with paperbacks. Generally the popular library is conceived of as a small browsing collection with emphasis on recreational reading and currency. But in those very large libraries which treat subject departments as informational centres handling all the specific needs of the library, the popular library is much larger and more encompassing, handling, as was stated earlier, all the general needs of the library. The Free Library of Philadelphia is planning to provide a popular library with approximately 30,000 to 40,000 volumes, including a general reference collection at the undergraduate level.[9] The Boston Public Library is presently building a very large addition which will house principally their general library which will offer circulating materials for the general reader. The collection will be extensive and will complement the great reference collections which will serve the scholar and the researcher. The relationship between the reference, general library and branches of the Boston Public Library is shown in Fig. 22.1.

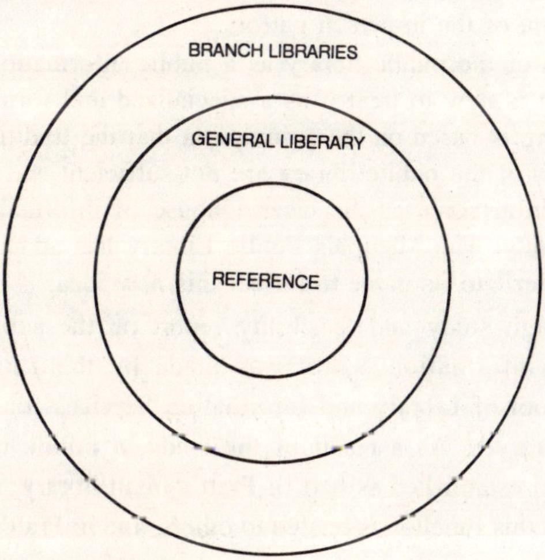

Fig. 22.1. Boston Public Library Relationships

A current trend for resource responsibilities for major urban libraries beyond the city proper is offering whole new dimensions and with these the need for organizational readjustment. The large city library collections offer a reservoir of specialized materials which give strength to the new library networks developing in many parts of the country. Inter-library loan sections are an important aspect of this direct service, as are consultation services. To assist in coordinating these services, some have a coordinator to supervise this operation and its relations with the cooperating libraries.

The extensive growth of main library telephone reference service has caused a heavy burden upon the staffs of the subject departments.[10] This is very expensive use of professional time for rather routine and simple reference service. To avoid this, libraries are increasingly following the practice of setting up telephone reference services. This service is frequently staffed by college graduates and siphons off simple repetitive questions leaving the serious in-depth research questions to be answered by the professional subject librarians. Those queries which are not easily answered and require specialized attention are passed on to the subject specialist professionals in the subject department. This technique is one method which is used in an attempt to give better service. With the rapid growth of telephone inquiries in recent years, it has been difficult task to decide which deserves better service, the telephone patron or the in-person patron.

The idea of the public library as a public information centre is not new, but it is new to treat it as a specialized and formal project. Current thinking is based on the assumption that the traditional information services of the public library are not sufficient and the library should in addition serve as the clearinghouse of information for its whole community. The Memphis Public Library has added "and Information Center" to its name to reflect this new idea.

A thorough study and feasibility report on the subject of the library as an information centre was made by the University of Maryland School of Library and Information Services for the Enoch Pratt Free Library.[11] As a result of the study, a public information centre has been established as part of Pratt's main library. Experience has shown that this function is related to others, and in Pratt's proposed organizational structure it will be a part of the informational services department.

There is currently a great deal of concern with service to children in main buildings in large cities. Emphasis in main libraries is shifting to serious, scholarly and in-depth research. Most libraries have realized that each year fewer children are visiting the main library except on tours and school visits, and some libraries are planning organizational changes to compensate for these shifts in use. Pratt is planning a small book collection for children in the fiction and popular reading department.[8] The St. Louis Public Library curtailed its services at the main building for children and young adults because demand was down and opened a new children's literature room in the main library for service to scholars, writers and artists interested in the field of children's literature, and for the few children interested in browsing.[12] In Dallas the young adult department has been discontinued as separate department and the collections have been integrated in the adult and young people's collections. The former children's department has been designated as the youth department.[13]

Every library, no matter how small, needs an administrative organizational framework to assure direction. In large libraries the organizational structure is usually rather conventional with several executives sharing the administrative function. Beyond the director and assistant director positions, the most commonly used titles are coordinators of adult and children's services. Coordination is a tremendous problem with subject departmentalization because of the increased supervision span which is inherent in this organizational arrangement. One method which is used to cope with this problem and which is in common use today is to assign to one person the responsibility for the whole main library public service operation. Some libraries have this responsibility assigned to the assistant director. This can be a great burden if the assistant director is in addition the deputy director of a library system. A number of libraries have an additional position, sometimes designated chief of the main library, to supervise directly the main public departments.

In Denver four subject departments relating to general service to adults report to the director of public service while four special departments report directly to the city librarian. Coordinators of children's work and young adult work supervise the departments for the two age groups.[14]

The Dallas Public Library in reorganizing in 1968 divided the position of assistant director into the two positions of associate director for public services and associate director for management services. Supervision of the main library and the branches were under the new associated director for public service and technical services, while

- LIBRARY COMMISSION
- LIBRARIAN
  - DIRECTOR OF ADMIN. SERVICES
    - METHODS ANALYST
    - BUILDINGS DEPT.
      - DELEVERY SERVICE
      - MAIL RECEVING AND SENDING
      - MAINTANCE AND REPAIR
      - — CUSTODIAL UNITS
    - ACCOUNTING OFFICE
      - ACCOUNTING
      - OFFICE AND LIB. SUPPLIES
      - SWITCHBOARD
      - — BOOK PROCUREMENT UNIT
      - — PRINT SHOP
      - — SECURITY UNIT
      - — SHELVING UNIT
    - CIRCULATION AND REGISTRATION DIV.
      - — CIRCULATION CONTROL UNIT
    - PERSONNEL OFFICE
      - — PAYROLL ACCOUNTING
  - DIRECTOR OF PUBLIC SERVICES AND ASST. LIBRARIAN
    - COOR. OF ADULT SERVICES
    - COOR. OF YOUNG ADULT SERVICES — YOUNG ADULT DIV.
    - COOR. OF CHILDREN'S SERVICES — CHILDREN'S LIB.
    - ART AND MUSIC DEPT. — AUDIO VISUAL CENTER
    - LIT. AND HISTORY DEPT. — GENEALOGY DIV.
    - SCIENCE AND ENGR. DEPT.
    - SOC. AND BUS. DEPT.
      - — BUSINESS DIV.
      - — DOCUMENTS DIV.
    - *REGION NO. 1*
    - PARK HILL. REG. LIB.
      - WARREN BRANCH LIB.
      - MONTCLAIR NEIGHBORHOOD LIB.
      - DAHLIA NEIGHBORHOOD LIB.
    - REGION NO. 2
    - ROSS-CHERRY CREKK RED. LIB.
      - ROSS-BROADWAY BRANCH LIB.
      - BYERS NEIGHBORHOOD LIB.
    - REGION NO. 3
    - ROSS-UNIV. HILLS REG. LIB.
      - DECKER BRANCH LIB.
      - FIELD BRANCH LIB.
      - VIRGINIA VILLAGE NGHBR LIB.
    - REGION NO. 4
    - CHALMER HADLEY REG. LIB.
      - ROSS-BARNUM BRANCH LIB.
      - BEAR VALLEY NGHBR LIB.
      - ATHMAR PARK NGHBR LIB.
    - REGION NO. 5
    - WOODBURY REG. LIB.
      - SMILEY BRANCH LIB.
    - EXTENSION SERVICES OFFICE
      - — BOOK MOBILES
      - — INTERLIBRARY LOAN
    - HEALTH AND HOSP. MED. LIB.
  - WESTERN HIST. DEPT.
  - SPECIAL COLLECTIONS
  - BOOK SELECTION CENTER
  - CONSERVATIN LIB. CENTER USDI PROJECT
  - DIRECTOR OF TECHNICAL SERVICES
    - CATALOGING DEPT.
    - PRODUCTION DEPT.
      - CARD PREPARATION UNIT
      - BOOK PREPARATION UNIT
    - SERIALS DIV.
  - DIRECTOR OF COMMUNITY SERVICES AND ASST. LIBRARIAN
    - PUBLIC INFORMATION OFFICE — STAFF ARTIST
    - GROUP SERVICES — PROGRAM SPECIALIST
    - GREAT BOOKS PROGRAM
    - COMMUNITY AIDES
    - DPL FRIENDS
    - DPL FOUNDATION

DENVER PUBLIC LIBRARY, DENVER, COLORADO

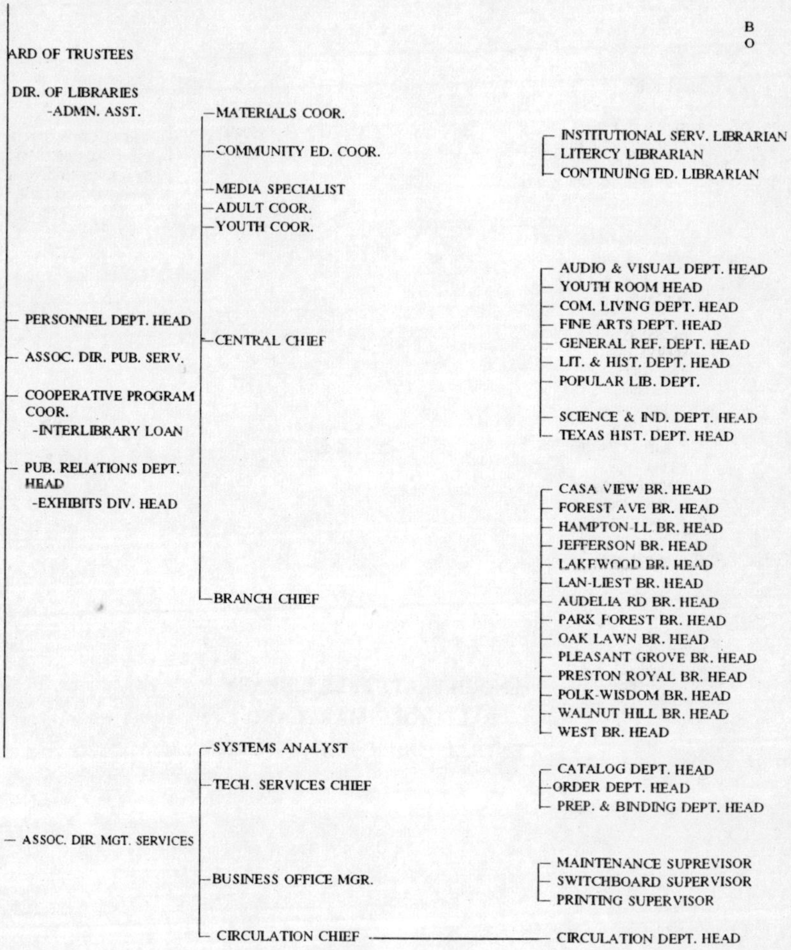

DALLAS PUBLIC LIBRARY, DALLAS, TEXAS

ASST. DIRECTOR

- GENERAL REF.
  - TELEPHONE REF.
  - CATALOG SERVICE
  - INTERLIBRARY LOAN
  - NEWSPAPERS
  - SERIALS
  - MICROFORMS
- POPULAR LIB.
  - YOUNG ADULTS
- SOCIALSCI. & HIST.
  - EDUCATION
- BUSINESS SCI. & TECH.
- MARYLAND
- FINE ARTS
  - MUSIC
  - RECORDS
- HUMANITIES
  - LIB. SCIENCE
- FILMS
- CHILDREN'S ROOM
  - HIST. COLL., ETC.
- PEABODY LIB.
  - RARE BOOKS
  - PICTURES

ASST. TO ASST. DIRECTOR

- CIRCULATION CONTROL
- CENTRAL CIRCULATION
- STACKS & SHELVING
- INFORMATION DESK*

* INCLUDES PUBLIC INFO. CENTER

ENOCH PRATT FREE LIBRARY
BALTIMORE, MARYLAND
CENTRAL PUBLIC DEPARTMENTS

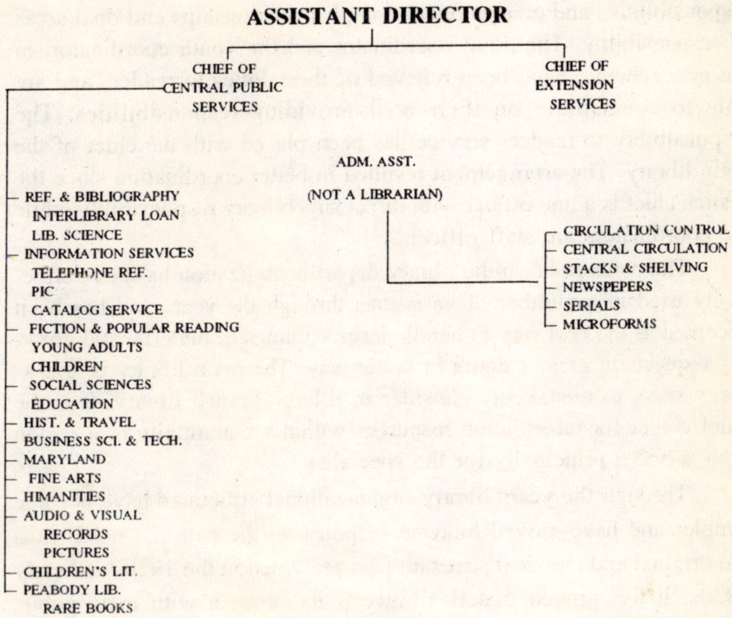

ENOCH PRATT FREE LIBRARY
BALTIMORE, MARYLAND
CENTRAL PUBLIC DEPARTMENTS
PROPOSED PLAN

business and maintenance management operations were under the director for administrative services. This plan logically divides the responsibilities and creates fewer complex relationships and dual areas of responsibility. The adult coordinator and the youth coordinator, in the new scheme, have been relieved of their duties to readers and are able to concentrate on their book-providing responsibilities. The responsibility to readers service has been placed with the chief of the main library. The arrangement resulted in better coordination since the branch chief is a line officer with direct supervisory responsibility while the coordinators are staff officers.[13]

The concept of public library departmentalization has been effectively tried in a number of variations through the years and has been accepted as the best way to handle large volumes of material and growing requests in greater depth in better way. The main library is not, as many seem to mistakenly consider it, a large branch library. It is the chief center for information resources within a community or a region with services principally for the specialist.

Through the years library organizational structures have become simpler and have moved more in response to the patron's needs than the original and classical structure first presented in the 1920s and early 1930s. It has proven that flexibility is its strength with main public libraries better structured today to meet the needs of the community. Undoubtedly continual change through experimentation will keep this unique institution alive and a vital part of community life.

REFERENCE

1. Keyes D. Metcalf, "Departmental Organization in Libraries." *In* Chicago. University. Graduate Library School. Library Institute. *Current Issues in Library Administration; Paper Presented before the Library Institute at the University of Chicago, August 1-12, 1938* (The University of Chicago Studies in Library Science). Carleton B. Joeckel, ed. Chicago, University of Chicago Press, 1940, pp. 90-110.
2. E. W. McDiarmid, and John McDiarmid, *The Administration of the American Public Library* (Illinois Contributions to Librarianship, no. 3). Chicago, ALA, and the University of Illinois Press, 1943, pp. 69-143.
3. Overington, Michael A. *The Subject Departmentalized Public Library.* London, Library Association, 1969.

4. Mary N. Barton, "Administrative Problems in Reference Work." *In* Chicago. University. Graduate Library School. Library. *The Reference Function of the Library; Papers Presented before the Library Institute at the University of Chicago, June 29 to July 10, 1942* (The University of Chicago Studies in Library Science). Pierce Butler, ed. Chicago, University of Chicago Press, 1943, pp. 218-48.
5. Overington, *op. cit.*, p. 53.
6. Stanley E. Gwynn, "Departmentalization and Circulation Work: Problems and Relationship," *Library Trends*, 6:87-100 1957.
7. Gertrude E. Gscheidle, "Departments in Public Libraries," *Library Trends*, 7:437-47, Jan. 1959.
8. Grace Slocum, Letter dated July 16, 1971.
9. Marie A. Davis, Letter dated July 8, 1971.
10. *Enoch Pratt's Gift, from Town to Library to State Resource Center*, Baltimore, Enoch Pratt Free Library, 1971.
11. J. C. Donahue, and Carole Peppi, *The Public Information Center Project Final Report.* Baltimore, Enoch Pratt Free Library, 1971.
12. Allan Angoff, ed. "Big Library Children's Services: Circulation Down—Reference Up," *Teaneck Points of Reference*, 6:9-10, May 1971.
13. D. L. Reich, Letter dated July 1, 1971.
14. Henry G. Shearouse, Jr. Letter dated July 26, 1971.

